HOLLYWOOD
and the GREAT
FAN MAGAZINES

HOLLYWOOD
and the GREAT
FAN MAGAZINES

edited by Martin Levin

HARRISON HOUSE
New York

This 1991 edition is published by Harrison House, distributed by Outlet Book
Company, Inc., a Random House Company, 225 Park Avenue South, New York,
New York 10003, by arrangement with the author.

Printed and bound in the United States of America

Library of Congress Cataloging-in-Publication Data

Hollywood and the great fan magazines / edited by Martin Levin.
    p.   cm.
    Reprint. Originally published: New York : Arbor House, 1970.
    ISBN 0-517-05785-9
    1. Motion picture actors and actresses – United States –
Miscellanea.   I. Levin, Martin.
PN1998.2.H66   1991
791.43′028′092273 – dc20   91-13266
                                                            CIP

                    8   7   6   5   4   3   2   1

The following selections are reprinted with the permission of
Macfadden Bartell Corp., 205 East 42nd Street, New York:

from Photoplay
TO THE NAVY
BOGEY
HOLLYWOOD'S UNMARRIED HUSBANDS AND WIVES
NO MORE DIVORCES
WHAT HOLLYWOOD IS THINKING
WHY THE PERFECT WIFE'S MARRIAGE FAILED
ROUND-UP OF ROMANCES
THE NEW MYSTERY OF MR & MRS CHAPLIN
IT'S LONELY BEING A CHILD PRODIGY
WHY FIFTH AVENUE LAUGHS AT HOLLYWOOD SOCIETY
THIS YEAR'S LOVE MARKET
SCOOP
THE INTIMATE LIFE OF A GENTLEMAN REBEL
SHIRLEY TEMPLE'S LETTER TO SANTA

from Motion Picture
DIETRICH IS STILL SELLING GLAMOR
DON'T BE AFRAID OF A BROKEN HEART
CAN HOLLYWOOD HOLD ERROLL FLYNN?
GINGER ROGERS ASKS "DID I GET WHAT I WANTED FROM
    LIFE?"
RONALD COLMAN GIVES THE LOWDOWN ON HIMSELF
WHY GIRLS FALL IN LOVE WITH ROBERT TAYLOR
THE STANWYCK COURT CASE
FAY WRAY'S DESIGN FOR MARRIAGE
WHO'S WHOSE IN HOLLYWOOD
CAREER COMES FIRST WITH LORETTA

from Silver Screen
TWO CLEVER FELLOWS WHO FOUND IT BETTER TO BEND
    THAN TO BREAK
BETTE FROM BOSTON
THE PRICE THEY PAY FOR FAME
FOUR RULES OF MARRIED LOVE
THE OPENING CHORUS

READY FOR LOVE
WHY GIRLS SAY YES

from Screenland
CHARLIE CHAPLIN'S KIDS
STUDIO SWEETHEARTS
JOAN GRABS THE BENNETT SPOTLIGHT
I'M NO GIGOLO, SAYS GEORGE RAFT
WHAT ABOUT CLARK GABLE NOW?
WATCH YOUR STEP, ANN DVORAK

from Screen Book
DANGER SIGNAL
THE STORY JEAN HARLOW HAS NEVER TOLD
MYSTERY TALES OF THE STARS
THE TRUTH ABOUT WILLIAM POWELL
NORMA TAKES A DARE
THE STAR WHO IS MORE MYSTERIOUS THAN GARBO
WHY GARBO HAS NEVER MARRIED
FIGURING THE STARS' SALARIES
WHAT I WILL TELL MY BABY
OUT OF TRAGEDY TO HAPPINESS
MARLENE DIETRICH ANSWERS HER CRITICS
JEAN HARLOW – FROM EXTRA TO STAR
MOTHERHOOD – WHAT IT MEANS TO HELEN TWELVETREES
THE BENNETS ANSWER HOLLYWOOD GOSSIP
THE TRUE STORY OF MY CHILDREN
HOW THE STARS SPEND THEIR FORTUNES
THE FIRST TRUE STORY OF GARBO'S CHILDHOOD
CHANEY'S SON MAKES GOOD
THE ONE STAR WHO HAS NO ENEMIES
LET ME GROW UP!
KAY'S DREAM OF ROMANCE
TARZAN SEEKS A DIVORCE
JEAN HARLOW CARRIES ON
CHAPLIN WINS

The following selections are reprinted with the permission of
Dell Publishing Co., 666 Fifth Avenue, New York:

from Modern Screen
AN OPEN LETTER FROM NORMA SHEARER
HE WANTS TO BE ALONE
I'M NOT MARRIED BECAUSE
THE TRUTH ABOUT THE MYSTERIOUS MISS LOY
WHY DID I SLIP?
THAT MARITAL VACATION
MARLENE ANSWERS ALL YOUR QUESTIONS
I WANT TO TALK ABOUT MY BABY

THE MOST REVEALING INTERVIEW JANET GAYNOR EVER
    GAVE
WHAT'S WRONG WITH HOLLYWOOD LOVE?
WHAT'S THE MATTER WITH LOMBARD
WHY I STAY MARRIED?
IT'S RUBY'S TURN NOW
THE INSIDE STORY OF JOAN'S DIVORCE
MY HUSBAND IS MY BEST FRIEND

for Andrea and Edmund

BACKWARD

In Santa Monica, Calif., where I lived as a boy in the early thirties, poppies grew wild in the vacant lots, hardly anyone's father had a job, and down on the Pacific Palisades—Marion Davies had a white and green mansion with gold faucets. Gold faucets! We knew this for a fact from the fan literature that our mothers absorbed in the Wilshire Beauty Salon (35¢ an item), along with their marcels, permanents and Edna Wallace Hopper beauty mud packs. Some of our more affluent moms even subscribed to Photoplay, Modern Screen, et al, at $1 a year, but few ever sprang for more than an occasional newsstand copy and a big read in the beauty shop.

So how come, if we were so poor, we didn't all go down to Marion Davies' place and smash her green shutters and heist her spigots? Or rustle Will Rogers' polo ponies, which grazed on his private polo field in our town? Or make off with James Dunn's brand new Stinson Reliant airplane which we read about in Silver Screen? Why? Because these appurtenances of the stars were part of an instant mythology which inspired not envy but admiration and aspiration. Movies were America's glorious pipe dream, and they were part of a double illusion. First came the make-believe of the pictures themselves. Then came the make believe *about* the pictures and their players, mass produced for and by the fan magazines. The movies produced demi-gods and goddesses, the fan magazines fabricated their epic qualities, and a movie enthusiast could extract limitless euphoria from the resultant fantasy. The movies and their mythmakers were part of a permanent dream, but a gold faucet is only a piece of plumbing.

Did I say *permanent* dream? A pardonable exaggeration. Fan magazines begin in 1911 with the establishment of PHOTOPLAY by the significantly named Cloud Publishing Company, spinning dreams out of Chicago, Illinois. And many are still publishing and thriving today. But the wonderful, nonsensical catalysis of films and ballyhoo hits its apogee in the 1930's and begins to lose altitude rapidly in 1941.The movie dream crystalized between 1929 and 1941, between the Depression and the War. In this dismal decade, "progress" in the USA ground to a halt and hardly anything changed except the double bill at the Bijou.

The fan literature of the 30's *creates* the Hollywood style and character. How else would you know that William Powell is a recluse who shuns publicity unless you read about it in four lavishly illustrated stories in four movie magazines during the same month? How else would you learn that Joan Bennett is hot tempered, favors blue and white in her beach house, and took Gene Markey from Ina Claire who married John Gilbert, who later married Virginia Bruce, who then married director J. Walter Reuben? How else would you learn of the indispositions of the stars, so delicately hinted? Only after bigtime movies are on the skids do we hear intimations of abortions rather than appendectomies.

The visions of Movieland, as whipped up in PHOTOPLAY, SILVER SCREEN, SCREEN BOOK, SCREENLAND, MODERN SCREEN, MOTION PICTURE and whatall indoctrinated their true believers with the notions that women were beautiful, men were manly, crime didn't pay, lovers lived happily ever after time after time, and Lana Turner was "discovered" eating a sundae at Schwab's Drug Store. The success of the fan magazine phenomenon of the 1930's was a cooperative venture between the myth makers and an army of readers willing to be mythtified. The magazines rewarded their true believers with a Parnassus of celluloid deities who climbed out of an instant seashell like Boticelli's Aphrodite. They were bigger, better and worse than you or I. They had Everything. But they wanted us to share in their lives. In the floor plans of their beach palaces at Malibu. In their firm resolves to stay married to their first wife, like Clark Gable. In their decision not to trade on their father's name, like Creighton Chaney. In their personal miscalculations, like the countretemps recorded in a boxed message to the fans in a 1931 *Screen Book:*

"I regret more than I can say that my marriage with Hal Rosson didn't work out."

Jean Harlow

The stars wanted their fans to know that in spite of their wealth, they had heart. Constance Bennett admitted to supporting "four needy families." Clara Bow outlined her approach to motherhood; ditto Joan Blondell and Helen Twelvetrees. Shirley Temple, pushing 12, wrote a letter to Santa, her last. (Did you know that Shirley had two brothers, Sonny and Jack?) Loretta Young was the breadwinner of her large family. And notwithstanding the splendors of stardom, the stars themselves assured you that *you* wouldn't really like it. It was too tough. In the wonderful words of a Silver Screen headline "In Hollywood, Health, Friends, Beauty, even Life Itself are Sacrificed On the Terrible Altar of Ambition." Some performers contracted real ailments, like Edwina Booth, who was never the same after "Trader Horn." But most ran the danger of coming unstuck by nervous debilities as mysterious and scary as the nameless pathology of radio soap opera, whose characters became inexplicably *hors de combat.* Fredric March's physician prescribed six months of rest after his diagnosis of "nerves shot." Milton Sills was hounded by "the curse of nerves." Ronald Colman required extensive rest and rehabilitation after the psychological demands of "Lost Horizon." William Powell needed solitude just to rest up. And we know about Garbo's therapeutic need for privacy.

What is more—the stars envied the fans, so they said. Deanna Durbin longed for a fudge party, just like an ordinary 14 year old without an agent. But fudge isn't the same when one "has found fame and has paid fame's price." Ginger Rogers wished she could be more of a homebody. ("I do manage a certain amount of knitting and crocheting and hooking rugs and doing petit point and things like that . . ."). Myrna Loy wistfully envied the L. A. secretaries who had the leisure and anonymity to shop on their lunch hour.

This two way dialogue between the stars and the fans is one of the purest examples since Gutenberg of perfect communication. Its instrument was made up of the fan magazine writers and editors who did an utterly heroic job of message carrying and image making. Communication faltered with the arrival of affluence, when the credit card and an increasingly gross national product seemed to make individual dreams more realizable, and the big Hollywood dream superfluous. Fan magazines still survive, but on a different plane. (Still, if one can believe the back-of-the-book ads, today's fans may well look the same. The nostrums for acne, oversize bust, undersize bust, overweight, underweight, etc. haven't changed at all.)

This book is a memento of the wonderfully ebullient communication that once was. It is an appreciation and not an analysis. That is why I have avoided arranging the material in any socio-historical pattern by category or chronology. If the collection has any form at all, you might call it pre-browsed. The reader is invited to turn on his Tiffany lamp and wander ad lib into movieland.

Spring, 1970   Martin Levin

My special thanks to Frederick A. Klein, president of MacFadden-Bartell Corporation, and to Mark J. Greenberg, vice president, for their kindness and cooperation. To Mrs. Helen Meyer, president of Dell Publishing Company, for her words of wisdom. To Rose Friedman of the Astor Place Book and Magazine Shop for her help in tracking down the dustier archives.

M. L.

CONTENTS

How the Stars Spend Their Fortunes 12
The First True Story of Garbo's Childhood 14
Chaney's Son Makes Good 16
The True Story of My Children, The Bennett Sisters .. 17
What About Clark Gable Now? 20
I'm No Gigolo! Says George Raft 22
The One Star Who Has No Enemies 24
Joan Grabs the Bennett Spotlight! 26
The Bennetts Answer Hollywood Gossip 28
The Inside Story of Joan's Divorce 30
Ready For Love 32
Studio Sweethearts 34
Motherhood—What It Means To Helen Twelvetrees .. 37

FAN FARE

Movie Fan's Crossword Puzzle 39
Here We Go For the Basic Step of La Conga 40
Prize Contest! 42

Jean Harlow—From Extra To Star 43
Shirley Temple's Letter To Santa 45
Marlene Dietrich Answers Her Critics 47
Bogie 48
It's Ruby's Turn Now! 50
Let Me Grow Up! 53
Why I Stay Married 54
What's the Matter With Lombard? 56
Kay's Dream of Romance 58
Out of Tragedy To Happiness 59
What's Wrong With Hollywood Love? 60
What I Will Tell My Baby 63

FAN FARE

Movie Fan's Crossword Puzzle 65
Dancing School 66

Figuring the Stars' Salaries 68
Charlie Chaplin's Kids 70
Chaplin Wins 72
The Most Revealing Interview Janet Gaynor
   Ever Gave! 73
Why Garbo Has Never Married 74
The Star Who Is More Mysterious Than Garbo ... 76
Norma Takes A Dare 77
Jean Harlow Carries On 78
Four Rules of Married Love 80
The Intimate Life of A Gentleman Rebel 81
The Opening Chorus 84

Career Comes First With Loretta 85
Who's Whose in Hollywood 86
I Want To Talk About My Baby! 89

FAN FARE

A Movie Fan's Crossword Puzzle 90
Win A Watch! 91
The Lowdown Chart 92
Love and Hisses 93

The Price They Pay For Fame 94
The Truth About William Powell 97
Mystery Tales of the Stars 98
The Story Jean Harlow Never Told 101
Danger Signal! 103
Marlene Answers All Your Questions 104
Tarzan Seeks A Divorce! 106
Fay Wray's Design For Marriage 108
Bette From Boston 109
That Marital Vacation 110
Scoop! 113
This Year's Love Market 114
The Stanwyck Court Case 116

FAN FARE

A Movie Fan's Crossword Puzzle 118
Win A Personal Check From Joan Crawford 119

Why Fifth Avenue Laughs at Hollywood Society .. 120
Why Girls Fall In Love With Robert Taylor 123
Why Did I Slip? 124
Watch Your Step, Ann Dvorak! 126
Ronald Colman Gives the Lowdown On Himself .. 128
Ginger Rogers Asks, "Did I Get What I Wanted Out
   of Life?" 130
Can Hollywood Hold Errol Flynn? 131
It's Lonely Being A Child Prodigy 132
The Truth About the Mysterious Miss Loy 134
The New Mystery of Mr & Mrs Chaplin 136
I'm Not Married Because 138
Roundup of Romances 140
So You'd Like To Be A Star? 142
Why the Perfect Wife's Marriage Failed 144
My Husband Is My Best Friend 146
Don't Be Afraid of A Broken Heart 148

FAN FARE

A Movie Fan's Crossword Puzzle 150
Shirley Temple Wins 151
Another Hollywood Date Test 152

What Hollywood Is Thinking 154

He Wants To Be Alone 156

Dietrich Is Still Selling Glamor 159

An Open Letter From Norma Shearer 160

Two Clever Fellows Who Found It Better To Bend
 Than To Break 162

Why Girls Say Yes! 164

No More Divorces! 166

Hollywood's Unmarried Husbands and Wives 168

To the Navy! 170

HOLLYWOOD and the GREAT FAN MAGAZINES

How Stars Spend

A frankly written article shedding new light on the subject so frequently discussed by movie-goers

IN A VILLAGE near Hollywood, the Chamber of Commerce has erected a huge sign, which reads: "Don't wait for 'good times'—spend *now* and keep business alive!" Hollywood doesn't need that advice.

Many screen stars earn salaries so fabulous that they stagger the imagination of the average business man. They also incur expenses just as incredible. The studio scale of wages, in general, is high, but of necessity so is the scale of living. As long as a dollar is kept in circulation, it stimulates business and gives to each merchant who receives and uses it a measure of prosperity and profit.

There is food for thought in the expenditures of a "Hollywood Millionaire." Tom Mix, for example.

For the past five years, at least, Tom has been paid approximately $500,000 a year. He has spent it lavishly.

During those five years he has paid to the United States government in income tax $574,000. He owns an estate in Beverly Hills which is valued at approximately $500,000; also, a number of small residences and ranches. What his annual property taxes amount to, Allah alone knows. He owns nineteen horses and three mules, and spends $600 a month for their feed and stable space. He employs thirteen people—three grooms, three riders and seven house servants. I don't know their exact salaries, but the aggregate is undoubtedly in the neighborhood of $18,000 a year. Last year he gave more than $20,000 to organized charities, without counting his contributions to the Boy Scouts of America, an organization which has always had first place on his list. He also gave private gifts to needy friends, which amounted to $22,000. He spends $1,000 a year for the white sombreros that he gives to his admirers, and it costs him $12,000 a year to take care of his overwhelming fan mail. His wardrobe expenditures are estimated at about $8,000 a year, groceries at $7,000 (remember that small army of retainers to be fed), and physical conditioning (doctors' bills, gymnasium expenses, etc.), at about $4,000 during an average year.

—Hurrell

Wallace Beery has suffered terrific losses in the stock market, and pays a tax amounting to almost half his income. His financial problems would stagger the average business man, yet he spends freely for pleasures he enjoys most—and no one can deny that Wallie earns what he is getting

Constance Bennett spends about $15,000 a year to maintain this beach home and her Beverly Hills residence. Entertainment, clothes and pleasure trips cost her thousands of dollars each year, yet she lives on a strict budget and spends only what is necessary to maintain her position as a star

Their Fortunes

By
Jan Vantol

In five years Tom Mix has poured $574,000 into the United States treasury in income taxes. Entertainment, upkeep on his Beverly estate, ranches and other residences cut deep inroads into his pay check

Marion Davies, one of Hollywood's wealthiest stars, spends thousands of dollars each year for charity, supporting a child's clinic in California and a large foundling home in New York

IN THE foregoing maelstrom of figures, the $574,000 paid in income tax is worthy of especial note. No wage-earners in the United States pay so large a proportion of their lifetime incomes to the government as do the screen stars. The average star's professional span is short, usually about five years, but in that period he earns a sensational salary and pays a sensational tax. With the new tax schedules established this year, many of the highest salaried stars will pay nearly one-half of their total incomes to Uncle Sam.

Incidentally, because of the California "Community Property Law," a screen star actually saves money by being married—unless his mate happens to make a still larger income. As you know, the percentage of income tax paid increases quite drastically with the amount of the income. In California, the total income of a family is divided equally between the husband and wife, and each member of the connubial partnership is taxed separately. A star who earns enough to pay a forty per cent income tax (Harold Lloyd, for instance) saves about $35,000 a year by being wed to a non-professional.

CONSTANCE BENNETT has an undeserved reputation for extravagance, thanks largely to a certain imaginative article which claimed that she spends a quarter of a million each year on clothes. As a matter of fact, she is an exceed-

---

THESE STARS PAY INCOME TAXES OF APPROXIMATELY $100,000 EACH YEAR

Doug Fairbanks Sr.	Marion Davies
Will Rogers	Ann Harding
Harold Lloyd	Constance Bennett
Norma Shearer	Richard Barthelmess
Greta Garbo	Janet Gaynor

EDITOR'S NOTE: Many stars pay as much as half of their earnings to the government in taxes, the total amounting to several millions. Hundreds of thousands of dollars are expended by them yearly on charities. Proportionately they are able to save less than the average business man, due to the constant demands on their pay checks. The public at large is prone to over-estimate greatly the wealth of movie folk.

---

ingly shrewd business woman, who invests wisely and keeps her expenses well within the limits of her income.

Her salary, according to the best available reports, is approximately $8,000 a week. This year her income tax will probably be far in excess of $100,000. She rents a large home in Beverly Hills, owns a house at Malibu Beach and estimates that the two residences cost about $15,000 a year.

Connie budgets her expenses. Three-fourths of her salary is invested by the Equitable Investment Corporation, which handles her business as well as that of many other stars. She allows herself $100 a week for pocket money to take care of tips, café and theatre parties, and [Continued on page 172]

13

The First True Story of GARBO'S

How the career of a great actress really began

—*Clarence Sinclair Bull*

Greta Garbo always has been an actress since the earliest days of her childhood. "It is difficult for me to think of her as a famous person now," her brother, Sven, says. "She will always be, to me, my little sister, in whom I couldn't help but believe"

STOCKHOLM, the great capital of Sweden. In a small courtyard, in the rear of an apartment house, a small girl plays with her dolls. She talks to them, admonishing, cajoling, threatening. She walks back and forth. Her hands move. Her mood changes. Her voice is soft, then high-pitched, then laughing. She lives through various emotions. Pretending. Always pretending.

The courtyard is no different than hundreds of others in Stockholm. A patch of green grass, worn to the soil in some places. A place where the sunlight comes filtering down with its cheer and its warmth. A sheltered little place, especially in the sweet coolness of a summer evening.

But the girl who plays with the dolls adds distinction to that courtyard.

The girl is Greta Gustafsson.

The years drift by, happy, uneventful. The girl grows more mature. She has put away the dolls, and there are school books to attend to, but the love of pretending is as strong as ever. Stronger, perhaps.

The little courtyard is still her playground; still the center of all her dreams, her ambitions, her hopes. It has now become a stage, for here she gathers other children for dramatic games. She tells them how to stand, what to do. She flys here and there, laughing, happy, eager.

"You are the mother," she instructs. "And you are the father, and you are the little brother. . . ."

In a circle of children—and older people—the games are acted out. Childish imagination, and childish love of make-believe. But with one mind dominating the whole.

AGAIN the years pass. The girl sits now, on a summer evening, in a little open air theatre near her home, watching actors and actresses portray their rôles. She is intent, interested. It is more than pleasure for her. It is the expression of an urge that she has within herself.

A few years more. Friends of the girl learn that she is taking part in motion pictures, and they are not surprised. They expected something like that. They talk about the afternoons and evenings in the little courtyard, and nod their heads knowingly.

Still later. And Greta's career explodes into fame. She leaves Stockholm, leaves the little courtyard, the parks, and the shady walks, but she comes back to her home city on long strips of celluloid. In darkened theaters the people with whom she played as a child watch her interpret life for them. And her childhood friends applaud, and remark that they are not surprised that Greta should become famous.

For if one thing is certain about Greta Garbo, it is that she is living out a childhood ambition. A realization that she wanted nothing in life so much as a chance to act.

I sat with her brother in the veranda café of the famous Grand hotel in Stockholm. To our right, across a canal, was the royal castle, a warm silhouette in the sunlight. Straight ahead, a mass of rooftops, pointed and pyramiding, was the section of the city were Garbo was born. Three tables away, in a corner of the café, sat the crown prince of Sweden with a party of friends.

THE whole setting was symbolical of the Stockholm that Garbo must love, in her natural rôle of Stockholmer.

I suggested to her brother that it was strange—or at least

By PETER JOEL, SCREEN BOOK'S EXCLUSIVE SWEDISH CORRESPONDENT

CHILDHOOD!

Above: Where Garbo was born, in an apartment house, 32 Blekingegatan in Stockholm. The white arrow points to the third floor suite in which her family lived

Right: The doorway of the building in which Garbo first saw the light of day. Through the entrance can be glimpsed the courtyard where Greta, as a little child, unconsciously trained herself for the great career ahead

Garbo at the age of eleven—a serious little girl, still occupied with childish pastimes. A natural leader among her playmates. Even at this age, those who knew Greta well, believed that she would one day become famous

interesting—that his sister should attain her present fame as an actress.

Her brother, who is seven years her senior, good-looking, charming in manner and speech, shook his head. His blue eyes lighted up, and he smiled.

"Yes, I suppose it is strange."

He toyed with a cigarette.

"And still I'm not surprised. When she was young you couldn't help but believe in her. You couldn't help but have confidence in her. I speak as her brother, of course, but there was something about her that made you have faith in her."

"But how did she happen to choose a theatrical career? Was it by accident or did she have that idea for a long time?"

Garbo's brother smiled.

"She always wanted to act. Even when she was very young." He spread his hands. "It was just in her, I guess."

We talked, then, about careers; about the way that some people hew their way through to success with a guiding ambition to help them. Again I made mention of his sister's career,

and this time it brought forth a beautiful bit of sentiment.

"Sometimes it does seem strange that she should be as popular as you say she is. You see, I can't help but think of her as my little sister. It's difficult for me to think of her as a famous person. She will always be, to me, my little sister, in whom I couldn't help but believe."

In all of this there was a natural modesty, a charm of manner, blended with intelligent understanding, that was pleasing. For Garbo's brother, known here as Sven Gustafsson, is an interesting person. He is married to a girl born in America, has traveled on the continent, but has yet to visit the United States.

But this, after all, was Garbo's brother, a member of her family. I determined to talk to someone else who knew Garbo as a child. In the house at 32 Blekingegatan, where Garbo was born and where she spent her childhood, I talked with Mrs. Emanuel Lönn, who remembers well when a girl who was christened Greta was born in the next apartment to her own. [Continued on page 172]

Chaney's Son Makes Good

Creighton Chaney carries on the illustrious screen name

By

J. Eugene Chrisman

—*Robert W. Coburn*

Creighton Chaney refuses to use his father's name and rebels against comparison to Gable

BLOOD will tell and Creighton, stalwart son of Lon Chaney, has become an actor. He has finished his first RKO-Pathé picture, *The Roadhouse Murder* and more recently completed *The Most Dangerous Game.*

In spite of the fact that it was pointed out to him that by using the name of Lon Chaney, Junior on the screen, his boxoffice value would be greatly enhanced, Creighton flatly refused.

"I positively will not cash in on the fame which my dad earned by his years of hard work and suffering in the grotesque roles he played. I know that I wouldn't have received a contract so soon if I hadn't been his son but that's as far as I want to travel on that basis."

A handsome six-footer is this twenty-six-year-old lad who bears the illustrious name of Chaney. His hair is dark and straight, his chin firm and his eyes clear and sparkling beneath heavy brows. He bears little resemblance to Lon, although there are times when a certain expression brings back the memory of the Old Master.

Creighton was born in Oklahoma City. His mother, Cleva Creighton, was a member of the "smalltime" troupe for which Lon worked as stage manager, hoofer and general handy man. He was raised in the theatre, his first cradle being the lid of Lon's old theatrical trunk. Between scenes, Lon would hurry backstage, warm milk over a gas jet and feed the baby. The stage hands were his first playmates, the lore of the stage his first education.

Until he was nearly seven, Creighton toured the tank towns with his parents. His first garments were fashioned by Lon's own hands from odds and ends of theatrical costumes.

Then Lon and Cleva were divorced. Lon got custody of the boy and the name of the mother was never permitted to pass his lips. During the years before Lon's second marriage, he was both mother and father to the lad.

"Dad won his spurs in a hard school," says Creighton, "and he wanted me to learn the same lessons. As I grew up, dad became famous and his earnings ran into big money, but I had nothing given me to indicate that I was the son of a rich man.

"I had to earn my own spending money in grade and high school and buy most of my own clothes. I never drove a car until I was twenty years old. My only vacations were those spent with dad in the mountain cabin he loved so well. I didn't rebel or feel abused, because dad had taught me his own philosophy of life."

Lon Chaney did not want his son to be an actor. No one knew better than he the hardships of a professional career. When Creighton finished high school, he was apprenticed to a boilermaker and it was this rough work which built up his great physique.

Later, he became a plumber and six years ago he married the daughter of his employer. His industry soon earned him a place in the firm and until his father died, he had no contact with studio life or the people who make pictures. Lon died believing that the son whom he loved was firmly established in business.

"I don't think dad would have objected had I told him I wanted to be an actor," says Creighton. "I knew he would rather see me in business, so while he lived, I did not reveal my desire to go on the screen. If he were here today, he would cuss a little, grin a bit and then tell me to go to it."

Young Chaney resents being told he resembles Clark Gable.

"I suppose I am of the same type as Gable," he admits, "but why make a comparison? He's Gable and I'm Chaney, and let the matter end there. I don't care what sort of pictures they put me in, only I hope I'm to play virile, he-man types. I feel better in a pair of riding pants than I do in a full-dress suit."

THE most refreshing thing about Creighton Chaney is his modesty. Never has he presumed on the fact that he is the son of a famous man. His associates at the golf courses and bridge tables played with him for months before finding out that he was Lon's boy. He would rather play golf than eat and he's devoted to his wife and two boys. Until recently he had been inside a studio gate only three times. The second Mrs. Lon Chaney is mother to him and he relies upon her for advice and guidance.

"I wouldn't be in pictures if mother and my wife hadn't advised me to go to it. I don't know what's going to happen. I may be an actor or I may be just a good plumber, but I'm going to find out. I've burned all my bridges behind me and if I do flop, it means starting at the bottom again."

The theatre is in Creighton's blood. Whether the father's great talent has been handed down to the son is yet to be seen, but at least he means to find out.

Adrienne
Morrison
Bennett

In this intensely human story the mother of the famous Bennett sisters, herself a celebrated actress, reveals for the first time many intimate facts about the family a whole world has learned to love

By Adrienne Morrison Bennett
as told to
VIRGINIA MAXWELL

SCREEN BOOK SCOOP

The True Story of
My Children,
the
Bennett Sisters

"Joan is one of the most fastidious housekeepers"

"Few people understand Constance and she doesn't particularly care whether they do or not"

"Barbara is a born mother . . . she would have been as successful as Joan or Constance"

"I T SEEMS only yesterday they were such little tots," Mrs. Adrienne Morrison Bennett said to me the other day.

"In no time at all little Joan has grown up; now she's the mother of two children and she was my tiniest baby only a few years back.

"Constance was the terror of the neighborhood, a wild little tomboy until she reached fifteen. She began then to realize boys liked her and thought her pretty. Then Constance changed. A complete turnabout of her behavior. After this, instead of coming in with her hair smeared back and her best frock torn to shreds, she started putting on 'grand lady' manners, spending hours before the mirror doing her hair in curls and crimpers."

We sat back in easy chairs in the ex-Mrs. Richard Bennett's finely appointed office high in one of New York's skyscrapers. Mrs. Bennett was known on the stage as Adrienne Morrison and it is this name she uses today in her very success-

Barbara Bennett, now the wife of Morton Downey, and Constance

ful literary brokerage office. She began digging through old photographs brought down from her country place. These pictures had reposed for many years in dusty trunks until the world began to ask so many questions about her daughters, those girls who have brought their mother's dreams to fulfillment.

About Barbara Bennett, their sister, the picture public know least. Yet Barbara is rated one of the Bennett beauties in New York smart society where Broadway and Park Avenue mingle. She is married to Morton Downey of radio fame and is the proud mother of a tiny son.

"Tell me about the girls as children," I coaxed as Miss Morrison drew forth some of their charming baby portraits.

"Well," she smiled, "nobody would believe it, but all my daughters have always had a terrific mother complex. They were flung into the maelstrom of Hollywood life when they were just on the brink of girlhood. That they have survived it and gone ahead living sane,

A previously unpublished photograph of Mr. and Mrs. Richard Bennett with Joan and Constance taken at their summer home near New York

Richard

Adrienne

Barbara

Connie

Joan

Barbara, Joan and Constance were inseparable as children. Even today, the illness or misfortune of one will bring the others flying swiftly across the continent

domesticated lives seems to me proof enough of that instinct.

"Joan, you know, is one of the most fastidious housekeepers I've ever seen. She's always been that way about dolls and dishes. Every morning now before going to the studio she writes out her grocery list and checks up on things in general in her pretty little home.

"I've watched Joan examining silverware to see that it was carefully polished. And going over linen to see that it was laundered to perfection. Now, honestly, you'd scarcely expect that of a movie star, would you?"

"HOW about Constance? Is she domesticated, too?" I asked.

Constance, who has been front-paged since her screen career began, had scarcely gained the reputation of being a "home" girl. Yet this is what her own mother said:

"Few people understand Constance. And Constance doesn't particularly care whether they do or not. She's like her father in that respect. But I can tell you that beneath the apparently helter-skelter existence she might seem to live, Constance is a very motherly sort of girl.

"She has come home, night after night, from the studio and gone directly to Peter's room so they could romp and play together. Peter is the idol of her life. And I think the love Constance has given to her child is reciprocated beautifully by the youngster himself.

"One morning while I was visiting my girls in

"To my own adorable mother," reads the autograph on this portrait presented to Mrs. Bennett by Connie, "with so many more hearts full of love than there are people to have hearts that only she can understand what I say"

California, I brought Peter a train with a whistle. I handed it to him, expecting him to wind it up and start it going at once. He looked longingly at the train, then at the stairs and said: 'Please Ditto, better wait till Mommy is awake, the noise might spoil her sleep . . .'

"THERE is a close tie between me and my girls, a tie which has grown steadily through the years since they were youngsters together in the old Washington Square house.

"Too bad there had to be a such a thing as divorce to disrupt our family life. But at least, two such opposite temperaments as Richard Bennett's and mine were adjustable enough for the good of the children. We adjusted our own personal difficulties until the youngest, little Joan, heir to all the temperaments on both sides of our families, had reached the age for boarding school.

"I think," she reflected, as if her level-headed business mind had wandered back to more sentimental things for a moment, "the children more than compensated me for any personal unhappiness I have known. I think all children should. But my girls have fulfilled the dreams I saw as future realities when they were babies.

"I don't mean their picture success entirely. I'm proud of that—immensely proud. But the greater thing, it seems, is that they have grown to womanhood retaining the finer characteristics which I tried to inculcate while they were still developing.

"Barbara is a born mother. Yet I believe if she had chosen to follow the stage or pictures she would have been as successful as Constance or Joan.

"Constance was always very close to me," her mother confided. "And in spite of the fact that she was the reddest of red flappers in those wild post-war days, it was she who would come to me when she was only eighteen years old and caution me about letting little Joan go here and there when Joan was beginning to attend her first parties.

"Constance is entirely uninhibited; affectionate, loving with a depth only those very close to her could understand.

"When she was only eight years old she used to don a little nurse's uniform to take care of her ailing puppy. To him she wrote reams and reams of romantic, sentimental poetry which she would read to Barbara and Joan with tears in her great, big, blue eyes.

"She is to those who know her only as a Hollywood movie star the glitter girl of glamour and sophistication. But I smile when I see her strutting about on the screen. For, deep down beneath the pose she has acquired from her worldliness, Constance is yet the little girl I cuddled in my arms when she cried over a sick puppy who died.

"Yet it seems strange, even to me now, that pent up inside of her dramatic little makeup Constance was a very unsentimental tomboy too. She's that way yet. Hard-headed in business deals, driving hard bargains with studio executives, yet tender and gentle as a lamb when she leaves the tomboy rôle behind and opens up that dramatic emotional side of hers. I love her for that combination of personality. I can see so many sides to my own daughters and with Constance there's always been a conflicting cross current which she inherits from both sides of her parentage.

"BARBARA has an intensely dramatic sense but she is repressed. She's more stolid, a little less impulsive, less quick to response than Constance. But Joan has a dynamic little personality which she has yet to show.

"I want Joan to come back to the stage. I want her to leave Hollywood and the studios and let me find her a play to do—something in which she can really prove the dramatic intensity of which she is capable.

"But little Joan wants to remain in Hollywood. I can always visit her there, she claims. She wants to be near Constance. They're next door neighbors at Santa Monica, you know. And Constance is forever running over to borrow things from Joan's perfectly oiled household. I don't believe the girls could get along without each other, despite the gossip writers who are always cooking up little enmities between the two girls.

"I've always been an impartial mother," she said. "And I hope I have been an understanding one.

"I don't forgive the newspapers for things they have printed about my girls. Most of those unkind things are untrue, especially in the stories written about Constance.

"You can't believe a girl could be too terribly sophisticated when she writes her mother a letter like this every year on her own birthday . . ."

Miss Morrison held out a letter which she had been carrying in her pocketbook and a little scent of rich French perfume wafted from it. The letter was from Constance. Thanking her mother, not so much for the pretty undies she had sent, but for the magnificent gift of her birth.

"That is worth the price of my own career," she said happily. "That marvelous sense of understanding and closeness which I instilled into my girls from babyhood.

"I WAS only sixteen, and already in Charles Frohman's company, when I married Richard Bennett.

"You see, I come from a family of theater people—seven generations of them. My mother was Rose Wood, the well-known stage star in the old Lester Wallach stock company days. My father was Louis Morrison, who played in *Faust* for seventeen years. That couldn't be done today," she laughed, "not from what I know of new faces and new fancies in the theater and pictures.

"I adored the theater. But I was willing to forfeit the right to our family tradition to devote my energies to my girls. I used to accept minor rôles in the plays in which Richard Bennett was the star, that I might travel with him and have the girls along at the same time.

"We lived in trunks for years. But I mannged to have my daughters know the peace and comfort of a home life too. It required no end of planning to be home for Christmas and vacations in the country, etc. But I managed.

"And today, when I steal into some little movie house and slip quietly into my seat for a view of Constance or Joan on the screen, my heart pounds a little at sight of them, even now. For they are my dreams come true. And in that rare fulfillment, I feel as if I have been truly blessed.

"You know," she went on, after a little reflection, "children never owe parents anything. Parents owe their own happiness and contentment to their children. That is really their compensation for a lifetime of work and sacrifice."

What *about* Clark Gable Now?

Here's the great he-man of the movies at a Hollywood first night. No, no—not Jimmie Durante! Clark Gable, with Mrs. Gable. Jimmy's the runner-upper.

Gable, Today! Has he Changed? Is he Happy? What's New?

By Ben Maddox

MEET Clark Gable *today!*
This he-man with dimples ; this gangster who went heroic by feminine demand ; this most desired of all current screen lovers—where does he go from here?

His powerful performance in "Strange Interlude" has clinched his right to stardom. Unofficially M-G-M's biggest male draw for the past six months, he is on his own for the first time in the just completed "China Seas."

What is Hollywood doing to him? How has this amazing whirl from obscurity to the foremost position in the talkies affected him? Can he possibly live up to all the grand breaks he has had so far? And, to be personal, is it true that fame is splitting up his second marriage?

Some other stellar men about town have been saying, "Poor Clark! We feel sorry for him. No one could keep a level head with all the publicity and adulation that have been showered on him!"

Logical, but after you meet and talk to Clark Gable you're ready to answer, "Sour grapes!"

Hollywood has affected him, certainly! What's more, he's man enough to admit it. But the change is a sensible, admirable one!

Every actress yearns to play opposite Gable. Every honest male star recognizes the potent appeal Clark exerts in pictures. And you and I know that he is one of the best topics in any social gathering. The Gable craze can be likened only to the Valentino boom of yester-year.

I wanted to know what he, himself, thinks of all the excitement he has stirred up. Learn his own conception of how popularity has altered him. There's nothing quite so authentic as letting a man speak for himself.

The first thing he said was the most unusual statement I've ever heard from the lips of a star. I've interviewed most of them, and Gable is the very first who ever announced, "I haven't done anything big yet!"

This from the fellow who has teamed with Garbo, Shearer, Crawford, Davies—and won equal honors with these long acclaimed ladies!

"I have never carried a pic- [Continued on page 173]

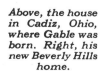

Above, the house in Cadiz, Ohio, where Gable was born. Right, his new Beverly Hills home.

"I'M NO GIGOLO!"
Says George Raft

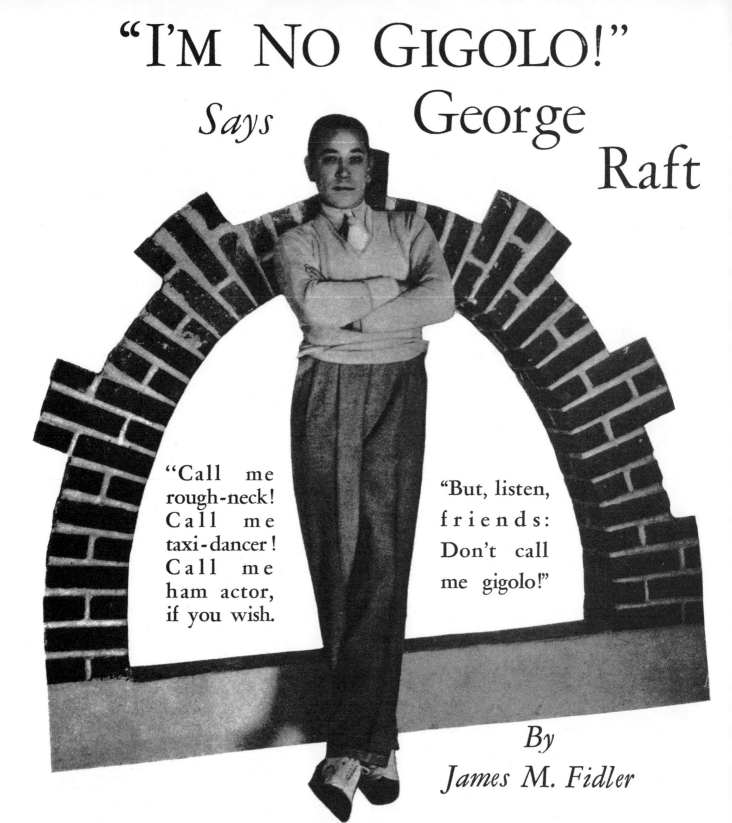

"Call me rough-neck! Call me taxi-dancer! Call me ham actor, if you wish.

"But, listen, friends: Don't call me gigolo!"

By
James M. Fidler

IN "THE VIRGINIAN," the title rôlist says to *Trampas,* "When you call me that, SMILE!" He delivers this ultimatum directly after *Trampas* hurls an insulting term that begins with *son* and doesn't end with *shine.*

Likewise, George Raft boils when the term *gigolo* is applied to him. That's his fighting word. Of course, Raft will fight at the drop of a hat, even during his most peaceful moods, and if there is no hat to drop, that is all right, too—George will fight regardless. But he is particularly pugnacious when he hears himself called *gigolo.*

"I am not a gigolo! I never was one! I will punch the nose of any man who says I am or was—try me!"

Thus, in no uncertain terms, does Raft deliver himself. Furthermore, he declares that the American public confuses the definition of the word. A *gigolo,* in this country, has come to include practically all men who earn their livelihood in professions that depend strictly upon feminine trade. The original and true meaning was descriptive of a class of males who were supported by women; in other words, *kept men.* This meaning was gradually broadened to include young men who married wealthy old dowagers.

"One writer stated that I glorify the gigolo," muttered

Here's the frankest story ever written about a motion picture actor

Raft. He spat savagely, as if to clear his mouth of a bad taste. "Can you glorify a sewer rat? I know only disgust for such men; why would I exalt them?

"To be frank, I recently rejected one of the finest motion picture stories I ever read because my rôle would have been that of a gigolo. Had not such an unfortunate publicity blast made it appear I was once one of the breed, I might have taken the rôle and perhaps won renown. But I don't want to be known as a gigolo, and I am positive that the picture, combined with the publicity that has been broadcast, would confirm me in the public mind as a first-class kept man!"

That Raft look! Here it is levelled on pretty Gertrude Messinger while George holds her make-up box for her. This picture answers the question, "Why do movie actresses like to work on the Paramount lot?"

The term gigolo was first applied to Raft when it was learned that several years ago he worked as a taxi-dancer in a public restaurant-dance palace. It was his duty, as one of several gentlemen employed by the management, to dance with unaccompanied feminine patrons who felt the urge of Terpsichore. For this duty, sometimes pleasant but more often irksome, he received a ticket for each dance. At the end of an afternoon or evening, the management paid him for his tickets; the more tickets, of course, the more money. The majority of ladies who danced were middle-aged and homely; the sort of women who *must* pay. Few were good dancers; most were clumsy; many were fat. When Raft went home each night, he soaked his numbed, trampled feet in hot water, after which he rubbed them with olive oil.

"But I was no gigolo," he insists. "I earned an honest living. As a taxi-dancer, I made seventy-five dollars or more every week. As a clerk in a store, I might have earned twenty-five. Whatever else I may be, I am not dumb; I'll take seventy-five in preference to twenty-five any day, provided it is honestly earned."

Raft learned patience when [*Continued on page 174*]

George Raft's new home is in the heart of Beverly Hills—and here's George in front of it.

The One Star Who

Jean Harlow tells the philosophy of life which has helped her survive tragedy and escape petty entanglements in Hollywood

"I love the sun," says Jean. "I'd always rather walk than ride." Here she is walking to the sound stage after lunch

YOU know how Jean Harlow gets her men on the screen. This is going to be the story of how she got her interviewer!

When I was asked to question Jean on her philosophy as to the right way to live in the movie whirl, the editor instructed me, "Please give us a new slant on life in Hollywood from Jean, and don't send me the same old stuff." I am taking him at his word, which gives me an excuse to be extraordinarily unconventional.

To start at the beginning, I must identify myself as an unusual fellow. So far I've been the one interviewer who has *not* praised Jean Harlow! One of those indifferent types? Not at all. But somehow I just couldn't believe in Jean.

I have enjoyed her pictures, especially since she's revealed that sense of humor. But I couldn't reconcile the "headline" Harlow with the girl the writers persistently described a vamp whose personal affairs have been front-page material, yet whose mother calls her "Baby", a woman who is obviously a magnet for love, and yet ticketed "a regular girl" by her friends.

This being red-hot on celluloid and good clean fun in person annoyed me. I deliberately steered clear until, finally, I started thinking maybe I was wrong. After all, Jean Harlow has had more spectacular ups and downs than any other young star. She *must* have some successful philosophy to have bucked Hollywood so successfully. I went out to her home, I confess, in a Missouri frame of mind. I reassured myself that she couldn't fool *me*.

Smiling, her hand stretched forth for a firm, cordial handshake, she welcomed me—and I must report that she is as genuinely devastating "off" as "on." Her house is a white and gold setting for her platinum beauty.

To counteract the friendliness she radiated, I hurriedly turned on my most professional manner as I questioned her.

"The two hardest things I've had to learn in Hollywood," she said, "are how to smile, and how to talk about myself. I used to think I had the homeliest smile—and for that reason all my early portraits were glum affairs. Eventually, I practiced cheering up before my mirror, and now I can grin without feeling like a darn' fool!"

Was I melting at this good humor? I crossed my fingers!

"And then, about telling my thoughts. That was hard, too. One day a writer advised me that it would be infinitely easier all the way around if I'd speak up instead of forcing the poor interviewer to drag every detail out of me!"

I NEEDN'T have worried about "new stuff." Jean's opinions tripped forth and they proved as fresh and sparkling as her blue eyes.

"One important thing I've discovered about the right way to live here is the necessity for variety in one's life. There's a terrible chance of becoming a one-track soul. When you're acting for the movies, you're apt not to quit when you leave the studio. You continuously fret over a million problems.

"Everything from the way they lighted you in that last sequence to the kind of a gown you'll wear to a première can bother you. Your actions are so public that you have to be a jump ahead all the time. And that's why I've found it essential to seek outside interests.

"To be personal, I try to broaden my perspective by reading

24

Has No Enemies

By
Ben Maddox

She lays down the rules of good behavior for Oscar the Peke, evidently an excellent listener

"When health is of such great importance, movie stars can't afford to burn the candle at both ends. It's no wonder visitors think us provincial!"

as many good books as I can, by always studying something. At present it is French. You know how it is when you're growing up and in school. You are lazy. Until I was five I spoke French almost exclusively, as I had a Parisian governess. Recently I've been embarrassed to death at my inadequacy in French, so I have a tutor who comes to the house daily. In the future I'm going to resume piano lessons. It isn't *what* you study. It's that you get away from the temptation to concentrate on yourself, which makes you selfish and, therefore, unattractive to others." [Continued on page 174]

—Grimes

TO MY SCREEN BOOK FRIENDS—

"I regret more than I can say that my marriage with Hal Rosson did not work out. Believe me, this is no frivolous matter—but the only way out for both of us. We are uncongenial, and while there is no ill feeling between us we realize that it is best for us to separate."

JEAN HARLOW

Joan, at twenty-one, has been a bride, a mother, a divorcée, the apex of a famous triangle—and now a bride again. Who can match her career to date?

Joan Grabs the Bennett Spotlight!

Sister Connie has our cover— here's where Joan stars

By Helen Harrison

ON HOLLYWOOD'S marry-go-round Joan Bennett has pulled the golden ring!

True, on the spirited chargers that so gaily pirouette to a mad jazz rhythm, vaguely reminiscent of Mendelssohn, one only goes round-and-round —grasping at new rings, hopeful that the next will be better than the last, throwing the past aside for "just one more chance."

Joan Bennett Fox Markey, at twenty-one, has been

the central figure of at least two famous triangles—but in her quiet, wide-eyed manner the little blonde sophisticate has plucked Hollywood's (and points East) most eligible bachelor with all the ease she has consistently exercised since, at sixteen, she left the confines of a French convent to marry John Martin Fox, then matriculating at an English college.

That was five years ago—enough time for an upstanding Bennett to annex a wee daughter—Adrienne, blonde elf—named for her grandmama, to divorce her husband, time indeed to declare she was "through with romance," and then to figure prominently in the John Considine-Carmen Pantages triangle. There are those who have felt Carmen, as Mrs. Considine, came off the victor in that hot-cold-luke-warm-hot-again romance— but I share the opinion of most that Joan had ceased to care, or else there might have been a different ending to that story. Considine, you will recall, was the one to first sign Joan to her contract, when she was immediately cast opposite Ronald Colman in "Bulldog Drummond." She had had other plans then, had actually studied interior decorating and endeavored to persuade her mother to go into business with her. Since then *exterior* decorating has been Joan's line—and what grand curves and divine color schemes she has accomplished.

At all events, last autumn Joan found herself wholehearted and single—long-distanced daily by a famous political play-boy and a first-water critic, and shortstopped nightly by several of California's most regal Romeos!

Back in 1929, when Joan was seriously considering the movies as a means of earning her sarouks and sables, a nebulous triangle was forming across the continent. Ina Claire, blonde, beautiful, and bewitching had done just that to Gene Markey, gifted magazine writer and coming premier scenarist. For many years Ina and Gene had been a familiar pair at the Algonquin, and week-ends at Ina's beautiful Portchester menage were unfailingly graced by the certain charm of Markey. Here, on the broad lawns of Westchester, Ina would sit, a script in hand, her lovely dogs grouped at her feet —Gene figuratively so—the centre of admiring friends, and it seemed to those who knew them best that life would go on so forever—that Ina Claire (née Fagan), the sensation of the 1912 Follies, the scintillating star of innumerable Broadway successes, would soon be Ina

Some of the Bennetts at play. Joan's mother (now
Mrs. Eric Pinker); Joan herself; Gene Markey, her
husband; and Sister Connie. Don't the Markeys make
an impressive couple?

Markey, and Gene's bachelor days would be at an end.

And then another famous star, the recent husband of Leatrice Joy, the adored of Garbo, twisted that papier-mâché triangle into a cocked hat!

It was in the summer of that same '29 that prosperity, the Claire-Markey combine and Wall Street all took a nose dive. Ina had been signed by Pathé for two pictures and was sent to the Coast to begin "The Awful Truth." Gene followed soon after, stopping off at Chicago for some trousseau miscellany. It was there he received a preview of "The Awful Truth"—the horrible, irrefutable reality of his shattered romance—Ina Claire had married John Gilbert!

There are those who believe Gene had dallied too long, but I do know it was thought by those "in the know" that Ina's previous marriage and more recent divorce had violated Gene's religious scruples. It may have been that time was needed to reconcile Gene's Catholicism to Ina's situation—and that Ina was irked. Yet there may have been other reasons—for Joan, Mrs. Markey that is, is also a divorcée!

Gene was deeply shocked and sincerely hurt when Ina Claire married John Gilbert, but he's a swell person—sporting, regular. He became a friend of the Gilberts, was entertained by them and entertained them. And then the Gilbert romance ended in a draw. But where was Gene? Writing in Hollywood. And where was Ina? Appearing in Paramount pictures. And where, indeed, was Joan? Working for Fox.

It was at the home of the Marquis de la Falaise de la Coudraye that Joan and Gene met, the home of that other glamorous Bennett—Con-

stance. And that, children, is how *that* started.

One cannot help wondering if Joan's blonde beauty was not, at first, reminiscent of Gene's former love. Both are blondes, both are women who dress exquisitely, are abundantly intelligent, the natural companions of men of fastidious discernment. Ina, with her wise, twisted smile, delicately cynical; Joan with her disarming pout, her almost naïve glance, seem very different types of women—yet they are both inherent sophisticates. Joan is a 1932 edition of a still young Ina.

As for Joan—Markey, she felt, was at last a man to trust and to believe in. Her loss of faith in men was real when her first marriage proved disastrous. Still an adolescent, in spite of her participation in adult life, Joan was as malleable as are most young girls of sixteen, and the unhappy turn of events to her romance plumbed unsounded depths in the soul of this impressionable girl. Her romance with Considine was probably a rebound from her divorcement. She was finding men again. Finding life and its eternal riddle intriguing. When she was apparently jealous, inconsiderate, and sometimes even conspicuously dramatic, her conduct must be condoned as that of severe readjustment. To me it seems that neither John Fox nor Considine were really *men* in Joan's life. They stand, rather, as ideals of a romantic girl's first love and as the re-birth of romance. Markey seems surely the first real

[Continued on page 175]

The mother of the Bennett girls, the former Adrienne Morrison, photographed with her volatile young daughter on a recent visit to Hollywood.

The Bennetts Answer

"I Am Not Facing Divorce!"

By Constance Bennett

"I am not facing divorce," says Constance Bennett. "I am quite happily married"

THIS magazine, in its September issue, printed two articles entitled respectively—but not respectfully— "Divorce: Is Connie Facing It?" and "Divorce: Can Joan Avoid It?" I read them with mingled wonder, understanding and disgust. Principally disgust!

The editors of SCREEN BOOK have convinced me of their sincere regret and promised a complete retraction. And to make assurance doubly sure, I am taking this opportunity to tell the public exactly how I feel about such malicious insinuation and misrepresentation.

Being a "business woman," I can understand, for instance, the purpose which inspired the editor to print such irresponsible rumors and ridiculous conclusions; I can understand the author's reasons for writing the article—and, having lived for four years in Hollywood, I certainly can understand the ease with which appropriate rumors were harvested. Hollywood produces a truly prolific rumor crop. Practically any rumor needed for any purpose can be had here for the asking —and the fact that most of them are stupid and untrue apparently enhances their value in the estimation of some editors. Those of us who are "public property" have become inured to reading about our own plans and actions long before the plans are born or the actions are performed.

My "wonder" was aroused by the fact that the author of that ingenious article carefully avoided me while collecting the "material," and by the further fact that her editors did not request its verification. Perhaps she decided that I would not know the truth of any rumors concerning myself; or, perhaps,

she merely wished to save me the bother of an interview and believed that I would not be interested in an innocuous little article which glorified me as a triple-threat woman, a delightful combination of unfaithful wife, mercenary huzzy and social snob.

And imagine! For years I've been deluding myself, believing that I had honestly earned a reputation for dealing fairly and frankly with the press.

IT SEEMS that she was equally careful to avoid an interview with my sister, notwithstanding the fact that she actually quoted Joan!

Had she questioned me, I should have told her that:

I am not "facing divorce"; that, on the contrary, I am quite happily married and that my husband has failed to give me the least hint that *he* regards our marriage as a failure.

I should have "confessed" that I *actually was guilty* of planning a vacation trip to Honolulu and that my immodest plans included my maid, my secretary, one of my friends, her son and my son. And I would have assured her that so large a party would seriously overcrowd that mythical but oh-so-romantic "love nest on the beach at Waikiki." I should have confirmed the studio's announcement that my trip was deferred because of retakes, and I might have persuaded her to come on the set and be convinced that those retakes were a very sweltering reality.

For a person who is reported (truthfully, for once) to have a quick temper, I failed to be greatly infuriated by the rumors of my "Honolulu romance" and my "inevitable divorce." Such rumors have become more boresome than annoying. In the past four years, Hollywood's gossip-mongers have gleefully reported me as being in the arms of first one lover, then another. Anyone who habitually reads the fan magazine and newspaper chatter-columns might well conclude that I am a female Casanova, and that I cry my loves from the housetops.

The author of the imaginative masterpiece published in this magazine apparently was afraid to mention the name of the man who has been linked with me in the present barrage of romantic ravings. She meant Gilbert Roland. The rumors were first kindled by the hideously insinuating fact that he played opposite me in *Our Betters*, and they were fanned into a blaze when he escorted me to the Hollywood Legion fights and to a preview. Undoubtedly, it was our consciousness of guilt and our fear of gossip which prompted us to "hide-out" in such lonely places!

Frankly, I like Mr. Roland. I have reached the age of discretion, and I do not choose to become a recluse merely because my husband happens to be out of the city, or otherwise engaged, and because "people might talk."

ONE of the more unfortunate phases of a screen star's life is that it is easier to drive a famished cat away from a saucer of cream than to check the wagging [*Continued on page 175*]

Hollywood Gossip

Joan Denounces Hollywood Gossip

By Muriel Babcock

"I welcome this opportunity to condemn the whole vicious circle of Hollywood gossip," says Joan Bennett

THE other day, Joan Bennett quite casually opened a copy of the September issue of this magazine and found, to her great amazement, she was reading an article entitled "Divorce—Is Joan Bennett Facing It?"

Joan was horrified, shocked, astounded.

More than that, she was furious.

She and Gene Markey had been married on March 16, 1932; they were happily married and the thought of divorce had never entered their heads.

In five minutes she was on the telephone, investigating, trying to find the source of the story, calling upon friends who might help her.

It was six o'clock in the evening.

I was sitting in the broadcasting chamber of KHJ waiting for Elissa Landi to go on the air, when an attendant tapped me on the shoulder and said I was wanted on the telephone.

"This," said a strained voice, which I did not recognize, "is Joan Bennett—something terrible has happened! Can you come at once?"

The "something terrible" was the article in the magazine which Joan resented, and rightly so. She and Gene immediately went about taking steps to refute the article, but anything like that, as you know, is like locking the barn after the horse is stolen. The damage has been done—in this case, not so much damage, for it seems as if nothing can effect the happiness of these two people—but hurt to them had been accomplished. They were both really shocked.

Other people near and dear to them were shocked and hurt, too. In fact, all Hollywood was aroused and indignant. Letters and telegrams and phone calls from people Joan didn't even know poured in, as well as from friends and business associates.

A FEW days later, Gene had a letter from his mother in Chicago. Now the senior Markeys are devoted to Joan. They love her very much and were amazed and troubled to read that Gene and Joan were considering divorce.

They didn't stop—as people outside Hollywood don't —to reckon with the vicious rumor mart of the town. They hoped the story was not true, but they couldn't understand why it started.

RETRACTION

In the September, 1933, issue of SCREEN BOOK, there appeared an article entitled "Divorce! Is Connie facing it? Will Joan avoid it?" by Virginia Sinclaire.

Misses Constance and Joan Bennett insist that the double article is false and untrue, and injurious to their names and reputations. It appears to have hurt their pride and sensitiveness, all of which SCREEN BOOK exceedingly regrets. Consequently, we retract the said articles in their entirety.

In this same spirit of repentance, and believing in the bigness of their minds and estates, and likewise believing that any article submitted by them would point out with specificness all statements which they claim to be false, we gladly consented to run their two personal defense articles in this issue, with the hope that such articles would be free from all vindictiveness and vituperation. We present these articles as they were submitted to us.

If any mistake has occurred, we trust that these articles will clarify such mistake. We have never entertained the slightest intention to injure or harm the great Bennetts. We have always and now have great affection and admiration for them, and wish them well in all their undertakings—a wish which we trust is jointly shared by all of our readers.

Gene sat down and wrote his mother a long letter. Joan did the same. They wrote to Joan's mother.

And they took steps to get in touch with the editor of this magazine whom I am told was also shocked and grieved to think that, through lack of careful editorial check, something had been printed that was not true to facts. Through her attorney, Joan told him she was prepared to take legal action.

He asked me to write this story and he asked Joan to comment—if she would—on the vicious circle of Hollywood gossip that attacks Hollywood homes, that causes heartbreaks and anguish of soul and mind, that is apt, in the case of married movie stars, to destroy confidence in one another. He wanted her to give the star's side of the story.

Meantime, further investigation of the story led to discovery of how it started.

[Continued on page 176]

THE INSIDE STORY

Joan Bennett was once Hollywood's outstanding example of a two-career girl. That's over! Below is a recent picture of the Markey family. Left to right, Gene, Melinda, Joan and Diana.

FROM THE beginning, on March 16, 1932, until the end, on April 29, 1937, one adjective was used to describe the marriage of Joan Bennett and Gene Markey. The adjective was "ideal." Even the headline that heralded their parting read, "Rift Climaxes Ideal Screen Marriage."

That headline appeared with an unexpectedness and suddenness that stunned all except those close to Joan and Gene. Those close to them were prepared.

But for five years, as far as the outside world was concerned, there was nothing to hint that the marriage of the Markeys was not everything that it appeared to be.

Until very near the end, no gossip marred the illusion. There were no hints of quarrels, no intimations even of the usual temperamental differences of the usual husband and wife. They were not exactly labeled as recluses, but everyone was convinced that they preferred their own home life to Hollywood party life. There were no outward symptoms of restlessness or discontent or incompatibility. There was no more doubt of their love for each other than there was of their love for their children —Diana, Joan's child by her first marriage, whose name

OF JOAN'S DIVORCE

Here are the real facts behind the break-up of this once happy marriage

By George Benjamin

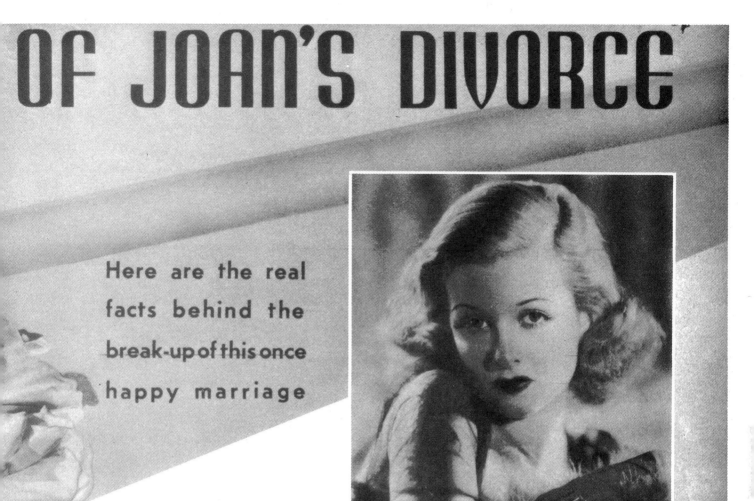

Joan heads a cast of "pretties" in one of the big musicals of the year, "Vogues of 1938."

had been legally changed to Markey, and the baby, Melinda.

Whenever Joan gave an interview, she did something that few actresses (thinking of their box-office appeal) had the courage to do. She talked of her husband and her children. There was something infinitely appealing about Joan, the glamorous young movie modern, also being Joan, the girl-wife and girl-mother. She became Hollywood's most radiant example of a two-career girl. Her happiness became legend.

Now, suddenly, the legend has exploded. Joan and Gene have rung down the curtain on the saga of love, in the middle of the second act. The show won't go on. They feel that they can't give convincing performances any longer. They are "incompatible."

Incompatibility is Hollywood's most popular, most polite and least convincing explanation for divorce. In the case of Joan Bennett and Gene Markey, it satisfies no one.

Joan may owe the public a fuller explanation, after all those interviews stressing her happiness; but she will give none.

The real explanation is so simple—yet so blunt, so difficult to make. . . .

It does not strictly follow the familiar Hollywood pattern. Joan's marriage has not conflicted with her career. If anything, her marriage to Gene, the dramatist, has made her a better actress.

It is not a case of wife becoming more important than husband. Gene has never suffered the title "Mr. Bennett." He has never earned less than Joan. He has never ranked lower in the Hollywood scheme of things. Today he is a producer—and, as such, controls the destinies of stars.

Neither is it a case of violent clash of temperaments. The Bennetts—Joan included—have earned a reputation for being unpredictable, but Gene's mordant sense of humor has never allowed temperament to be one of his weaknesses.

The explanation is, simply and bluntly, that Joan—who is said never to have been really in love with Gene, as he has been in love with her—has found someone else. The "someone else" is a big name in moviedom.

Ironically, it seems as if Joan Bennett has not really been in love with either of the men she has married.

The first time, that she repeated a bride's responses, Joan thought she was in love. She was sixteen at the time. She had a lonely, [Continued on page 176]

31

READY
FOR
LOVE

Olivia de Havilland
Says That Her Career
Would End If The
Right Man Came Along.

By Dena Reed

IT WAS precisely five minutes
of ten of a Saturday morning
when I glanced up at the
Ritz Towers wondering, as I
entered, if a screen star has any
legal rights to take pop shots at
an early interviewer, or whether
the usual procedure is to turn
over and ignore the animal
until the decency of a midday
sun makes all sweetness and
light.

The publicity department at
Warner's had said I might see
Olivia de Havilland at ten, if
. . . and when . . . and as she
would be "available."

Announcing myself I was told
to "go right up." I've heard the
maid's sister tell the scrubwoman's assistant to do that, in a pinch, and it didn't
comfort me any as I whirled up in the
elevator, my mind running something
like this:

I'll probably sit around for two hours
when there'll be stirrings and mutterings
and finally, 'long about one o'clock, the
object of my dejection will emerge, yawn-
ing behind a dainty white hand held up
limply for the occasion—and the business
of living will idle along from there. . . .

Letters which sprawled at my feet in
front of the de Havilland suite didn't
cheer me any either. I glanced down at
the postmarks as I toed them between my
first and second and third rings at the
door. "Waukegan, Warner Brothers, points
West. . . ."

. . . And then the door opened!

It opened just a mite and in the slit appeared two
brown eyes bright as a press agent's blurb, and, as the
opening widened, I discovered it was Olivia de Havilland,
her light brown hair in a fluffy halo about her head and
her full, curving mouth forming a smile of welcome as
she asked me to come in. For all the world she looked
like some small child who was filling in until mother
appeared on the scene!

There was something excitingly fresh and young and terribly
vibrant about her (at ten!). *Smash-bang* went my visions of a star
lolling on her beautiful satin divan.

Before I knew it I was "zipping" up her dress. It had a black
skirt and a blue top with a fascinating buckle that closed at the
throat and which Olivia fastened and unfastened continuously
during our conversation, giving added feeling that here was just
a cute kid, albeit a grand looking one!

"I'm so glad you've come," she said unceremoniously, with the
voice of one who is accustomed to eating much earlier as a general rule, "because now we can order our breakfast! What do

you like?" she smiled.

"Oh, I've had breakfast," I answered,
"go right ahead and order yours."

"But you *haven't*," she frowned her
disappointment. "Why, we had a
breakfast appointment!"

"Well, I'll have some milk and we can go gay over that."

"I made a personal appearance at the Strand last night," she
explained when we sat down to the business of talking, "and that
always upsets me terribly. I never seem to get used to personal
appearances and suffer terrible stage fright every time! You can
probably see the effects."

There were, I remarked, no tangible bruises.

"How did you ever manage to appear in 'A Midsummer Night's
Dream?'" I asked, "out there at the Bowl in front of so many
thousands of people, including the whole   [*Continued on next page*]

Her rise from
babyhood in To-
kyo to starhood
in Hollywood is
a "miracle" to
Olivia.

32

picture colony?" And, for all her breath-taking beauty, the question that arose in my mind was how such extraordinary good fortune had gravitated to her!

"I don't know," she answered slowly, as though considering her dastardly deed for the very first time. "I suppose it was because I'd just come from high school and didn't know much of what it was all about. And, too, because it was only very late when Gloria Stuart withdrew from the cast and I was actually given the rôle of Hermia, which I understudied."

Not least among the strange incidents which have crowded into her full young life is the fact that she was born in Tokyo, Japan, on July 1st, 1916, although only three years later her parents returned to America and eventually to Saratoga, California. There she attended grammar school, and, in rapid sequence, Notre Dame Convent, Los Gatos Union High School and then won a scholarship to Mills College at Berkeley—which, because of higher histrionics, she never took advantage of, though not to her regret!

It was while she was at Los Gatos that she was given the rôle of Puck (shades of Mickey Rooney) in the school production of "A Midsummer Night's Dream," and one of Professor Max Reinhardt's better scouts watched her work and decided that she'd do nicely to understudy the rôle of Hermia, which, without further ado, she proceeded to do!

So much has happened to the little de Havilland since! There has been a long term contract, first for five years and then, on her agent's advice, she signed for seven years—and a long and impressive "financial program" to say nothing of a formidable list of picture successes which, in the last two years, have included such amazing *coups de theatre* as "A Midsummer Night's Dream," "Captain Blood" and the memorable "Anthony Adverse," to say nothing of her current and brilliant performance in 'The Charge of the Light Brigade."

Olivia told me, amid much laughter, how she had spent her last birthday falling in and out of a "river" on the lot at Warner's realistically enacting her part for "The Light Brigade."

"How did you like playing with the dashing Errol Flynn?" I asked

"Delightful!" she assured me. "He is so pleasant and such good fun that, in the spirit of the whole thing, I didn't even mind getting wet and drying off by turns!"

"Well, it's good to know you're not going temperamental on us!"

"I've made up my mind to face my future with a practical viewpoint," she confided. (If you could ever hear the word "practical" coming from the un-

believably lovely Olivia!) "A star should realize she has just so many years to work and be popular and then——"

"And then," I asked, "what is your real objective? What have you always wanted to do?"

"I used to want to be a teacher, an English teacher, probably because my father was an English teacher who, because he was practical, later took over a law firm. But now," she finished impulsively, "I want to act for the rest of my life!"—which is as charmingly unpredictable an answer as are her moods!

In came the waiter and before long we were sitting down in front of a hastily improvised table and I was reaching for a napkin.

Drawing it out briskly to whisk across my lap I soon discovered, to my mixed emotions, that it was the napkin which so cozily had covered the toast, and looking down I saw I was all over toast and so was the rug.

I'm no de Havilland. I don't blush prettily. Embarrassment with me is just that. And toast on the rug is only one shade better than toast crumbs in bed.

Then *I* came in for a surprise.

Olivia rose grandly to the occasion. She said all the right things, assuring me that she loathed toast, that it was the very bane of her existence, that, indeed, I had done her, in a manner of speaking, almost as great a turn as had the intrepid Max Reinhardt, who started her on her career! In short, when I later met her mother, a charming, cultured woman, who has also been a dramatic coach, I realized that breeding and background *do* tell. Here was a little girl in modern clothes who, I felt, could be suddenly quite at home in the sweeping gowns and mannerisms of a grand lady! Here, I felt sure, was the answer to the enigma of the so-called de Havilland "luck." She was a natural born actress who, in the rôle of Hermia, had found a part which fitted her talents, ability and breeding as snugly as had the costumes her smooth young curves!

Just then the telephone rang, as it was doing continuously, and Olivia, who has no secretary (because of her "financial program"), answered it herself. Disguising her voice she assured an unknown caller that "Nobody is here." As she put the phone down she wore the guiltiest of expressions and her tongue curled from one side of her mouth to the other like some very wicked imp.

"I don't know what to do about them all," she explained, as it rang again.

This time it was different.

Obviously it was a boy friend calling "long distance," and, like some college freshman, her excitement, as she held on, was palpable. From her answers,

which I really tried not to hear—do you believe me?—well I tried not to be *too* curious, he was very anxious to see her, wanted to know if she were coming to his town for personal appearances? Olivia, now dignified and in complete possession of the situation, told him unfortunately she was not— and then, after relating how much she had enjoyed his letters, inquired if he were "happy"?

For one moment I fully realized how serious is this business of being a bright, new, and shiny star with (at twenty) a contract that seems to reach to the very border of senility (twenty-five). And as she put the receiver down I asked if she had many such young worshippers?

"I have no suitors," she answered, guilelessly, the very use of the word showing what an old-fashioned romanticist is this charming and capable young modern! "And I'm immensely grateful that's true. I meet probably the most attractive and intelligent men in Hollywood, but none has clicked with me romantically, and I'm very thankful for that at this stage of my career! My friendships are confined to men on my own lot because I'm so thoroughly tired when the business of acting, posing for stills, standing for fittings, being made up, having my hair dressed, being interviewed, studying my rôles, having story conferences with the director and all the other fascinating details that go into picture-making are through, I'm content to go straight home to bed—and call it a day! (advertisement)."

Her next part is in "Call It a Day," as the elder of two sisters, a rôle which she plays in real life.

"My own sister," she said, "wants to go on the stage now, though she's still busy at school and it's really too soon to know if she is fitted for acting."

In "Call It a Day" Olivia is supposed to be a young girl in love with Roland Young, who plays a mature, much-sought-after artist for whom she poses. This rôle should do much to popularize her in more modern stories—of which she expects to do three successively— returning then to costume parts, which are her favorites.

"People," she says, "knew how to live a century or two or three ago, graciously, with artfulness and taste. When I play in costume pictures it seems I have returned to those days and feel in sympathy and tune with them."

There is a flow of warmth about this young player that augurs well for her dramatic future, for it is plain to see that only the surface of her latent acting ability has been tapped. And (old softie that I am), I believe that she *is* sincerely grateful love has not made more complex her already involved existence.

"I'm sure if I were to fall in love,"

[Continued on page 177]

It was Betty Compson, one of the prettiest blondes ever seen on the screen, who said: "I have a sweetheart in every part!" Here's Betty with Hugh Trevor, when these two were believing their own love scenes.

By
James
Marion

Studio Sweethearts

THERE are three distinct classes of romance in Hollywood. First, there is the old-fashioned, hand-in-hand love that leads eventually to the altar. Then there is the "secret love" that seems to go nowhere in particular—but to the divorce courts in general. And there is the *third,* that keeps Hollywood and the gossips on tiptoe, and makes for all the silly rumors that continually exude from the film city. This last but decidedly not least type of romance is hectic but seldom permanent. Hollywood has a special name for stars in this group: *Studio Sweethearts.*

To Betty Compson must go credit for the discovery and exploitation of this new and handy idea. Betty's disclosure of studio romances has given Hollywood's famous sons and daughters a new method of whiling away otherwise weary hours during production of pictures, to say nothing of the publicity accrued. It all began with Miss Compson's remark to a very stunned and astonished writer:

"I don't know what I would do without my studio romances. I have never made a picture that I did not fall in love with some man in the cast. None of these harmless affairs ever lasted beyond the length of the production, but I think all concerned enjoyed them thoroughly. Nothing really serious—just like the sailors: *I have a sweetheart in every part!*"

With that explanation, Betty answered all the gossip about herself and Hugh Trevor, Grant Withers, and other leading men. In addition, she supplied the rest of the boys and girls with either an idea or an excuse. Since then? Well, let us see!

Take Joan Blondell and George Barnes, the Goldwyn cameraman. They met during the production of "The Greeks Had a Word For Them." Joan, always considered cute and talented, but never beautiful, was suddenly transformed into a gorgeous woman on the screen, and George, the cameraman, was the reason. Another studio romance, whispered Hollywood. True, Joan and George seldom went out in public, but they constantly lunched together. One day a newspaper reporter saw them and immediately published a "reported engagement." That was unfortunate for the reason that Barnes was in the process of getting a final divorce decree, so Joan denied a pending marriage. She and George were not seen together so much after that, but—you want to know a secret? They are to be married soon! Joan admits it openly, and as soon as her George is free to wed, she'll be Mrs. Barnes.

But here's one that will show you how trivial some of them really are—and how soon they stop and start again! Take the case of Lupe Velez and Lawrence Tibbett. That romance developed out of a playful attempt on the part of the vivacious Mexican to show the rest of the cast in "The Cuban" that she could turn the heart of the famous singer. It had been said that he was afraid of women—that he wanted no more of women after his divorce. Lupe was sure that she was able to make him fall and fall hard!

She tried, at first, to break down his natural reserve by saying things that would either make him laugh or embarrass him. He went her one better on every occasion by coming back with a

A studio romance that came true: John Gilbert and his Virginia, who met during the filming of Jack's picture, "Downstairs."

Connie Bennett and Joel McCrea, when Connie thought Joel was a pretty nice boy. But now she's La Marquise (Marquise de la Falaise.) (Left.)

Loretta Young and Grant Withers fell in love while making love in "Too Young to Marry." But it didn't last. (Below.)

fast retort that would leave Lupe sagging on her heels. With the net result: *She fell for him instead!* Every day they were seen to rush up to each other with a good-morning kiss. Luncheon? Always! Lupe even followed him into the men's barber shop and held one hand while he had the other one manicured. "Lupe and Larry have it bad," said the best of the insiders. But hardly had the studio romance reached the point where everyone in town was talking about them and conjecturing as to when they would become secretly married—*when Lupe went off to New York on the same train with John Gilbert!* That's how permanent they are—now they are and now they aren't. Maybe it is all done with mirrors.

If you will recall, Lupe and Gary Cooper started their romance during the making of a picture called "The Wolf

Song" in which they played together! At the start they were just Studio Sweethearts. No one expected that romance to survive the length of the production, but it did, and more. That is where this type of romance has Hollywood fooled! So many of them flash on and off during a picture schedule, Hollywood expects *all* will end with the final camera crank.

Connie Bennett and Joel McCrea, according to a once hot rumor, were to take the long plunge down to the altar. Gossip actually had this couple married. Joel was seen lying on the sands in front of Connie's beach place at Malibu with none other than the famous blonde lady herself. They were seen dancing, dining, first-nighting, and what have you. Oh, it was a hectic romance all right. And what happened?

Connie ups and marries the Marquis! We can't say at the moment whether or not this started out as a studio romance. Surely they were both working at the same studio, and were together a great portion of the time while this was possible. But we are inclined to believe that they were really in love long before they worked at the same studio—in fact, we are inclined to put a bit of credence in what [*Continued on next page*]

Joel used to say when questioned on his romance with Connie: *I think that Miss Bennett is really much in love with the Marquis. I don't believe she has a real, serious thought for me.* That will show you just how small these studio romances really are most of the time. Joel and Connie were involved in a studio romance while Connie and the Marquis *were already in love!*

Mention of Studio Sweethearts cannot fail to conjure up the names of Janet Gaynor and Charlie Farrell! We have often alluded to the fact that theirs was nothing but a casual studio romance, but the world chose to believe differently. It has since turned out that they were actually in love with other people at the very top of their private studio romance. Janet and Charlie were together during the making of several pictures. Hollywood liked the team off the screen just as well as the fans liked them *on!* Thus it is an easy matter to understand how their casual romance developed into a hectic bit of headline material. Those who still protest their views to the effect that these two are in love are just the type of people who don't believe in signs—after all, they are married, and *not* to each other!

And how about Frances Dee and Josef Von Sternberg?

There is a cute little scramble to untangle! As you will no doubt remember, Von Sternberg, the director, is the gentleman presumed to be so violently smitten by Marlene Dietrich. This is attested to by the fact that she was named in Josef's former wife's suit for alienation of affections. They were seen at every event of any importance for weeks on end. Then came the filing of the six hundred thousand dollar suit. It was probably thought best for Marlene and her director to give up their tête-à-têtes, at least for the time being. So, a studio romance developed between—Frances Dee and her director! Just a momentary flutter of the heart, nothing more. Von Sternberg began taking Frances all of the places he had formerly taken the beautiful German star. They were together constantly on the set and off during the production of "An American Tragedy." There was quite a good deal of talk to the effect that she was cutting out Marlene entirely—but now that the picture is finished and released the romance, if any, came to an end.

You remember the hectic love that developed between Loretta Young and Grant Withers during the filming of "Too Young to Marry." The kids eloped despite the strenuous opposition of Loretta's mother, and all went well for a while. Then it began to look as if Mother knew best. The Young-Withers romance went on the rocks, with Loretta getting a divorce.

But a studio romance that looks as if it might last is the alliance of Jack Gilbert and the pretty blonde Virginia Bruce. She was assigned the rôle of leading lady in Jack's picture. "Downstairs," adapted from the star's own story, and Jack proceeded to fall in love with her. She is an entirely different type from the former Mrs. John Gilberts and half of Hollywood is betting that she will make the temperamental Jack happy.

Then there's the studio romance of Norma Shearer and Irving Thalberg. Their romance started at Metro-Goldwyn-Mayer studio, and continued until they had reached the altar. This marriage is one of the points of interest in Hollywood—because it is a happy one. The colony is apt to be caught "pointing with pride" to this romance at any moment. It all started on that certain Christmas Eve when Norma finished working at eleven o'clock and was climbing the long stairs to her dressing-room with the thought that perhaps everyone else in the world was enjoying a sane night-before-Christmas. When she reached her dressing-room she looked out the window and saw her boss, Irving Thalberg, still working at his desk across the way. Hardly had she taken notice of this comforting fact when the telephone rang. It was Mr. Thalberg, who called to wish Miss Shearer a very merry Christmas. From then on it was considered a studio romance until the time came for the actual wedding.

And so Norma and Irving fooled the town and went the Studio Sweethearts a little better by becoming man and wife. However, this is one of the exceptions that prove the rule. Most of our very best Studio Romantics are just out for the ride—merely a method of passing a few hours together. The main reason you and I hear anything about them at all, is the fact that the "whispering chorus" works day and night spreading the news. Every season is rush season among the studio romance gossipers! And it's not advisable to place bets on these romances.

Helen Twelve-trees, in an exclusive interview, says: "Motherhood is of far greater importance than a career to me. Even if bearing a child means that I will have to retire definitely from the screen it will still be worth while"

By
Sonia Lee

Motherhood . . .
What it means to Helen Twelvetrees

AN EMOTIONAL revolution! Forgetting herself and gaining spiritual values! That's what having a baby is meaning to Helen Twelvetrees!

She spoke slowly, weaving dreams into the reality of sentences—of hopes for her child—what coming motherhood means to her. How having a child with its intimate and complete relationship will change the pattern of her life. What quota of happiness and growth she expects from the experience!

"Having a baby means," she explained, "that you can no longer be self-centered. A screen star thinks too much of herself—of her hair, her complexion, her clothes. It is the most essential part of her life. Of necessity she must think of these things if she is successful—and wants to make progress. The ego must be developed—or she is buried under small criticisms, biting sarcasms, those frightful moments when she doubts her own abilities."

The dusk deepened as she talked. The comfortably unostentatious room told more potently than words of this girl's background. Her father is advertising manager of the largest newspaper in New York City; her mother has that social equilibrium which expresses itself in her daughter's choice of quiet domestic life as the wife of Frank Woody Jr.—Hollywood real-estate broker.

"When I knew I was going to have a baby—so much that was important became of not the least importance," Helen continued. "Now I see myself, my career, the people around me from a different angle entirely.

"Motherhood is of far greater consequence than a career! Even if bearing a child will mean that I have to retire from the screen for a year, it will still be worth it. I have no illusions about lasting fame. If I should disappear from the screen for twelve months, I know that at the end of that time, I should have to start all over again—from the bottom—as I started before. The public would forget me. Producers and studios would forget me. But somehow, even such a price in payment for one thing that is always and forever your own is not too great. I would gladly, [Continued on next page] willingly—begin to rebuild the career it has taken me years to establish.

"For having a baby is being a woman —entering into a woman's estate!

"I know that my emotional and mental life is being broadened. I have developed a tolerant spirit. Until recently if an actor in a scene with me went up in his lines, or was difficult to work with I was impatient and angry. Today, I can make allowances for human frailties. For I have another interest!

"Child-bearing is a woman's ultimate experience. It should make her a greater personality. To an actress it is an indispensable journey—from which she should come back with farther-reaching horizons. With a capacity to understand pain and joy, and kindness and pity, and to interpret them more movingly than she ever could before.

"TO ME—planning for my baby—the emotional benefits are just by-thoughts. They are pleasantly drifting clouds. They are part of the dreams for my baby—dreams which soon will be gorgeous reality."

For her baby—and she doesn't care whether it's a boy or a girl—she has definite expectations. If it's a girl—she visualizes her as a great actress—but without vanity.

"I feel," she explains, "if I give her the correct psychological mould while she is young, I can achieve a young, unspoiled girl—no matter what her career may be. If it's a boy—I want him to go out in the world of business—where problems are to be faced and solved. I don't want my son to be an actor. I don't think, somehow, it's a man's work. Although," she adds with a smile, "how could we have screen dramas without our Gables and our Barrymores?

"I trust,' she says, "that I'll have my mother's clear insight regarding my child. Even though mother hoped that I would become an artist, yet when she realized that my entire ambition centered on the stage—her sole comment was 'in that event, you must be as good as possible; you must have the right training.' And so I went to the Sargent School in New York, where I learned the principles and the rudiments of acting. In no way has my mother tried to live my life for me.

"I want to be a successful mother. Not in the small matters of guarding my child's physical welfare—but in the larger realm of spiritual accord. For that reason—having one child or having many—will never take me permanently from the screen. Today motherhood alone is not enough. But to earn the lasting affection and respect of your children you must be a rounded-out personality, so that your viewpoint breaks the limiting bonds of a home alone."

The sunlit room which will soon be a nursery in the Woody's Brentwood home, is being measured for delicate pastel curtains. The wardrobe for the coming king or queen is to be all in white—and there are minute woolen shirts in the dresser drawers. The nurse will be the capable woman who took care of Helen as a child. She will come from New York in a short time.

And apart from dreams—Helen Twelvetrees is making very practical plans for her child. It involves a trust fund from her salary—to start the day of the infant's birth—a certain financial arrangement which will assure the Woody heir of a tangible measure of a mothers aspirations for it.

A Movie Fan's Crossword Puzzle
By Charlotte Herbert

The Final Fling

Garbo © INTERNATIONAL

IT IS, we are sure, impossible to be great part of the time and revert to commonplaceness the rest of the time. Greatness is built in, and a great person can never be caught off guard. When Garbo passed through New York on her vacation to her homeland, she permitted the press photographers to take her picture. The result is a delightful proof of our theory. Garbo is such an actress that her every thought pulls and tugs at the muscles of her face, and it is beyond her to conceal her emotional nature. Look at the photograph which the hounds of the press took of Garbo. You will see that she did not want to pose. (That settles for all time the insinuation that her hiding is a publicity gesture.) She makes herself face the cameras. See her clenched hand and defensively bent elbow. There is no ease to her figure. The most graceful woman in the world is taut and nervous. The disdain of her mouth fairly screams "Who says I dare not pose?" The out-thrust jaw is a lesson to anyone who thinks that bashfulness and timidity mean weakness, for they do not. Garbo could no more think of smiling than she could of whimpering, yet she has posed for hundreds of portraits and knows the value of an ingratiating friendly smile.

Garbo is a great actress because her sensitive mind is emotional and these emotions she is able to convey to you. She is returning shortly to make more pictures.

* * *

We told you last month to get "State Fair" and read it, so that your evening at this picture will be the culmination of weeks of anticipation. Janet Gaynor, Will Rogers, Charlie Farrell, James Dunn, Sally Eilers and Robert Montgomery will be in the picture.

The Editor

Precipitous

Erect

ACROSS

1 Shakespearian King
5 Music composers' favorite river
11 Last name of famous actress who played with Sir Henry Irving
12 He played in "The Expert"
14 A dress trimming
15 Every star has at least one
16 Seventeen hundred and sixty yards
18 Her latest picture is "Guilty as Hell"
19 To solicit
20 Her new picture will be "Those We Love" (initials)
22 A young actor on the Universal lot
23 Irate
24 The bleat of sheep
25 Aspect
27 Bill Boyd's wife (initials)
28 Before
29 Name of actor in "Radio Patrol"
31 Secure
33 An English player in "Five Star Final" (initials)
34 His latest picture is "Tiger Shark" (initials)
35 Relative of the Barrymore family
38 She was the widow in "So Big"
41 A tree
42 Behold!
44 To verify
45 Altitude (abbr.)
46 Roman numerals for 901
47 Advertisements
49 Like
50 Suffix denoting a native or citizen of
51 Uproar
52 Her last picture was "A Woman Commands"
54 Hail!
55 Name of famous American frontiersman
56 Hero of "Is My Face Red?"
59 Arrogant
60 She is noted for her wonderful mother characterizations
61 Great quantities

DOWN

1 A player in "The Gay Diplomat"
2 God of Love
3 Skill
4 A subtle and amusing actor (initials)
5 Automobiles replaced it
6 Conflict
7 A former serial star (initials)
8 Negative
9 A tree
10 To revise
11 First name of Paramount actress
13 The odic force of electricity
14 He could not have "dunn" better in "Society Girl"
15 To climb with difficulty
17 Printers' measures
19 They come Big and Wet out in Hollywood
20 A supernatural occurrence
21 Bustle
24 Ben Alexander (initials)
25 Marked with striae
26 Completion
30 Affable
32 Period of time
36 She will soon be seen in "Thirteen Women"
37 An actress in "The Widow from Chicago"
39 One of Harriet Beecher Stowe's characters
40 Clara Bow started it
42 To lick up
43 Stench
48 Nickname of comedian in soldier comedies
50 An Actor in M-G-M pictures
51 Basic
53 A unit
54 American Humorist
55 Brother (abbr.)
57 A suffix
58 She will soon be Mrs. George Brent (initials)
59 He hails from Budapest (initials)

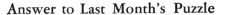

Answer to Last Month's Puzzle

HERE WE GO!

Count 4. In Hollywood you add a "bump" toward the left, consisting of pulling right hip up quickly, balancing with right toe, which pulls right foot back slightly, leaving weight on left foot. For official La Conga, swing or kick your right foot in front of your left. (See picture at the left, with Bob "bumping" to the left, right foot released)

Count 3: Step left with left foot, shifting weight to it, still moving left

Count 2. Cross your right foot over, in front of the left, moving leftward again

Count 1. Step left on your left foot, shifting the weight to it, moving leftward. (Note: We aren't dancing yet. This is just to show the foot movement)

Count 5. Now we're going to repeat pattern to right. At end of Count 4 weight was on left foot. So step right on right foot for Count 5, shifting weight to it, moving to the right

Count 6. Cross left foot over in front of right, moving to right

Count 7. Step right with right foot again, still moving to right

Count 8. "Bump" or kick with left foot in front of right. (See picture, right, with Bob "bumping" to right, his left foot released)

The girl does the same pattern, but begins by stepping right with right foot, crossing left foot over and in front of right, moving right, stepping again on right and "bumping" or kicking with left. Then she repeats the pattern to the left, thus covering the 8 counts.

So much for the foot movement of the basic step. Now's the time to put some swing into it. Legs move easily with not too much bend at the knees. Shoulders are carried level during 1-2-3, 5-6-7 counts. On 4 and 8, the "bumps," the shoulders do a quick horizontal swing—left shoulder moves slightly forward and back as the right shoulder comes forward in almost a jerk. The body is slightly

forward from hips up and the leg holding weight on the "bump" is rather straight. It is the "bump" or kick, together with the quick shoulder movement on counts 4 and 8, that form the outstanding characteristic of the Conga.

We're ready now to start dancing. The man takes his partner in a loose hold and leads her for several of the basic steps (repeating 1 to 8 several times) until they both have caught the rhythm and are moving smoothly together.

Then both drop arms and, still facing each other, start to do the basic step in opposite directions. The general movement after you are into this next step will be to the right for the girl and to the left for the boy. In order to do this, the boy must shift his weight, since after he finishes 1 to 8 counts his weight is on the right foot. He accomplishes this shift step by

stepping left as in the basic step to count 1, but instead of crossing over with right, he merely swings his right foot across, retaining weight on the left for count 2, steps right on right foot for count 3 and "bumps" or kicks with left on count 4. You'll note this holds man on place while girl is dancing to right, leaving them apart at end of first 4 counts. They cross each other on counts 5 to 8, still ending up apart. (Note: When the boy wants to dance again in unison with his partner, he does his shift step by stepping right on 1, swinging left across on 2 but holding weight on right, stepping left on 3, and "bumping" left on 4, which leaves right foot free to start to his right with the girl who moves with him to her left.)

Go back and forth with this step as many times as desired. A pleasant variation is to catch left hands on the "bump" right and right hands on the "bump" left.

A twosome variation: Mary Beth and Bob make their own arch. They start facing, La Conga for two or three steps . . .

. . . then the man turns to the left, the girl to the right, still holding hands until they are halfway around. Then . . .

. . . he takes his right hand back again and they come out of it facing, go right on with the regular steps of dance

A further variation is for each partner to make a complete turn on the 1-2-3, 5-6-7 counts while moving from side to side. I.e., step right with right foot on 1; put enough steam behind your next step left on count 2 to carry you halfway around a circle which you'll be completing to the right; finish circle on right foot count 3 and "bump" on count 4. Repeat, going to the left.

In the Conga line everyone on the floor gets in a queue and follows the leader, until the leader and his partner form an arch with their arms; whereupon every one dances under the arch and comes out in a circle, from which individual couples step out and shine. The picture below shows the way you look in the queue. Don't let the arch bother you—at home or on a casual floor you can do a twosome variation by making your own arch and skinning the cat under it.

A. Stand facing each other, hands meeting clasped in front of you, the way Bob and Mary Beth do it above. La Conga in this position for two or three steps, then

B. The man turns to the left and the girl to the right, still holding hands until

C. You get halfway around. Then he should take his right hand back again. If he doesn't you'll both end the step with a sprained back.

D. Come out of it facing each other and go right on with your dancing.

We might add that when you wish to progress around the room, the girl crosses her foot over in back instead of in front, when doing basic step.

This is the way you'll look in the Conga line when you're scrunching along, following the leader

The Boopsie-Doodle step: You end up by "bumping" each other. See directions at the left

WE sort of like this Boopsie-Doodle step.

Stand side by side, as you did up there in the beginning, but instead of both walking to the left, the girl should take that direction and the man should go to the right. At the fourth step, kick in toward each other, the girl with her right foot, the boy with his left. When you start back, turn as you step so that when you do your little "bump" and kick on the fourth step, you do indeed bump into each other, right there on the derrière. It's silly, but it's lots of fun!

Photographs by Hyman Fink

PRIZE CONTEST!

Can You Describe

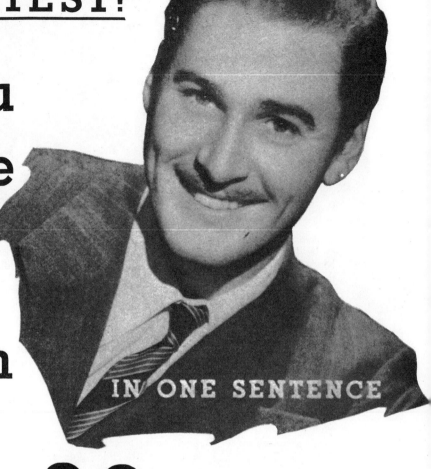

Errol Flynn

IN ONE SENTENCE

Using Just 20 Words?

HOW proficient are you in the use of adjectives? In order to describe Errol Flynn most effectively at least three descriptive adjectives should be used. For instance, here's a sample sentence of 20 words containing three adjectives which we think fit his type and personality:

One of the most *debonair* and *adventurous* Hollywood actors is *attractive* Errol Flynn whose hobby is travelling in strange places.

There are dozens of adjectives equally descriptive of Errol Flynn. All you have to do is think up three which you think describe him most aptly and incorporate them into a well-rounded sentence of your own, using not more and not less than 20 words. Write your sentence on the coupon below.

There will be four prizes awarded to the writers of the four best sentences, in our opinion. These prizes consist of four beautiful gold wrist watches made by the Longines-Wittnauer Company. They are watches which everyone of you would be proud to own.

PRIZES TO BE AWARDED

FIRST PRIZE
Lady's wrist watch, valued at $40.

SECOND PRIZE
Man's wrist watch, valued at $37.50

THIRD PRIZE
Lady's wrist watch, valued at $25.

FOURTH PRIZE
Man's wrist watch, valued at $25.

USE THIS COUPON TO SEND IN YOUR ENTRIES

(Write Plainly)

....

....

Submitted by ....

Street .... City .... State ......

c/o SILVER SCREEN, 45 W. 45th St., New York, N. Y.

CONDITIONS

1. Sentences must not be more and not less than 20 words. Three or more adjectives must be used.

2. Contest closes Midnight, May 25.

3. In the event of a tie, prizes of equal value will be given to each tying contestant.

4. Address your contribution to, Adjective Contest Editor, Silver Screen, 45 W. 45th St., New York, N. Y.

JEAN HARLOW
—from EXTRA to STAR

By Sonia Lee

A Jean Harlow you never see on the screen —spontaneously gay, full of zest and charm. Neither fame nor sorrow have dimmed the sparkle in the mind and heart of the girl all Hollywood sincerely loves

LAST month you read of Jean Harlean Carpenter's remarkable childhood, the unusual understanding and companionship with her mother. These things were to have an unusual influence on Jean's life in the future. Although she went away to school and her parents separated, Jean remained more like a sister than a daughter to Mrs. Carpenter. Even Jean's marriage to Charles Freemont McGrew at the age of sixteen did not disturb her mother. A true mother, she realized that disapproval of the elopement might mean bitter, lasting disillusionment to her daughter. Bravely, she put her arms around Jean and Chuck McGrew and wished them every happiness. Now go on with the story:

JEAN and Chuck went to New York on their honeymoon, and from there sailed through the Panama Canal to Los Angeles. Much has happened in those six years since Jean Harlow, a little school girl, eloped!

The newlyweds found a charming little house in Beverly Hills. Soon they were in the midst of a gay young set, whose only concern was what excitement could be organized for their amusement and diversion.

It wasn't long before Chuck and Jean began to drift apart. Jean was restless and eager. A round of amusement wasn't enough to fill her heart or her soul or her days. But her letters to her mother never breathed a word of her dissatisfaction, nor admitted that her marriage had already begun to fail.

Mrs. Bello (Jean's mother had wed again following her divorce), with the intuition of a mother, knew that Jean needed her. Marino Bello sold his manufacturing business in Chicago, and he and his wife moved to California to be near Jean. Certainly she needed them, needed them desperately in this chaotic period.

Her introduction to the studios came quite by accident. One of Jean's guests at a luncheon she was giving, played occasional

Jean Harlow's beautiful white colonial home—a monument to her sensational success in Hollywood

parts in motion pictures and that day had to leave the party early to keep an appointment at the Fox Studios. Jean drove her to the studio and went through the gates with her. She was fascinated by the place, by the sense that here was achievement, here was occupation both for the mind and the spirit.

While on the lot she was introduced to three men who were impressed with her astounding beauty and offered to give her letters to the Central Casting Bureau, the clearing house for extra players, and to several studio casting directors. She waited while the letters were written, carried them home with her, put them in her bureau drawer and promptly forgot them.

Several weeks later she told some friends of hers about the letters and they taunted her that she lacked the courage to present them. She made a bet that she wasn't afraid, and the next day presented herself at the studio gates. She gave her name as Jean Harlow.

Before long she was being called frequently for extra work, and after her first hesitation, she accepted the calls.

Right: Jean Harlow has her picture snapped on the diving board of the huge swimming pool on her estate where she spends hours in the company of the many friends who have discovered her to be one of Hollywood's most lovable personalities

THE Casting Director at the Hal Roach Studios spotted her in *Moran of the Marines* and offered her the feminine lead in two Laurel and Hardy comedies. She acquitted herself so well that a five-year contract followed.

Here was the thing, she thought, which would still the nameless craving which she could neither define nor stop. Social routine merely set her nerves on edge. But this demanding, relentless "movie" business had a quieting effect on her. Here at last was something she wanted to do. Here at last was a chance to do something with her life. In work, in a career, she would find respite from the emotional disturbances of her unfortunate marriage.

But the career she had begun in such gaiety found an objector in her grandfather, who had been kept in ignorance of her new activities until he saw her in scanty black underthings on one of his rare visits to a theater. He lost no time in 'phoning to California and in expressing his displeasure in thunderous wrath.

There was nothing left for Jean to do but to ask Hal Roach to release her from her contract, which he did. For eight long months Jean wandered around trying to fill her days with things which had some purpose. She and Chuck were drifting apart daily, and finally they decided to part, and Jean went to her mother's home.

Shortly thereafter she received a quite unexpected call to play in a picture with Clara Bow. It was almost like an answer to a prayer. She accepted it, after consulting with her mother and deciding that they would not tell her grandfather of her return to pictures until such time as her fame might prove that [Continued on page 177]

SHIRLEY TEMPLE'S LAST LETTER TO SANTA

DEAR SANTA:

Every year I write you a letter and on every Christmas you've always remembered what I ask for. I know it's not nice to ask for things but I've decided that telling you what I want might save you a lot of trouble. So this is a sort of shopping list and if you have time to get around to me after taking care of all the other little girls I'll be very glad if you take this list along.

But there is something I have to explain first. It is about last year. I didn't mean to play a trick on you. I just wanted to *see* you, Santa. Just once. That's why I put the bell on the toe of

ILLUSTRATION BY VINCENTINI

my stocking and hung it by my bed (instead of the usual place on the mantel) so I'd be sure to hear it. But I didn't. You filled it without ever making a sound—with those candy nuts I

love so, and little glass figures for my collectchun and the small silver tea set. Remember?

And maybe I'd better explain about that stocking too. Mine isn't very big. Sonny and Jack (they are my brothers) only wear socks but they hold more. So I told a friend of mother's and she made me that glazed chintz stocking two feet long. I hope you don't mind because I'd like to use it again this year.

45

WHAT I want more than anything, Santa (even more than a double-folding sleeping bag and one of those jiffy tents) is another Jimmy. O I know it will be hard to find and you will have to look all over because Jimmy was the dearest baby doll in the world. He went to Honolulu with me and he was so good. But on the trip we took last summer I left my Jimmy sitting in the car right in the sun when we went to the Grand Canyon. I never should a done that because my dad locked the car and it got pretty hot. When we came back Jimmy's cheeks were cracked. The paint had run onto his little white rompers and when I picked him up his lashes fell out. I just could not help crying. My dad sent him back to the doll hospital in Hollywood but they couldn't fix him. When I got home I buried my Jimmy in our backyard and Mary Lou Isleib (she is my best friend and stand-in) was pallbarer. So please let me have another Jimmy.

And I would like to have:
1 pr dungaries (blue)
1 shirt (blue and red check like Bill's the cowboy at Hillsdale ranch)
1 pr 6-shooters.

That is to wear when I ride the pony Mr. Schenck gave me. (We play G-men of the West. The pony is awful smart.)

And if it's not asking to much I certainly would like the wardrobe that goes with Lottie. I bought Lottie myself last week with money I saved up. But when I went to the store after her the clerk said—This doll's clothes are extra. And I did not have enough. They are on the 4th floor so you will know and they are in a big hatbox marked My Dates. She has a dress for every day in the week. A blue one with a brown fur jacket (my favorite) and a red swow suit.

LAST year I went to that store to see a man who *said* he was you. But I told mother He is not the real Santa because he said—Well, Shirley I see all your pictures—and I know you cannot do that up at the North Pole. But mother said He is a stand-in for Santa. I guess you have a lot of stand-ins.

We had a swell time last Christmas. I went to the Assistance League the day

before and they let me help push the wagons and fill the baskets. Then we went home to supper but I could not eat much. We always have the Tree on Christmas Eve. A big green one (I do not like the white they smell so funny) with electric candles and balls on it. My dad puts it on a turn-table which plays Silent Night. Only it did not work last year. The tree was to heavy.

Did you see the Star of Bethelehem lit up on the pine tree outside? Sonny put that up. He nearly fell.

We never open presents before Christmas morning but *one* kind of opened itself up. There was a terrible scream in the kitchen and we all ran out and sitting right on the floor in a cage was a big red macaw. Somebody had brought him for me around by the back and he had pecked through his paper covering. He was screaming at Elizabeth May (she is our cook) and Elizabeth May was screaming right back at him with a broom. My brother Jack said Haha and the macaw said Ha ha to and everybody laughed.

Once I got a very nice cow for Christmas. It was from the children of Tillamook where the cheese comes from. The Xpressman brought it to the studio and mother said My goodness where are we going to keep it? We tied it to the little fence outside my bungalow but it ate all the tops off the flowers and the studio gardener was pretty mad. I wanted to take it home it was so beautiful, only we lived in the house on 19 St in Santa Monica then and when we phoned dad about it he said Well it is a case of keeping the cow or the car. We have not room for both! So a milk farm man came and got it. It has little cows now.

Every Christmas morning when I was a little girl mother woke me with sleigh bells. Now she lets me ring them. My dad says 5 is to early so I wait till 6. We all go in the room together where the family presents are (The other presents are downstairs). Granny gave me a green sweater she knitted herself last year. And there was the nicest kitchen store from You with tiny jars and little potatoes and lemons and everything for my playhouse. I am just learning to

knit. I made my dad a tie but he has not worn it yet. He says he is saving it.

I LOVE Christmas dinner. Sometimes Elizabeth May lets me help. I can not cook much xcept biscuits. I make those on my little stove out in the playhouse. I did when Miss Carrie Jacobs Bond came to tea last Monday. (She is coming to visit me on the set of The Little Princess to.

But Santa when I was washing my dishes afterwards my dog Rowdy jumped up and broke three cups and the tea pot cover. I would like very much to have another tea set if it is not to much trouble. There is a very pretty one (blue with yellow flowers) on the 4th floor of that store I told you about. And in case your not in a hurry could you just sort of look over the new Wizard of Oz book? And some of the Ranger series?

Mother says Christmas is a family day so we do not go out. We play and open presents and it is the Best day of the year. But the next day Mary Lou and my friends come over. We make Christmas last the whole week! In the evening my dad drives us around to see all the trees lit up outdoors and they are so beautiful. One house in Beverly Hills has studio snow piled all over the yard and raindeer in front. Sometime I would like to see real snow on Christmas.

Did you see our wreath? A lumber Jack man up north made it for me with my name on it. It must have been hard because holly pricks. People are awful good. So are you. Please give all my friends (like the cripple boy in Spokane and the lady from DeTroit who writes me every week) extra presents. Thank you Santa.

Love,

Shirley Temple.

P. S. Mother says Please don't bring any more rabbits. I got two darling Chinese ones last year and when we came back from Honolulu there were 45.

Marlene Dietrich Answers Her Critics

By Jack Grant

SCREEN BOOK SCOOP

Marlene's most recent portrait

"**B**UT I don't mind being misunderstood," Marlene Dietrich told me. "In fact, if offered a choice, I am sure I should prefer to be misunderstood.

"More than a year ago, I stopped giving interviews. I felt I had nothing new to say. I also felt there was much too much being written about me. Writers were thoroughly familiar with my life story and they no longer asked me about it. Instead, they told me about themselves, very intimate things, preparatory to questioning me about matters equally intimate. This I did not like.

"My private life as it affects my public life cannot be kept secret. That it has become public property does not annoy me. But what I do when I am alone, what I think about and how I conduct myself—these things are strictly my own affair.

"Imagine changing places with me. How would you enjoy picking up a magazine—practically any magazine—to read 'All About Marlene Dietrich' for ten cents?

"You would not like it? No, of course, you would not. Nor do I.

Preferred Silence

"**I** DO not like to talk about myself at any time and I particularly dislike to talk of intimate matters for publication. Once you have told your fans everything, they say, 'Well, we know all about her now. Let's find somebody else, somebody new.' Too often when this happens, actors blame the public, charge their fans with fickleness. It is not fickle to lose interest when no mystery remains.

"I do not care if I am misunderstood as you say I am. I do not care how many stories are written about me giving wrong ideas—that is, if they are interesting ideas. But I do not want to be

so well-known as to be uninteresting."

Marlene Dietrich treated me to another of her fascinating smiles. It was her smile that had started all of this in the first place. Seeing the impish grin that seems to be constantly lurking in the corners of her mouth, I realized the Dietrich I had believed to be a rather humorless person was really the possessor of a rare sense of humor. This discovery startled me into the statement that she was grossly misunderstood.

Her answer, as recorded, was, however, even more astounding. In the years I have been interviewing in Hollywood, I have written countless thousands of words in which stars have pleaded to be

understood by their public. Marlene Dietrich is the first one I have encountered who does not worry about misunderstanding. And her reasons are certainly excellent.

The only faulty part of her reasoning is that she could ever be "too well-known to be interesting." The man who pretends to "know" the many faceted Dietrich personality is a fool.

A Strange Personality

SHE meets you with great charm and poise. From the moment of meeting, her attention is all yours. She appears to exclude everything and everybody to devote herself entirely to you. Whether you are a man or a woman, you are pleased and flattered by her attention. You had no idea she was such a friendly person. Her command of the English language and the ease with which she uses it also surprise you.

Then suddenly her mood changes. To say that she becomes a different individual is as true as the expression is hackneyed. You still have her attention but she has eluded you, is now remote.

You start to rearrange your impressions. But before you are through, there is another chamelon-like change. During the hour I spent talking to her in her Paramount bungalow—in the first interview she has granted in more than a year—I met a whole room full of Marlene Dietrichs. And the only similarities I saw in their characters were a friendliness and a constantly-present sense of humor.

Oh no, my friends, don't accept these stories you read "All About Marlene Dietrich for ten cents" entirely upon their face value. If the writers "reveal" her personality, they give you only one Dietrich. There are many Dietrichs.

[*Continued on page 178*]

The star breaks her long silence for the first time to speak for herself in reply to many false stories—

"Bogie"

A great author writes of a great friendship with a great actor, HUMPHREY BOGART

Mr. and Mrs. Bogart (the former Mayo Methot). "He has a great love for animals"

DON'T know when I first met "Bogie" but he has been a friend for a very long time—about as long as any friend I have. And it has been the kind of friendship that is real and based on granite rock, because out of the past twenty years I doubt that we have been in the same place at the same time for longer than a few months.

Friendship is a curious thing and abused by a great many people. Above all it is not possessive and separation has nothing to do with it.

A friend remains a friend, even though 10,000 miles separate him in space and ten years in time. The kind of friend I like, the kind of friend who endures, is the kind with whom time and space make no difference. After ten years you can walk into a room and meet again and say, "Hello, Jim" and take up again exactly where you left off. That's the kind of friend Bogie is and there aren't many like him.

I have an idea that all this is going to sound too perfect, too good to be true. All I can say in reply is that I wouldn't be writing it if I didn't believe as much as I do in Humphrey Bogart as a person and as a friend. I'm writing it because I've never read anywhere anything about Bogie that gave any idea of what he is really like and because there are a good many people who admire him as an actor, I thought they might want to know what sort of a person he is.

There aren't many like him in Hollywood or elsewhere for that matter. I've known him when he didn't

Above: On the stage with Leslie Howard in "The Petrified Forest." Says Mr. Bromfield: "He had sacrificed his good looks by cropping his hair"

Culver

After "The Petrified Forest," Hollywood wanted him. Below: With Ida Lupino in "High Sierra"

know where his next meal was coming from and I've known him with plenty of money, and I've never noticed the least difference. Bogie is not one of those stars who was discovered overnight. He came up the hard way and by the time he reached Hollywood he was already a fine trained actor.

He went into acting half by accident because he had gone to school with young Bill Brady and between them existed the kind of friendship with which Bogie's life is rich. Young Bill's father, William Brady, is one of America's great theatrical producers and Bogie began his career with bit parts. Then he discovered that he liked the business and began to put his heart into it and almost at once they began to discover along Broadway that there was a new young juvenile with talent. Only they hadn't discovered yet that the young juvenile was exactly Bogie's role.

Nevertheless, he did very well, because Bogie is a worker. Anyone who has ever had anything to do with him on the stage or in pictures knows that I don't mean he's one of those actors who has to carry a "mood chamber" about with him to sit in before he goes on. He belongs to that great tradition of actors who can rise from a poker game, walk on the stage or before the cameras and give a great performance. That's because he is a natural actor and sincere one and because he has as good a sense of wit and humor as anyone I've ever known.

In those [Continued on page 178]

IT'S RUBY'S TURN NOW . . . !

By CAROLINE SOMERS HOYT

This story tells how Ruby takes her new fame . . . and the picture (top of page) illustrates it . . . Al and Ruby arriving in New York recently.

ONE day I was having lunch in the First National commissary with Ruby Keeler. Her husband, Al Jolson, attired in golf knickers and white cap, came up to the table.

"Want to play golf this afternoon, honey?" he asked.

"I'm sorry, darling, I can't," she said. "I've got to rehearse the dance routines for 'Golddiggers.' Then I've got a fitting later." She saw the look of disappointment on his face. "But maybe if I hurry I could meet you about five and we could have one round."

And there was Al Jolson with a glorious California afternoon on his hands and nothing to do with it but wait for Ruby to finish her studio activities.

When Ruby Keeler and Al Jolson arrived in New York not long ago to attend the opening of Ruby's latest picture, she was interviewed by dozens of reporters.

Hundreds of eager fans stood in the lobby of their hotel and begged for her autograph.

The news cameramen snapped dozens of pictures of her.

During their stay in New York I called Ruby on the telephone. Al answered and told me that Ruby was out and could not see me that day. He might have been Ruby's business manager or press agent—the way he spoke to me. And I was disappointed. I had wanted to see Ruby.

Then suddenly I remembered that just a few years ago I had turned heaven and earth in an attempt to get an appointment with the busy, the sought-after, the important Al Jolson.

FOR behind these three apparently simple and average incidents there is a story as tragic as the history of show business.

Al Jolson and Ruby Keeler. Five years ago you said it that way, if you said it at all. Five years ago it was the great Al Jolson and "who was that little chorus girl he married?"

But now it is Ruby Keeler. Al Jolson is her husband.

Even before talkies Al was the greatest entertainer in the world. He made more money than any of the then-great. Came talkies and he was the one great star. "The Singing Fool"—his picture—will go down in motion picture history. Being a part of history, however, is scant

... Ruby Keeler has fulfilled most every girl's dream of instant and unusual success. But to her, at least, husband Al Jolson is still the Big Shot of the family

After her big success in "42nd Street" Warner Brothers hurried Ruby into "Golddiggers of 1933" in which you see her opposite crooner Dick Powell (top picture). Above, Marland Stone paints Ruby for this month's cover of MODERN SCREEN. Success!

consolation when one is still alive. When Al appeared on the street thousands followed him and begged for his autograph and laughed at his wisecracks. And just the other day I was disappointed when he answered the 'phone and told me Ruby Keeler was out. Isn't it amazing that now this slip of a girl, not much over twenty, erstwhile Texas Guinan chorus girl, is now the star of the family and Al Jolson—the great Jolson—makes appointments for her, answers her telephone and languishes away a California afternoon waiting while she rehearses and has fittings at her studio?

But the curious part of this strange, topsy-turvy pattern is that Ruby doesn't know it is different from what it was. To Ruby, Al is as great as he was that night, years ago, when he came to Guinan's night club and asked somebody who the cute little tap dancer was.

So perhaps that is what makes it possible for Al to go on. Perhaps that is why he can watch Ruby's fame grow and his diminish. Ruby adores him, admires him and respects him. To her he is still the greatest showman of his time.

You should have seen them when they arrived in New York. The news cameramen swooped down to take their pictures. It was Ruby they wanted, but Ruby stepped behind Al, let him take center stage, with a big broad smile, and just looked over his shoulder. Ruby wanted it that way, because that's the sort of girl Ruby is.

IF it hadn't been for the fact that she was born with dancing feet, Ruby would never, never have chosen the theatre as a career. She just isn't the type. But in school her teachers watched her going through the dull routine of "drill" and saw how lithe her body was, how quick her step and that she turned the stupid exercise into a thing of rhythmic beauty.

It was those teachers who persuaded her to go to the Professional Children's School. At thirteen she was a chorus girl in "The Rise of Rosy O'Reilly." And not much longer after that was a dancer in Texas Guinan's night club.

I'm sure you'd say that that was no place for a young and inexperienced girl to work. But you wouldn't know Ruby. She tells you now—her soft eyes lit by the fire of sincerity—that the girls at [Continued on next page]

Guinan's were "awfully nice girls." And she isn't putting on an act. To Ruby, they were.

Ruby managed, somehow, to remain immune to the sinister and sometimes sordid atmosphere she breathed. She danced at Guinan's but she was never a part of it. I'll give you a typical incident.

One night there was a fight in the club, the reason for which remains a tawdry secret of the underworld. Guns were drawn. Hatred charged the air. Everyone in the place was filled with terror.

And Ruby? Well, Ruby was down in the grill room. She didn't know there had been a fight until the other girls told her about it later, for Ruby was always somewhere else when these spectacular events occurred.

Ruby worked at Guinan's—that was all. The life was never an actual part of her life.

And that, of course, was partly because of her family.

For Ruby had lots more fun telling her brothers and sisters about the celebrities that came to the club than she had stepping out after the show. Besides, she was too tired to do much stepping out.

Ruby's working day at the club began at twelve-thirty and ended at half past four in the morning. The rest of the morning and the better part of the day were the child's sleeping hours. She usually got up at five and told the family everything that had happened the night before.

It was one of those big, jolly, Irish families and with them Ruby felt much more at home than in the world of glittering tinsel in which she worked.

ONE day Ruby asked her sisters, "Guess who came in last night?"

Ruby couldn't wait for them to guess.

"Al Jolson," she said, with a note of due awe in her voice.

"Al Jolson!" they repeated.

Yes, the great Al Jolson had been to Texas' Club—the greatest entertainer in the world, the big shot of the theatrical business and—what's more—he had definitely noticed Ruby. He had asked who she was. It was all very exciting and thrilling and her sisters sat wide-eyed and listened as she told the story.

And that was how the romance began —the romance between the big entertainer and the little chorus girl.

Ruby was so thrilled to be seen in company with the great Al Jolson. For she had never overcome her awe of celebrities and a feeling of her own unworthiness.

She was so shy, so unsure of herself that when Ziegfield asked her to star in "Show Girl" she told him she could neither sing nor act and that he was making a mistake in putting her in the part. But he patted her on the back and persuaded her to take the stellar rôle.

She suffered such torments that when she would look out into the audience and discover two heads together, people whispering and laughing, she was quite sure that they were laughing at her. In spite of encouragement from Ziegfeld she died a thousand deaths of self-consciousness whenever she stepped on the stage and finally, her nervousness was so great, she became physically ill and a doctor told her she must leave the show.

Ruby didn't want to be anything but just Al Jolson's wife, to shine only in his reflected glory.

But the executives begged her to work in pictures. The first offer came to play opposite Al in one of his films. Ruby refused that flatly. She knew Al was nervous when he worked and she thought the added worry of her would trouble him. Besides, now that she and Al were married she had no desire for a career.

They broke down her resistance

finally and she consented to "Forty-Second Street."

Again she suffered from stage fright, although she was thrilled to meet the stars and asked for autographs like any high school girl. And still, as her popularity on the lot grew, she believed that it was just because of Al.

WITH the utmost sincerity she told me, People hardly ever remember me. But they all know Al and it's fun meeting them through him."

You see? To Ruby there is no change. Their relationships are exactly the same. She does not realize what has happened.

But these are the facts. With the release of "Forty-Second Street" Ruby's star ascended. It was one of the smash hits of the season and Ruby became an instantaneous success. She was rushed into "Golddiggers of 1933" and other films are in preparation for her.

In the meantime—and even long before—Al's star had been waning. The novelty of his work in the first talkies having worn off, he is no longer the greatest entertainer in the world.

But the curious part is that Ruby doesn't know it. The beautiful part of the story is that Ruby still sees Al as the greatest entertainer and her picture triumphs are merely secondary to the glory of being Al Jolson's wife.

The important part of her life is being with Al.

She actually doesn't realize that he is answering the 'phone for *her* and waiting on *her* while she rehearses and has fittings, for Ruby is still the little girl in the night club who was awed when Al Jolson asked her name.

As his popularity with the public fades, his popularity with Ruby grows. In her heart he is the great one, she the lesser. She still thinks that it is only because she is Al Jolson's wife that anyone is interested in her.

And so, perhaps, Al is compensated.

Let Me Grow Up!

Bette Davis pleads for a chance to act her age

With Richard Barthelmess in *Cabin in the Cotton*, Bette Davis gives the finished performance of a seasoned actress. Yet, casting directors, she says, refuse to believe, because of her youthful appearance, that she can portray mature rôles

By Miriam Gibson

—*Irving Lippman*

Most women are anxious to appear younger than they actually are, but not Bette Davis. Her youthful appearance is a hindrance rather than a help to her career. She is twenty-four but directors won't believe she is old enough to play that age on the screen

MOST women want to be known as younger than their actual age. But not so with golden-haired, blue-eyed Bette Davis.

"My very youthful appearance is a hindrance rather than a help," she laments. "When casting directors are looking for a girl to fill a serious rôle, they take one look at me and say 'No.' They seem to think that I can't portray the proper balance for a girl of twenty-four. No one will believe that I am that age.

"Unusually youthful appearance is a characteristic of our entire family. My grandmother is seventy years old and looks not a day over fifty."

Imagine! And thousands of women all over the world are spending millions of dollars every year to look more youthful. But Bette Davis is one of those girls who wants to be herself.

"When I was on the stage with Richard Bennett he told me one day that I looked just like two of his daughters. Of course he considered it a great compliment—and it was. But I don't want to be like someone else. When I first went to Hollywood, everyone mistook me for Constance Bennett. It grew to be very embarrassing at times. It's not so bad now, but it still happens frequently."

She flicked the ashes from her cigarette and tucked her foot more securely under her. She was curled up in a big armchair—which seemed to swallow her—in lounging pajamas of maroon and white, lined with green, her dainty little feet in green satin sandals and her only jewelry a deep red stone bracelet.

"You know, I loathe beads and jewelry in general. But I must always wear a bracelet—I adore them. I like long drooping earrings with formal evening clothes. And I love pretty clothes. I never had so many until I went to Hollywood. In New York I always wore black and white—really my favorite. But in Hollywood everyone goes in for bright colors, and I've joined the ranks. Of course, being a blonde my favorite color is blue." [*Continued on page 180*]

Mrs. Gable never visits the set to check up on Clark's big clinches such as this one (above) with Joan Crawford in "Forsaking All Others." She is neither jealous nor suspicious and is content to remain in the background of his public life, serene in the knowledge that she is first in his private one.

Why I Stay Married

Are you wives on the spot? Jealous of your husbands?

A famous husband named Gable tells his side of the story

IF you have an attractive husband—or contemplate annexing one—you have the same problems that beset Ria Gable. She has the constant worry of predatory women—so have you. She has to fear flattery that turns a man's head, ego that breeds superiority—so do you. Her husband's reactions must be your husband's reactions, so I sought out Clark. His answer is revealing, helpful to us all.

I said to Clark, over the luncheon table, "What kind of a woman do you think an actor should marry? In order to make marriage successful, I mean?"

Clark said, without an instant's hesitation, "The kind of a woman I am married to—my wife."

We had been talking about Hollywood marriages and their failures and the why of their failures—Kay Francis and Kenneth MacKenna, Ruth Chatterton and George Brent, Ann Harding and Harry Bannister, Gloria Swanson and her exes, Jean Harlow and Hal Rosson, the sadly swelling list of them.

Clark said, "It's all predicated, I believe, on the basic law of things—where the husband, or in our business the 'star,' is the breadwinner, the marriage has a seventy-five

The Gables in a party mood (left). She likes social life—he likes hunting, yet they never reach an impasse.

ing's, Gloria Swanson's, and so on, the wives were the stars. The men were known as 'the husbands of . . .' To be 'a husband of' means the divorce court even as you stand at the altar. You can't get away from the fundamental laws separating and governing men and women. Grease paint on the face does not alter immutable laws. Man is born with a dominant ego—offend that ego or compete with it in the same field and, if you are a woman, you will soon be a divorcée."

I said, "You've never talked, specifically, about your own marriage, Clark, or your own wife. Do you mind?"

Clark said, "Not at all. You've asked me what kind of a woman an actor should marry and the only way I *can* answer that question is to describe my own wife.

TO begin, then, I am the 'star,' Ria is my wife. But she is a wife, who though not in my profession *is* in it—for me, not for herself. She is interested in it and she is thoroughly informed about every phase of it. She is ambitious about it for me. She is interested in it as she would be interested in medicine, in law, or in banking if any one of these were my life work.

"She is, also, a very self-sufficient woman, which is very important in the making of a successful 'movie marriage.' She has her own interests, her own friends, she has her bridge clubs and parties and children and our home. She doesn't seize hold of my life with idle, and therefore morbidly curious, [*Continued on page 180*]

per cent chance of success. You can look about and make, off hand, a list of vital statistics proving this contention. For instance, the Jean Hersholts, the Clive Brooks, the Leslie Howards, the John Boles, the Warner Baxters, the Morgans, Frank and Ralph—in every one of these marriages the husband is the one in the arena and the wife is just the wife. And in every one of these marriages, too, the marriage has stood and appears to be standing on the firm bedrock of many years. Also, in every one of these marriages the husbands and wives are of approximately the same respective ages and the wives are intelligent, self-sufficient women who have been around and know what it is all about. They are real people, neither jealous rivals nor paper-doll appendages.

"On the other hand, and in such cases as Ann Hard-

WHAT'S THE MATTER WITH

Is it true that her marriage to Clark Gable is responsible for Carole's re-

THERE ARE persons in Hollywood who are sore at Lombard. She doesn't care, however, because she probably doesn't know of her misfortune. If she did, she would doubtless do something about it, because Carole is too good a business woman to wilfully make anyone sore at her and too warm-hearted to deliberately give offense to anyone. It never pays to make enemies. Least of all in Hollywood where that little, old office boy you've heard about today may be a producer tomorrow. Lombard knows all this. Yet she is making folks mad. What's the matter with Lombard? That's what Hollywood is asking.

Carole has long been a particular pet of the boys and girls who write stories about the stars, because she was always cooperative, because she always gave swell, honest copy, told the truth and didn't blue-pencil every word she spoke that was more pithy than a nursery rhyme. Lately all is changed. There is, these days, an un-Lombardian evasiveness, a disregard of matters she once attended to richly and generously.

Perhaps, you may say, Lombard has been shy of people, of the Press,

because she has not wanted to discuss her recent marriage with Gable. But that is no good, for Carole has gone out socially, and has given interviews since the beginning of her romance with Gable.

In my effort to diagnose the case of Carole I've talked to her best friends. I've talked to Fieldsie, now Mrs. Walter Lang. And Fieldsie, as every Lombard fan knows, is Carole's most intimate friend. Carole and Fieldsie were Sennett girls together, sharing the same custard pie, driving to and from the studio in Fieldsie's car so that they could pool the expense of gasoline. Later, they shared a house together, and Fieldsie acted as Carole's business manager. And so, from Fieldsie and one or two other old pals, I garnered the material I needed to answer the question, "What is the matter with Lombard?" Out of it all, came these pertinent facts—and they are facts:

In the first place, Carole, so her friends believe, is being badly advised of late concerning her relations with Press and Public. They say that she is being counseled to be difficult, aloof, hard-to-get; advice which

neither fits nor becomes the good fellow who is Lombard. But if she hearkens to this counsel, one might say, isn't she of the same stripe herself? The truth of the matter is, she doesn't hear it. Not properly. Not so she makes sense of it.

Carole doesn't rightly pay heed to what is said to her. Not unless she is backed up against a wall and told about appointments in good trenchant words of one syllable. She doesn't heed because she hears so much all the time, so many demands—requests buzz around her until there is confusion in her head. Fieldsie told me that, after being away from Carole and the studio for some months, she went back one day and wondered how she had ever kept her reason in the mêlée which is Lombard's life.

She said, "It's a wonder people didn't hate both of us, Carole and me. You get so lost in that world of too much to do." Phones ringing incessantly. Agents calling. Conferences. Telegrams. Fittings. Noise. So that, when someone says to Carole, "Will you come to my baby shower next Tuesday?" or "Will you give me an interview next Friday?" her natural

Mr. and Mrs. Clark Gable snapped at Cafe Lamaze on one of their very rare night club appearances.

Carole goes dramatic again in "The Kind Men Marry," with Cary Grant. Few people realize how seriously she takes her work.

LOMBARD ?

cent unprecedented behavior?

and impulsive generosity of spirit says, "Yes, sure." Her necessarily limited number of hours and powers of attention fail to make note of the promises and they are lost in the mad shuffle of stardom's demands. And we find ourselves asking, "What's the matter with Lombard?"

Fieldsie told me that when she was with Carole constantly, she would cut through the mesh of people, tell Carole that she had made such and such appointments for today and that they must be kept. And when Carole would say, dazedly, "Tomorrow, I'll do them tomorrow," Fieldsie would say, firmly, "No, not tomorrow—to-day." And Carole, her attention thus riveted, would answer good naturedly, "Okay, let's go." Now Fieldsie is no longer with Carole. Now Carole's advisers do not pin her down to her promises, but feed her natural non-chalance by telling her to "forget 'em." This is one of the answers.

For another thing, Lombard is the busiest little woman in all Holly-wood. She always has seven times more places to go and things to do than there are hours on the clock. It's simple [Continued on page 181]

When Carole goes hunting with Clark, she is no delicate doll leaning on Gable's broad shoulder. Not if *he* knows it!

BY

GLADYS HALL

KAY'S DREAM of ROMANCE

Kay Francis outlines her conception of an ideal honeymoon

By Jewel Smith

YOU can cease calling her "Clothes-horse" right now, and more appropriately rename her "Race-horse." She looks like a winner!

Kay Francis, aristocrat of the screen, tall, graceful, young, one of Hollywood's best-dressed actresses, might well be insulted at being compared to a horse. But she should not mind being branded "thoroughbred." There's something about the proud beauty of her head, the round, firm curves of her well-kept figure, and her unhaltered amount of grit which reminds one of a Kentucky pride stepping out to win the race.

And Kay is stepping out to win the greatest race of her life. She has never worked so hard, so untiringly, so ambitiously. In two months, she has completed three pictures at Warner Brothers under her new contract—a record to quake the strength of a male, let alone that of one hundred and twenty-eight pounds of feminine flesh.

But Kay has not wavered either mentally or physically. Where a less well-equipped actress undoubtedly would break under the strain of all-day and all-night work, Kay, long years ago, prepared herself for such a task. During college days, she was an all-round athlete and knew the fundamentals of physical perfection. At that time she ran the 100-yard dash in twelve seconds flat. In the years following, she has kept up her athletic attainments through the equally strenuous game of tennis. She is Hollywood's most excellent player. Her health secrets are simple—exercise, sunshine, and fresh air.

Mentally, she is equipped with an honest and ambitious mind, backed by the courage of her own convictions.

Knowing these things, one will understand that Kay is not drifting away on a tide of enthusiasm. Her feet are sound on the turf. She is off at full speed ahead, taking no detours, and following only the right road to the definite goal which she has in mind.

Why this terrific speed, this break-neck race to somewhere? This absolute disregard of rest between pictures? The answer is easy.

At the end of that road there is a prize—and Kay is exerting her entire physical fitness and ability to reach it.

A LITTLE over a year ago, when I interviewed this Blue Ribbon girl, she talked of her recent marriage to Kenneth MacKenna and their complete happiness.

Today, she talks of but one thing—to take her husband and to get away from it all.

Naturally, the first conclusion Hollywood drew when Kay Fran-

[Continued on page 182]

David Manners appeared with Kay Francis in *Man Wanted*, one of the three pictures which Kay has completed in two months' time in her frantic race to reach the goal of her dreams

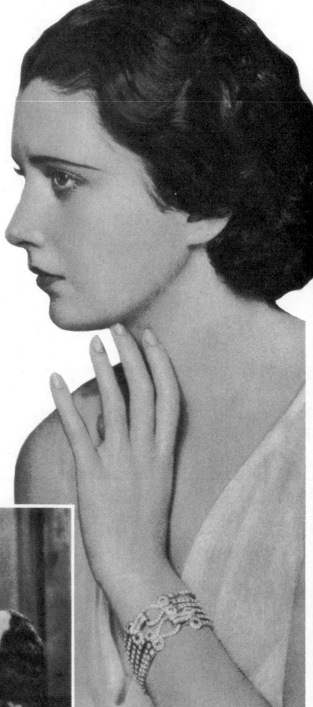

—*Elmer Fryer*

Kay Francis, tall, graceful and one of Hollywood's best dressed actresses, is truly an aristocrat of the screen

Out of Tragedy to Happiness

By J. Eugene Chrisman

IN SPITE of the fact that Hollywood, the place they call *Heartbreak Town*, has brought nothing but sorrow, disillusionment and discontent to thousands, it brought happiness to Helen Twelvetrees. She came to Hollywood a broken, tragic figure for whom the fires of romance had died. She remained to become a radiantly happy wife and mother. Helen Twelvetrees has reversed the usual order of procedure.

The press had assembled to see a studio preview of *A Bedtime Story*. Half way through the picture, a woman representative of a great newspaper syndicate who was seated next to me. turned to her neighbor and whispered,

"What has happened to Helen Twelvetrees? She positively radiates happiness. Marriage and motherhood must have worked wonders with her."

And the Helen Twelvetrees who appeared in the rôle of the nurse in *A Bedtime Story* was a new Twelvetrees. No longer did her fragile shoulders droop like those of an over-burdened Atlas. It was as though a shadow had been lifted and the radiance of a new soul were permitted to shine through.

"It's no secret and there's nothing mysterious about it." smiled Helen as I sat with her on the set at Columbia studios where she is making *His Woman*, a title strangely reversing that of her first big hit, *Her Man*. "Of course I'm happy. I think I'm really happy for the first time in my life. I have my husband, my baby and my career and what more could a girl want?"

But to understand Helen's present happiness, one must also understand the experiences which first brought her to Hollywood, a broken disillusioned girl. One cannot appreciate the sunshine without the rain and the earlier tragedy which all but wrecked Helen's life. brings a double appreciation of her present happiness.

Helen was but a child of sixteen when she married Clark Twelvetrees. She had been carefully raised in an atmosphere which, if it did not give luxury, was at least secure and comfortable. Then came her marriage and the drab routine of a small town stock company. The dirty ill-kept rooms, the failure of their combined salaries to make ends meet and the fact that Clark, himself but a kid, sought solace in the gin bottle. And then, as if this were not enough,

Clark's attempt at suicide when he leaped from the window of their room on the seventh floor of a cheap theatrical hotel in New York. Clark lived but Helen was at first accused of having pushed him from the window! Is it any wonder that when she came to Hollywood, after her separation from Clark, that she cared little what happened.

And Hollywood did not receive the little girl from Brooklyn with open arms. In three pictures for Fox she failed miserably to register. Then, at last. Edmund Goulding selected her for a rôle in *Grand Parade* which raised her to the ranks of stardom for Pathé.

But it remained for a picture called *Her Man* to really give Helen her opportunity. She knew that it was the hit of her career before the first week's shooting was over but that was not the greatest thing that *Her Man* was to do for little Twelvetrees.

PHILLIPS HOLMES was a member of the cast. One day, when he had a luncheon date with Helen, he absent-mindedly made another with a young real estate man named Frank Woody. Laughing it off, the three went to lunch together.

Frank Woody fell in love with Helen at first sight and she with him but the memories of that first unfortunate infatuation stood between them. Helen was a f r a i d and why not? Woody was gentle, persistent and his wooing was a decided contrast to the impetuous ardor of young Twelvetrees. Helen decided to wait a year to be sure. At last they were married.

Hollywood turned up its nose in its usual cynical sneer. Another one of

Helen Twelvetrees, who appreciates happiness now, having suffered tragedy in early life

those things. Frank and Helen settled down in a home on Bristol Avenue in Brentwood Heights
[Continued on page 182]

EXTRA

. . . These Hollywood romances (are you up to date on them?) start out like yours and mine—but a sword of Damocles hangs over them! Here's the really authentic low-down

Myrna Loy and Ramon Novarro's liking for each other promises to be a real Hollywood romance. Phillips Holmes and Florence Rice are rumored secretly married.

WHAT'S WRONG WITH HOLLYWOOD

Below you see pictured four Hollywood couples. (Left to right) Lilian Harvey and Gary Cooper. William Janney and Helen Mack. John Warburton and Alice White. Marjorie King and George Raft. Each couple is rumored "that way." But—according to this story — "how long can it last?"

THE other day a group of us were sitting around the luncheon table when one of the women in the party, who has never been to Hollywood and whose knowledge of picture people is obtained through reading about them, said to me:

"What's wrong with love in Hollywood? Why can't those nice young people keep on being in love? Honestly, I can't keep up with them. One minute I hear that Janet Gaynor and Charlie Farrell are in love and then Janet marries Lydell Peck and Charlie marries Virginia Valli, but pretty soon Janet and Lydell are divorced and Janet is running around with . . . with . . ."

"Lew Ayres," I supplied.

"Oh, no! Not really," she said, amazed.

I went on to tell her about it. "It's sort of confused. The other night at a party someone asked Lola Lane, Lew's ex-wife, where Lew was these days and she said that he was going places with Ginger Rogers, but although this romance is supposed to

J. B. Scott

LOVE?

By

KATHERINE

ALBERT

be hot there is the shadow of little Janet in the background. You see, Lew and Janet met on the set of 'State Fair' and since then she's been many times to Lew's lovely hillside home—always with her mother, of course.

"Once she told Lew that they could never be happily married because their temperaments would clash but that because they were two of a kind and nobody understood them they could be understanding friends but that they shouldn't marry. So bets are on Ginger."

"That's just what I mean," persisted my friend. "Why can't they fall in love and stay in love? What's wrong with romance out there?"

It was on the tip of my tongue to give her the age old reason: "It isn't that they change partners more often than other people, it's simply because, since they are famous, you hear more about it." That's the usual and the easy excuse. And then, suddenly, it occurred to me that that wasn't the reason, really. That much, much more entered into it and that there is something definitely wrong with Hollywood love.

I N the first place real love thrives on romantic secrecy. You know how it is in your set. You meet a boy at a party. You look at him and think, "Now here's a nice fellow. I could like him." But you're not sure.

Then maybe he comes over and asks you to dance and he makes a date for later in the week. Well, you go J. B. Scott out with him and you like him but he's still on trial. The romance hasn't actually "taken" yet. You don't know him well enough. But he calls you up later and you have another date and this time some chord of understanding is
struck

and you realize that you like him very, very much.

Lots of dates follow. You're getting acquainted and then he begins to pay compliments to you and to send you little gifts—a book you've mentioned, a dozen roses. But you don't tell a soul the things he said to you when you sat out that dance. Those things were precious and it's such fun to treasure them, to be in a room full of people and cast knowing glances back and forth, to hold hands for a second under the table—all those dear, intimate little gestures shared by just you two.

But this ordinary courting is impossible in Hollywood. Now visualize yourself in the film town. Imagine you're a great picture star and see how the same little romance progresses. Don't forget that the stars are just like you and would love those important clandestine trysts. But can they have them? Not on your life.

If you're a star and hold hands with another star under the table there's a photographer lurking somewhere to record the event. And when the boy-friend whispers a sweet nothing in your ear, you'll read it in the paper the next day. There are exactly 150 cinema news gatherers in Hollywood and so quick are the chatter columnists to record every romance, no matter how incipient, that love doesn't have a chance to "take." Before you've really made up your mind whether you like a new man or not Hollywood gossip has you secretly married to him.

Joan Crawford is free now to go out with whom she pleases. Joan is on the eligible list. So what happens? "Joan is seen dancing and dining with Franchot Tone. It must be a romance." But, honestly, has Joan had time

J. B. Scott

to find out whether or not she is in love with Franchot? Hollywood tells her she is before she knows it herself.

One night Joan was out dancing with Franchot and he leaned over and whispered something to her—something very sweet and tender. I give you my word that the next day eight people asked me if I knew what Franchot said to Joan when they were dancing. How would you like everybody in your set to know everything that the boys said to you while dancing?

AND then the gossips said, "You know, my dear, he's not really in love with Joan. He is just using her for publicity. He's new on the screen and whenever he takes her out he gets his name in the paper. It's good business." I know Franchot well. I know that isn't true but the very voicing of such cynicism brings us to another reason why there is so little lasting love in Hollywood.

When, in your town, a boy asks you for a date you're pretty sure that it's because he likes you and that nobody is going to tell you later he was using you as a political campaign. But bitter Hollywood always raises this doubt —"Their romance is just a publicity stunt." Good heavens, how can young people buck a remark like that!

And yet precedent has been set. There have been publicity romances—so Hollywood is skeptical of young love. Remember the Clara Bow-Harry Richman case? As you know, publicity men evolved the idea of having Richman—who had not made his mark in pictures—rush Clara, who was a big star. Perhaps what you didn't know is that Clara was the innocent sufferer. So subject was she to sweet words and tenderness that she was really in love with Richman and—eventually—he with her. But the roots of that romance were embedded in the soil of press agentry. How can love grow like that? The answer is it can't.

Maureen O'Sullivan and Johnnie Wiessmuller were seen dancing and dining together. What a nice, handsome couple they made. You could get very sentimental about them until you knew that Johnny was telling Lupe Velez, via long distance telephone, all about it and that Maureen was being seen with Johnnie to try to counteract the unfortunate publicity he had at the time when the Weissmuller-Velez romance was hottest. Now Maureen is back with her old love, Johnnie Farrow, who was once Lila Lee's sweetheart.

They say that Jack LaRue and Glenda Farrell are romancing but I've got a strong hunch that that is sired by publicity, since Glenda is being seen places with Gene Raymond. You see what I'm doing? I'm doubting. I'm being terribly, terribly Hollywood. But that's the way it is.

You must, for instance, doubt [Continued on page 183]

J. B. Scott   J. B. Scott

What I Will Tell My Baby

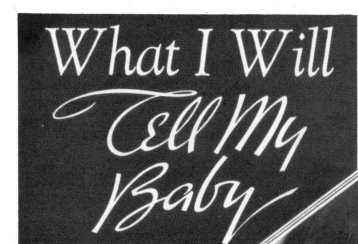

Every mother and daughter should read this outspoken story by the star who has embarked on the greatest adventure of her lifetime—motherhood

By *Clara Bow*

As told to JEWEL SMITH

SCREEN BOOK Scoop

I SUPPOSE every mother has spent months figuring on what she would tell her first child. I know I am no different from all others, but each one figures from her own experiences. And there, I believe I have a right to think I am different. Not many mothers have had exactly the same experiences. I'm *pretty* sure no other mother has had mine or anything like it. So what I tell my child will be based upon things that haven't happened to other people.

First, I take this very seriously. All my life I have wanted a baby and now that I'm going to have one I realize I have to be very careful what I do with it—especially what I say to it. Because I lost my own mother so young, I know that no one else can ever take her place. You can have a dozen husbands; you can have more children if anything happens to one. But you can never have but one mother.

You've read how lonesome I've always been. I used to tell how I wanted to marry a man who would stroke my hair and talk softly and let me tell him things. I remember the first time I read an interview I'd given about that. I went to bed with the magazine under my pillow and cried myself to sleep.

I was too young and too emotional to understand just why I wanted that kind of a husband. I do now. I know I was hunting a man who would be a *mother* even more than a husband. I wanted someone to confide in; to cry to—someone who would sympathize and understand me no matter what I did. I thought that was a husband—I know, now, it was a mother.

Motherhood Serious To Clara

THE first thing I'm going to tell a child, whether it's a boy or a girl, is that he has a mother. I'm going to make myself sort of a safety valve for that baby from the very beginning. Whenever it cries, from the very first, I'm going to be the one it sees standing over the cradle. A nurse may be there,

too. A nurse may give him his bottle or change the pins and do the practical things that must be done for a baby. But that baby is not going to look into a nurse's eyes for sympathy and understanding. He's going to look into his mother's. That's the reason making another picture isn't as important as it used to be. I wouldn't make one if it interfered with my being with my baby. That baby is going to know, from the very first breath he draws, that he's more important to me than work or bridge or women's clubs or anything else that keep mothers busy.

I know a lot of people think a woman like me won't make a good mother. They probably think, "God help that child." That's where people are wrong. Girls like me make the best mothers, if we have any common sense. We know about things and you can only help your children from what you know. I've been reading a lot of books on taking care of children. I've had a lot of laughs from them. What do professors and nurses, who haven't loved and laughed and cried and suffered and starved and spent thousands of dollars really know about living? You'd think

Clara Bow Today

Almost two years have passed since the name of Clara Bow was last featured in lurid newspaper headlines. In that time the Clara Bow of Flaming Flapper days has completely vanished. Clara today is a purposeful young lady who has retired from pictures—not permanently as certain unfounded stories have stated—to become a mother. Your editor has known Clara for many years, from her hey-hey days to the present. I feel that the public should know her as she really is and that the opportunity presents itself for the first time in this story.

Roscoe Fawcett

from what I've read that all babies have is bodies. Well, I know different. It's a child's soul, his thoughts, that are the most important.

Clara's Careful Plans

I'VE been reading recently a lot about too much love giving children mother complexes. And I think that's a lot of bunk. Of course, there's two kinds of mother love. [*Continued on next page*]

63

One is done because the mother is selfish. She says "I love you so much so you have to do what I say." I can understand how that kind of love might ruin a kid. It isn't real love. It's love for the mother rather than the baby. Mine won't be that kind. It'll be the kind that just says, "I love you. You know that. No matter what you do, whether you cry, whether you fight, whether you get into mischief, whether you get married to the right girl or wrong, whether you become a big, honest man or whether you happen to get into prison accidentally or *on purpose,* there's one person you can always trust to love you. And that's your mother. And if he understands that—I don't think he'll be as apt to have bad luck.

That goes for a boy or a girl, but from then on things are different.

An Honest Education

HE'S even going to understand there are good snakes that you mustn't kill, poisonous ones you step on the second you see 'em. And he's going to be told humans are about the same! "If you can learn to tell a kind snake from a poisonous one, you can learn to tell a kind human from a poisonous one in the same way. Be good to the good ones and step on the others. Step on them before they get a chance to step on you!"

There isn't going to be anything left for him to find out if I can help it when he's ready to step into the world and fight his own battle. If he wants to fight when he's going to school and he's got common sense enough to pick the mean ones to fight, he's going to be encouraged. I'll tell him "Okay, that was a bad snake. You did right to step on it." But he's got to pick his own snakes! I'm not going to take the initiative and wisdom out of him by trying to pick 'em for him.

And I hope he knows women well enough, by the time he's ready to marry, so he'll understand them the same way. To do that he's got to mix with them just like he's got to mix with snakes on the ranch to tell a rattler from a gopher. There'd be no sense in trying to keep him from it, anyway, because I know men. They are always men. Men are about the same now as they were when Cleopatra was playing with her generals. And for a mother to think she's going to create a new kind is foolish.

I'm glad I'm not a very wealthy woman. My boy will know there's enough to help him get started but not enough to keep him from having to make some of his own. If he knows that from the beginning he's going to start using part of the energy and brains God gave him to think about it. He'll make his own choice there. He'll know I'm standing behind him but he'll know, too, it's his life, and I can't live it for him.

Girls Must Have Romance

WHEN it comes to a girl—I'm not so sure. As I see it, the place of women hasn't been exactly decided. It's a tough time to raise a girl. I suppose that's one reason why I sort of hope it'll be a boy. I see Mussolini is putting the ladies back into the home to do the cooking, rear families, and care for their men. And although I've worked most of my life, I sort of think that Mussolini must have decided God knows more than he does about that matter. After all, it was God who decided about women in the first place, wasn't it?

You see, I'm a girl and I know that there's nothing as important to a girl as romance. And since romance is so important, you've got to be very careful not to take it away from your daughter.

I hope I can send my daughter to private schools and dress her in dainty dresses and have her learn how to play the piano and sew. I'm going to teach my daughter to be a dainty lady. I tell you a woman isn't created physically to stand the strain of a career. In the business world you are apt to be brought into suits, for example. A woman's emotions rule her feelings. She carries her emotions into a court room instead of her common sense or brains. She can't help it. She shouldn't help it. Woman was made to feel and man to think. I want my daughter to have the chance to live as God intended. Woman cannot struggle and battle and compete—she shouldn't have to.

I have been called over-emotional. I suppose I am. That's a compliment to a woman. It should be. But it's not good in the business world. I'm called impulsive. I am. But that's a drawback, too, when you're working. Of course, if my daughter wanted to work, wanted a screen career, for example, I wouldn't stop her. I wouldn't have the right. It's her life.

I guess I'm a little old-fashioned but I think most girls who have lived life, as I have, get old-fashioned when they are old enough to see that happiness is all you want here. Glory and fame, even money, don't bring happiness. And, in the long run, I only want my child to be happy!

The Final Fling

L UISE RAINER'S great performance in "The Good Earth" was not marred by the desire on her part to appear, at least once, as the beautiful girl that she is. She really threw herself unreservedly into the part of the timid down-trodden coolie woman. The complete unself-consciousness of Rainer in the role was marvelous. She bent down, hiding her face, as the woman, O-lan, would have done in life, completely disregarding the camera.

However, in humble lives it is the nobility of *thought* that moulds the faces of the poor into the outlines of loveliness. Because of this, Rainer appears at times transfigured and her face shines with true Beauty.

* * * *

A ND now to boast a little about this magazine, particularly concerning an important feature that will be in SILVER SCREEN next month. We do not pretend to introduce you to Dana Burnet. You two have met before. You have read his stories in all the best magazines, you have seen his plays on Broadway and his scenarios on the screen. Dana Burnet now lives in Hollywood and his typewriter is going like a machine gun, capturing the important and colorful doings in the studios and lining them up against sheets of paper. All right! All right! We admit we are enthusiastic. We will leave the rest for you to discover for yourself next month.

How's that, Dana? Is that editorial gusto, or what?

* * * *

T HERE is a war that never ceases. It goes on day and night in Hollywood—the scheming, blackguards of the underworld against the highly paid players of the studios. The story of the various swindles makes one realize the risks that are a part of the life of each popular star. Read Helen Louise Walker's article on this subject in SILVER SCREEN for May.

Also in the May issue, Elizabeth Wilson writes a "Projection" of Madge Evans that makes our well-loved Madge dearer than ever.

Did you think those perfectly proportioned girls just grew that way? Read about the many exercises that are used by the players to prepare their beautiful figures for the severe test of the summer beaches. It's a Ben Maddox story.

The studios hum with activity and S. R. Mook listens to the din. He hears the voices of the directors and the banter of the actors. Read his survey of the new productions in the making in "Pictures on the Fire."

* * * *

You don't mind if we drop a hint?

Elliot Keen

EDITOR.

A MOVIE FAN'S CROSSWORD PUZZLE
By Charlotte Herbert

ACROSS

1 The dim-witted worker in "Black Legion"
6 Tree
9 Loved by Don Ameche in "One in a Million"
14 Exclusively
15 The originator of "Come up and see me sometime"
16 Weird
17 Now working in "The Prince and the Pauper"
19 One wielding an ax
21 Patrons of a restaurant
23 An American humorist
25 He portrayed "Daniel Boone'
27 Thoroughfares (abbr.)
28 Buffalo Bill in "The Plainsman"
31 Public roads (abbr.)
32 Meadow
34 Associate of Arts (abbr.)
35 Ruby Keeler's husband
37 A beast of burden
39 Within
40 "Tarzan"
45 A three-toed sloth
46 Direction of compass
47 Head coverings
48 An opera by Verdi
49 Measure of length (abbr.)
50 Beverage
51 One of the submarine divers in "Depths Below"
52 The twenty-third letter of Greek alphabet
53 "The Jungle Princess" (initials)
54 Parent
56 Like
57 North Western State (abbr.)
59 To whom Merle Oberon seems devoted
61 French article
63 Masculine pronoun
64 "Old Hutch"
66 The doctor in "Ladies in Love"
67 A very special friend of Robert Taylor's
70 Royal Academy of Arts (abbr.)
71 Either
72 "John Meade's Woman"
74 North River (abbr.)
75 Janet in "Great Guy"
76 He recently returned to the screen
78 Request
79 With George Brent in "God's Country and the Woman"
80 Part of verb "to be"

DOWN

1 Hopalong Cassidy
2 Upon
3 The newspaper woman in "Smart Blonde"
4 Now making "Danger, Men Working"
5 Plural of that
6 Type measure
7 The pathetic widow in "After the Thin Man"
8 Personal pronoun
9 Handsome tap dancer in "Gold Diggers of 1937"
10 Approaches
11 The snobbish mother in "Rainbow on the River"
12 Suffix
13 Lovely Universal player
18 Method of transportation (abbr.)
20 Team mate of Charles Ruggles (initials)
22 The novelist in "Theodora Goes Wild"
23 Expression of sorrow
24 Jacob's brother (Bib.)
26 Short written composition
29 Young girl
30 Spanish cooking pot
32 Cecilia Parker's beau in "Old Hutch"
33 The innocent prisoner in "We Who Are About to Die"
36 Radicals
38 Excellent in "You Only Live Once"
40 Sports reporter in "Woman Wise"
41 Separate article
42 The hostess in "Fugitive in the Sky"
43 Borders of the mouth
44 Bride of Clifford Odets
53 The faithful sweetheart in "We Who Are About to Die"
55 Wing-shaped
56 Pertaining to aeronautics
58 The fourteen year old star of "Three Smart Girls"
60 Sacred images
62 To wander
63 Thigh of a hog
65 More unusual
67 A former world's heavyweight champion
68 To wait for
69 Curved lines
72 Popular male player (initials)
73 Every (abbr.)
75 Country north of the U. S.
77 Pronoun

Answer to Last Month's Puzzle

FAN FARE

A favorite Lindy Hop variation by Jackie and Bunny is shown in the two pictures at the right

Bright examples of the new dance are Jackie Cooper and Bonita Granville. In the two pictures below they are doing the off-beat fox trot (see diagram and text explanation)

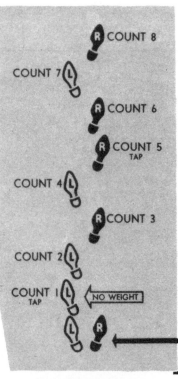

PHOTOPLAY—MOVIE MIRROR

Dancing School

Ground Plan for Basic Step of Off-Beat Fox Trot

```
                        R COUNT 8
COUNT 7 L

                        R COUNT 6

                        R COUNT 5
                           TAP
COUNT 4 L

                        R COUNT 3

COUNT 2 L

COUNT 1    ← NO WEIGHT
   TAP
        L
           R
```

Boy Starts Here
(Girl Does Opposite)

THERE'S a dance in America today for which even the Greeks would have trouble finding a name —but not the Americans. The Easterners call it the Slow Lindy Hop; on the West Coast it's the Balboa, because all such steps start at the Rendezvous Ballroom in Balboa out there. We don't know what they think they're doing in the corn belt.

If you're still just fox-trotting with variations of the Charleston or the hoary Big Apple, you'd better get busy. Just turn the radio dial until you've got the music—Kay Kyser, Glenn Miller, Artie Shaw.

Our guest stars this month are Jackie Cooper and Bonita Granville. They're just going to dance, the way they would, and we're going to tell you what they're doing and how to do it too.

Let's leave a name for it to future historians, eh?

The original fox trot was the simple, four-beat step done in a brisk fashion to fast or popular music. *One two, three, four,* and repeat. Then you maintained the step through turns or whatever variation you felt like making.

But when jazz turned into swing,

The Granville-Cooper version of the famous Balboa is shown in the three pictures on this page. See text for directions

If you're still just fox-trotting along, you better wake up. There's a new dance swinging across America—and here's how you do it

Conducted by HOWARD SHARPE

PHOTOGRAPHS BY HYMAN FINK

We acknowledge with gratitude the careful check which was given this feature by the Arthur Murray Studios

the subtle change of emphasis from the down-beat to the off-beat gave all the guys and gals an impulse to get a different rhythm into it. So they started holding—waiting—on the first beat; then they gave a little acknowledgment of that kind-of-neglected first beat with a quick touch of the toe to the floor and went right on.

Now that off-beat step is the basis for all modern dancing to popular music. From it came such variations as the Lindy Hop, first fast and then slow; the Balboa, which is more of a shuffle variation; and all the jitterbug steps.

Dorsey's "Melancholy Baby," or better yet, Artie Shaw's platter of "Begin the Beguine," is what to stick on the phonograph. Turn the knob to "repeat" and stand facing each other. We're going to give the man's routine; you girls learn to do it backwards, starting on the other foot.

At the beginning, we'll just worry you with the actual steps, starting with that basic pause-and-catch-it-up fox trot above-mentioned and working into the slow Lindy Hop, the Balboa and anything else you want to make of it. After you've learned these you can cope with the instructions that

Ground Plan for Basic Step of Slow Lindy Hop

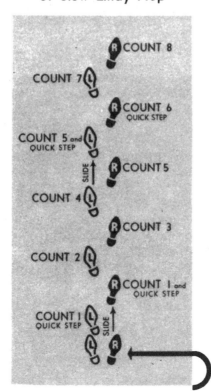

R COUNT 8

COUNT 7 L

R COUNT 6
QUICK STEP

COUNT 5 and L
QUICK STEP

SLIDE

R COUNT 5

COUNT 4 L

R COUNT 3

COUNT 2 L

R COUNT 1 and
QUICK STEP

COUNT 1 L
QUICK STEP

SLIDE

L R

**Boy Starts Here
(Girl Does Opposite)**

turn them from walking steps into honest-to-pete dancing about which friend Arthur Murray would probably say: "That's the speed, boy, that's the speed."

Now look at the diagram on the left side of the opposite page. Start following the steps for the basic off-beat fox trot, counting to the rhythm of the music, *One*, two, *three*, four—emphasizing the off-beat. Just walk forward for a while until you're used to it, then, on the count of one, instead of taking a step, just tap your left toe very quickly on the floor without putting any weight on it; then step forward for the count of two on your *left* foot, forward on your right foot for the count of three, forward left foot on four; then, for the second group of four, do the tap on your right foot for Count 5, step forward on Count 6 with the same foot, shifting the weight to it—and so on.

Try doing this backward, and then in a simple square. In the pictures (1 and 2) Jackie and Bunny are doing the square and of course you simply turn right or left in the same rhythm, never breaking the step at all. Finally, when you're proficient, you'll be able to [Continued on page 184]

Will Rogers—$15,000

Figuring *the* Stars' Salaries

Huge Pay Checks May be Reduced by Government to Lower Theatre Admissions and Open Dark Houses—Why Some Stars Get Big Money

By Jay Brien Chapman

Greta Garbo—$13,000

John Gilbert—$13,000

Chevalier—$10,000

A CERTAIN male star who gets lots of fan mail, and personally reads more of it than any other screen idol I know, pointed to a big pile of letters he had just read.

"For the first time in my long career as a fan-mail reader," said he, "movie-goers *en masse* are demanding an explanation for big stellar salaries. They're even asking—some a bit peevishly—about *mine!*

"It had to come. Human beings demand reasons for everything now, even the weather! In here, they're asking me lots of embarrassing questions. What I do with my $5,500 a week? How come I get that now, when in my most *popular* days I got only $750?" He took one letter from the pile, hesitated a moment, then passed it on to me.

"Read this. It's the sort that almost brings tears to my eyes. It's from a typical fan—the kind to whom we owe the success of the whole industry."

I quote the letter literally:

"Dear Mr. ———: I'm one of your most loyal fans, so feel free to bother you with a problem that must be troubling countless others. Our little town had two shows. Both are now closed. The managers said people wouldn't pay 25 cents admission, and when they charged 15 cents they lost money, even with good crowds. They said picture rentals were too high.

"I read about you getting a new contract at higher salary, and other stars demanding more thousands weekly. The

papers said all stars might strike, because of threatened salary reductions.

"I don't begrudge you your fine salary, but with the closing of our nearby theatres, the only other is 16 miles away and charges 20 cents admission. We so far have managed to keep our little old auto, but there is engine and tire trouble all the time and it uses so much gas and oil. Getting to the show and back costs at least 30 cents, even if we have no breakdown or blowout. So we can hardly afford movies any more. My husband and I love them, and the children miss them terribly. All need them more than ever in these hard times, to cheer us up.

"Don't you think all *big* salaries might be lowered—maybe to $1,000 a week? If what the paper says is true, you earn in one week *five times what most of us earn in a year!*"

When I had read the letter, the star handed me a clipping from *Variety*. I saw the connection immediately, for here is the skeleton of the long, scare-headed article:

"Picture scouts returning from Washington . . . report special records being kept of salaries which are out of proportion. . . . Top film salaries as much an official concern as minimum wage . . . 350 Hollywood salaries over $100,000 a year . . . before a major feature starts about forty-seven per cent of the budget is written off for salaries . . . this write-off is conceded tremendous . . . there will have to be an explanation."

Ruth Chatterton—$9,375

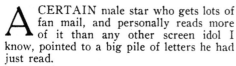

Will the Government Cut Hollywood Star Salaries?

Ann Harding—$9,000

Richard Barthelmess—$8,750

Mae West—$8,500

Ronald Colman—$6,500

Constance Bennett—$8,000

"You see what it's coming to?" the star asked. "Standardized salaries! Well, it can't harm *me*, personally. I was never so broke in the old days as I am now."

"Let me answer your fans in a magazine article," I challenged. "Tell me why you're broke, what you do with your money, and how salary reduction would affect you. I'll tell them."

"I will, but I can't let you use my name," he replied. "If you named me, an army of parasites that take most of my money away from me would be after my blood, next."

I SHALL quote other stars and many odd facts and figures on stellar salary problems in this article. The star I cannot name, however, gave me such interesting data that, despite his anonymity I am forced to quote him further:

"My relatives began the great migration to Hollywood when they first heard my salary had been raised to $2,000 per week," he said. "Most of them developed strange illnesses that keep them from earning their own livings. My former wife is supporting many of her relatives on the alimony I pay her, but some of them are still dependent directly upon me. My present wife's relatives are gradually arriving in golden California, too, like the '49ers! And my various friends, and relatives' friends are often thirsty, sometimes hungry, and occasionally in need of financial aid.

"Then there are the parasites of the acting profession. One is my agent, who battles my salary up so his commissions will be higher. Ten per cent—$550 weekly—goes to him. Another share of my salary goes to my direct employer, the studio executive who has me under contract to him personally, while sub-letting me, as it were, to the company that hires both of us. Then there's my press agent, secretary, stenographer, business manager; also a lawyer kept on a retaining fee basis. Besides this drain, I shell out to charity—a heavy item nowadays—and to Uncle Sam, for income tax.

"Of these, only an agent was bleeding me back in the days when I got $750 per week. I spend no more today on the little comforts and luxuries of life than I did then."

"So you're no better off?"

"If I am, I can't see it. Yet I'm powerless to change matters now. The parasites depend on me. I must go on earning a big salary."

How Today's Stars Rank Differently In Salary And Box Office Value

Star	Salary	Salary Rank	Popularity Rank
Will Rogers	$15,000	1	2
Greta Garbo	13,000	2	3
John Gilbert	13,000	3	10
Maurice Chevalier	10,000	4	5
Ruth Chatterton	9,375	5	6
Ann Harding	9,000	6	7
Richard Barthelmess	8,750	7	9
Mae West	8,500	8	1
Constance Bennett	8,000	9	4
Ronald Colman	6,500	10	8

A general salary reduction to $1,000 per week (in case the government sets such a top on movie salaries) might help rather than hinder stars' screen careers, he admitted.

"After all, real artists and troupers don't require riches for happiness, and our art seldom thrives on them. Most of us could struggle along on $52,000 per year. Our parasites might then have to work for their livings, but that would improve *their* health, too!

"My best work was done when I was getting less than a grand a week. Worrying about handling a quarter-million-dollar yearly income doesn't help one's screen work. It's too much responsibility for anyone of an actor's temperament. Clark Gable, in my opinion, was at his best when he was earning $750 weekly. Before Jimmy Cagney made Warners boost the ante from $450 to $3,000, he was a much more arresting screen personality. Ruth Chatterton was better in *The Doctor's Secret* and other early films, earning $1,500 weekly, than in recent pictures at about $9,000."

IT IS true in many cases that stars have received their lowest salaries when they were most valuable to their employers, and their highest salaries long after their value had diminished This, many explain, is due to the signing of long-term contracts, with upward-sliding salary scales. Before the contract expires the star's popularity has time to wane, while the salary automatically increases on the agreed scale.

Some amazing examples are available. Charles "Buddy" Rogers rode to fame on *Wings* at $75 weekly, was paid $150 weekly during the months he reigned as the industry's most popular male star, and drew $2,500 weekly during the period of his decline to zero—when in despair he quit the screen for the stage. Corinne Griffith, Clara Bow and Greta Garbo got about $1,500 weekly at the time of their greatest fame, and their latest recorded salaries are $10,000, $4,500 and $13,000 weekly!

But why should popularity wane so quickly as some stars' popularity waned? "Buddy" Rogers lasted in top favor about a year. Producers don't anticipate such speedy declines, or they wouldn't write such contracts. The only obvious conclusion is that in many cases, a high salary robs the stars of their normal span of years in the limelight.

Stars like Richard Barthelmess can "take it." Big salaries haven't affected him adversely—and instead of fading in popularity, he has gained or held his [Continued on page 184]

Charlie

Scoop! SCREENLAND gives you the first intimate story about the Chaplin children, who will soon be seen on the screen

By Ida Zeitlin

The two subjects of this story—Sydney Earl Chaplin, nicknamed Tommy, and Charles Chaplin, Jr. Read every word of this interview! It is the most enchanting we have ever given you.

The one and only Charlie Chaplin. What does he think of his sons going into pictures? Does he know that Charlie, Jr., does a perfect imitation of his dad?

IF I were stood against a wall and ordered to name in the flash of an eye, or perish, the screen's most enchanting figure—the sweetest and rarest, the most brilliant and beautiful, the pearl without price and the glory of Hollywood, past, present and (for my part) to come—I should answer, with a fleeting regret, perhaps, that I hadn't been allowed to name two, but still without hesitation—"Charlie Chaplin!"

I now rise to proclaim that the father's charm has descended upon the children. Which isn't quite fair, since their mother is equally involved. Not knowing the lady, I can only compliment her on the beauty, the breeding and the intelligence of her sons. And while I'm handing out compliments, I should like to bestow an accolade on their grandmother who has brought them up and is certainly entitled to a solid slice of credit in the finished product.

I am no child-fan. Children embarrass me, I don't know what to say to them, and I'd much rather leave them than take them. But I defy the surliest misanthrope to spend an hour with Charlie Chaplin's boys and come away without a smile in his eyes and a sense of warmth around what was once his heart.

I should like to share with the readers of SCREENLAND the delight of my experience in meeting the Chaplin children. And I think I can best do that by taking you with me and trying to show them to you as I saw them that hot day in New York, just after their return from France whence they had been brought to be launched on their screen careers.

I ring the bell of the hotel room, and wait. The door is suddenly flung wide to reveal two small figures, armed with boxing gloves, and clad in brief summer suits—one yellow, one blue. Two pairs of friendly dark eyes are raised to mine, and the slightly taller of the figures—the one whose front teeth are missing—does the honors. "I'm Charlie—he's Tommy—please come in."

Their grandmother, Mrs. Grey, emerges from the bedroom, where she's been packing. Tiny and dark, with short curling hair, a gentle manner and a deliciously soft voice, she looks much too young to be anyone's grandmother.

I ask her how Tommy came to be Tommy, since his real name is Sydney Earl. "Oh," she replies, with a shrug which must be a heritage from her Spanish mother, "only because he's such a tomboy."

The children listen with grave attention for a moment, then go about their business. Neither shy nor forward, and utterly unselfconscious, they seem to take everything

Chaplin's Kids!

for granted. If, through all your short life, people have crowded about you and asked you questions and taken your picture and inquired about your daddy, it becomes as much a matter of course as eating and sleeping; though even then you might conceivably balk in the end, as Charlie did, and cry to your grandmother: "I'm tired of them taking pictures of me, Nana. Haven't they taken enough?"

At first glance, the boys seem to me so much alike that I feel I might have difficulty in telling them apart, except for the difference in height and those front teeth! The same lustrous brown eyes—not quite the same, either, for Charlie's have an attractive Oriental tilt—the same silky brown hair, the same delicate chins and sensitive mouths and delectable baby contours—even though they *are* six and seven; the same clarity of enunciation, the same admirable choice of words, the same excellent manners. But this surface similarity fades on very brief acquaintance, to reveal two distinct and distinctive personalities.

A tall grizzled Irishman enters. "That man's a detective." Charlie looks up from his stereoscope to volunteer the information. "He's watching me, in case anything happens to me." Then he buries his nose in the stereoscope again.

The detective and a newspaper man had taken them to the Zoo that morning to have their pictures taken. They had been given peanuts and popcorn to feed to the animals. Charlie hadn't been sure at first that he wanted to stick his hand right under the wet mouth of a deer, but Tommy had leaped at the chance. It was Charlie, though, who, having conquered his timidity, quivered with happiness as the deer licked his outstretched paw. "See! He likes me now!" he cried rapturously. "He's nice, isn't he? He's a nice little animool, isn't he? When I come next time, he'll know me." His voice broke with excitement.

He's telling his grandmother about it now, his eyes kindling. "I fed a little calf right in his mouth, Nana. I fed him this way. He liked me." That's obviously the all-important thing to Charlie.

"The man brought me a bird," Tommy contributes,

Lita Grey Chaplin, the young mother of Charlie Chaplin's two sons. She has been touring in vaudeville, but will soon be in Hollywood making "The Little Teacher."

Below, the Chaplin kids making a news talkie on their return from Europe.

"but his tail fell off. He took our picture with popcorn and then we ate some." He eyes his grandmother speculatively, not quite sure how this piece of news will be received. "But not peanuts, Nana," he added virtuously. "I told him to not give us any peanuts."

Tommy is lively and venturesome, where Charlie is reflective and reserved. With Tommy, to have an idea is to act on it, but Charlie will think twice before he moves. Tommy is restless, turbulent, independent—Charlie is sensitive, high-strung, and craves affection. Nothing is safe with Tommy—his toys have a habit of breaking apart in his hands. Charlie's clothes are always folded neatly at night and his small shoes placed carefully side by side. Tommy would sleep sweetly, says his grandmother, through an explosion, but there aren't many nights when she isn't awakened by an apprehensive little voice from Charlie's bed: "Are you there, Nana?" And only on being reassured, does Charlie fall asleep again. Charlie has his father's troubled temperament—Tommy, like his mother, is equable; and if signs mean anything, life is going to be considerably harder on Charlie than on his

The latest portrait of Lita Grey Chaplin, who returns to the screen in "The Little Teacher," the Fox picture in which she will play with her sons.

little brother Tommy.

Tommy's grown tired of rolling two perfectly good apples around the floor, and comes to sit cross-legged in front of me.

"Now you have to speak a little about me," he suggests. "I like trains."

Charlie joins us. "And I like boats. Big boats to cross the ocean with."

These children know how to make things easy for the interviewer.

"I like big buildings," Tommy says helpfully. "I like the Empire State building." And he looks at his brother to indicate that it's his turn now.

"I have been to the Zoo," Charlie chimes in obediently. "I saw a monkey and a little calf." Oh, that "calf" that has found her way deep into Charlie's heart! "I put my hand right in his mouth. It was the mama calf. It feeled good."

Tommy decides it's time to branch off.

"We used to live in Bronxville—years and years and years ago—before we lived in France."

"We had a chauffeur." Charlie's eyes turned dreamy. "His name was Albert—the chauffeur's name."

"We had a cook too." [Continued on page 185]

Charlie Chaplin Wins In First Skirmish To Keep His Sons Out Of Motion Pictures

Youngsters May Still Work if Verdict is Reversed

Sidney Earl and Charles Spencer Chaplin Jr. will not become child movie stars if their famous comedian father can help it.

Hearing that his two sons were soon to appear in pictures with their mother, Lita Grey Chaplin, Charlie went to court and secured an order restraining these plans. Fox studio executives, to whom the youngsters are under contract, are hoping that a reversal of the court judgment may be secured soon as extensive plans have already been made to start the younger Chaplins off on their careers.

—*Wide World Photo*
CHARLIE CHAPLIN as he appeared in court, determined to keep his sons out of the movies. The famous comedian argued that he wanted the children to develop normally and lead happy lives as children. Acting, he intimated, is very bad for children at the impressionable ages of five and seven

THE CENTER OF A RAGING LEGAL BATTLE, Charlie (seven) and Tommy (five) still hope their movie careers will begin soon

—*Wide World Photo*
SELFISH MOTIVES, Lita Grey Chaplin charges, are back of her ex-husband's legal battle to keep Sidney and Charles Jr. off the screen. She declares that Charlie has always been indifferent to his two sons and that his sudden interest now develops because he fears they may detract from his fame

The most revealing interview
JANET GAYNOR
ever gave...!

. . . . At last! Janet breaks down and tells you all the things you've been wanting to know about her: Is she bitter about life—and love? What of her screen career? An honest, intimate chat

By GLADYS HALL

Janet wanted Henri Garat to play opposite her in "Adorable" as part of a well-thought-out plan.

I TALKED with Janet in her Irish cottage "dressing room" on the Fox lot. A thatched and fairly-tale cottage once used by John McCormack of the golden voice. Janet wore a jade-green dressing gown and whiffs of lavender mules. Her feet are the only things about her that have not grown-up. Her heavy, red-gold hair hung in a Garbo-length bob to her shoulders. Her eyes are steady and aware. She doesn't laugh as often as she used to. Her face is firmer and more definite. And when her mouth is in repose it wears a slightly ironical expression.

I said, "Have you been hurt by—by things—Janet? Are you broken hearted? Are you disillusioned? Are you happy, as you used to be?"

Janet said, "I'll answer the last question first. No, of course I'm not happy, as I used to be. I don't suppose I'm happy at all. The more we learn the sadder we become. And we must learn or be classed as morons.

"I think you begin to lose happiness when life begins to take off its masks. When you find that there is no Santa Claus but, instead, a mother or a father or both who are worried to death lest they may not have the money to *be* Santa Clauses with. You begin to lose happiness when you find that there are no fairies; that friends can be fair-weather friends, that success has as many rough spots as failure.

"I don't believe in fairy tales any longer. That about covers everything. I don't believe that black is black or white white. Which makes everything confusing. *I don't believe in people any longer,* not as I did. I know, now, that I can count my real friends on the fingers of one hand—and have some fingers to spare.

"I used to have ideals and expect people to live up to them and be bitterly hurt and disappointed if they didn't. I haven't any ideals now and I can't be disappointed. I used to be critical and exacting. People had to fit, exactly, the pattern I'd cut for them or I'd have none of them. I know better now.

"Now, if I like a person at all, for this quality or for that and if he doesn't fit perfectly into the pattern, I lop off an edge here or a rough corner there and say, 'Oh, well, he has a lot of things about him I do like and I'll just *make him fit.*'

"You can't live through the major experiences of life and remain untouched by them. They should not make you bitter. They should make you, what I hope they have made me, more tolerant of others, kinder, more understanding. If experiences do not soften your heart and harden your spirit you might better never have had them—"

There was a time, Janet told me, when she was a very poor business woman. In that respect she was, then, the "child" they called her. Now, she knows what it is all about. She knows a script when she reads one and she reads every script and criticizes it and makes suggestions which must be adopted. She knows what stories she can do and what stories she has outgrown. She knows her own capacities and her own limitations.

And she advises every girl in business or the professions or the Arts to do the same; to know what they can do and believe in what they can do but to realize, also, that there are certain things they cannot be or do.

Janet was especially indignant because a writer once said of her that she secretly [*Continued on page 186*]

WHY GARBO HAS

Has Garbo ever been really in love? Why has she never taken a mate? Read the answers here

WHY is it that the most alluring woman on the screen today has never married?

What strange reason exists which keeps the most excitingly beautiful Garbo from committing matrimony?

Search as you may, you cannot find any woman—any actress—who arouses the myriad passions which this glamorous Swedish actress is capable of arousing. Garbo tops them all. She always will continue to be more alluring than any other woman.

There is Gloria Swanson, with a terrific magnetic attraction for the opposite sex. There is Norma Shearer, who represents the most polished, the most ultra-modern note when it comes to being a sex-menace. There is the slim, golden Constance Bennett, whose romantic affairs have whipped up an international furore. There is a delectable list of charming women, whose feminine qualities have swooped them to the starriest heights, romantically and financially.

But Garbo goes her silent way—alone. She has been the theme for countless stories. The colorful, far-away lady has not found protection behind her wall of exclusiveness. Never has she been able to draw her mantle of reserve closely enough about her.

Those exquisite features of hers have been analyzed by some of the most famous analysts in the country. Her horoscope has been cast as many times as the proverbial fishermen's nets of Galilee. Astrologists have to admit that they

Garbo has turned platinum blonde! But only for her new picture, *As You Desire Me*. She has flatly denied that following this film she will return to Sweden to wed Wilhelm Sorensen, who was for a time her most intimate friend in Hollywood

The whole world thrilled to the romance of Greta Garbo and John Gilbert, when these two figured as the principals in such torrid love scenes as this from *Flesh and the Devil*. In private life, Gilbert swept her off her feet

NEVER MARRIED

By Marcella Burke

do not know the exact hour of Garbo's birth. Such a detail is of the utmost importance, they say, if a horoscope is to be accurate. Some astrologists have said that Garbo has great success in love, as well as in her career. Others say she will never marry, but that great loves will be an integral part of her existence.

When Garbo was only sixteen years old, Mauritz Stiller, the director, discovered her. It was through him that Garbo was persuaded to take up acting. He made one picture with her in Sweden.

When Metro-Goldwyn-Mayer wanted this talented director to come all the way to America to make pictures for them, he consented only if they permitted Greta Garbo to accompany him. If Stiller accepted a contract, Garbo must have one. Anxious to procure Stiller at any cost, the Metro-Goldwyn-Mayer officials accepted his proposition. And so it was that these two foreigners sailed for America.

Garbo was shy and frightened. She clung to her beloved Sweden. Perhaps because of the terrific wrench of leaving her mother and little brother and sister, Garbo clung more tenaciously than ever to the man who was bringing her to a strange country. From the very beginning Stiller comforted and guarded her faltering footsteps. It is all part of the history of Hollywood—the romance of Stiller and Garbo.

THE strange way that Garbo was ignored upon her arrival in the little cinematic city of Hollywood is also history. She was given flowers at the station and photographed, but it was upon Mauritz Stiller, the great director, that the real attentions were showered. Garbo was not smartly dressed. She was awkward and timid. She shrank then, as she does now, from the crowds.

America was bedlam. It was a vast, crowded place of loneliness and misery to the homesick Swedish girl. A test was made of Garbo a few weeks later which caused the Metro-Goldwyn-Mayer officials to shake their heads. The timid young Swede was "out," as far as they were concerned. They began to wonder if Stiller was in his right mind.

And don't ever believe for a minute that Garbo didn't resent their criticism, their superiority and indifference. It all cut deeply. When she told Mauritz what had occurred he was thrown into a black rage. He whipped into the head office and announced, in no uncertain manner, that Garbo was the greatest actress in the world and that none other than he, Stiller, would direct her in a test. This he did.

Garbo glowed under his careful direction. Here was the great man who not only worshipped her, but who spoke her language.

It was only a few weeks when lo! Garbo's name was on everyone's tongue. She became the rage of the American public. Today she is the most popular actress throughout the entire world. Utter one adverse criticism of Garbo and international complications are imminent.

As the months passed, Garbo's salary jumped from two hundred and fifty dollars a week to six thousand dollars. Later this was even increased. She was a great success. Stiller was forced into the background. He was in no way the success that Garbo was. It was this same success which finally separated Garbo and Stiller. It was John Gilbert who widened the breach between the two.

It was inevitable that Stiller should bow to the obvious. With true Continental grace he took his departure for Sweden. He died a short while afterwards. His friends say death was due to a broken heart. At the time of his demise Garbo was involved in a seething grand passion for John Gilbert. For Gilbert, the handsome, dashing young man, had figuratively swept Garbo off her feet.

Mauritz Stiller, perhaps Sweden's greatest directorial contribution to Hollywood, was directly responsible for the career upon which Garbo engaged. He brought her to this country, fought for her, directed her, worshipped her

Their pictures exploded on the public like a tumultuous volcano. Their love scenes were the most torrid ever shot in Hollywood. People gasped but wanted more. Even the censors were numbed into delightful acceptance of these sexiest pictures.

The Garbo era came in, as did the Gilbert era. These two stars became household words. Young, old and in-between fell captive to their romantic spell.

THE next bombshell which exploded brought more synthetic enjoyment to their fans. The story leaked out that these hot, fierce love scenes were not turned on merely at the given word of a director. No, sir! Garbo and Gilbert had fallen in love with each other.

Their romance thrilled the whole world. When John kissed Greta the audience felt like tip-toeing out as the lights came on in the theatre. They felt like "peeping Toms."

Nothing more perfect could have happened for Metro-Goldwyn-Mayer. Garbo and Gilbert were the biggest box-office attractions in the country. Gold poured into the producers' coffers.

Then this romance came to an end. Gilbert promised Garbo everything he owned if she would only marry him. He pleaded with her time after time. Rumors were that Garbo finally went to some little Mexican town quite prepared to marry Gilbert. At the last moment, very much frightened, she ran away and hid until the train arrived to carry her back to Hollywood. However, that is only one story.

Another is that Garbo succumbed to John's pleading and got as far as the Santa Ana marriage bureau but turned and fled, leaving John a heartbroken bachelor. Whatever the real truth is no one will ever know, unless Garbo chooses to tell the story herself. But to cherish an idea that this might ever happen, would be as ridiculous as imagining that historical bit of stone in the Egyptian desert becoming garrulous.

The one thing we do know is [Continued on page 186]

The star who is MORE *Mysterious* than GARBO

Hollywood has never been able to learn the private life secrets of Fay Wray...no idle gossip touches her ...this story tells why

F AY WRAY is the most normal young person in Hollywood . . . yet, she is the enigma woman of the film capital.

This paradox may sound rather startling to those of you who live without the borders of Cinemania. You may feel inclined to take exception to this statement and enumerate other actresses whom you consider more enigmatical than Fay Wray.

There's Garbo, you say, the Swedish lady lynx, undoubtedly Hollywood's own mystery woman. . . . Dietrich and Sten, respectively German and Russian, whose backgrounds loom in shadowy shades.

All very well and good, BUT . . . stop a moment and consider carefully. Off-hand, you can tell much more about these three delectable strangers to our shores than you can about Fay Wray. Each has had so many stories printed about her, particularly Garbo, that little remains to know.

Friendly, yes, but no star in Hollywood is more a mystery than Fay, despite the fact that she has lived there twelve years

By Whitney Williams

Who, though, can claim familiarity with the life of Fay Wray? She came from Canada, got her first real break in Von Stroheim's masterpiece, *The Wedding March*, married John Monk Saunders, the writer, and seems to make a great many pictures yearly . . . everybody is cognizant of these facts. BUT . . . what else do you know about her, who are her friends, how does she live, what does she do in her spare time?

Nobody, even in Hollywood, really knows Fay. Her life is more of a mystery than the very ones whose allure is based upon that quality. She has resided in the film colony more than twelve years . . . she might as well have just arrived, for all that anyone has learned of her during these years.

E ARLY in her career, prior to being selected by Von Stroheim for his epic, Fay determined in her own mind that she would keep her private life her own. She reached this decision, not because she [*Continued on page 187*]

NORMA TAKES A DARE

By
J. Eugene Chrisman

Young women who become intrigued by the sophisticated characterizations of Norma Shearer are advised by the actress not to follow her precept

Norma Shearer braves public opinion in the most daring rôle of her career

This scene of Norma Shearer and Cobert Kirkland in *Strange Interlude*, pictures *The Divorcée* in anything but the beguiling rôles she is noted for. Yet, none more daring has ever been enacted by Miss Shearer than in her latest vehicle

NORMA SHEARER, noted since *The Divorcée* as the most daring of screen sophisticates, has just completed the most daring rôle of her career. Not even the heroine of *A Free Soul* or *Let Us Be Gay* can compare in shocking power to Nina, the sex-tortured woman of Eugene O'Neil's *Strange Interlude*.

"I admit that it is far more daring in conception than any of my previous rôles," says Miss Shearer, "but probably even Nina is not to be my most sophisticated.

"It was during the filming of *The Divorcée* that I learned I was to become a mother. My contract was nearly fulfilled and I had decided to retire to be a mother to my baby and a wife to my husband, for at that time I did not believe that marriage, motherhood and a career could be combined. I have, as you see, learned that they can. Sophisticated parts have done it."

If Nina is not to be the end of Norma Shearer's daring, where *will* it stop? Those who know the tragic story of *Strange Interlude,* realize that no such character as Nina has ever been put on the screen—Nina with her frustrations, her search for sexual expression, her unrestrained giving of her body to the maimed and the final tragedy of her illegitimate son. It is doubtful if any other actress would attempt it. However, Miss Shearer is not dismayed.

"I think my previous rôles will prove that sophistication does not need smutty lines, lewd scenes or display that is vulgar. The sophistication lies rather in that they deal with the real emotions which sway men and women and complicate their lives. We should not be afraid of sex on the screen, so long as it avoids vulgarity. I would be the first to decry vulgarity in pictures, but it is the more daring and more sophisticated side of life which forms the most interest."

THAT Norma Shearer's ability to portray such characters does not come from experience of her own, is shown by a study of her life and her career. In her first search for screen fame, she did not run away from home, as so many girls have. On the contrary, her mother accompanied her from their Canadian home to New York. When she came to Hollywood, her mother also lived with her, quietly and conservatively. [*Continued on page 187*]

JEAN HARLOW CARRIES ON

Star Strives to Forget Recent Tragedy in Future Plans

—*Wide World Photo*

WITH HER STEPFATHER, Marino Bello, Jean Harlow is seen leaving the little chapel where she said a last goodbye to Paul Bern

GRIEF-STRICKEN, Jean Harlow sought to deaden her sorrow by long hours of work in *Red Dust*, in which she appears with Clark Gable

"The show must go on!" This famous phrase, known to every actor and actress, echoes these days in the ears of Jean Harlow as she steadfastly finishes her job as leading lady opposite Clark Gable in *Red Dust*.

Following the sad train of events which robbed the star of her beloved husband and Hollywood of its most admired movie executive, many predicted that Paul Bern's suicide meant the sudden end of Jean Harlow's career. But with admirable courage, the platinum blonde star quieted all these prophecies by insisting on immediate resumption of her studio duties.

Like Billie Burke, whose husband, Florenz Ziegfeld, died suddenly while she was appearing in her first talking picture, *Bill of Divorcement,* Jean has admirably obeyed theatrical tradition by going quietly, courageously on with the show.

All through that first day of her return to the studio Jean was cared for by a special nurse who watched carefully for any signs of nervous fatigue. Jean's stepfather, Marino Bello, was with her constantly, ready to summon a physician immediately if she collapsed. Fellow actors and studio workers tenderly and graciously extended themselves to make things as easy as possible for her.

Jean, with inborn courage, knew that the show must go on. She insisted on working through the full day and did her best to deliver a convincing performance. Her first scene was of a somewhat wistful nature and one scene was of light comedy nature but Jean saw it through, never letting down.

With her emotional and nervous system taut—at the breaking point—she never once gave in to a moment of weakness. The show went on.

Hollywood Throngs Pay Last Tribute to Paul Bern

—*Wide World Photos*

The little chapel in which last respects were paid to Paul Bern was submerged in flowers—costly orchids from cinema's brightest lights—and tiny floral sprigs from grieving folk the kind-hearted producer had befriended

More than a thousand persons, the great and the small, b i d farewell to Paul Bern

John Gilbert, one of Paul Bern's c l o s e s t friends, entering t h e chapel

Joan Bennett, among the many who mourn with Jean Harlow, as s h e stepped from her car to attend the services

4 RULES OF Married Love

*Hollywood's Happiest
Husband Tells How
He Stays That Way*

By
DOUGLAS FAIRBANKS, Jr.
as told to DORA ALBERT.

DOUGLAS FAIRBANKS, JR., in a red dressing gown, discovered in the act of clipping reviews from the newspapers about his father's latest picture. Joan Crawford in a dark blue serge dress but still wearing loose, flopping mules moves gracefully across the room.

The scene is the suite of the St. Moritz Hotel in New York, where one of Hollywood's most romantic couples spent a belated honeymoon. The time—eleven o'clock in the morning—a ghastly hour to ask people how they hope to make a success of marriage.

"I hate to be interviewed about marriage," confessed young Doug frankly. (Candor is his forte, but it is a charming sort of candor, and never brusque.) "Articles about marriage are always being written."

"But people are always getting married," I interposed.

"And writers write such mushy, oogly-woogly stuff about Joan and me."

It was decided in solemn conclave that this wasn't going to be an oogly-woogly article. That wasn't what I wanted, anyway. The world knows about the personal happiness of Joan and Douglas. But I wanted to know any rules young Doug had by which he was going to try to steer the frail craft

of marriage through all the shoals that beset it.

"Now when Mencken was married," I reminded Fairbanks, Jr., "he said that there was just one rule for marital success, 'Be polite.' What do you think?"

"It's all a matter of the personalities concerned," said young Doug, looking out at me from his incredibly blue eyes. "If two personalities click, other things can be adjusted if you have intelligence enough.

"I don't think that married people ought to be conscious of the fact that they are married. They ought to live in sin, so to speak."

Right there I almost forgot my promise. I could see a swell headline. "LIVE IN SIN" SAYS DOUGLAS FAIRBANKS, JR.

But Doug has a devastating smile and I have a conscience, so I warned him, "That might be misinterpreted, you know."

"I mean that after marriage it is a very good thing to attempt to keep up the same relationship that existed before marriage—to keep right on courting your wife."

"Do you mean that a husband ought to send his wife orchids when she goes to the theater or a dance?"

"Yes, why take your wife for granted? The moment you [Continued on page 188]

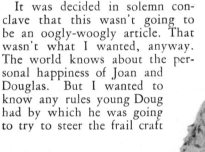

Hollywood's perpetual honeymooners, Joan Crawford and Douglas Fairbanks, Jr.

"Married people really ought to live in sin," says young Doug

[Continued on page 188]

THE INTIMATE LIFE OF A

Gentleman Rebel

The event of greatest consequence in the career of Franchot Tone
was the invaluable lesson he learned—from the woman he loves

By WALTER RAMSEY

FRANCHOT'S first official protest was aired February 27, 1905, at the home of Frank J. Tone at 426 Buffalo Avenue, Niagara Falls, N. Y. It was an interesting household in which everyone, including the newly arrived Franchot and his older brother Jerry, was expected to develop interests of his own and begin living his own life as soon as possible.

Franchot's first memory of the spotlight came at the age of three, when his brother's mind went blank at a Christmas party and Franchot recited the lines he had heard Jerry practice.

Before Master Tone was five, he was practically a world traveler. Then, on his return to Niagara Falls, came school—first, Miss Otis', later, the Hill School, a boys' academy.

He had been allowed to return home two weeks early because of excellent grades.

"I took that extra leave with a great deal of poo-ba around the family," smiles Franchot. "Then, the day before Christmas, a letter arrived for me I read it through. I read it again. It was from the Head Master. I remember the words indelibly:

"*.   is hereby notified of his dismissal from the student body of the Hill School for being a subtle influence for disorder throughout the fall term. . . .*"

THAT first moody reaction from being kicked out of the Hill School for being: ". . . a subtle influence for disorder . . ." stayed with Franchot but temporarily. After the first shock, no one in the family seemed to mind much. His father, perhaps, might have taken it rather hard but for the statement made by Franchot's older brother. Jerry said:

"What a break! Now you can start right in at Cornell without waiting that extra half year."

Thus, Father Tone's reaction was tempered immediately to: "Well, it'll save me a damned expensive half term!"

Jerry had already been at Cornell several terms and was on good pal grounds with the Registrar—this because Jerry was on the baseball team and the registrar was by way of being a baseball nut. So it was arranged that Franchot was to come immediately to Ithaca and begin a two-week cram session so that he could pass the entrance examinations.

It was the dead of winter when he arrived at Ithaca. He took quarters in a combination room-and-board house and began his cramming. But despite his hard work and study, it seemed for a time that he might come closer to freezing than to mental perfection. The house had porous walls and the wind—starting at the far end of one of the Finger Lakes—hit the house and zoomed right on in. Night after night, Franchot sat in bed bundled to the ears in blankets and poured over his studies; at the same time, he was promising himself that if he was lucky enough to pass the exams he'd go on a toot by way of

From the very first Joan was a revelation to this discontented young actor from New York, who had been put under contract by M-G-M after he had appeared in such Broadway successes as "The Pagan Lady" with Lenore Ulric, and with June Walker and Helen Westley in that hit of 1931, "Green Grow the Lilacs"

making up for these awful freezing weeks. The wind, unmindful, continued to wail off Lake Cayuga and straight into his room.

That he finally passed the examinations with flying honors was no particular surprise to him. Self-confidence and young Tone were to be considered as interchangeable terms.

Outwardly, Franchot must have appeared a likable, quiet sort of a chap to his fellow first-termers at Cornell. Inwardly, though, he was a different person—sure of himself, of his values and even slightly egoistic concerning his place in the scheme of things. In fact, in a less conspicuous way, he was as much of a rebel at Cornell as he had been at The Hill.

He was rather flattered when invited to join his brother's fraternity, *Alpha Delta Phi,* but it didn't matter to him that the fraternity felt let-down when he, their youngest member, went out for the tame dramatic club instead of seeking glory and honor for both the fraternity and the school on the athletic field. Athletics-for-honors bored Franchot. The dramatic club, scorned though it was as an activity, did not. And to his credit it must be said that the presidency of the Club (which he finally held) soon became one of the most coveted of honors and that before he left school, the Club was recognized as one of the finest in the country.

THE first year or so of Cornell went by swiftly for the young and experimental Tone. He studied diligently the subjects that interested him, thumbed through those that didn't and poured his whole heart into the Dramatic Club. Occasionally he imagined himself in love with one of the many pretty girls in Ithaca. But even if he could remember any one of their names, he wouldn't tell them—though he swears the only one he sincerely remembers is the beautiful girl who bid him be true as she left Ithaca for a try at Broadway after a hectic summer romance. This morbidly-happy ending so impressed Tone that he actually was true to her—for six months.

When Franchot was halfway through his sophomore year, he and three other "free souls" went in together and rented a house on the westerly boundary of the Cornell quadrangle and promptly named it "The Little Gray Home In The West."

"If that paints a quiet, sentimental picture, it's a false one," grins Tone. "If The Little Gray House could talk, it would certainly have tales to tell of Saturday night beer busts, of dishes that were never washed, floors that were left unswept and of a big, blazing fireplace that soon became the focal point of every mentally undigested idea or notion in the clan."

Franchot loved the free and easy life of The Little Gray Home In The West. It was a grand bachelor existence. Bachelor, chiefly, because all four of the male occupants were carrying the torch for some out-of-town girl; so women were never permitted within the doors.

"We had grand times, great talks and sometimes a heavy beer hang-over," Franchot admits. "The four of us did almost everything—including joining the Book & Bowl Club and acquiring a model T Ford. When a fire broke out in The Little Gray Home, we spent three winter weeks with nothing but a canvas flap over the burned-away front door. And I'll never forget the night my Ford went 'nuts' and chased the night watchman all over the campus—well, no one knows the truth of that little incident but model T and myself."

His third summer at Cornell, Franchot decided to drag himself away from The Home and take a fling at European education. He enrolled in a school about eight hours out of Paris. Four days out of each week he labored studiously and then hiked quickly to Paris for a long week end. He was, supposedly, gaining a knowledge of the French language at the school but actually . . .

". . . I got most of my French lessons from a cute little girl at *Zelli's* in Montmartre. There, at a small table in a far and dimly-lighted corner, we'd sit over a bottle of wine and she would speak to me in French. I learned a lot from her—about French, I mean—and I grew rather fond of her in the bargain." .

Her name was Yvonne. Franchot might have had quite a romance, had he not been still in the throes of carrying the torch for the girl Broadway had taken from him. As it was, "nothing." And I suppose he still thinks of the very cute little Yvonne and mentally kicks himself around the block for not taking a more active interest. But, as Franchot puts it: "When I woke up, I was back in America and Yvonne was still in Paris."

College days came to an end for Franchot with real pangs of regret. The school, the Dramatic Club and The Little Gray Home In The West had so completely filled his life for over three years that he was at a loss to adjust himself when those days were over and done forever. One thing he was sure of, however: He wanted to be an actor. During college, he had appeared in over forty University plays. He was at home behind the footlights. It was the career that interested him. When he broached the matter to his family, no one forbade him his chance to carry Broadway by storm. In fact, Franchot never knew until much later that his family had given in to his plans with the idea that he would "out-grow" the stage notions and return to take his place (along with

Jerry) in father's Carborundum plant. Knowing Franchot, I suppose they considered it wiser to let him try—feeling certain that he would tire with failure. And he almost did!

HIS first two years as a "professional" were certainly drab enough. Through the intervention of a cousin who was backing a stock company known as The Gary-McGary Players in Buffalo, Tone secured a job as stage manager at the puzzling salary of $15.00 a week. His duties were to write down all stage business during the rehearsals, announce half-hour, and prompt the actors from the wings. In fact, he was paid to do everything but the one thing he wanted to do—act!

His first break came when the juvenile of the company got an offer from Broadway and the director (Ralph Murphy, now a motion picture director in Hollywood) was left without a romantic lead for a play that was to open in a couple of nights. Luckily, being so anxious to play the rôle, Franchot had learned every line and every gesture of the now-unfilled rôle. So, in desperation, Murphy allowed him to play it. And Tone was so exhausted from an all-night cram session, that he was sufficiently relaxed to give an excellent performance. Even his mother who occupied (quite skeptically) a front row seat, was forced to admit that Franchot *might* be headed in the right direction.

Being a new play, the critics were there as well. Were enthusiastic, too. And when those two "Bibles" of the theater, *Billboard* and *Variety* deigned to carry short-but-laudatory reviews of his work, Franchot considered himself on the way. He spent the entire day, following this minor triumph, cutting out his "notices" and pasting them in a scrapbook. This book, he planned, was to be his main weapon of attack on Broadway producers.

But Broadway was not yet for the eager Franchot. For six weeks he remained with The Gary-McGary Players at $40.00 weekly before he was offered $60.00 by a New York group called the New Playwrights Theater. The promise of those twenty extra dollars was his undoing for, after six weary days of rehearsals, the manager let him go with the excuse that he was too young and inexperienced for the tough rôle, after all! For weeks, he made the rounds of the agencies and producers—his notices always hopefully displayed. The managers who bothered to read them were totally unimpressed. No contracts, no salary. For the first time in his life, a discouraged young Franchot entertained doubts that the world was his particular oyster.

"But those tough breaks were good for me. I had them coming. Up to that time, things I had wanted had come too easily to me. I shall never forget one awful day; it was the day I had been released after six days of rehearsal and I had to ride the subway back to town. Lord, I was blue. But on that subway, I had it out with myself. I knew I could do one of two things: Return to Niagara Falls and a good job with Father, or stick it out in New York and wait for the break that was to be quite a long time showing up. I'm not saying that I was too courageous to quit. But at least I was too stubborn."

His real career didn't get under way until after almost eighteen months of "backing and filling"—backing into assorted, cheap stock companies and filling into minor rôles with such lesser Broadway plays as "The Ladder." Matter of fact, it wasn't until an agent sent him to Guthrie McClintic (husband of Katharine Cornell) for a rôle in the great Cornell's starring vehicle "The Age Of Innocence," that Franchot skated, even lightly, on the thin ice of Broadway success.

The Cornell play was a hit with the critics and even more a hit with Franchot because it paid him $100.00 weekly in addition to the great pride he felt in appearing with the first lady of the New York stage. Of that period, he says: "Oddly enough, I stayed away from the more-or-less gay spots and saved my money. In fact, I saved more that year, in proportion, than I've ever been able to save since. I wound up with $2,000 in a savings account which I promptly lost in the stock market boom-boom of 1929!"

The season of 1930-31 saw Franchot in "Cross Roads" with Sylvia Sydney and Peggy Shannon, both of whom tried Hollywood before he did. Following that, he appeared in "Red Rust" for the Theater Guild and after a brief run with Phillip Barrie's "Hotel Universe," the Theater Guild signed him to a three-year contract.

Success had come upon him in such gradual doses that Franchot was a sought-after and popular actor on Broadway almost without realizing how far he had come. Though he was not starred, he drew laudatory notices for his work opposite such stars as Lenore Ulric in "The Pagan Lady," Jane Cowl in "A Thousand Summers." It was while touring the road with Miss Cowl that he had the terrific thrill of playing in Ithaca before the old gang from Cornell. The regular theater had been too small to hold the advance sale and a huge auditorium had been taken over for the play. The name "Franchot Tone" was prominent in lights beside the famous name Jane Cowl . . . which is an experience akin to returning to your hometown and driving a Rolls-

[Continued on page 189]

The Opening Chorus

A LETTER FROM LIZA

DEAR BOSS:
I have just returned from a shopping bender with Joan Crawford, which is an experience well worth writing home about, not that I consider your termite-eaten desk and over-crowded waste paper basket home. I have been entering shops, and exclusive shops, too, I daresay, for well nigh on to, we won't go into that, years, and not once has my entrance caused the least bit of a flurry, though I did see two detectives edge in on me the day I looked at cigarette cases at Cartier's.

But the very second Joan Crawford entered Magnin's this morning, with me bringing up the rear as sort of a backdrop, as we say in the theatre, I suddenly found myself in the midst of the most excitement I have seen in all those years we won't go into. Salesladies rushed hither and thither like mad, models dove into tasty little numbers, and despite the fact that Joan had really come to buy a hat, sort of a combination Easter bonnet and chapeau for her cocktail party, in honor of the famous conductor Leopold Stokowski, practically everything in the store was paraded in front of her.

Joan said I came to buy a hat out loud and they said

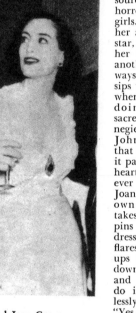

Wide World

Franchot Tone and Joan Crawford step out at the Biltmore Hotel, an unusual occurrence in the Tone family.

that's what you think under their breath. Before an hour had elapsed Joan had hats, dresses, pajamas, hosiery, lingerie, slippers, perfumes, powder, bags and even gadgets. Joan is a most amazing shopper. The slightly mad type. As I sat over in the corner on a couch, trying to persuade Pupchen and Baby, Joan's two puppy dachshunds, not to chew up the frou-frou on a little Hattie Carnegie something for the cocktail hour, I simply went into one amazement after another. And here's how Joanie shops . . .

When she finds a hat she likes she immediately has it copied in a dozen or more colors. She buys expensive straws and brings them back year after year to be re-blocked. She prefers simple tailored hats and vagabond hats, but, of course, if the *Occasion* demands a picture hat Joan wears a picture hat. Her Stokowski party hat, which she selected the day I was with her, was one of the loveliest I have ever seen her wear. It was an enormous, floppy blue straw, worn back on her head *sans* crown and showing the top of her head. (Not for the subways, dearie.)

Joan hates waiting for anything, she's the impatient sort, so she rarely has the shop deliver things to her home—she simply stacks them up, as she buys them, and insists upon carting them herself out to her big black Cadillac waiting in front of the store. She also slips her feet out of her slippers while she is shopping, and you can well imagine the out-of-town tourists' surprise when they see their favorite Glamour Girl, quite shoeless, dashing about the store with her arms piled high with dresses, lingerie, robes, and things, and with Pupchen and Baby, with bits of Schiaparelli dangling from their teeth, yapping wildly at her feet.

Joan is both a source of joy and horror to the salesgirls. They worship her as a big movie star, and they love her as one girl to another (Joan always chats and gossips with them) but when it comes to doing over their sacred Hattie Carnegies, Chanels, and John Fredericks that Crawford buys, it pains them to the heart. No one is ever allowed to fit Joan. She does her own fittings. She takes charge of the pins and tucks the dress in here and flares it there and ups the hem and downs the neckline and all they can do is to sit hopelessly by and say, "Yes, Miss Crawford."

Ever since she was a little girl and played on the floor, Joan has adored making and designing clothes, first for her dolls and then for herself, and when she can do over and improve upon the most exclusive and expensive models in the country, ah that is fiesta day for Joan. But I leave it to you, her public, isn't she always dressed with the most exquisite taste? Pooh to the couturiers.

Another of Joan's annoying little habits is waiting on herself. She never misses a chance to dart behind the counter and pick out just exactly what she wants without any of the chi chi of having it sold to her. And to the floorwalker's horror, often she disappears, when no one is looking, into the holy of holies—the stock room. Through all this shopping orgy (even when a customer, not recognizing her behind the counter, asks to see something in washable gloves) Joan keeps in a gay, rollicking humor. The one and only way to make her furious is to try to sell her something that looks like what the cat dragged in. She's definitely not a push-over for truck. And speaking of truck I got a date to go truckin' . . .

Liza

Loretta Young isn't sure yet whether she will mix career and marriage again

Loretta's marriage to Grant Withers (left) didn't take. Eddie Sutherland is the new love

Career Comes First with LORETTA

By DAN CAMP

THERE'S a lovely white Colonial house atop one of those rolling hills of Bel-Air, on Hollywood's borders. It's a grand house, a warm house, a friendly house, a house fine to live in.

BUT—it's a pretty certain bet that before long, now, that house is going to be deserted, cold and empty. And then, when superstitious ones pass it by (and who, in this luck-and-fate-ruled Hollywood isn't superstitious, I ask!). they'll be able to point to it as a monument to filmland's pet superstition—"the Law of Threes."

You know that Law of Three's, don't you? It's simply this —that when any one outstanding event happens in Hollywood, two other similar events must happen within a short time, before the fate-cycle is complete. If one star elopes, they believe two others will elope soon. If there's one blessed event of top-rank prominence, the wise ones expect two more stork announcements pretty quick. And, strange as it seems, the rule works out pretty consistently . . . !

And that house—Three lovely sisters used to live in that house. Three famous sisters, named Polly and Sally and Loretta. You know 'em as Polly Ann Young, Sally Blane, and Loretta Young . . .

They were happy there, and they loved the house. But then the Cupid kid, who hasn't any respect at all for home-ties and things like that, started shooting his hellish arrows about, and before you knew it, what happened?—why, Sally got married. And Polly got married. And Sally had a baby. And Polly had a baby. And there are Polly and Sally, with their hubbies, their babies, and their own homes. And there, still in the big white house on the hilltop, is Loretta—with no husband, no baby.

(But wait! Here's where the Law of Three's comes in.) There is, in the picture, a gentleman named Eddie Sutherland. Eddie's a big-shot director, as you [Continued on page 190]

32

FERNAND GRAVET

BRIAN AHERNE

ERROL FLYNN

NELSON EDDY

WHO'S WHOSE

AT LAST HERE IS THE DATA THAT YOU'VE BEEN
WAITING FOR—TOLD FOR THE FIRST TIME. LET'S
LOOK AT THE RECORD AND SEE WHO HAS
BELONGED (OR BELONGS) TO WHO IN HOLLY-
WOOD'S "400"

By JAMES REID

THIS is a directory to end all wrong impressions about
marriage in Hollywood.

Most articles about Hollywood marriage are written from
one of two viewpoints: (1) It can't succeed, or (2) It
can. Writers cite only the cases that "prove" the particular points they wish to prove. So now, for the first
time, let's face facts. Let's look at the actual record, in
black and white.

MOTION PICTURE herewith presents, for the first time in
any magazine, a *Who's Whose in Hollywood*. It is entertaining. It is illuminating. It answers questions you have
silently asked about this one or that. It is something you
will want to keep as a record, a reference.

There are four hundred names in this *Who's Whose*. They
are not names carefully culled to prove any particular case.
This *Who's Whose* is concerned with Hollywood's Top Four
Hundred—considered from three angles: their importance
in pictures, the publicity they are given, and the fan mail
they receive.

Read every item. Form your impressions of the success
or non-success of screen stars in their off-screen romances.
Then, at the end, check your impressions of Hollywood marriage, as a whole, with the actual statistics compiled from this
directory! It will appear in two installments of which this
from A to H inclusive is the first.—Editor's Note.

ABEL, WALTER—Married to Marietta Bitter, concert
harpist, since early acting days. Has two young sons.

AHERNE, BRIAN—Still in the market for marriage. Attentive to Olivia de Havilland, among others.

ALLAN, ELIZABETH—The "long-distance wife" of Wil-
fred James O'Bryen,, London theatrical agent.

ALLEN, FRED—His private-life partner is his public
heckler, Portland Hoffa.

ALLEN, GRACIE—She's from San Francisco, George
Burns is from New York; they first became vaudeville partners in Newark, N. J. Married four years later, in 1927. They
have two adopted children, Sandra Jean and Roland Jon.

ALLWYN, ASTRID—Lost Robert Kent in *Dimples*, won
him between scenes. They were married secretly January, 1937.

AMECHE, DON—Married his schoolday sweetheart,
Honore Prendergast, who had become a dietician while he
was becoming an actor. The date: November 26, 1932. They
have two sons, Donald and Ronald.

AMES, ADRIENNE—No. 1: Derward Truex,, by whom
she had a daughter, Barbara, now 13. No. 2: Stephen Ames,
broker. Divorced in 1933. No. 3: Bruce Cabot. Married,
1933. Her divorce will be final next April 6.

ANGEL, HEATHER—She and Ralph Forbes became the
"hitch-hike elopers" when their car broke down on the way

IN HOLLYWOOD

to Yuma, August 29, 1934. It's her first marriage, his second.

ANNABELLA—Twice married, briefly and unhappily, before marrying the French star, Jean Murat, two years ago. Has child by previous marriage.

ARLEN, RICHARD—Has a debutante daughter by an early, brief, pre-Hollywood marriage. His second wife: Jobyna Ralston. They have a son, Richard Jr., and scoff at recent divorce rumors.

ARNOLD, EDWARD—His first marriage, to Harriet Marshall, ended in divorce. Married now to Olive Emerson. Children: Betty, Edward, Dorothy.

ARNOLD, JACK—The former Vinton Haworth is Ginger Rogers' uncle by marriage. His wife is Lela Rogers' youngest sister, Jean Owens.

ARTHUR, JEAN—Never mentions her unhappy, month-long first marriage, which ended in annulment. Married since June 11, 1932 to Frank Ross, Jr.

ASTAIRE, FRED—Stepped to the altar in 1933 with socialite divorcee, Phyllis Livingston Potter. They have one child, Fred, Jr.

ASTOR, MARY—Widowed when Director Kenneth Hawks was killed in an air crash. Dr. Franklyn Thorpe restored her health. She married him in 1931, had a daughter, Marylyn, who became center of bitter custody battle in 1936. Eloped to Yuma February 18, 1937, with actor-writer Manuel Del Campo.

AUER, MISCHA—He makes those amusing faces first for wife Norma Tillman and son Anthony, aged 3.

AUTRY, GENE—The singing cowboy married the girl whose name was Ina Mae Spivey.

AYRES, LEW—Married Lola Lane September 15, 1931. Divorced February 3, 1933. Married Ginger Rogers November 11, 1934. Separated after two years, but still not divorced.

BAKER, KENNY—His high-school sweetheart, Geraldine Churchill, was willing to starve with him—so they were married May 6, 1933. Then the breaks started coming his way.

BALL, LUCILLE—Still single, but that romance with Director Alexander Hall looks serious.

BANCROFT, GEORGE—Married and divorced Edna Brothers in his salad days. Married to Octavia Broske since May 30, 1916. Has a grown daughter, Georgette.

BARNES, BINNIE—Her first husband was Samuel Joseph, London antique dealer. They married January, 1931, divorced October, 1937. Her next will be painter Jean Negulesco.

BARRIE, WENDY—Hasn't made The Great Decision yet.

BARRYMORE, John—No. 1: Katherine Carri Harris. No. 2: Writer Blanche Oelrichs (pen name "Michael Strange"), by whom he had a daughter. No. 3: Dolores Costello, by whom he had a daughter and a son. No. 4: Elaine Barrie (nee Jacobs), whose Ariel-and-Caliban romance culminated in marriage November 11, 1936, an interlocutory divorce April 23, 1937, then a reconciliation, which still holds.

BARRYMORE, LIONEL—His first marriage—a remote and unhappy memory—was to one Doris Rankin. On July 14, 1923 he married actress Irene Fenwick, who died Christmas Eve, 1936.

BAXTER, WARNER—Very early, and very briefly, married to one Viola Caldwell, who later died. Married for years to actress Winifred Bryson.

BEAL, JOHN—Hollywood's most ardent commuting husband. Married since 1934 to Helen Craig, young Broadway actress.

ANNABELLA

GRETA GARBO

MARLENE DIETRICH

MARY ASTOR

87

BECK, TOMMY—Still one of Hollywood's handsomest bachelors.

BEERY, WALLACE—In February, 1916, married Gloria Swanson. It lasted about a year. His present marriage (to Rita Gillman) looks perpetual. Has an adopted 6-year-old, Carol Ann, around whom his world revolves.

BELLAMY, RALPH—Married to Catherine Willard, English actress, who calls him "Ralphalf." His first marriage, her second.

BENNETT, CONSTANCE—Her first marriage, to Chester H. Moorhead, University of Virginia student—was annulled. Her second—to Philip Plant, millionaire playboy—ended in divorce and a handsome property settlement. On January 9, 1932, she adopted a child, Peter. On November 22, 1932, she married Marquis Henri de la Falaise, who now makes travel pictures. Contrary to popular impression, they are not divorced—yet.

BENNETT, JOAN—At 16, Joan married John Fox, at 17 was a mother, at 18 was divorced. To earn a living (she wanted no alimony), she became an actress. Married writer Gene Markey in March, 1932, had a second daughter, was credited with two successful careers. Received interlocutory divorce, May, 1937.

BENNY, JACK—Since January 12, 1927, he has been listening to Mary Livingstone's poetry. This one looks permanent. They have an adopted 3-year-old, Joan.

BERGEN, EDGAR—Single. (Business of knocking on Charlie McCarthy's head.)

BERNIE, BEN—He married a Palm Beach girl, Dorothy Westley, which explains all those Florida visits. They have a grown son, Jason.

BLANE, SALLY—Her first and only husband is Norman Foster, who used to be married to Claudette Colbert. Daughter Gretchen born June 7, 1936.

BLONDELL, JOAN—When she married cameraman George Barnes on January 4, 1933, she wanted to change her screen name to Joan Barnes. They had a son, Norman. Then, in September, 1936, they had a divorce. The same month, she married Dick Powell—and they had Hollywood's most hectic honeymoon.

BLORE, ERIC—In 1917 he married a London actress, Violet Winter. She died, childless, in 1919. In 1926 he married Clara Mackin, also an actress. They had a son, Eric, Jr., in 1927. Recently separated.

BOGART, HUMPHREY—The first Mrs. Bogart was actress Helen Mencken (div. 1925). The second, actress Mary Phillips (div. 1937). The third—when the second divorce is final—will be actress Mayo Methot.

BOLAND, MARY—Has always lived alone and liked it.

BOLES, JOHN—Married to Marcelite Dobbs since the day he graduated from college, in 1917. They have two deb. daughters, Marcelite and Janet.

BOWMAN, LEE—Eligible. Currently the favored escort of Ginger Rogers.

BOYD, BILL—When he married Grace Bradley, newspapers credited him with four ex-wives. Two ex Mrs. Boyds: Elinor Fair and Dorothy Sebastian.

BOYER, CHARLES—Long a bachelor, he finally married in haste, courting Pat Paterson just three weeks before they eloped to Mexico, February, 1934.

BRADLEY, GRACE—As a schoolgirl, she used to paste Bill Boyd's picture in her schoolbooks. Last June 5, she married him.

BRADNA, OLYMPE—Seventeen-year-old "O'Lamp" isn't even thinking of marriage yet.

BRADY, ALICE—Love Alice, and you have to love her dogs. Maybe James L. Crane didn't. Anyway, their marriage lasted only two and a half years.

BRENNAN, WALTER—In 1920 Ruth Wells risked sharing his struggle. Now she's sharing his success. Children: Wells, Walter, Jr., and Ruth.

BRENT, GEORGE—He hasn't been lucky in love. After a brief marriage, divorced from one Helen Campbell in 1929. On August 13, 1932, married Ruth Chatterton. On October 4, 1934, divorced. On May 10, 1937, eloped to Mexico with Constance Worth, Australian actress.. Two months later he asked for an annulment. The court turned him down. She obtained divorce. December, 1937.

BRICE, FANNY—First sang My Man when married to mystery-man Nicholas (Nicky) Arnstein, by whom she had two children, William Jules and Frances. Later married showman Billy Rose, who recently announced candidly, if ungallantly, he was divorcing her to marry Eleanor Holm.

BRODERICK, HELEN—Since 1916, Mrs.

Lester Crawford, They were a famous vaudeville team. They have a big boy—Broderick Crawford, who is achieving Broadway fame in the smash hit, Of Mice and Men.

BROOKS, PHYLLIS—The next Mrs. Cary Grant, if they haven't already eloped.

BROWN, JOHNNY MACK—Mrs. Johnny was nee Cornelia Foster. They have a son born in 1933.

BROWN, JOE E.—Claims he has been married as long as he can remember—and to the same woman, Kathryn McGraw. They have two grown boys, and two little girls (one adopted to replace baby they lost).

BROWN, TOM—Married twice to Natalie Draper. First, on July 5, 1937, aboard a yacht. Then, ten days later, on land. Now honeymooning in England.

BRUCE, NIGEL—Married since May 10, 1921, to Violet Campbell, actress. They have two daughters, Pauline and Jenifer.

BRUCE, VIRGINIA—She was 21 when, on August 10, 1932, she became the fourth wife of John Gilbert, by whom she had a daughter, Susan Ann, in 1933. They were divorced May 25, 1934, only shortly before his death. While working on Bad Man of Brimstone, she and Director J. Walter Ruben fell in love, married him December 18, 1937.

BRYAN, JANE—Being strenuously courted by one of the Kellogg heirs.

BURKE, BILLIE—Widow of Florenz Ziegfeld, mother of Patricia Ziegfeld.

BURNS, BOB—His first wife, Elizabeth Fisher, mother of his 13-year-old son, died August 1, 1936, just when luck was turning in his favor after years of struggle. On May 31, 1937, lonely Bob married his secretary, Harriet Foster. Now heir-conditioning their home.

BURNS, GEORGE—See Gracie Allen.

BUTTERWORTH, CHARLES—After 5-year acquaintance, married Ethel Kenyon Sutherland, December, 1932. Divorce rumors currently popping.

BYINGTON, SPRING—Believes a divorcee should get alimony only in proportion to time she was married. Divorced herself, from a gentleman named Chandler. Has two daughters in college, Phyllis and Lois.

CABOT, BRUCE—Married Adrienne Ames in 1933, legally adopted her daughter, then was divorced April, 1937.

CAGNEY, JAMES—It was love at first sight with Jimmy and his actress-wife, Frances Vernon—and that was more than a decade ago.

CANTOR, EDDIE—When he married Ida Tobias in 1914, Eddie had hardly five dollars. Now he has five daughters, Marjorie, Natalie, Edna, Marilyn and Janet.

CARLISLE, MARY—Still keeping the boys guessing.

CARRADINE, JOHN—After the movies finally found John, in 1935, he soon found a wife, Ardanelle Cosner. They have a little John, born December, 1936.

CARRILLO, LEO—His rivals for California's governorship, probing his record, will find only one marriage—to Edith Shakespeare. They have an adopted daughter, Marie Antoinette.

CARROLL, MADELEINE—Married since 1931 to wealthy Philip Astley of the Chequers, England, Astleys. One of the more successful long-distance marriages.

CARVER, LYNNE—As Virginia Reid, she gave up films in 1935 to marry Dr. R. C. McClung of Birmingham, Ala. Divorced in 1936, she came back with a new name. On July 18, 1937, married Nicholas Nayfack, young M-G-M executive.

CHAPLIN, CHARLIE—No one was certain he had married Mildred Harris in 1918 until she divorced him in 1920. His second marriage—to Lita Grey—was no secret. She gave him two sons, Charles, Jr., and Sydney, before their divorce in 1927, when she won boys' custody. Everybody suspects Paulette Goddard is Wife No. 3—but they won't talk.

CHATTERTON, RUTH—"Still good friends" after 8 years of matrimony, Ralph Forbes gave Ruth a Nevada divorce, August 12, 1932. The next day she wed their mutual good friend, George Brent, whom she divorced October 4, 1934. Denies being engaged to Portuguese millionaire wine exporter.

CHURCHILL, MARGUERITE—Became Mrs. George O'Brien in 1933. They lost their first child, born in 1934, now have a second.

CIANNELLI, EDUARDO—Hadn't been in America a week when he fell in love with socialite Alma Wolfe and wooed her with gestures, not knowing the language. They have two boys in

their early teens.

COLBERT, CLAUDETTE—Secretly married a long time, Claudette and Norman Foster finally took a world-tour-by-freighter honeymoon, then tried the separate-house type of matrimony It didn't work. She's now married to Dr. Joel Pressman.

COLMAN RONALD—Because he was a recluse, long thought a bachelor Instead, was long separated from Thelma Raye, English actress, who divorced him in 1934. Still a recluse. Denies any and all romance rumors.

CONKLIN, PEGGY—Married to James Thompson of the New York "400."

CONNOLLY, WALTER—Long and happily married to actress Nedda Harrigan. They have a 13-year-old named Anne

COOGAN, JACKIE—"The Kid" has grown up. A married man since November 20, 1937, when Betty Grable said "I do."

COOPER, GARY—Old-timers remember his long, hectic romance with Lupe Velez, which ended this side of the altar in 1931. Married socialite-actress Veronica Balfe in 1933. Daughter born September 15, 1937.

CORTEZ, RICARDO—First wife, actress Alma Rubens, who died tragically in 1930. Married socialite divorcee, Mrs. Christine Lee, January 8, 1934. Recently rumored apart, more recently rumored reconciled.

COSTELLO, DOLORES—Received final decree of divorce from John Barrymore, and custody of two children, October 27, 1936. Friends predict she will soon marry Dr. John Vruwink.

COWAN, JEROME—Quietly, but definitely married.

CRABBE, LARRY—Married his pre-movie sweetheart, Adah Held, in 1933. Has a year-old daughter.

CRAWFORD, JOAN—On January 3, 1929, married Douglas Fairbanks, Jr. On May 12, 1933, divorced him. Two years later, married the world's most persistent suitor, Franchot Tone.

CROMWELL, RICHARD—Still looking them over.

CROSBY, BING—Sang I Surrender Dear to Dixie Lee, for keeps, in 1932. Son Gary born 1933. Twins, Philip and Dennis, born 1934. Expecting again.

CUMMINGS, ROBERT—Young, tall, handsome, wealthy, but—already married, to Vivienne Audrey.

CURTIS, ALAN—M-G-M's new white hope loves Priscilla Lawson more than "romantic rave" publicity. He's marrying (just married?) the girl.

D'ARCY, ALEXANDER—Young Man-About-Hollywood, 1938 model.

DARRIEUX, DANIELLE—"The rage of Paris" is married to Henri Decoin, French writer-director.

DARWELL, JANE—Won't 'fess up to an early brief marriage, but is suspected of one.

DAVIES, MARION—Holds the Hollywood bachelor-girl record.

DAVIS, BETTE—Quietly and successfully married to orchestra-leader Harmon O. Nelson, Jr., since 1932. Another case of schoolday sweethearts.

DAVIS, JOAN—She and Serenus (Si) Wills, late of vaudeville, still are partners and have a 4-year-old, Beverly.

DEANE, SHIRLEY—Engaged to cameraman Russell Bowditch, but a "no-marriage-until-a-certain-date" contract clause is delaying the wedding.

DEE, FRANCES—Happily Mrs. Joel McCrea since 1933. They have two sons.

DE HAVILLAND, OLIVIA—Love requires leisure. And Olivia is busy.

DEL RIO, DOLORES—Came to Hollywood as the wife of Jaime Del Rio, who later died tragically in Paris. In 1931, she married scenic designer Cedric Gibbons.

DE MILLE, KATHERINE—Her adopted father, Cecil B., introduced her to Anthony Quinn a year ago. She married him October 2, 1937.

DENNY, REGINALD—When he isn't acting or inventing model airplanes, he's married to Isobel Steiffel. Previously wed to Irene Haisman.

DESTE, LULI—Widow of Baron Gottfried Hohenburg, who was killed in a European air crash just before she came to the U. S. A.

DEVINE, ANDY—Eloped to Las Vegas October 28, 1933, with Dorothy House. Son Timothy born November 26, 1934.

DIETRICH, MARLENE—Just returned from yearly reunion with husband Rudolf Sieber, a director abroad. Married May 17, 1923. Daughter Maria born 1925. Year after year Marlene and her escorts baffle the divorce prophets.

[Continued on page 191]

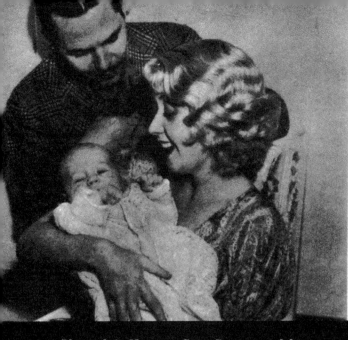

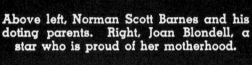
Above left, Norman Scott Barnes and his doting parents. Right, Joan Blondell, a star who is proud of her motherhood.

"I want to talk about my *baby!*"

Says Joan Blondell, smashing Hollywood's pet taboo

By Kay Osborn

IT just never occurred to me to seek out Joan on the subject of her baby—for publication, that is. It's sort of understood out here that women stars with babies don't like to talk about them to the press. A lot of other writers weren't asking about the baby either, because they, too, considered the subject taboo.

I ran into Joan one day and asked her about the baby, carefully explaining that my interest was personal, not professional. I told her I knew she didn't want to have a story written about him. So you can imagine my surprise when Joan protested, "Who says I don't!" and her blue eyes flashed. "As a matter of fact, I've been quite hurt that nobody has come to me, wanting an interview about me and my baby. What is this, anyway? Doesn't anyone want to hear about him? Of course I'll talk about my baby! *He's the most important thing that's ever happened to me, or ever will happen!*

"This business of a baby spoiling the fans' interest in a female star is all the bunk. Audiences today are more intelligent than they used to

be. They like to see an actress give a good performance, more than anything else. And a baby helps a woman to become a better actress. My baby is helping me. He takes me out of myself. Makes me understand many more emotions than I have ever felt before. Why shouldn't I talk about him?"

Well! We plopped into the nearest chairs, and, believe it or not, I never got another word in edgewise.

It seems that Joan's baby is the cutest, the cleverest, the prettiest and the healthiest baby that ever shook a rattle. Oh yes, I know you've heard that story before. But this time it's so, says Joan.

"Do you know that right this minute, and at this minute he is exactly five months, three days, and five hours old, he is every bit as big as a year-old baby? Why, he never could wear any of the lovely things which were given to me at my shower. I've had to give all his presents away. The doctor comes in to look at him on his weekly visits, and laughs. Just laughs! And Normie laughs right [Continued on page 192]

The Final Fling

A MOVIE FAN'S CROSSWORD PUZZLE

By Charlotte Herbert

Charles Laughton

CAN a person act a part unless that part has an echo inside his own soul? Is Bette Davis no relation to the mean girl in "Of Human Bondage" and is Charles Laughton without a drop of the acid of Captain Bligh?

We have met Bette and she was a very pleasant person from our own Massachusetts. Laughton, during the making of "Mutiny On The Bounty," was the life of the party at the camp at Catalina and well liked by everyone.

One is quite ready to see the true soul of a player when the part he is playing is lovable or goes heroic, so naturally we are likewise apt to imagine the villainy is not make-believe.

After Peter Lorre made "M" people would get up and leave a restaurant if he entered. All of which makes us eager to see Charles Laughton as *Cyrano de Bergerac*, a favorite well-loved character of ours.

* * *

The picture theatre has a certain function, which is to entertain you by stimulating your imagination so skillfully that you are lifted out of yourself.

To go to see Lily Pons just to hear her voice, is to have missed the point. In other words, you could have enjoyed her voice by hearing her sing (in person) or on a radio. You went to the theatre for something real and not for make-believe.

But the picture theatre is great when it does *more* than reflect the real person. Claudette Colbert in every day life is just a nice girl. But when in—say "Imitation Of Life," she stakes Ned Sparks to a stack of wheats, she breathes life into a character and creates, by the magic of the theatre, *a new time and place* to enchant you. That is the appeal of the movies at their best.

* * *

Lily Pons is real without our imagination. Captain Bligh is real too, but our imagination, tortured, twisted and goaded by a great actor, made him so.

THE EDITOR

ACROSS

2-7 "The Man Who Broke the Bank at Monte Carlo"
13 Morning (abbr.)
15 Dr. Felix in "The Invisible Ray"
17 To be afraid of
18 The sun god
19 The poor manicurist in "Hands Across the Table"
20 The originator of "Come up and see me some time"
21 Her latest picture is "If Only You Could Cook"
22 The queen of "Three Kids and a Queen" (init.)
23 A suffix used to form many plurals
26 Exists
27 Masculine title of respect (abbr.)
28 Our country (abbr.)
29 Tarzan's mate
32 Star of "I Found Stella Parrish"
33 He is now appearing on the stage (initials)
34 To break suddenly
35 A precious stone
37 A South Western state (abbr.)
38 The reformed gangster in "Rich Girl's Folly"
40 Looking-glasses
43 Star of "Here's to Romance"
45 A large river in Siberia
46 A Celtic Scotch Highlander
48 Removes with a sudden pull
50 A range of mountains in Arkansas, Missouri and Oklahoma
52 In that place
54 Head (abbr.)
56 Before
58 Denial
59 The lovely Constance in "The Three Musketeers"
62 Large Spanish vessel of the Fifteenth Century
65 Either
66 A girl's name
69 Nickel (abbr.)
70 The Russian girl portrayed by Garbo in her last picture
72 The Chase and Sanborn Coffee Slogan :— "It's _____"
73 Beheld
75 Acts again
77 Station (abbr.)
78 She is married to Hal Mohr
79 Near
80 She will soon appear in "Romeo and Juliet"
81 Thoroughfare (abbr.)

DOWN

1 Shared honors with Lombard in "Hands Across the Table"
3 A musical wind instrument
4 Bruce, of the Canadian Mounted, in "Rose Marie"
5 A beverage
6 Huey Long's home state (abbr.)
8 Belonging to
9 A meadow
10 The Duchess of Kent
11 Branches of learning
12 His next starring vehicle is "The Voice of Ann Bugle"
14 A Paramount player
16 He is featured in "The Magnificent Obsession"
18 He's in "East of Java"
24 Agnes in "Peter Ibbetson"
25 She dances with Patsy Kelly in "Thanks a Million"
30 Identical
31 Semi-circular recess of a church
34 Thoroughfare (abbr.)
36 The reporter in "Atlantic Adventure" (init.)
39 Featured with Lily Pons in her first picture
41 To level with the ground
42 An imaginary monster
44 She will be starred in "Show Boat"
45 The disgraced ex-captain in "China Seas"
47 Army officer (abbr.)
49 He portrayed an archeologist in "I Live My Life"
51 Tony Orsatti in "Three Kids and a Queen"
53 Puck in "A Midsummer Night's Dream"
55 Twelfth month (abbr.)
57 The cry of a sheep
59 To gather and store away
60 He played opposite Jean Harlow in "Riffraff"
61 A color
62 A disease of sheep
63 One who is defeated
64 A simpleton
67 A box in which things may be kept
68 A Shakespearean king
71 Seize unexpectedly
74 Old times (poet.)
76 Star of "Mary Burns, Fugitive" (initials)
78 Speech of hesitancy

Answer To Last Month's Puzzle

WIN A WATCH!

WHO WAS IT?

WHO?

WHICH STAR?

WHEN

A Prize Contest To Test Your Knowledge Of The Stars.

HAVE you kept track of their doings and if so, how much do you remember? Just to enable you to check on your own answer, the correct version of the following paragraphs will be printed in a later issue of SILVER SCREEN.

Can you tell which players are referred to? For a reward you may receive a beautiful watch as a prize. There will be just one watch given for the prize, but such a watch! It may be either a man's or woman's watch, as the winner prefers. They are *Wittnauers* and that means that if you win one of them your days will be timed by as fine a watch as the watchmaker's art has produced in its class. The watches retail for $25.00.

Fill in the blank spaces with the names of the stars that you think the items refer to and, in addition, write a fifty word letter to accompany your answer.

Fill in the name of the star referred to in the answer column at the right.

Otto Kruger is puzzled—What was her name?

---

1. What former stage actress played many leading rôles in films but did not reach real success until she was cast in a picture with Clark Gable?

2. What unmarried male star went to Hollywood and was unable to get a break in pictures? He returned to Broadway, secured a part with Katharine Cornell, then went back to Hollywood and became the idol of millions of movie fans?

3. What versatile actress has won applause for her beautiful singing, for her dramatic ability and for her flair for high comedy? She has sung at the Metropolitan Opera House in New York.

4. Tell the name of the American woman who first had her hair bobbed, and started something! She's in Hollywood now, but not acting.

5. There is a great artist in pictures, so loved and respected that authors prepare their stories so that he will not be required to over-exert himself in his part. Who is he?

6. In the quiet rolling hill country of Tennessee, a pretty little girl was born and raised. She used to sing in church. She has made musical pictures successfully and has sung at the great opera houses, Covent Garden for one. Her name is . . .

7. Myrna Loy once rejected a certain rôle and the girl to whom it was given sprang into prominence and later won higher honors than Myrna ever did. Who is the girl?

8. What is her name? She used to be a night club dancer. She has made many pictures—all dramatic and good, too.

9. Who is the very successful star whose restless spirit of adventure took him to strange places? This restless spirit he comes by quite honestly, for he is a descendant of Fletcher Christian, who led the famous mutiny on the Bounty.

10. The picture plots centering around a famous home circle have brought one man to the peak of popularity. It is the break that he has been waiting for during the twenty-three years that he has been in pictures. What's his name?

1. _____
2. _____
3. _____
4. _____
5. _____
6. _____
7. _____
8. _____
9. _____
10. _____

Write A 50 Word Letter To Accompany Your List Of Names, In Which You Explain: **Why I Read Silver Screen.**

CONDITIONS

1. There is one prize—a lady's or a man's wrist watch. The best letter on "Why I Read Silver Screen," accompanying the list that is nearest to correct, of stars' names, will be awarded the prize watch. Specify your choice.

2. Contest closes Jan. 26, 1939.

3. In the event of a tie, prizes of equal value will be awarded to each tying contestant.

4. Letters must not be longer than fifty words. No letter will be returned.

Address: STAR INFORMATION CONTEST, Silver Screen

45 W. 45th St., New York, N. Y.

SCREEN BOOK'S LOWDOWN CHART

Questions	Grace Moore	Jean Parker	Joan Crawford
Age?	Won't tell	18	26
Birthplace?	Jellico, Tenn.	Deer Lodge, Montana	San Antonio, Texas
Real name?	Grace Moore	Mae Green	Lucille Le Sueur
Nickname?	None	Robin	None
Brothers and sisters?	Four	One half-brother, one sister	One brother
Married or single at present?	Married	Single	Divorced
Number of marriages?	One	None	One
Husband's name and profession?	Valentin Parera, actor	None	Douglas Fairbanks, Jr., actor (ex)
Best friend?	Ruth Chatterton	Frank Phillips	Franchot Tone
Began career?	Opera work	On a float in Pasadena Tournament of Roses parade	Dancer
How long in Hollywood?	Four years	Two years	Seven years
Studio address?	Columbia Studio	M-G-M Studio	M-G-M Studio
Lives in?	Colonial house	House	House
Servants?	Six	One	Three
Cars?	Three	One	Two
Musical instruments played?	Piano	Piano	Piano, harp
Favorite sports?	Golf	Swimming, riding	Swimming, tennis
Hobby?	Cooking	Interpretative dancing	Hooked-rugs
What do you collect?	Emeralds	Miniature wire-haired terriers	Symphonic records
Favorite food?	Pineapple mousse	Tea and crumpets	Mustard on saltines
Favorite color?	Green	Green	Blue
What do you dislike most?	Poorly-laid tables	Cynics and people who use sarcasm	Dishonesty
Color of hair?	Golden	Brown	Medium brown
Color of eyes?	Blue	Blue-gray	Brilliant blue
Color lipstick worn?	Vermillion	Tinge of orange	Carmine
Color nail polish?	Carmine	None	Deep rose
Size gloves?	6½	6	6¼
Size shoes?	5B	4½B	4C
Height?	5 ft. 4 in.	5 ft. 3 in.	5 ft. 4 in.
Weight?	132 pounds	108 pounds	115 pounds
Bust measure?	36 in.	33 in.	35 in.
Waist measure?	28½ in.	24 in.	25 in.
Hip measure?	38½ in.	34 in.	35 in.
What do you sleep in?	Won't tell	Nighty	Pajamas

Editor's Note: If there is any star from whom you'd particularly like answers to the above questions, write today to The Lowdown Chart Editor, SCREEN BOOK, 52 Vanderbilt Ave., New York City. Your letter may also include any additional questions you may want answered.

LOVE AND HISSES!!

THIS is a real fan department—Love on one side and Hisses on the other. Write what you think about pictures you've seen and players you've heard— and don't pull your punches. Three prizes each month for letters not longer than 200 words. $15 First Prize; $10 Second and $5 Third.

Prize Winners

FIRST PRIZE

Oakland, Calif.

A STEP-MOTHER to success—that's what the motion pictures have been to me—a finishing school in modes and manners.

Not that I expect to be rich, beautiful and courted like the stars of the screen, to whom these gracious gifts come as by magic, but because of my admiration for these lovely ladies, I keep myself better groomed; I watch my carriage and my complexion.

No one will ever mistake me for Jeanette Mac-Donald, but with practice, her grace of carriage can be mine. Corinne Griffith's aristocratic simplicity has taught me to avoid extreme styles and imitation fur. At least with thought, I, too, can be immaculate and artistic in dress. It is really just a mental step up—something hardly tangible, of the stuff of which inspiration is made, but these beautifully kept and cultivated women make me *want* to have their charm and wanting anything is the first jewel in the crown of achievement.

Eva Lovel Dunbar

WE, WE, MAURICE

Portland, Ore.

WHY don't they give Maurice Chevalier better pictures? Maurice is one of the finest actors on the screen but the terrible plays they give him are making his fans less anxious to see him. "The Love Parade" was wonderful. "The Big Pond" only fair. And "Playboy of Paris" was a terrible story. If any other actor had been given that story it would have flopped completely. I surely hope to see Maurice in better pictures from now on.

Jane Brown

FIRST AID TO BOY FRIENDS

Baltimore, Md.

I CAN only dance a waltz and that poorly. I have little money to spend and I hate lounge lizards. Then what a boon the movies are. They are the only economical and congenial way for me to entertain a girl for the evening.

They also help me overcome my self-consciousness and save embarrassing lulls in the conversation, because I need only turn the subject to the movies and thanks to your magazine I can talk easily on all subjects pertaining to them.

Three cheers to SILVER SCREEN and the movies.

James Quinlan

SECOND PRIZE

Palms, Calif.

I ADORE the talkies. In day-dreams I associate the voice with each beloved artist, an automaton no longer.

Our children may now have the open country. the flowers, animals. Yet we no longer envy city folks since we step into our nearby movie house and get all their joys.

We travel miles in minutes to foreign climes and begrudge not the tourists their travels.

A few humble suggestions:

1. That Clive Brook, an excellent artist, may not portray a drunk again. Unconvincing.

2. That H. B. Warner and Raymond Hackett clarify their voices.

3. That Lawrence Tibbett of the marvellous voice refuse to play opposite Catherine Dale Owen, the blinking beauty.

4. May Marie Dressler forever remain the Savior of Suicides as well as a liver cure!

5. Why not produce La Poupee, the Story of a French Mechanical doll with Ramon Novarro as the monk and Dorothy Jordan as the doll?

Mabel Ford

A WORD TO MARY

Knoxville. Tenn.

HOW we old-timers do hate to see Mary Pickford—peerless Mary—pull the house down over her head!

Doesn't she realize there is no counterfeit for youth? Because she won her way into the hearts of the world by her portrayal of lonely, impish roles, does she expect to get acclaim tap-dancing at forty?

The first movie the writer ever saw (and it was away back yonder, I tell you!) was Mary as "Tess of the Storm Country". Since then—an ardent follower.

The first great contrast of age was painfully apparent in "My Best Girl", where she played opposite a youth about half her years. She holds an enviable position—one hard to equal, or excel. Why risk it for one or two grabs at the skirts of fleeting youth?

Mary is our favorite. But she, the beautiful, gracious, intelligent hostess to Presidents and crowned heads, should stick to stately and dignified roles.

M. Sevier

THIRD PRIZE

Washington, D. C.

I BELIEVE, as the mother of three small children manager, chief cook and bottle-washer of the home (and I own a husband, too) that I can give a vote of thanks to the movies.

You see, it's this way: There isn't always enough money left over from buying three pairs of shoes or paying a two-ton coal bill to attend the opera or the latest stage hit, but—there are the movies!

It is my favorite means of escape from a much-involved, workaday life, and my husband and I often take this one little chance of being together and living again our own romance.

We like them all, for, as you know, "variety is the spice of life", and we leave with a new feeling—"Life's wonderful, isn't it?"

Vee Williams

KNOCKING THE CRITICS

Savannah, Ga.

THE critics may condemn the talkies and say what they will, but I shall always be a grateful worshipper of the microphone. For talking pictures taught my father really to speak English. Until he heard the perfect speech of some of the screen actors, his English was much the same as that of any other Chinese who came to this country twenty years ago. But now his vocabulary is considerably enlarged, his pronunciation almost without accent. and I am very proud of him.

So, when we consider the talkies from the educational standpoint alone, shall we not give three cheers?

Chung Kahm Yeng

MOVIES WITH EXAMS

Alamosa, Colo.

I AM a high school student and I wish to tell you why I like pictures. Every time examination week comes around I make it a point to go to the show every night. It makes me forget about the low grades I received, that is if I received any, which I most generally do. That is why I like to go to a show on examination night. It makes me dream pleasant dreams instead of dreaming of the professor chasing you with an examination paper marked zero.

Helen Jarrett

The PRICE

In Hollywood, Health, Friends, Beauty, even Life Itself, are Sacrificed on the Altar of Terrible Ambition

To his art Lon Chaney gave everything without stint. One role nearly destroyed his eyesight. Another left him temporarily lame. The suffering he endured in all of them undoubtedly caused this great actor's untimely and sorrowful end early last autumn

After several unlucky years, Lila Lee staged a vivid comeback. She worked constantly, until her health broke. Einar Hansen died, friendless and alone, in an automobile accident. Edwina Booth braved the jungle for a great role. Fever has kept her from working since

MAYBE after all it is enough—just a few short days, or years in the burning searchlight of motion picture fame. Days when people turn to watch you in the streets; nights when your name flashes on a thousand theater marquees. Perhaps those few days and nights make everything worthwhile. Perhaps what comes after really doesn't matter. It must be so. Every day many young people pour into Hollywood. They want to be stars. They are eager to pay any price to achieve their goal. But do they stop to ponder how terrible that price may be?

It is a cruel, heartbreaking game and the cards are stacked. Fame is the consolation prize which is given when everything else has been sacrificed. It is a killing pace, this winning and holding success on the silver screen. Not many of the glittering figures of filmland have withstood it for more than a few years. There have been far too many who have dropped by the wayside, health gone, beauty gone, money gone, youth gone before its time. Far, far too often it has meant that the paths of glory lead but to the grave.

Many players have paid with their lives for a fleeting taste of renown. More have sacrificed their health to the fickle Lady Fame.

Just in the closing months of last year Lon Chaney and Milton Sills paid the supreme price of popularity.

There isn't a doubt in the world that those unbelievably exacting roles played by Lon Chaney hastened his death. He had built a reputation for grotesque characterization, and his fans clamored for even more difficult and health-destroying portrayals. Chaney was too good a trouper to disappoint them. His fame, the fact that there was but one Lon Chaney, and there can never be another, cost dearly. He was only 47 when he answered the last and greatest curtain call. He had hoped to retire soon and enjoy some of the fortune he had worked so hard to accumulate.

Even as far back as "The Hunchback of Notre Dame", Lon Chaney had begun to injure his health by his torturing makeup. He wore in that picture a harness that gripped his shoulders in a vise-like mould. For not more than three moments at a time was he supposed to keep on that cruel harness. However, if a scene were going well, Chaney would never complain. They worked on for half hours.

He suffered agonies in "The Penalty", when his legs

they PAY for FAME

By Marquis Busby

Fame imposed on Milton Sills the curse of nerves. Scholar, fine actor, gentleman, he forced himself through picture after picture,when he should have been resting. Finally came a nervous breakdown, an enforced retirement, return for a single picture—and the end

Lower left, Dorothy Seastrom, whose health failed her as she stood on the brink of stardom. Next, vivacious Renee Adoree, who is now in a sanitarium. Top, Olive Thomas, the most beautiful girl in filmdom, who had the most tragic death. What price fame?

were strapped underneath him. It was said that his spine received an injury then from which recovery was impossible.

Those brutal rôles were beginning to tell on him, but he went on. He left a hospital bed for "The Unholy Three". He returned there when the picture was finished. He never saw again the studio where he had climbed to world fame. Lon Chaney paid an awful price for being distinct and alone on the stellar mountain top.

Continual worry over financial matters hastened the death of Milton Sills. He faced grave charges in the income tax investigation which dragged the names of so many stars across the pages of newspapers. He suffered a breakdown and for months he was not able to go to the studio. Then he came back, apparently as strong and as stalwart as ever. But worry had left an indelible mark.

Edwina Booth is now recovering slowly from the fever, the languors of the jungle. She was left broken in health after the long period she spent in Africa during the filming of "Trader Horn". She risked her life to take this dangerous trip into the Dark Continent, but the risk seemed worthwhile to her. The prize was success on the screen. Life itself was an unimportant pawn with that prize at stake.

After struggling for so long to regain a foothold in the industry, Lila Lee suddenly became one of the most popular figures on the screen. Every studio was calling for her services. Lila rushed without rest from one rôle to another. Now she is paying for it. For many months she has been in a remote sanitarium in Arizona, fighting to win back her health. Her physician promises that Lila will be back before very long, back to the whirlpool of life in Hollywood.

At that same sanitarium you will find Renee Adoree. Not long ago a frail Renee came back to camera-town to resume the threads of life. She had been ill for many months, but Hollywood would not let her rest and regain her health. She was forced to give up and go back to the sanitarium.

That exacting life, the rapid pace of the Hollywood colony has sent many stars to hospitals and sanitariums. It sent Mabel Normand away and she never came back.

Many screen stars have died under circumstances as dramatic as the plots they enacted on the screen. There seems some sort of cruel, relentless [*Cont'd on next page*] fate which sweeps so many players to swift, tragic deaths. It is something to think about. It has occurred too many times to remain in the realm of sheer happenstance.

There may be many people who have forgotten Robert Harron, but there must be many more who will remember this familiar figure of the old D. W. Griffith pictures. There was a winning, unworldly quality about Bobby. He lived for his work—for his work and Dorothy Gish. People said they would be married. But Bobby's fame was just a brief flash of sunlight on a gray day. One morning he was cleaning his gun—it is the old oft-repeated story, but none the less tragic. There were rumors that it wasn't accidental—that Bobby was brokenhearted.

There was Martha Mansfield. She was just climbing the ladder of fame. The fan letters were beginning to pour in on her. Critics had commented on her youthful beauty. It didn't seem that there could be a cloud in the horizon on the day she left Hollywood for San Antonio. She was to have her greatest opportunity in the Fox picture, "The Warrens of Virginia." She never came back. On a warm, southern Thanksgiving Day Martha Mansfield breathed her last in a Texas hospital, far from home and friends. Someone on the set had lighted a match near her. The flimsy costume of hoops and frills which she wore caught fire, and in an instant Martha was a slender, human torch.

Atlantic cables carried back the shocking news of Olive Thomas's death in Paris. Vivid, lovely Olive—her beauty had been a white flame on the screen for a little while. She had taken poison at her height of beauty and fame. To add a deeper note of sadness to her sudden death, just a few days before, she had blithely left New York harbor for Paris with Jack Pickford. It was to have been a belated honeymoon trip. Olive was another victim of that deadly fate which shadows so many.

"Rough Riders" promised to mark the turn in the road for Charles Emmett Mack. This serious, young actor had struggled up the road to success. There had been no overnight triumph for him. He had fought for everything he had won. But in "Rough Riders" he had given a superb performance. In it was a death scene of almost unbearable poignancy. It represented a high mark in screen art. There must have been something prophetic in that scene for very soon after Charlie Mack set on the great journey, and this time it was not acting.

He was in Riverside, California, on location. A gay crowd had gone to the Mission Inn for luncheon, and they were returning to the race track location. There was a sudden grinding of brakes, skidding tires, a crash. It was the end of the road for Charlie, just as fame was within his grasp.

A death-bed scene in an early Warner Brothers talking picture also presaged the end for Gladys Brockwell. It was the tragic finale of a tragic career. This fine actress had almost dropped from sight. Talking pictures brought her back. A new and greater career was at hand, but fate willed differently. She died following a dreadful automobile accident on Ventura Boulevard, a few miles from Hollywood.

Clarine Seymour had just one short year of fame before she fell a victim to the white plague. Perhaps the long work she put in on "Scarlet Days" hastened her end. Clarine might have been one of the greater of screen stars. She was so full of life.

Another girl to pay heavily for a brief taste of the elixir of success was Dorothy Seastrom. Ambition drove her toward the heights. She was given a contract with First National, then her health broke. For several months she was absent from the screen, fighting to regain her health in a quiet sanitarium in the valley. She came back but for only a little while. Her health was gone. Just a few weeks ago she died in a little Texas town, forgotten in the glittering parade of fame.

Success came to Einar Hansen while he was very young, and then death took the prize away as suddenly as it had been bestowed. Hansen met death in an automobile accident.

Then there was Barbara La Marr—the too-beautiful girl. Her career was a brilliant meteor across the sky, lighting the whole film horizon for a short time, then falling into darkness. Her own fame intoxicated her. She reached with both hands for life. For some reason she believed that she would not live long. Very well, then, she would live while she could, draining everything from life. More than anyone else the dazzling Barbara with the white, oval face recalls the Edna St. Vincent Millay poem:

"My candle burns at both ends;
It will not last the night;
But ah, my foes, and oh, my friends—
It gives a lovely light!"

Those nights along the primrose trail began to tell on Barbara. She was put-

ting on weight at an alarming speed. Then it was that she began one of the most dramatic diet regimes ever undertaken by any woman. It ruined her health. At twenty-seven the brilliant meteor that was Barbara La Marr had destroyed itself. The pace had been too fast.

And poor Wally Reid. He, too, was his own worst enemy—Good Time Wally. His health, so magnificent when he played the rugged blacksmith in "The Birth of a Nation," was failing him. Dissipation had already left a lasting mark, but his popularity continued to scale the immortal heights. Millions of ardent fans clamored for more pictures. Toward the end they actually propped Wally Reid before a camera to finish a picture. A long rest might have saved his life, but instead he had to pay the toll of fame.

Yet, perhaps those that remain behind should not sorrow too much for the great ones who have gone. They had escaped the hand of unscrupulous Time, more cruel than Death. Death has cut in lasting marble what would have become dust. Many players have climbed to the heights and have lived to see their fame dwindle to nothing—forgotten by the very people who once acclaimed them. To them that must be worse than death.

Innumerable players are trying now to keep up the pace—hard work, long hours, society, the many, varied demands made upon the famous. They face the camera. They take the knocks and bruises. Stars like Bebe Daniels, Monte Blue and George O'Brien have been injured dozens of times. They go on, but some day those injuries may exact a payment. Raoul Walsh lost the sight of one eye while directing "In Old Arizona." Mary Pickford believes that her mother sacrificed herself in her hard work and unlagging interest in the career of "America's Sweetheart." Undoubtedly the appearance of Mrs. Pickford at the premiere of "My Best Girl" hastened the end. She was practically carried into the theater that night. But it is all in the game, this killing pace up the steep road to success.

When one player drops out, there are hundreds to take his place. They are ready to pay the price, no matter what it may be.

Is Fame, the fickle jade, worth the winning?

Those that have gone on might answer.

Those that remain behind do not know.

The TRUTH About William Powell

By JIM TULLY

Who can see in the polished, successful actor of today the completely disillusioned youth who seriously contemplated suicide?

HE IS a rather melancholy man, with a droll sense of humor.

His versatility on the screen is explained by the fact that in two years with one stock company he appeared in over two hundred thirty-seven different rôles. His work has been exercise enough for him.

"I keep in physical trim with my swimming pool," smiled William Powell. "Every day I go up to it and give it a long piercing look. Also I think a lot about tennis, and I talk a very good game of golf."

When asked about his present ambition, he replied, "Security of principal."

This explains the suave actor. He is never so hurried that he fails to be urbane. He has been mellowed by time and hardship into what Walter Winchell would call "a regular guy."

Except when he does a villain, Powell is always in character on the screen. For he is the kind of a chap who would give a dollar to a beggar and not bother to be thanked.

He is never exuberant in real life, and never insincere. If I were to go on a long journey with any man in Hollywood, I would just as soon it would be Bill Powell.

When William Powell was a youngster he made a speech in high school and his parents decided to have him enter the University of Kansas to study law. The inevitable happened.

Shortly afterward he was given a part in a school production of *The Rivals*. He received so much praise that he decided that there already were too many young men studying for the profession of law; so he decided to be an actor.

He had heard of the American Academy of Dramatic Art in New York. The tuition was four hundred dollars a year. An additional amount would be required for his upkeep.

His father, after a lifetime of accounting for the money of others, had none himself.

William decided to go to work. He got a job with the telephone company in Kansas City at fifty dollars a month. By this time, as bad luck would have it, he had a sweetheart. He found it difficult to entertain a girl in Kansas City without money.

He dreaded his work with the telephone company. As month followed month he was unable to save any money toward the fulfillment of his cherished ambition.

WILLIAM POWELL'S aunt had no earthly use for appendages known as relatives. She was also wealthy enough to be fortified against intimate association with them.

Young Powell knew all these things. But what has an aunt's attitude to do with a young man's ambition? He hugged his secret as if it were a leading lady. He would write to his aunt, who lived, secure from relatives, in a Pennsylvania town. He would tell her that he was a *different* relative, that he came not as a relative— *but to borrow money.*

The days merged into weeks. He divided his spare time between ushering at the Grand Opera House, his sweetheart, and writing a letter to his aunt.

It was not a simple matter to induce an old lady into sending money to a young relative who wished to embark on so preposterous a career as acting.

The letter was finally finished. It was twenty-three pages long. It was tactful, pleading, and proud. No young man with such a burning desire to get on in the world should stand convicted of his aunt's hate— [*Continued on page 193*]

It took William Powell thirteen years to pay back the $700 he borrowed from an aunt to start his career. Today he earns many thousands a year and is just now building a luxurious home in which to enjoy the fruits of his success

MYSTERY TALES

Nine famous stars relate their weird, occult experiences

IT ALL began one evening at the Lyon's beach home. The waves were singing a lullaby out in their front yard, and inside, the guests were chatting in that pleasant, relaxed mood that follows a thoroughly enjoyable dinner. The soft lamp-light threw an iridescent glow about Bebe Daniels' head as she leaned back in her chair, when someone suddenly remarked, "Bebe, you have a perfect aura around you tonight. Have you a sixth sense?" And Bebe replied jestingly, "Of course! I have in-cense, too, and occasionally I like a bit of non-sense."

She thought for a moment and then she said seriously, "Yes, I believe I *must* have a sixth sense. At any rate something forewarned me once of a disaster or I wouldn't be here now to tell about it." The story she told was singularly curious, particularly in view of the fact that so many departed stars figured in it.

"I was working in *Speed Girl* and one night I had an extraordinary dream. It was one of those vivid dreams where everything is intensely real so that when you wake up you're lost for an instant. It seemed as if I were going up a gravel walk toward an enormous white Colonial house that was surrounded by a wide-spreading lawn. The rooms were filled with actors I knew who were dead— John Bunny and Barbara LaMarr among them. The only two there who were alive at the time were Valentino and Mabel Normand. They came to meet me and asked if I intended to join them. I told them I was sorry but I couldn't stay.

"The whole thing made such an impression upon me that I felt groggy in the morning. I could see that white house wherever I looked. After breakfast, though, I stopped thinking about it and left for location.

"We were some miles away from Los Angeles in a section that was entirely new to me. I had never been there before. I was supposed to drive a car at racing speed in that particular scene and

the director told me that the girl who was to 'double' for me had been taken ill. We were behind in our production schedule so, without any premonition whatever, I took the wheel and said, 'Let's go!'

"Theodore Roberts rode beside me and a cameraman straddled the hood. We were going ninety miles an hour when my coat collar started blowing up against my face. I shouted to Theodore to put it down and he accidentally stuck his finger in my eye. It began to water. The other one watered in sympathy. Mascara got into them and my eyes became so inflamed I could scarcely see.

"I swerved to an eight-foot ditch on the side of the road and, in that instant, I caught a glimpse of a white house. A white Colonial house with a wide-spreading lawn! In terror I realized we were facing Death. I've never known quite how

The night before an aërial battle was to be filmed for *Hell's Angels,* Ben Lyon dreamed of falling to his death and, consequently, refused to fly. The plane he would have occupied crashed and one man was killed

A bronze Buddha in Clara Bow's Chinese den, her favorite room, exerted a mysterious and malign influence in the lives of all who came in contact with it. Five men who loved the room's exotic atmosphere met tragic deaths

OF THE STARS

By Jerry Lane

Sylvia Sidney declares that mental telepathy brought her father to her aid when she was suddenly taken ill while playing with a road show

On two occasions, a strange presentiment has prevented Joel McCrea from meeting accidental death. Now he obeys such hunches religiously

Ruth Chatterton frequently has been puzzled by an unaccountable, subconscious familiarity with places and people entirely unknown to her

I managed to get the car back to the center of the road. I pushed on the brakes with all my strength. When we came to a stop I fainted."

WHAT was it that warned Bebe of danger? Certainly not her sub-conscious mind, because the night before she had not expected to do the fast driving. Perhaps it was that elusive, psychic something referred to as "sixth sense." Whatever caused it, the presentiment saved Bebe by making her immediately aware of her peril.

"I had a similar experience," observed Ben from where he lounged at his wife's feet. "It occurred during the making of *Hell's Angels*. As much as I've flown, I have never dreamed about it except the time I had this nightmare. *That* was enough to last a lifetime. I thought I had been forced to bail out of a 'plane and my parachute wouldn't open. There appeared to be thousands of 'chutes around me—all sailing smoothly—and I tried wildly to grab one. Each time it would slip out of my grasp just as I imagined I had it. I woke up with the cold sweat streaming from me and my body tensed as if I were actually falling. It didn't make me any too happy to remember we were due to take shots in the big Gotha that day. The hunch not to go up was so strong I decided to play it. Lucky for me I did," Ben patted Bebe's hand reassuringly. "The Gotha crashed that morning . . . one man was killed . . . others were injured , . . Boy, since then I heed my hunches!"

It may be that actors—like aviators and artists—are more psychic than the rest of us, for since that after-dinner hour at the Lyon's I've discovered a number of them who have had unexplainable forebodings, and strangely mysterious occurrences in their lives that are beyond human interpretations.

Joel McCrea, in spite of his healthy tan, always turns a little pale when he relates this incident. As a lark one summer, he and two of his friends shipped as deckhands aboard a Panama liner. They were given shore leave when the boat docked at Colon. It was hot, insufferably hot, and the boys decided, true sailors that they were, to spend the afternoon at the ocean. They found a cool, blue lagoon that looked especially enticing. After days of being *on* the water, it would be heaven to be *in* it, Joel thought, as he stripped off his shirt. Not for nothing does he hold several west coast swimming records—he's a true amphibian.

"Last one in is a scared cat!" called one of the boys in the time-honored custom. Joel rushed to the edge of the embankment, prepared to dive . . . and paused. A light surf scudded merrily over the rocks on either side of the lagoon; it was a tempting sight. Joel turned and slowly walked back to where he had thrown his clothes. His pals were already in the water yelling lustily for him. But something held Joel back. He couldn't go in. What was the matter with him anyway? "The heat must have made me cuckoo," he told himself angrily as he pulled on his shirt.

There was a piercing scream from below. Joel rushed to the rocks. The youngest of the trio was fighting for his life—fighting a hideous, white-bellied monster . . . When Joel and the other boy dragged him free, they saw the shark had bitten off their pal's hand . . .

"And that," said Joel quietly, "is why I follow these queer impulses that keep me from doing what I'm all set to do. They saved me a second time—" That happened just a year ago when he was returning from a week-end party at a Northern California ranch. "I had planned to come back with the other guests in a car and, at the last minute, I changed my mind for no reason at all. I said I'd take the train down and they laughed at me so I gave as an excuse that I had some scripts to read. That night, when I got into Los Angeles, the newspaper headlines seemed to rise up and hit me. The whole party had been killed when the auto was struck by a trans-continental train . . ."

Then there's the hair-raising experience Maureen O'Sullivan and her family went through three years ago. They took a house for the summer at [Continued on next page]

Brighton Beach in England. It was a cheery, pleasant house at *113* Brighton Drive and they wondered why it had stood vacant so long before they moved in. They had the answer the first night they were there. Shortly after twelve (why do ghosts and such things love the midnight hour so?) Maureen was awakened by a rhythmic pounding that grew louder and louder as it came down the hall. When it reached the door of the nursery where her baby sister and the nurse slept, it was like thunder. Maureen was so terrified she couldn't move until her mother came rushing into her room, and together they went to the nursery. The noise stopped as they approached. They found the nurse hugging the baby in a paroxysm of fear. "It's probably something wrong with the plumbing," Mrs. O'Sullivan said, trying to be practical. The household went back to bed and the next morning everyone was inclined to treat it as a joke. But that night it ceased to be a laughing matter. The same thing happened again. They summoned electricians and plumbers, but the wires and pipes appeared to be in perfect working order. After the third night the nurse gave notice.

"I can't stand it any longer. I'm a nervous wreck!"

So were the others. Mr. O'Sullivan came down from London and the first thing he heard about was the terrible rapping. He was highly amused at what he termed "superstitious absurdity." At twelve that night he was not so amused. The noise was actually weird. As much as they searched they could find nothing to create it. The baby was sleeping in Maureen's room and they had a new nurse. The rapping, however, continued to end with a grand finale at the nursery door.

Unfortunately, the O'Sullivans had a two months' lease on the place so they didn't want to move. It was not until the last day of their stay that a solution—a very gruesome one—was given. They learned that the man who had built the place had shot his infant daughter accidentally while cleaning a gun and, in his despair, had then turned the gun on himself. What connection had that with the noise? Enough to satisfy Maureen, at least.

Often, when families are closely united, there's a sort of mental telepathy among them. Perhaps you've noticed it in your own. Sylvia Sidney declares it's uncanny at times. For instance, she was taken very ill while on the road with a show, and her mother, who accompanied her, telephoned her father in New York. The operator reported there was no response at their apartment. Mrs. Sidney tried all night to reach him without success . . . and at seven-thirty in the morning Dr. Sidney strolled into their hotel.

"I just felt you needed me," he explained. "I was playing bridge at the club last night and all of a sudden I got up and told the men I had to catch the next train for Washington. And here I am."

Sylvia *did* need him. They were to operate on her for appendicitis within the hour. Her father called in the capital's leading physician for consultation and he diagnosed her trouble as a sprained ligament in her back. Her appendix was perfectly normal!

Sue Carol says she can't stub her toe without receiving a wire from her mother in Chicago—"Are you hurt seriously, dear? Do you want me?" She didn't write her mother when she had to have her tonsils out, but the day she entered the hospital Mrs. Lederer arrived. "I knew something was wrong with you, darling. I came as fast as I could."

Ruth Chatterton frequently has the unique sensation when she visits houses or places new to her, of recognizing them. Sometimes it becomes embarrassing. Not long ago she attended a dinner at a Pasadena home for the first time. When she went into the drawing room, she was startled to find that she knew intuitively that the baby grand piano was a rosewood Chickering—that the walls were panelled with green satin brocade. To test herself she asked her hostess— "You have some very wonderful Sevres plate, have you not?" "Yes, but how did you know?" And Ruth found it a bit difficult to explain just how she *did* known! At dinner she carried on an animated conversation with a famous pianist. Finally she said in a puzzled manner—"I've never met you before, but I remember this conversation and I have anticipated every one of your answers." What surprised her more was his remark—"Yes, I remember it, too!"

What's back of it all?

There is just one reason why Richard Arlen has respect for spiritualistic mediums . . . and it's the same reason why he wouldn't go near one again for a fortune.

He was vacationing with his family at one of the lakes in Minnesota when he encountered his first and only medium. The man also claimed to be able to tell fortunes through crystal gazing, and he had quite a following in the summer colony. Dick and a couple of his friends decided, boy fashion, to call the man's bluff. They hopped in a canoe and paddled a mile across the lake to pay him an impromptu visit. Much to their disappointment the man looked like any ordinary human being. He entertained them with all kinds of stories but, as they were preparing to leave, he said very seriously—

"You boys take my advice and stay out of the water tomorrow!"

Naturally, it was nothing but a dare to them. Early the next day all three were splashing about in the lake. Before ten o'clock one of Dick's chums had drowned . . . no one knew just how. "It might have been merely a coincident," Dick observes, "and then again, it might not!"

Of all the mysteries in Hollywood (and they are legion in number) there is not one with so many dramatic highlights as the mystery of Clara Bow's Chinese den. Nor one quite so unfathomable. I saw the den only once. It was just off the living room in Clara's small bungalow. It had lighted candlesticks and incense burning before a fat bronze Buddha. There were other Buddhas and Sivas nodding from their brackets in the wall. The windows were covered with scarlet velvet and a pie-shaped divan occupied most of the space. I thought of it at the time as "Clara's retreat." She adored it. Something in its oriental, mystic atmosphere soothed her.

Yet, *five men who learned to love that room—to find peace in it—met tragic deaths.* One of them was Ian Hansen . . . killed on the beach road late one night . . . The Buddha has a ghastly grin . . .

Rex Bell never cared for it particularly. It was Clara's "make-believe" room to him. He laughed at the Buddha and strummed the red-lacquered guitar. Rex has been able to do more for Clara than any other person. He brought a clean gust of air with him when he came . . . shooed away the oriental bogies. I don't suppose anyone will ever know what the spell of that Chinese den was. It's dismantled now—gone.

But the other mysteries remain intact, unsolved. Have you any answer?

Every word of this dramatic account of the star's narrow escape from tragedy is true! You will have a better understanding of Jean Harlow when you have finished it!

The Story Jean Harlow Has Never TOLD

SCREEN BOOK Scoop

By
Jack Grant

FOR nearly four years, Jean Harlow has been in constant danger of losing her eyesight. For nearly four years, she has carried on without saying a word to anyone about it. Only the members of her immediate family have known the pain and suffering she has endured.

Now the story can be told, for Jean recently has had assurance from her doctors that all danger is past. The dread threat of being stricken blind no longer hangs over her head. Even so, you and I might never have heard this story had it not been for another accident.

Series Of Accidents

IT IS fairly well-known that three bones in Jean's foot were broken during the making of *Hell's Angels*. The bones knit improperly and frequently cause her to lose her footing with resultant injuries in falls. One such tumble occurred only last month. She fell from the garden wall of her hillside home, wrenching and skinning her leg. She needed a cane for several weeks to walk at all.

During this period, I called to see her and took occasion to offer commiserations upon the strange quirk of fate that brought her, at the same time, a troublesome injury and screen fame through the medium of the same motion picture.

"The accident in which my foot was broken is nothing compared to what happened to my eyes," Jean replied, then paused. "That's a story I never thought I'd tell anyone but as long as part of it has slipped out, I might as well continue.

"Before I go on, however, I want it distinctly understood that I blame no one for what happened. It was an accident pure and simple.

"You may remember that the final sequence of *Hell's Angels* was filmed in color. They didn't know as much about color photography in those days as they do now. They were still experimenting with it. All they knew was that several times as much light is required to shoot scenes in color. There was scarcely room for the actors to walk around, so many big arc lights cluttered up the sets.

An Unknown Danger

"I HAD a number of large close-ups to do. For these shots big batteries of lights were arranged on each side of the camera. I had to face these lights, looking directly into them. The heat was terrific, but I didn't fully realize how terrific until later.

"We worked for two successive days on my close-ups and each night I went home with inflamed eyes and a headache. I believed the headaches were the normal result of eye-strain. But as the days went by, my headaches became more frequent rather than diminishing. Soon my [Continued on next page] vision began seriously troubling me. I had always had exceptionally strong eyesight. Now it was cloudy and blurred.

"Finally I went to see a doctor. His diagnosis was almost unbelievable. *My eyes were burned.*

"What is known as the conjunctiva, I believe that is the correct name for the mucous membrane covering the eyeball with a transparent epithelium or film—had been burned by the excessive lights just as the exposed skin of your body becomes sunburned. And like sunburn, it was peeling. The grease-paint in my makeup had protected my face against burn but my eyes were unprotected.

"Doubtless you have never heard of such a thing. I know I never had before nor have I since. The doctor admitted it was an unusual and rare case. He prescribed an operation to remove the burned and peeling membrane covering the eyeball. It was becoming hard and encrusted.

"As soon as the picture was finished, I submitted to this operation. Then for more than *eleven months,* I had to wear dark glasses day and night while a new film grew over my eyes. I wasn't permitted to read or to use my eyes more than was absolutely necessary."

Jean Endures Agony

HELL'S ANGELS was completed in November of 1930. It was released the following May and Jean was sent on a fifteen weeks personal appearance tour by her studio. Naturally, she did not wish to make an entrance wearing dark glasses. She wore them right up to the moment she went on the stage and donned them again the minute her act was over. But the glare of the theater footlights was an agony that had to be endured.

Always her eyes were blood-shot as she came off stage. The weakened condition of her smarting eyes often caused tears to stream down her cheeks. Healing lotions had to be applied and the eyes given complete rest before her next appearance. Sometimes there was no time for rest for Jean was doing five, occasionally six, shows a day. Then, too, there were city officials and other local figures to be met and greeted.

Only those of us who have experienced trouble with our own eyes can appreciate fully the suffering Jean Harlow went through during these weeks of her tour. Added to the physical pain

and discomfort was the mental worry that she might be doing irreparable harm to her sight—might even be inviting permanent blindness. Jean never talks of blindness even today, but it is easy to read between the lines and sense that her dread of this horrible affliction still remains with her, has not even vanished now with the assurance of her doctors that she is cured.

Yet Jean Harlow has carried bravely on, all these years, *without ever once mentioning her injury.* There exist but few more courageous examples of compliance to he creed of all public entertainers—the show must go on.

"It *was* a temptation to tell people occasionally," Jean admitted with her usual candor. "Whenever I was accused of being high hat and not speaking to friends who would wave at me from a distance, I did want to offer the true explanation—that I couldn't see them in

Secret Battle Won

"I can't put my happiness into words," Jean Harlow says, now that she knows the danger of blindness is past

those periods of blurred vision. I could never tell, you know, when my eyes would unexpectedly fail me. There were no advance symptoms.

"The experience can best be likened to being abruptly engulfed in a fog. One minute I could see clearly and the next second everything was diffused. This might last an hour or several days then the lights would be bright again.

"The only time I could anticipate trouble with my eyes was during the last days of shooting a picture. As day after day of the shooting schedule passed my vision became worse and worse until, as we neared completion, I could hardly see at all. This was caused by the eye strain under the strong artificial lights, of course."

A Real Heroine!

REMEMBER the boys in *Beau Geste* and their expression, "stout fellow?" It was the highest compliment they could pay one another. And that's what we say to you now, Jean. Stout fellow!

Just one more question so that this history of the disaster that has threatened you for four long years may end on its happiest note. What were your re-actions to being told you were out of danger—had nothing more to fear?

"I can't put my happiness into words," Jean replied. "But surely you can imagine how I felt.

"The first thing I thought of was the joy my mother would express when I repeated to her the doctor's blessed verdict. I know she has been more worried than I over the outcome." (Which doubtless caused Jean to minimize the danger and often avoid even mention of the pain she was suffering rather than increase her mother's worry.)

"Mother was always urging me to retire from motion pictures before my eyes were permanently injured. It was I who wanted to go on, whatever the cost. I knew better than to tell anyone at the studio, fearing I might be made to quit.

"Secondly I thought of all the things I love to do that I had had to give up or at least curtail. I can now read all those books I have purchased and stored up in the hope that someday I could read them. I can now see all the good pictures instead of picking and choosing just those I had to see.

"It's like beginning a new life—a life that knows no restrictions after four years of constant restrictions. Can you wonder I'm happy?"

DANGER SIGNALS!

Revealing how the fire of genius threatens the brilliant screen career of Fredric March

By Potter Brayton

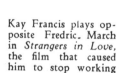

Kay Francis plays opposite Fredric March in *Strangers in Love*, the film that caused him to stop working

Freddie March put so much vitality into his picture rôles that he nearly suffered a nervous breakdown. After a long rest, he has finished *Merrily We Go To Hell* and is now in perfect health

THE fire of genius is threatening to ruin the career of Fredric March! His strenuous screen characterizations are consuming his vitality and undermining his health.

Worn out by the difficult dual rôles in *Dr. Jekyll and Mr. Hyde* and *Strangers in Love*, March barely escaped a physical collapse while preparing to begin work on *Merrily We Go To Hell*, his new picture.

Freddie thought he merely had a stomach ache. It persisted. He spent days in a Hollywood clinic, having a rigid checkup. "Nerves shot," came the verdict. If he didn't give up his strenuous picture schedule, they said, the trouble would spread from stomach regions to other parts of the body and result in a complete nervous breakdown.

"Go to some secluded spot and rest and play and put all thought of pictures out of your mind for at least five weeks," the doctors said. So Freddie and his wife, Florence Eldridge, packed their things and quietly slipped out of Hollywood.

Paramount, realizing the serious condition of his health, was forced to postpone for two months the production of *Merrily We Go To Hell*, for fear its strenuous dramatic requirements might prove too much for him.

FROM his appearance, you might guess that Fredric March is one of Hollywood's most *unactorish* actors. He is the type, who, were you to pass him on the street, would cause you to remark mentally, "There goes an up and coming junior member of some law firm—or else he's a young business executive."

In reality, seldom is a thespian so sincerely and intensely wrapped up in his art as is the tempestuous Mr. March. With more than respect due his charming and talented wife, I would go so far as to say that the turning out of an inspired performance is the most important thing to him in life.

Hollywood has come to associate art with long hair, temperamental demonstrations, and an excessive amount of "*boloney*" handed out around the studios by "arty" stars regarding the importance of "my career." This is true, solely because too many stars are more concerned about the riches

and glory of success than they are with giving a perfect performance to the screen.

Whatever drives Fredric March, drives from within. He is gifted with the creative power of genius, and he knows what to do with it. It wasn't in him to sign his John Henry to his Paramount contract, and then sit back and twiddle his thumbs. Every new rôle finds him striving to improve his art—and learning. Every bit of pantomime and every line he rehearses on the set is done with a determination and an emotional force that seems literally to sap his vitality.

[*Continued on page 194*]

I HAVE just had twenty minutes with Marlene Dietrich.

It took me three months to get them. But when I finally got to La Dietrich she talked as she has never talked before. So this, really, will have to be an unusual sort of story. Because the woman herself is so extraordinarily different.

An appointment with Marlene can only be made after the greatest maneuvering. Her agent sorts the sheep. So few are chosen that half a year has elapsed since she was last interviewed. I felt complimented when her agent telephoned me that he would be glad to have me interview her.

Then came one broken date after another, for three months. Finally I was told to appear at the studio. I was walked out to her dressing-room. She hadn't yet come off the set. In two minutes a large, gray Rolls-Royce drew up and out stepped a maid who expressed disappointment at her mistress' absence. A few more minutes and Marlene came walking around the corner from the sound stage.

We were left alone in her dressing-room.

She was attired in a striking black satin Spanish gown of elaborate design and over one ear she wore a red flower. But I didn't pay much attention to her costuming. I came to see Dietrich.

Sitting on a small straight chair beside her desk, she turned toward me. She was gorgeous. She has the biggest blue eyes, in which lurk a constant twinkle. There was a slight curve of merriment on her wide, lovely mouth. I suspected that she classes interviews as amusing.

Marlene isn't a terribly curious person herself. She is polite and kind. But she distinctly has enough in her own life to keep her occupied.

"You have been subjected to such a lot of criticism," I began, "that I thought you might like to give me a story on what your four years in Hollywood have meant to you. We've had everyone's opinion but yours."

She smiled a little. Just as she does on the screen. To myself I stated that they can protest all they wish about beauty being no longer a woman's major asset. See Dietrich and succumb!

Perhaps her remarkable charm is due in part to her serenity. She is still, not silent. And friendly, though not fluttery. Her voice is slow, caressingly rich in tone.

"I should not like to do the story in the first person, as if I were writing it. Somehow, that sounds conceited to me," she said.

The 'phone rang. Excusing herself, she answered it. It was a good old-fashioned instrument, not a coy French hand-piece. She uttered one word—"No." With no attempt to explain something which didn't concern

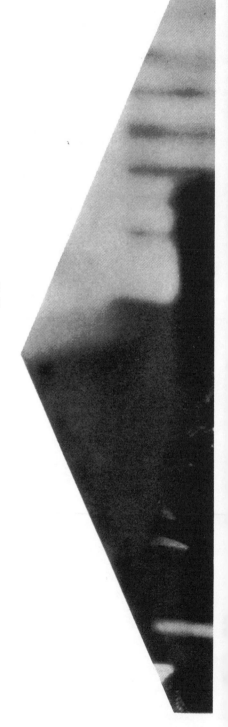

Marlene Answers all Your Questions

Von Sternberg?
Husband? Child?
Career? Future?

by
Ben Maddox

•

me, she faced me again, waiting for me to speak.

"In what ways do you feel that you have been changed by Hollywood?"

"I do not believe I have changed, except to grow older, of course. And I have more responsibilities. There is a realization that a whole production rests on one's shoulders. But Hollywood? It doesn't do anything drastic to people. Certainly not to those who have strong personalities and firm minds of their own."

"They say that you were dowdy when you arrived. And the Trilby legend has hung on."

Marlene smiled anew. A smile of hers can reveal so much. It makes questions suddenly seem trivial banter.

"That theory that I was dowdy, a dumb German housewife-kind-of-actress is absurd. I came from metropolitan Berlin. And I brought trunks full of Parisian

gowns. If you will compare photographs of me then and today, I do look better, now. But that isn't any Hollywood polish. That is the effect of time. You examine old photographs of yourself. They, too, will be quaint."

That was a long speech for Marlene. She hesitated, then continued:

"As for this Von Sternberg-Trilby chatter, it is

humorous to me. Anyone with intelligence can see that I'm not hypnotized. Obviously I have something of my own behind this face. You can't put a brain into a woman's head if it isn't there already."

I wondered about her approaching split with Von Sternberg. He has announced that she will not do her next film under his direction. Apparently, she will switch to Ernst Lubitsch. This report crops up every once in a while. It has come up again at this writing. Marlene stated, "People will make much of nothing. This is the situation: I do only one picture a year. Sometimes it has taken Mr. Von Sternberg nearly a year to find a proper vehicle. He will be a long time cutting and completing this one we are finishing now. He thinks I should not wait around when he hasn't a story for me. I did the one picture away from him, with Mamoulian, only because he telephoned me from abroad and advised me to. We are not separating now. If, until he is ready for me, I find something I like I will do it for another director."

All of which blasts beforehand the mystery that is apt to arise when she works in 1935 with a different man at the helm.

"How has Hollywood changed your mode of living?" I queried.

"Not at all. My parents had money. I live as I did in Germany, except that I have to have guards here."

She has been residing in the pretentious Colleen Moore place in Bel-Air and I had heard that she had leased it for two years, indicating permanency. So I inquired about it.

"But I just rent it from month to month," she retorted. "I never tie myself down. How do I know what will happen? Where I shall want to go?"

"But you do like Hollywood?"

"Oh, yes indeed. And this is strange. I am not bothered here as so many stars claim to be. Why, I am not even recognized on the streets. [Continued on page 195]

Tarzan Seeks

"I really loved him!"

Mourns Bobbe Arnst who spurred her husband on to screen success only to lose him because of it

By Clark Warren

Bobbe Arnst, stage dancer and social registrite before marrying Johnny Weissmuller, boasted that Hollywood could not wreck their happiness, but she underestimated filmdom's malign influences

TWO weeks after Johnny Weissmuller, world's champion swimmer, met Bobbe Arnst, popular dancer and social registrite, down in Miami, Florida, he married her. It seemed like blissful romance until they came to Hollywood and Johnny scored a sensational triumph in *Tarzan, the Apeman.* Then they separated and divorce rumors began to fly.

"Yes, Johnny and I are finished. He wants a Mexican divorce but I won't have it. We will get an honest-to-goodness California divorce though, just as soon as we can file the papers. Johnny is madly in love with Lupe Velez. I do not know whether or not she loves him or if they will get married but I've known about the affair for some time. I've tried to fight it out. It's no use, the gossips win. Marriage can't be victor in Hollywood!"

This is the story which Bobbe Arnst told me as we sat in her apartment. A week ago Bobbe still believed that she could beat the game but now she knows definitely that she has lost. A month ago she told SCREEN BOOK reporters that Johnny was her man, to have and to hold and that nothing could ever tear them apart. Bobbe was sincere. She believed that she could hold her man, in the face of anything Hollywood could do. She had no intention to deceive the press, she simply underestimated the malign influences arrayed against her.

"I've lost but I'll try to take it like a man," she smiled, "and if Lupe, or anyone else can make Johnny happier, I want him to have her. I loved him and I did what I could but Hollywood was too much for us. It breaks my heart to lose my boy but I'll play the game, no matter what it costs me."

That a romance existed between the stalwart *Tarzan* and the fiery Mexican was suspected before Lupe returned from New York. Both idols of the metropolitan populace, they were seen frequently in each other's company. Women by the hundreds demanded *Tarzan* but he showed a decided preference for the company of Lupe. Scenting romance, the New York reporters tried to pin it down but both Johnny and Lupe poo-pooed the idea and the matter was dropped.

When Lupe returned to Hollywood she went into seclusion. When Johnny also returned from his personal appearance tour, their meetings were frequent. Still they denied a romance and insisted that they just happened to be together in the same crowd and Hollywood, for once credulous, swallowed the bait. Now, from the lips of Johnny's own wife comes the statement that it is her husband's love for Lupe which has broken up their romance.

"It all happened so suddenly," she confessed, "that I was dumbfounded. While Johnny was in New York he wrote me long love letters almost every day and when he returned it

was like another honeymoon. We had never been so happy with each other—not even when we were first married."

Then came the bombshell! They had been out with a party of friends. As they returned to their apartment, Johnny suddenly turned to his wife, and spoke frankly.

"I want a divorce!"

Johnny did not intend to be unkind—it isn't in his nature—but in his honest desire to lay his cards on the table he had spoken too abruptly.

But imagine hearing those words from the lips of the husband and lover whom you adored and the man whom you were striving to hold in spite of insidious gossip. No wonder Bobbe was stunned! As the tragic import of that brief request penetrated her senses, it required all her courage to smile up at him.

"Why, Johnny? There must be a reason."

"No." It was hurting Johnny as much as it was the wife he had loved. "Only that I want to be free," he said.

For two days Bobbe Arnst was [*Continued on page 196*]

[*Continued on page 196*]

No one suspected that all was not well with the Weissmullers when they gaily attended picture premières and other social functions together after Johnny's success as *Tarzan*

a Divorce!

"I'm never going back!"

Cries Johnny Weissmuller, who finds his marriage
to Bobbe Arnst is stifling his freedom

By Marcella Burke

Johnny Weissmuller, who became an overnight
screen star as the stalwart *Tarzan, the Ape Man,*
now succumbs to the Hollywood divorce menace

HOLLYWOOD'S gone and done it again. This time it's
wrecked the Weissmuller marriage and fastened the
blame on Lupe Velez. Johnny avows that his marriage with Bobbe Arnst, cunning hot-cha dancer, who used
to step fast and pretty in Ted Lewis' show, is completely
washed up. But he adds that their wedded happiness had
become a thing of the past long before the scintillating little
Mexicano had come upon the scene. So that should exoner-
ate Lupe.

The day I talked with Johnny I was dumbfounded. He
acted like an embarrassed kid just playing hooky from school.
He ate cantaloupe à la mode and growled about marriage.
Johnny had no reticence at all. Said marriage wasn't in the
cards for him.

He scooped up a satisfying chunk of ice cream and scowled.
"It was down in Miami that I met Bobbe and it took only
two weeks for us to decide to get married. I loved her at
first but it began to fade when she always wanted to go every
place I went. Gosh, that's no fun.

"I like to get off with a gang of fellows and play around.
Two or three times a week to go to the beach with Bobbe was
enough. I got nasty about it after awhile. I'd say I was
going down to the club and that I'd be back for dinner. Then
I wouldn't show up. Then she would get sore and start nagging me. And I don't blame her. I guess I am spoiled. If
anyone wants to start an argument I don't take it. I finish
it—or walk out.

"You see the trouble with Bobbe is this. She tells people
I am a boy, that I don't know my own mind. She takes the
credit for making up my mind for me. Well, this time she
can't do it. I'm finished. When I'm divorced from her I
won't marry again."

Johnny's eyes laughed for the first time.

"Gee, I'm scared of marriage. I'm scared of everything
now. And it isn't about myself, but the others I've gotten
into this mess. Poor Lupe is all burned up and sore at me.
Somebody told Lupe the other day that she was breaking up
our marriage and she had better send me back to Bobbe.

"I didn't know what it was all about. I was at her house
swimming in the pool when Lupe came home and said, 'You
get out of here. I won't ever speak to you again.' Then she
threw all my clothes at me."

Johnny looked like a fellow who had just seen his best
friend commit suicide. Words seemed to fail him completely.
He sat there and looked sick all over. Then he started talking at random.

"'She's getting the divorce now. She wants twenty-five per
cent of my salary. That wouldn't leave very much for me.
You see I don't get very much—$350.00 a week.

"Anyway, this all started about two months after I got
married. It bothered me with my work. I wouldn't let Bobbe
go with me on location when I made *Tarzan*. She wanted to
go but I wouldn't let her.

"You see she thinks I'm going to change my mind and come
back home, but I'm never going back. It makes me sick when
I hear the things she says about me. She ought to know we're
all washed up."

Make no mistake about it, Johnny Weissmuller is sick. He's
green around the edges. He can't understand why anyone
he stops loving should continue to love him.

He isn't fit for marriage actually. No man is who can be
so unwittingly cruel. Underneath it all he means to be kind
but he wants his own way and that's that. He's proud of the
fact that he won't compromise.

Later on Lupe said plenty about how she felt.

"I can't even look at a man without everybody saying I'm
in love with him. One thing they [Continued on page 196]

The friendship of Johnny Weissmuller and Lupe Velez
began in New York and continued in Hollywood. Lupe
denies a romance and Johnny says he will not remarry
after his divorce

FAY WRAY'S
Design for Marriage

By Dorothy Spensley

To auburn-haired, Canada-born Fay Wray all this chatter about "how to hold your husband" and "how to indulge in a happy marriage" is so much unnecessary hooey. She has one simple, unwavering rule which she flaunts convincingly—because her marriage to novelist-scenarist-director John Monk Saunders is rated as one of Hollywood's "ten best." The rule is "freedom of thought, plus inter-dependence upon each other."

Two years ago I tried to wangle Fay into giving her matrimonial success secrets, and the only answer I could get was: "my marriage is successful because my husband is John Monk Saunders." She had been married, then, for six years. It takes eight years of wedded life to produce anything like a commandment, and Hollywood is a tough place in which to stay continuously married.

As a matter of record, statistics recently proved that West Coast wives (that does not mean Hollywood in particular, but the entire West Coast) had greater difficulty in keeping their legal mates than did East Coast wives. Whether it was the climate, or the temptations, was not said, but when a West Coast wife, like the stellar Mrs. Saunders, comes forth with a neat commandment for husband-holding, it's a good idea to listen: especially with the fresh crop of June (1936) brides settling down to the problem of Being a Good Wife to George.

Fay Wray's marriage was a love match. Realization that she loved this dark-haired, straight-nosed, handsome young writer came to her when she was playing with Gary Cooper in *Legion of the Condemned*. Saunders, author of *Wings*, had written this war aviation story, too. Fay was leading lady. "Until I saw John," she confessed, "I never thought I would marry. I had the usual vague, youthful ideas about matrimony. No man had ever stirred my imagination enough to set me to thinking that I wanted to be his wife. Then I met John."

If *Legion of the Condemned* was the picture that set the seal to the Saunders' romance, *The First Kiss* which took Fay and Gary

Fay Wray is currently appearing in Columbia's *Roaming Lady*

Here's an "easy-to-make" pattern from one of Hollywood's ten best unions. It's a fine formula if you know how to work it. Fay does

Cooper on location to Maryland in 1928 was the film that hastened the marriage. Saunders, like one of his own fictional heroes, couldn't bear the separation from Fay. She couldn't stand being parted from him. They were married in Easton, Maryland, on June 15th.

It has taken more than six years for Fay to learn to talk freely about her marriage. Fay, as you grow to know her, is deeply romantic, sentimental. She thrills to old tender memories and kindnesses long forgotten by others. She has a hidden emotional life beneath the beauty of her face, the perfection of her figure, that few ever penetrate. Within, she kept the real joy of her marriage. She was afraid to "tempt the gods" lest they destroy her happiness, if she gave forth her rules for marital bliss.

Now, she is not afraid to talk about it. Fay, the girl-wife, has become Fay, the very young matron. The obvious answer is that Fay has become more confident of herself. Blame it on her trips to England, the continent, Nassau. Travel broadens, they say. The change in Fay has been inward and mental.

As a youthful wife, not long out of Hollywood High School, with a background of "quickie" westerns [Cont'd on page 196]

Bette From BOSTON

By Virginia Wood

Bette Davis Wins The Academy Award for the Best Performance of 1935

Warren William and Bette Davis working out the theme of "Men on Her Mind."

S HE'S not the ordinary blue-eyed blonde, this Davis girl. She's ambitious, courageous, uncomplaining, with a distinct mind of her own. When Bette walks on the set, you get a definite reaction from the people with whom she works. There's a little sparkle of welcome for the girl who makes things just a bit easier for them all, and her winning of the coveted trophy has not changed her.

"Bette Davis?" they'll tell you, "she's swell! A darned good little trouper."

Off the screen, as Bette herself puts it, she and her husband, Harmon O. Nelson, Jr., are "simple people." They play no part in the Hollywood social life, and spend as much of their time together as possible. This hasn't been any too easy a matter, however, what with Bette working pretty consistently at her job, and with his career as a musician and orchestra leader to consider. For a long time, he was stationed in San Francisco, some five hundred miles away. Every minute she could possibly find, Bette would dash up to pay him a visit. They'd manage to duck away for a few days at a time to some nearby resort, where he could play golf, and they really had fun. It was somewhat of an ordeal, though, as the studio would invariably find something for Bette to do before they'd finished their visit.

"Thank goodness that's over," Bette said, gratefully. "I hope Ham won't ever have to go that far away again."

"Do you play golf together?" I asked her.

"No, not very often. I'm afraid I'm not very much good at that sort of thing. There are very few women who are really good golfers, and I think their husbands must get awfully sick of having to hold up their games for them."

"Spuds," as he calls Bette, and "Ham" live in a little cottage in a very nice, untheatrical section of Hollywood. It has a small white fence around it. There's a garden, too, where Bette loves to read during much of her spare time. They have two servants, a woman cook and a chauffeur.

"I'm not very domestic," Bette confided, smilingly. "I guess I've been fortunate in having people do that sort of thing for me, to a great extent. I do like to superintend the running of the house, though. That's about the extent of my domesticity."

Then there's the cottage down at the beach, where Bette's mother lives. When she's not working, she loves to run down for the day and get in a little sun-bathing and swimming.

"I think you simply have to get away from Hollywood and pictures occasionally," she said, firmly. "You get into such a terrific rut if you don't. People in this business live it twenty-four hours a day. It's practically impossible to keep your perspective unless you take a vacation whenever you possibly can.

"And it's always been a constant source of amazement to me," she added, wonderingly, "why most people here seek out the same places to go. I can't understand it. After all, the reason you want a vacation is to get away from the same things you've been doing for weeks on end.

"I used to go to Palm Springs all the time, until it got to be so fashionable. Why, you might just as well stay in Hollywood as go down there, nowadays. I love the desert. There's something so utterly peaceful about it. I've just heard of a grand place way out on the Mojave that I'm going to try, just as soon as I have an opportunity—you know, when I get that six weeks' vacation I've been after for so long!"

There's one thing I admire tremendously about Bette Davis—the biggest asset most anyone can have—and that is her remarkable patience—her ability to wait for things. Most of us become so utterly discouraged if success isn't handed us on a big silver platter—and instantly. But Bette has discovered the surer way and the safest. She has found that hard work is bound to bring its reward.

Bette was born in Boston and attended high school and the Cushing [Cont'd on page 197]

THAT *Marital* VACATION

Why is Bette living without her husband—after six compatible years?

THERE WASN'T anything surprising about Bette Davis' doing a disappearing act as soon as she finished "The Sisters." She had been working hard. She needed a rest. And her idea of a rest was a hideaway vacation.

There wasn't anything surprising about her vanishing; that is, except that her husband, Harmon Nelson, hadn't vanished with her. He still was around town. That was a bit odd. That hadn't happened before. He always seemed to arrange his working time to be free when she was free. Bette's vacations had a reputation of being "repeat" honeymoons. Even last year, when Bette suddenly cracked under the strain of overwork and had to take a long sun cure in the desert, "Ham" had been able to arrange to go away with her.

But this time Bette had gone away alone. A couple of columnists asked pointedly, What did this mean? Back came a couple of other columnists with pointed denials of any marital trouble between Bette and "Ham." Such rumors were silly. Why, they were the happiest couple in Hollywood. Then one of the news-seeking columnists heard where Bette was doing her hiding away. On a Nevada ranch.

Now, Nevada is a place not to go unless you want a divorce. Therefore, it was also barely possible that Bette might have divorce on her mind.

In search of a news scoop, this columnist got the telephone number of the Nevada ranch, called Bette long distance, asked her bluntly if she and "Ham" had parted. Just as bluntly, Bette answered, "There's absolutely no truth in any such rumor. I'm here for a rest. And I'm not alone. My sister's with me." Bette has always had a reputation for frankness with reporters. Her denial had to be accepted at its face value.

But, less than three weeks later, another reporter discovered Bette visiting her mother at Manhattan Beach, only a few miles from Hollywood. And, despite the fact that it was a weekend, "Ham" was not with her. The reporter asked her if, after all, she was contemplating a divorce. Fierily, Bette said, "If there were anything to the story, I would be the first to let the newspapers know about it."

That statement would have sounded reasonable enough, if the opposition paper hadn't carried a statement next morning by Harmon Nelson. He had told another reporter, "I can't say anything about a separation, except that there is none contemplated at this time and we'll just have to wait awhile for developments. When Bette comes home, she will probably have a statement to make about the situation."

Obviously, something was wrong. They weren't even getting together on their stories to the press. And "Ham's" quiet admission of discard made Bette's vociferous denials look a bit silly.

Returning home the next day, she wearily told a reporter, "We won't deny that we are having our troubles. But neither of us has made any decisions."

Her weariness made it sound as if she might have been frank before now, if she hadn't been trying desperately to hold the marriage together. Columnists were sympathetic. All of them suddenly forgot that Bette, not "Ham," was the one who had gone away without the other—which had precipitated all the rumors.

Eight days later, the columnists were completely re-convinced of Bette's liking for frankness. They received this wire: "Ham and I have definitely decided to take a vacation from each other. Signed, Bette Davis."

She had been "the first (*Continued on page 112*)

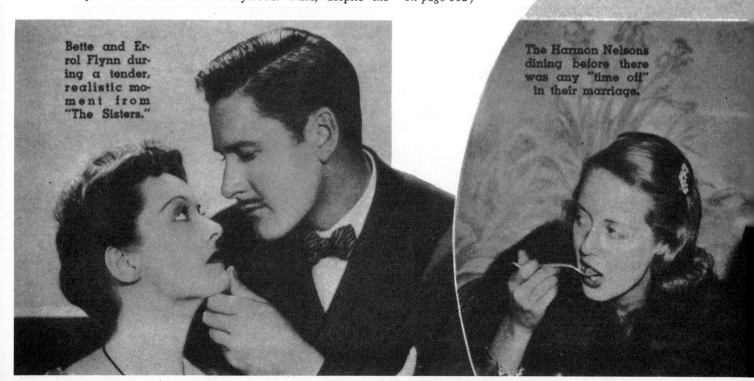

Bette and Errol Flynn during a tender, realistic moment from "The Sisters."

The Harmon Nelsons dining before there was any "time off" in their marriage.

by George Benjamin

Bette Davis, hitherto noted for her frankness, isn't talking too much at this point.

156

to let the papers know about it." Reporters were sent out to get the details. And the next morning's papers related the story.

All other attempts to settle their troubles having failed, Bette and "Ham" had agreed on a trial separation. She was still living in the new house in Coldwater Canyon. He was living with an associate in the agency by which he was employed. They hadn't discussed divorce, they said. They would let the trial separation decide whether they would be happier apart or together. They had to set no time limit for their "marital vacation." The only explanation they would give for their difficulties was incompatibility.

That probably is the explanation that one of them will later give to a judge. For, unless all Hollywood precedent is shattered, this "marital vacation" is the beginning of the end. It will wind up in court, not in reconciliation.

Incompatibility is a nice harmless explanation, which explains nothing. A blind man could see that Bette and "Ham" are incompatible, or they wouldn't have thought of a separation. But what made them incompatible so suddenly? That is the moot question.

"Ham" isn't answering. That is to be expected. A husband if he's a gentleman, and "Ham" is, doesn't say much in a situation like this. But Bette isn't answering, either. And that's unexpected.

Bette earned her reputation for frankness by being frank about her marriage. In interviews over the past six years, she has talked about it. Unembarrassed, she has gone into detail. She has discussed, not only marriage problems in general, but her own in particular. She has freely admitted all the obstacles to happiness in Hollywood, if only to prove how she and "Ham" have hurdled them.

Now, suddenly, she has nothing to say. The girl who always belittled any possible threat to her marriage, and always insisted that nothing could wreck it, is insistent now about something else altogether. Silence. She won't be interviewed on the subject. And this heavy silence would seem to indicate that something has come up that can't be belittled. Something that can't be talked about gracefully. Something that makes all her past talkativeness about her marriage embarrassing. But what? What is behind the sudden "incompatibility" in the Nelson-Davis household?

SOB sisters, shaking their heads sadly, say, "It's the same old Hollywood story —wife more important than husband. No man can take that."

Perhaps. It's asking a lot of a man to expect him to be the lesser half of a marital partnership indefinitely—the lesser in income, the lesser in prestige. No matter how much a man loves his wife, it's almost too much to expect him to be happy in the role of just-a-husband, in which people confuse him with just-a-gigolo, say he's living on her salary, and call him by her name with a "Mr." attached.

Many a movie marriage has foundered on those particular rocks. But not the Harmon Nelson marriage. For years, Bette and "Ham" have been steering away from that danger. Before they ever set out together, Bette saw it ahead. She saw it so clearly that, when "Ham" first asked her to marry him, that summer of 1932, she said, "No." She was terribly in love, so much in love that she thought of "Ham's" happiness, not her own. She was afraid for him, afraid of the mental punishment he would have to take, if star-conscious Hollywood tagged him "Mr. Bette Davis." She didn't say "Yes" until she was sure that they both could be happy, in spite of obstacles ahead.

Two things made her sure. Theirs wasn't a sudden infatuation, which could wane as suddenly as it had flamed. They had known each other for years. They had been sweethearts at Cushing Academy in Massachusetts, and later during a summer on Cape Cod, when she was trying to break into the theatre and he was trying to break into the orchestra game. Time had only deepened her feeling that "Ham" understood her as no one else ever had or would. And, "Ham" was of the same breed as she was. In his own quiet way, he was enough of a Yankee to be able to live his own life in spite of high water or Hollywood. So they were married, in Yuma, on August 18, 1932.

Harmon Nelson was a name fairly well known 'way down East, as an orchestra leader. But to Hollywood the name meant nothing. Hollywood promptly tagged him, for future identification, as "Mr. Bette Davis." And Hollywood assumed that Bette, having acquired a husband with a small income, had also acquired a sieve for her bankroll.

The Nelsons took it in stride. They didn't live like a movie star and her husband. They lived like an orchestra leader and his wife. They had a small house, drove a small car, gave small parties. During her working hours, she might be Bette Davis, movie star. But the rest of the time she was Mrs. Harmon Nelson. Emphatically.

One of the reasons for marrying the person you love is to be with that person constantly. But, the first few years of their marriage, Bette and "Ham" were apart more than they were together. That wasn't easy, particularly when a new crop of divorce rumors popped up every time "Ham" went

away. Crisply, Bette blew them all down. And, finally, Hollywood got the idea. She and "Ham" were in love, but he happened to be an individual in his own right, not just a husband.

When that idea did take hold, the biggest danger to their marriage passed. "Ham" indicated as much by making Hollywood his home, giving up orchestra-leading in the East to become a Hollywood agent.

Bette had said that she wasn't going to miss all the fun of a down-to-earth, partnership marriage just because she was a movie star. Hollywood had suspected an emotional "act," had said it wouldn't last. Sooner or later, ego would spoil it. Bette smirked at such a danger, and kept right on smirking.

They had a plan of living which would prevent either of them from ever feeling dominated or cheated of independence. "Ham" paid his way, Bette paid hers. They had separate savings accounts and separate expense accounts and shared household expenses. The plan worked for six years. It wouldn't fail now, over night. That isn't the cause of their sudden "incompatibility."

Fame and wealth do bizarre things to people sometimes. And Bette's fame and her pay check have been increasing steadily. But Bette has always been cynical about success. She has always made a point of saying that marriage might last, but stardom wouldn't. That has been one of her reasons for talking so much about her marriage.

Bette hasn't changed over night. She hasn't started concentrating on her career to the exclusion of everything else, including private life happiness. She isn't the type for that. She's too sane.

She rates today as Dramatic Actress No. 1. She wants to hang on to the title. She's ambitious. But this isn't something new. It was ambition that gave her the title in the first place. And "Ham" has been living with that kind of ambition for six years and not finding it a cause for incompatibility.

HAS one of them suddenly discovered faults in the other never suspected before? That isn't very likely. You can't live intimately with a person for years without finding out all of that person's shortcomings, as well as good traits. And Bette and "Ham" didn't start from scratch, as two infatuated strangers. They had known each other for years. They knew what they were getting in getting each other.

Have they run head-on into a big misunderstanding? Perhaps. But, like all married couples, they have had misunderstandings before this. And, big or little, they have weathered them all. Not long ago, Bette even revealed that she

[Continued on page 198]

Bette's "Farny": Arthur Farnsworth, aviator, violinist, sportsman

The Man Bette Davis Married

Photoplay-Movie Mirror stopped its presses to bring you this exclusive—the information you could not find in the newspapers

BY SALLY JEFFERSON

WHEN word was flashed to a thoroughly unexpectant world that at eight o'clock New Year's Eve in the ranch home of Mr. and Mrs. Justin Dart at Rockrim, Arizona, Bette Davis had become the bride of Arthur Farnsworth, one question was uppermost in the mind of every one: Who is Arthur Farnsworth? What does he do, what is he like, that he should win the hand of the screen's finest actress and Hollywood's most regular person? To answer this Photoplay-Movie Mirror stopped its presses and went to many sources to bring you a complete picture of the man and the event about which you all want to know.

Just a year before, to the very day, Jane Bryan, Bette's friend and protegée, had said good-by forever to Hollywood when she married the man she loved, Justin Dart. Now, in Janey's home, Bette was taking her vows and in a way was saying good-by, too, to many things—to struggle and heart-

ache and the intense concentration on work that she had previously placed above her personal life and happiness.

Bette was coming home again—to a life of peace with the man she loved, Arthur Farnsworth.

She met the tall and handsome 34-year-old New Englander two years ago when, weary to the point of complete exhaustion after strenuous years of picture-making, she went East for a rest.

First she had traveled to Boston and then on to the home of a school friend of her mother's at Bascom for several weeks. But still jangled nerves had refused to quiet down. Then she had remembered her mother's words as she left Hollywood, "If you feel yourself falling to pieces, go to Peckett's Lodge in Franconia, New Hampshire. You'll find rest there."

At the very sight of the Lodge, so peaceful and quiet, Bette indeed felt the cares of mind and body drop away. She knew that at last she had found

what she was seeking.

"Without a question, these kind people let me come home as one of them. They, stern Yankees all of them, accepted me, an actress, without a qualm. They asked no questions, made no demands. I dressed as I pleased, wore no make-up and revelled in peace. Ruthie, my mother, had been right," she said.

HERE she met the man who was to be her husband, for the assistant manager of the Lodge during the summer was Arthur Farnsworth. He was a light-haired chap with blue eyes, a well-groomed six-footer, rather stocky but very handsome. Typically New England, he had a natural charm, an easy sense of humor; a man's man, he was marked by a poise that had been acquired through his extensive travels.

The son of a retired and well-to-do dentist in Rutland, Vermont, he had been educated [Continued on page 199]

113

THIS YEAR'S

Photoplay turns back the Hollywood calendar to bring you the marital mergers and tangles, the Blessed and not-so-Blessed Events in a bulletin that's town talk

BY GRETTA PALMER

ILLUSTRATION BY JOANNE ADAMS

September, 1937: Saw the birth of a new Photoplay. The following months have brought record-breaking events. So the editors mark the close of its first fiscal year with these hilariously vital statistics. Romance opened strong, with marriage quotations giving the market a bullish trend. Announcement of the marriage of Miriam Hopkins to Director Anatole Litvak, early in the month, marked the beginning of the broad upswing. Cupid Common soared when Alice Faye and Tony Martin were wed. Other issues responded: Luise Rainer, in a statement, assailed bears who sold short her marriage to Clifford Odets, the plawright. The Tyrone Power-Loretta Young interests were reported firm, although a nervous tone prevailed over the Tyrone Power-Sonja Henie collaboration. Stork rallied with the new Gary Cooper-Veronica Balfe issue.

October: Marriage held firm, in spite of bearish interest in the Clark Gable ménage, with rumored participation by Carole Lombard. Hearts advanced when Francis Lederer wed Margo, showing strong foreign interests in the Domestic Hearts' market.

Rumors of a rise in Garbo-Stokowski, formerly unlisted, were denied by the company involved.

The Virginia Bruce-David Niven romance sagged. Conflicting rumors on the Robert Taylor-Barbara Stanwyck amalgamation confused observers.

November: Romances soared, with a firm undertone of wedding bells. The market for the month closed strong. Jackie Coogan's marriage to Betty Grable, Betty Furness' to orchestra leader Johnny Green and Alan Curtis' to Priscilla Lawson were pivotal points in the latter half of the session.

Public participation was marked. Traders and usually authoritative sources rumored new listings and the gossip tape lagged behind events. The new Tyrone Power consolidation mentioned Janet Gaynor. The Ginger Rogers-Playwright Robert Riskin deal attracted attention. Carole Lombard and Clark Gable were bracketed for a sharp rally. Robert Taylor's European interests included Barbara Stanwyck, according to London and domestic tipsters.

December: Matrimonial shares reached year's high when Virginia Bruce and Director J. Walter Ruben brought out a new and eagerly received gilt-edged debenture. The Hearts' Exchange reflected sentiment.

Continued upswing raised Romance averages to new highs on the year's movement. Early in the month several matrimonial issues were retired: Leopold Stokowski changed his listing and tape symbol from Husband to Divorcé. Gloria Holden released her holdings in Harold Winston. There was profit-taking in Stork Preferred by the firm of Henry Fonda and Wife.

Garbo denied plans for a Stokowski merger. Well-informed observers reflected coldness towards Lupe Velez-Weissmuller shares. Nervousness was expressed by the tape on the Clark Gable-Lombard company shares.

A broadly bullish tone prevailed, with Cary Grant-Phyllis Brooks and Loretta Young-Joe Mankiewicz moving briskly.

January, 1938: The New Year's Marriage Market opened sluggish, with little

OVE MARKET

remained firm. Hands-Holding received some support from the increased activities of the A. C. Blumenthal and June Lang interests.

April: Romance continued to lag, with many shares striking the low for the year on the Hearts' Exchange. Gossip-brokers were reluctant to take a position and the specialists' book showed few offerings. The tape reported bearish developments in Marriage Preferred when Herbert Marshall, handsome star, was sued by Eddy Brandt for alienating the affections of Mrs. Brandt (Lee Russell).

Eternal Triangle responded with a brief flurry of interest, but the Love market remained disappointingly stagnant for the session as a whole.

Infant Commodities attracted interest with the birth of a daughter to Doris Warner and M-G-M producer Mervyn LeRoy.

May: The Hearts' Exchange continued its recent listless tone, with few offerings. Shorts were vindicated when Luise Rainer and playwright Clifford Odets announced their separation early in the session.

Hearts advanced on a narrow front with the rumor of a rise in Melting Glances, Inc., sponsored by the strong Joan Fontaine and Conrad Nagel interests.

Slight gains were reported at the Fox lot, with Sonja Henie and Richard Greene said to be participating in Beating Hearts Preferred. Usually reliable sources did not authenticate the rumor that large interests were watching this issue.

support. The Stan Laurel wedding on the opening day was bullish, but general nervousness prevailed. Volatile issues, such as Robert Taylor-Barbara Stanwyck, remained unchanged. The Lili Damita-Errol Flynn romance encountered resistance.

The Stork Market showed an improved technical position. Stork Preferred announced four new listings when sons were born to Allan Jones, Bela Lugosi, Arline Judge and Bing Crosby. A daughter born to Claude Rains made this the outstanding month for stockholders in the Baby Commodity Market.

February: The Hearts' Exchange opened with little volume and scant outside participation. Traders were inclined to be bearish and Romance moved sluggishly.

Certain observers profited on the downside with the announcement of Fay Wray's separation from the writer, John Monk Saunders, and Walter Wanger's divorce from Justine Johnstone.

Valentine Common sagged sharply, in the dullest session of the year. News of Stokowski's sailing to join Garbo brought only a faint response.

March: The month opened with a bulge in Love, but Matrimony attracted few bidders. The Kay Francis engagement to Baron Eric Barnekow brought some public participation. Babies were bullish, with Bob Burns' new son attracting interest.

The Stokowski-Garbo issue moved sidewise, with conflicting rumors arousing uneasiness among gossip-brokers. The Tyrone Power-Janet Gaynor bond

June: Hearts advanced with a sharp rise and shorts scurrying to cover their positions. Love encountered little resistance in the almost perpendicular return.

All matrimonial issues shared in the most rapid upturn in months.

Leaders in the Matrimonial advance were Lily Pons-Andre Kostelanetz Nuptials, Frances Langford-Jon Hall Elopement, Inc., Gloria Dickson-Perc Westmore Knot, Cecilia Parker-Dick Baldwin Wedding-Bells, Virginia Walker-William Hawks Bridal Shares and Russell Gleason-Cynthia Hobart Honeymooner.

The strength of the movement was reflected among the Rumors, where Richard Greene was claimed on behalf of three important shareholders: Arleen Whelan, Loretta Young, Sonja Henie.

[Continued on page 199]

THE STANWYCK COURT CASE

THE TRUTH BEHIND

BARBARA STANWYCK FIGHTS TO GIVE HER ADOPTED SON, DION, HAPPINESS AND SECURITY SHE MISSED IN CHILDHOOD

By JOAN BONNER

"*I WANT my son to be happy. Above everything else I want him to have that sure sense of security in his home, that sense of peace and stability that I missed so much in my own childhood.*"

Barbara Stanwyck talking. Barbara fighting the greatest fight of her life for the custody of her adopted son, Dion. Carrying the case to the highest tribunal in the State, the Superior Court.

It would take a Zola to do justice to this story, to weave together all the human elements and highlight them as they should be highlighted by the supreme loyalty of one woman. I shall have to confine myself merely to the statement of facts.

The night before the first trial began Barbara said, "I'm so afraid that people may not understand. . . ."

Why shouldn't she let Dion see his foster father? Well, she had. The boy went to visit her former husband, Frank Fay, four times after their di-

Wide World
Barbara Stanwyck and Frank Fay, divorced husband, are fighting for the custody of their adopted son, Dion

vorce. And each time, according to the testimony which later came out in court, he returned home so ill that a doctor had to be called.

"I can't let him be a little emotional football tossed about this way and that. *I can't!*" It was a cry from the heart. And people understood. Thousands of letters poured in from all over the country. From other mothers, from clergymen of every denomination and people in every walk of life. As one woman wrote, "You were so *fine* . . . I have a greater respect for the whole acting profession."

They would have an even greater respect if they knew the entire inside story. I'll never forget last Christmas Eve out at Barbara's ranch, Marwyck —the same place that the opposing attorney tried to make sound like the Black Forest of Russia where a child might be crushed to death by horses' hoofs the minute he stepped out the door!

This is what Marwyck really looks like—picture to yourself 140 acres in one of California's most beautiful garden spots, a low ranch house splashed with sunlight and provided with every comfort and convenience. The stables are a mile and a half from the house (so the horses are not exactly up against the front door!) Dion has his own pony out there and each day Boris, an ex-Russian cavalry officer, comes to teach him the fine art of riding.

BUT Christmas Eve even his beloved pony was forgotten. Dion's blue eyes were round as saucers. He is six years old and probably the cutest freckle-faced youngster this side of Jordan.

"But the fireplace, mummy!" he protested. "We've got to put out the fire or Santa Claus will burn his whiskers!" Everybody solemnly agreed. Mr. Hart, who is in charge of the stables, saw to it that the flames were smothered and Dion, satisfied, was whisked away to his room.

Very carefully, the butler stole outdoors to ring the sleigh bells. There was a great hush. Then a sudden stir and commotion. Santa Claus had been there and Dion was tumbling downstairs to see his presents! You can imagine the sight—the Yule log afire again, the tremendous living-room bright with holly, and presents piled knee deep under the tall tree.

But every little while she excused herself and slipped away from the fun —to go into an adjoining room where Charles Cradick, her attorney, was waiting to confer with her about the trial.

Through years of the severest hard knocks ever directed at one girl, Barbara has built up a defense mechanism that is vulnerable only in one spot. *Dion.* Through him, you can strike at her because he has come to be the center of her whole life—as anyone in Hollywood can tell you.

"But can you *feel* this part? *Have you ever suffered over a child?*" Sam Goldwyn asked her when he was contemplating her for the lead in *Stella Dallas.*

"No," said Barbara. "But I can imagine how it would be." Ironic twist of fate! Before the year was out she was to *know* how it would be! Ironic too, that her greatest suffering should follow upon the heels of her greatest success in the most poignant mother-love story ever written . . .

Three years ago when Barbara found life with Frank Fay no longer possible, she walked out of one of the most elaborate estates in the southland and left him in possession. Even the choice antique pieces and the silver she had been collecting she left behind. Up to that time Barbara had made almost a million dollars in motion pictures. But due to the depression and other things she had practically nothing left. She had to start at scratch again—very nearly where she had started ten years before as a kid of fifteen in New York. But she saw to it that Dion had everything. A capable, sweet-faced English nurse looked after him and Barbara worked like mad. She took any part that came along whether it looked like "B" material or not. Just so she could build up again for her son.

"I want him happy. I want to try to give him the courage and confidence to face life and make a good job of it," Barbara told me on a spring afternoon recently when I went out to see her. "Oh, I know it takes hard knocks to develop! But he'll get those soon enough. I don't want him one of those so-called 'movie children.' The spoiled and pampered variety. Grief, no! That's why I'm sending him to military school soon." And Barbara's eyes took on a faraway look as if she were peering into the future.

But I was seeing the past. I was seeing a much too thin little kid with eyes too big for her face, sitting on a dirty curb in Brooklyn. A child of the tenements. Her name had been Ruby Stevens then. She'd never had a puppy. She had never even had a doll except the makeshift one she made from scraps gathered back of the gas works. When she was two, the fat old Irish woman from across the way had come after her one morning and patted her, not unkindly. "Ye poor thing, ye! They've kilt yere mother, so they have! A drunk pushed her off the street-car and now she's dead, God rest her soul!"

The words had no meaning for Ruby then. She was too young. But three years later she was old enough to understand when they told her that her father had died on the boat going to Panama. He had signed to work down there as a laborer. "Shure, there's gold to be had in a place like that," he had told his brood of five. "And when I come back we'll be afther havin' a feast and money t'burn!"

But that was the last bright thrill of her childhood. With his death, the three older girls went to work in a factory and "boarded out' Ruby and her brother, Byron.

"In eleven years I lived in fourteen different homes," the girl who is now Barbara Stanwyck once remarked. She said it in that straightforward way of her's that shuns self-pity. "My clearest memory is of the crowds, of spent old women bent over hot tubs and babies crying and men reeling drunk to their homes. Half the time I slept on a mattress on the kitchen floor."

And now her whole idea is to make up to Dion, once an orphan like herself, for what she missed.

As we sat there watching Dion on the terrace he fell suddenly and scraped his knee. For an instant tears welled up in the blue eyes. Barbara called him over. "It hurt you, son, I know." (She always calls him "son.") "But you're going to be hurt a lot because that's the way life is so you'll have to learn to take it." And then they were close in each other's arms and Dion wasn't crying anymore. He was patting her as if *she'd* been the one to stumble!

THERE was no sign of "smother love" in Barbara's devotion. She doesn't try to buy him the most expensive toys. The one whim she does cater to is his infatuation with men's neckties. All colors, all sizes. They make him feel so grown up! It's nothing to have Barbara stop the car and dash into a haberdashery because "my son will dote on that terrible yellow tie in the window!"

Last fall when the doctors ordered her away for a rest from her work she refused point blank at first. "I *can't* go. Dion might forget me!"

"You'll go," they told her, "or *you'll* forget the meaning of health!" So Barbara compromised. She was gone nearly six weeks and each day of that time she sent back to Dion a movie reel of herself taken with her 16 m.m. camera. He had a complete day-by-day record of his mother's travels. And every evening, just at the time she usually went in to say goodnight to him, a long distance call came. "*Mummy!*" Dion's ecstatic voice.

"Sleep tight, son!" A voice from 3,000 miles away.

The night before the trial came to an end Barbara was so agitated she paced the floor for hour after hour. Dozens of times she went in to look at the sleeping Dion, to straighten his blankets and kiss the outflung small hand ever so softly. If she could only keep him safe forever like that . . .

Towards morning she fell asleep and awoke just in time to dress and rush hurriedly to the courtroom. When she came back, weary, tired to the bone, Dion—who knows nothing at all about trials and courtrooms and such—met

[*Continued on page 200*]

117

The Final Fling

GRACIE ALLEN wants to know if "Gone With the Wind" will be a sequel to "The Hurricane."

JOAN BLONDELL'S small son, Normie, age three and a half years, has been begging for some luggage like Daddy Dick's, so with an afternoon off from the studio Joan dashed into town and bought Normie a small bag equipped with a flash light, two safety pins, and a tooth brush. Normie was delighted, but there was no peace in the Blondell-Powell home until Normie could take a trip on a train so he could use his luggage. So Joan and Dick took Normie down to the station, bought tickets to Santa Barbara, and took their young son for his first train trip. Hardly were they seated in the Pullman before Normie had his bag open and was on his way to the men's dressing room to brush his teeth. He wanted people to think he was an old-timer at this traveling business.

JEANETTE MacDONALD is superstitious and won't give out interviews on love and marriage. She also refuses to remove her wedding ring and when she is working in a picture she wears a strip of flesh colored tape over it.

DURING a recent vacation in the East Rosalind Russell was acclaimed by the New York designers as the best dressed Hollywood woman of the year. Of course she had to do a lot of shopping to live up to her title. Among the interesting items she brought back with her is a pair of green jersey shoes, made dressmaker fashion and stitched entirely by hand. She wears them with a silk jersey ensemble—and Hollywood drools with envy.

GARY COOPER certainly "does something" to feminine fandom. But it may be revealed in utter confidence that sitting on Gary's lap can be a tiresome procedure. Have it on the word of Claudette Colbert, who should know. For one scene in "Bluebeard's Eighth Wife" Claudette spent eight hours perched on Gary's knees. She found them a trifle too sharp for solid comfort.

THEY are telling the story around town about the eager young writer who bumped into Marlene Dietrich one day on the Paramount lot when she was under contract there. "Oh, Miss Dietrich," he said, "could you come into my office and let me read you the new script we have for your next picture. It's far more exciting than the play. Why when you come on the screen it is like the bursting of a bombshell. . . ."

"Naturally," said Marlene, and walked away.

EVER since Clark Gable won the popularity poll of a New York newspaper recently, and was actually crowned with a crown by the paper's western correspondent Spencer Tracy goes to great trouble to call Gable "King." Working in the same picture with Spencer and Clark, "Test Pilot," is Myrna Loy who was crowned "Queen" the same time that Clark was crowned. "It's very difficult," said Spencer winking furiously, "to have to work with so much royalty. But when they start ritzing me I always say, 'What have you two got that I haven't got? Ha, you've got Parnell.' That withers them." "Parnell," dear readers, is one of the colossal flops of the year, and a very sore point with both Gable and Loy, who starred in it.

118

A MOVIE FAN'S CROSSWORD PUZZLE
By Charlotte Herbert

ACROSS

1. Villain in "The Buccaneer"
4. Sea Captain in "Ebb Tide"
9. Ronnie Bowers in "Hollywood Hotel"
12. Direction of compass (abbr.)
13. Past
14. Partake of food
15. River (Sp.)
16. Regarding
17. A cog-wheel
18. District Attorney (abbr.)
20. Liquid Measure (abbr.)
21. Mountains in Russia
22. Type measure
23. Loiters
25. Branch of a deer's antler
27. "Man-Proof" is her latest picture (initials)
28. Nothing but
29. Wooden pin
31. Feminine first name
33. The taxi driver in "100 Men and a Girl"
34. Kingdom
36. In "Romance in the Dark"
38. An English actor
39. To bar
41. Terminate
42. Falsehood
43. Took precedence
45. Open (poet.)
46. Julien Stevens in "Dangerously Yours"
49. Dry
52. Luise Rainer's devoted husband in "The Big City"
55. With Irene Dunne in "The Awful Truth"
58. Wanderer
61. In "Hitting a New High"
63. Greek letter of the alphabet
64. In "The Great Garrick"
65. A word sacred to the Brahmins
66. Single individual or object
67. Unit of energy
68. Day of the week (abbr.)
69. The (Fr.)
70. Change direction
72. Ordnance Department (abbr.)
74. British India (abbr.)
75. Let it stand (pr.)
77. Before
78. Star of "Portia on Trial"
82. Self
83. The mad pearl trader in "Ebb Tide"
84. The murderer in "Dinner at the Ritz"
85. "Hawaii Calls" is his latest picture

DOWN

1. The defendant in "Portia on Trial"
2. Acute
3. Famous for her beautiful legs
4. Lovely newcomer in "Merry-Go-Round of 1938"
5. Myself
6. Comedian in "Fight for your Lady"
7. Army officer (abbr.)
8. The only woman director of films
9. With Grace Moore in "I'll Take Romance"
10. Pack tightly
11. A comedienne
19. Comparable to
20. Bone
24. Chests
26. On the sheltered side
28. Term used in pinochle
29. Remove outer covering
30. Viennese actress in "The Buccaneer"
32. Contralto
33. Star of "The Hurricane"
35. Utensil for washing floors
36. One of the great composers
37. Famous crooner
38. Tidy
40. Rich Indian in "Life Begins in College"
42. Southern state (abbr.)
44. Physician (abbr.)
46. Performer
47. Husband of Bebe Daniels
48. The rich girl in "Artists and Models"
50. Within
51. In "Thrill of a Lifetime"
53. In "Happy Landing"
54. Suffix
56. Wild (Scot.)
57. Find fault continually
59. Measure of distance (abbr.)
60. Affirm
62. Gaseous element
64. Mohammedan prince
71. Elongated fish
73. Eastern state (abbr.)
74. Public conveyance
76. Golf mound
78. Into
79. Day of the week (abbr.)
80. A character actor (initials)
81. Tiberius (abbr.)

Answer To Last Month's Puzzle

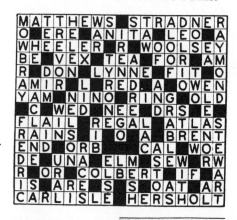

Win a Personal Check
from
Joan Crawford!

See Joan Crawford in her newest screen hit, *Sadie McKee*. Then try for a cash prize with a letter which expresses your opinion of her

How to Compete in this Fascinating Contest

WRITE in 200 words or less your opinion of Joan Crawford, telling frankly in your own language just what you think of Joan's personality and her pictures, suggesting if you wish ways in which she may improve her screen work. Your contribution may be written on typewriter or in longhand. Write exactly what you think, and remember that literary merit is not considered. The first prize winner's article will be published in September SCREEN BOOK and Miss Crawford will send personal checks promptly to the first six winning contestants. Send your entry today to *The Contest Editor*, SCREEN BOOK, 52 Vanderbilt Ave., New York City. Read the rules carefully.

THE RULES: Entries must be received before midnight of July 1, 1934.

Editors of SCREEN BOOK will be the sole judges. No entries will be returned. In case of tie, duplicate prizes will be awarded. All readers of SCREEN BOOK with the exception of employees of Fawcett Publications, or their relatives, are eligible to compete. Because of the great number of entries, SCREEN BOOK cannot enter into correspondence concerning the letters of individual contestants.

◆

Watch for the announcement of Joan Blondell contest winners in August SCREEN BOOK.

The Prizes
First $50.00
Second . . . 25.00
Third 10.00
Fourth, fifth, and sixth prizes . 5.00
Seventh to fifteenth prizes, autographed pictures of Joan Crawford.

WHY WAS ALFRED VANDERBILT

Anita Colby, Alfred Gwynne Vanderbilt

Every day in every way the stars get swankier and swankier—but is their wining and dining to the manner bought, not born, as this distinguished connoisseur claims?

WHY FIFTH AVENUE

LAUGHS

WHILE the white-tie set of Newport and Fifth Avenue disports itself in the gayest night spots of the East, California's most renowned white-tie set does its nocturnal reveling in and about the town called Hollywood. Once in a while the two sets meet, look each over, and report to the home field. But, for the most part, Fifth Avenue lifts a snooty eyebrow and emits a robust chuckle when anyone brings up the topic of movieland society.

As with everything else, there is a basic reason for this feeling—so take down your hair and harken to a few of the highfalutin' things I've seen hereabout in the past few weeks —then make your own decision.

STANDING in the midst of a gay Hollywood party the other evening, an ancient Oriental proverb that goes something like this, flashed through my mind: "Dignity begins where boasting ends."

All about me were the Four Hundred of Picturedom, cello-phane-wrapped and celluloid-displayed, pretending to have a good time. Grand people some of them, if only they would take time out to be themselves. No doubt in the depths of the modest little homes from which most of them emanated, they had for years been "just folks," the same as you and I. But once they'd made the grade to stardom and big money and come out of their warrens and permitted the world to give them the double O, the case was different.

In the past twenty years of coming to Hollywood once or twice every 365 days, I've been more struck by the pretensions of the bunch than by any other single issue. Hollywood and its hillbillies are a great deal grander than the cut-glass and ermine covered dandies who refer to Fifth Avenue as their place of permanent abode. Take it for what it is worth —these lads and lassies know how to put on the mustard with a vengeance.

Never in all my life of lapping the silver spoon have I seen the likes of Hollywood when it goes to town. It would put to

120

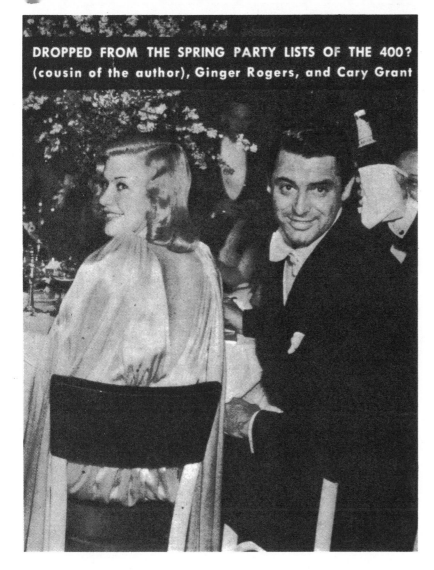

First to go British in this social tangle was Doug Fairbanks Sr. now married to Lady Ashley (far left with black glasses). Fred Astaire's wife was the ward of Henry Bull, which means something in Fifth Avenue jargon

he kept regularly in the house consisted of a butler, a footman, a chauffeur and two maids.

A case or so of champagne had been iced; nine other cases were cooled by cubed-ice in the glass. Two cases were imports, and of years that would not have been considered top-notch by any eastern host who knew his gravy, (or his champagne). The other eight represented the host's patriotic California spirit. Scotch, brandy and many liqueurs lay carelessly about the rooms. And I saw one guest make a souvenir of at least one bottle.

No New Yorker who valued the blue blood which permeated his veins would have for one moment given such a slipshod affair to so many locally important people. Certainly any Fifth Avenue party would have been duller, but you may be sure the host or hostess of the evening would have seen personally that every single detail was top-hole.

True it is that not one in a roomload of Hollywood guests knew, or even so much as cared, what was taking place back of the wings. All had preened their feathers at

AT HOLLYWOOD SOCIETY

by Cornelius Vanderbilt, Jr.

shame the turnouts of the dowagers Stuyvesant Fish, O. P. H. Belmont and any number of Astors, Van Rensselaers and Hamilton Fishes. Even architect Whitney Warren must get a chill up the spine and James Gordon Bennett turn in his grave, when hearing how Hollywood puts on the onions in 1937.

Of course it may be simply a case of "too much dough"; or perhaps they're in the first grade of from "shirt sleeves to shirt sleeves"; whatever it is, it's the comparisons that make Hollywood so refreshing. It's like paying your two-bits to sit in the peanut gallery down on Main and Seventh and watch the greatest show on earth (put on by a Cecil DeMille with a Cedric Gibbons and an Adrian costuming them), pass by, and then finding your next-seat neighbor, young Edsel Ford napping the ninety minutes through.

For all I know the particular party this evening may have cost the host fifty grand (in the public press); yet I learned (quite by accident I assure you) that all the domestic help servants, and a plain-clothes detective or two is even scattered in the ensemble. Concoctions may be served on Park Avenue; but they have not yet invaded the sanctum of Fifth; and it's doubtful if they ever will. Martinis, Bacardis, Old-fashioneds and whisky-soda are *de rigeur*. Take those or go around the corner to your favorite bar; no one cares, least of all your host.

Men or women who gain the reputation of not being able to hold their drinks are avoided like leprosy. Practically every New York hostess has a little red check beside their names. A few months after they have thus distinguished themselves, the Social Register lops them off its rolls. And it isn't long before they realize they are *de trop* wherever smart people go. They're shunned and shunted about as if their malady were an incurable case of something horrible.

But in Hollywood this sort of person is the life of the party. What Fifth Avenue dislikes stands the Hollywood party boy and girl in good stead. Their every word is dwelt upon. Producers sign them up for fabulous contracts and directors scan them from every angle for possible picture parts.

CHARITY affairs are the strangest parties of all in southern California's play city. You will find yourself seated beside one of the screen's greatest teasers, who will baby talk you to death the rest of the evening. An attendant will ask for your ticket. Certainly your hostess has provided that; but the attendant will assure you she hasn't; and instead of making a scene you'll fork up the ten bucks. But that's only gate money. All the night through you will be stuck for this or that, until the hole burned in your jeans will singe the hair off your leg.

Back in the city of the Statue of Liberty, at least you have your liberty with every charity dinner acceptance you receive. Not a nickel leaves your pocketbook from the time you sit down until they play "Old Lang Syne." It would be considered the height of something or other if any guests forked up so much as the hat-check fee on leaving the restaurant.

Back in 1932 when Franklin Roosevelt was the Democratic nominee for the Presidency, and I was campaigning as advance manager for his political train, I well remember receiving the shock of my life on arrival in Hollywood to find the manner in which Warner Brothers had then contributed to the campaign fund. A certain sum had been written down and affixed to it were the names of the studio executives.

Some weeks later I learned that everyone from plasterers, carpenters and electricians to gatemen, stars and extras had [*Continued on page 200*]

[*Continued on page 200*]

being asked. All could tell of their individual accomplishments, and boast for weeks to come of being included in the list of invited guests. All could lord it over the rest of Hollywood till the end of the season for having supped and wined with one of the world's best-known mugs.

AT one of those "Do come, I'm giving an itsy-bitsy cocktail party," I counted 186 itsy-bitsys, fully ninety-five per cent on the abyss. Ingredients had been mixed, diligently or otherwise. Various concoctions had been originated. Guests relaxed in the host's sleeping quarters at all points of the compass. A few had gone to sea, with sad results.

Hollywood had gone Hollywood with a vengeance, when word sped through the crowd that Walter Winchell had just entered the yard. Now, usually, in the best regulated Hollywood quarters, writers, press agents, photographers, and other scavengers keep pretty much to themselves. They're just about as welcome as Santa Claus on the Fourth of July. Winchell is feared more than any man in Hollywood, and respected for that reason. How or why he'd come, no one seemed to know; but the about-face of some of our better known celebrities was quite as remarkable as his appearance at the party.

Down along the broad Fifth Avenue that once housed more millions than the United States Treasury, cocktail parties are, to be sure, given. But they are very well arranged affairs. Every person passing the iron grille is known to the waiting

Howard Hughes, aviator, playboy, producer, who first put Jean Harlow into circulation, plays hands across the continent in this society game too. And Gary Cooper ploughed through the dowager circle and picked himself a peach, Veronica Balfe

The girls are keen for Bob Taylor—who is easily the young man of the hour. He slays them because he is natural, charming and typifies the ideal American youth

All feminine stars are clamoring for Bob Taylor to appear opposite them. Here he captures Loretta Young's heart in *Private Number*

Why Girls *Fall in Love* with

ROBERT TAYLOR

By Grace Mack

IT HAS happened again. You fans have picked a winner and through your concerted acclaim have lifted him right up to the top. This time it is a lad named Robert Taylor. In one short year he has made most phenomenal and dazzling progress. And while he may never achieve the romantic idolatry of Valentino there is no denying that he has taken feminine audiences by storm. His fan mail is pouring in at the rate of some 2,500 letters per week, which is just about tops. All over the country Robert Taylor fan clubs have sprung up like mushrooms. At the première of *The Great Ziegfeld* he was practically mobbed by enthusiastic fans. In fact, Robert Taylor is very much the young man of the hour.

A few years ago the same thing happened to a chap named Clark Gable. Overnight, he became the male sensation of the screen. Producers who had searched the highways and byways for another Valentino were puzzled. Gable wasn't handsome in any matinée idol way. Rather, in looks, he was what had formerly been labeled a "heavy." He suggested menace. As one writer in analyzing his appeal said: "He has a manner

which indicates that while he might kiss a woman's lips he might also, under provocation, slap her face." In fact, as *Ace Wilfong* in *A Free Soul*, the picture which sent Mr. Gable to stardom, audiences were treated to the somewhat unprecedented spectacle of seeing Norma Shearer receive a neat sock on the jaw from cave-man Gable. Women, apparently, adored it and it started a new cycle in screen lovers.

All of which brings us back to Bob Taylor. He, in no way, follows the original Gable pattern which girls were supposed to be so crazy about. There is nothing cave-mannish, nothing menacing about him. He hasn't slapped [*Continued on page 201*]

123

Was it ★★★½ Three Comrades bad acting,

bad stories or that "pretty boy" ★★½ Lucky Night

publicity ★★½ Lady of the Tropics that put Bob

on the ★★★½ Waterloo Bridge toboggan?

BY ROBERT TAYLOR

AS TOLD TO GLADYS HALL

ACTING is the most unstable of the professions. It and politics are the only two pursuits of man which depend solely upon public favor. In other lines of work, you fail or are fired because you are not efficient at your job. An actor may be completely efficient at his job but, if public favor veers away from him, that efficiency counts for nothing.

The question I want to ask my fans is this: What makes a star slip? What are the contributing factors that cause a star to fall? Do you get tired of his face? Is it a question of bad stories? How much does adverse publicity have to do with it? How great an influence is the star's private life? In other words, just what is it that *makes* a star and just what is it that *breaks* him?

Because I know my own case history best, I feel that if I can get the clue to my own toboggan, I can get the answer to the whole question. I don't know why I slipped. I know there are a dozen routine answers, but I'm not satisfied that they are the real ones.

I do know just when it all began. "They" said I was slipping before I went to England to make "A Yank at Oxford." The bad publicity I got in New York before I sailed, the "pretty boy" shrapnel they let me have was, "they" said, my death-knell. But curfew did not ring that night. Because, if I'd started to slip then as disastrously as was predicted, "A Yank at Oxford" wouldn't have done the business it did.

No, I skidded when I made "Stand Up and Fight," and well I knew it. Don't think we stars don't realize when we begin to wobble. We don't soar around with our heads blandly in the blue while our feet are walking the plank. Why I slipped with this picture is one of the things that confuses me. It was a good picture and brought in the shekels, yet it was not good for me. Which seems to indicate that, for the individual actor, the play's not always "the thing." You can slip even when you have a good picture.

Now it may be argued that the picture was no good for me because I played a tough guy in it—fighting with Beery, biting the dust and all that. I bet some of you said, "It's

Why did I slip?

too obvious that the studio is trying to disprove the 'pretty boy' publicity by giving Taylor a part where he can exhibit some beef and brawn." I thought of that, too, but it isn't a good enough reason, because "The Crowd Roars" was made before "Stand Up and Fight" and in that, if anyone remembers, I was a pugilist who was no palooka in the ring. If any of you had wanted to give it the "Hee-haw-they're-trying-to-prove-that-Taylor-can-take-it," that was your chance. You didn't take it. That picture was both good Box Office and good for me.

So, to a certain extent, my pictures have kept me on a see-saw, now up, now down. "Three Comrades" was a good picture for me. "Stand Up and Fight," "Lucky Night,"

"Lady of the Tropics" and "Remember" were bad for me. "Waterloo Bridge" gave me a swing up again and now I have hopes that "Escape" will put me on the up-end of the teeter-totter once again. But it's the *why* of the ups and downs that I'm trying to get at.

In my case it may well be said that I skidded because I'm not a fine actor. I know I'm not. I had no experience behind me when I came to Hollywood. I still haven't had enough training—it takes study and time to perfect any art or craft. I have a whale of a lot to learn.

Yet, you can't say an actor loses public favor just because he's not a fine actor. Naming no names, for courtesy's sake, we all know actors who make no [*Continued on page 203*]

Watch your step, ♦
♦ Ann Dvorak!

THIS editorial is dedicated to all sulky Hollywood girls, and to Ann Dvorak in particular.

Ann, you're a smart young thing—pretty, spirited, promising. You made a personal hit in "Scarface." You've become increasingly popular in several pictures. Hollywood considers you one of the best bets among the younger screen players. But, Ann Dvorak, you have not yet "arrived." And I think you should get wise to yourself—while there's still time.

Two years or so ago you were just one of the hundreds of Hollywood strugglers. Glad to get a job as a dancer in "The Hollywood Revue." Gladder to be made assistant on the Metro lot to dancing Director Sammy Lee. Coached Joan Crawford and other Metro stars for their movie dances. Worked hard. Made good. But all the time thinking—weren't you?—"Wish I could get *my* chance at acting!" Then Karen Morley helped you get a test, and "Scarface" was the result. Life suddenly opened up to you. People pointed you out. When Warners grabbed you for their pictures, no less a personage than Ruth Chatterton got down on her hands and knees to peek into the set where "that new Dvorak girl" was working. Fans pronounced your name a dozen different ways, but they pronounced it, which

was what counted. More power to you, we all said.

Romance, too. You eloped with Leslie Fenton. Your real friends said, "It's grand. She'll make him happy. He'll make her a great actress." The future looked as rosy as an extra's cheeks after a bawling-out by a third assistant director. And then—something happened to you. In a Barrymore it's temperament; in a little, new actress it's—something else. You came to New York with your husband, and why not? A honeymoon. But it began to look more like a business trip what with newspaper interviews quoting you complaining about your salary and Hollywood producers being slave drivers and all. A honeymoon—with the bride saying, "Why, a baby in one of my pictures earned more than I did"; and the groom, "There are other companies besides Warner Brothers." It was a rude shock, Miss Dvorak. Doing a Cagney? Anyway, it was "see my lawyer," and you went to Europe, shaking off the sordid dust of that commercial Hollywood.

And now let me tell *you* something! Success must be earned. Joan Crawford worked eight years in Hollywood to win the fame she has today — eight pretty hard years, too, with Joan striving and slaving to make good. She had her flurries of discontent, I know—but she was wise enough, or

Warning *to* Hollywood Girls!

Ann Dvorak and her husband, Leslie Fenton. Theirs was a real screen romance—they acted together in "The Strange Love of Molly Louvain," fell in love, and eloped. Now they have left Hollywood flat for foreign parts. Ann signed up to play in a British film, with Fenton opposite. Will they stay in England, or will they come home to Hollywood? It's our guess they will be back.

humble enough, not to let them sweep her off her path. She was afraid to do "Rain"—but she did; and *Sadie Thompson* is her greatest performance. And Crawford is still humble, and a little scared—even today. That's why we love her. Barrymore and Arliss, Barthelmess and Garbo, Shearer and Helen Hayes—years of hard work built their solid success, and nothing can take it away from them. James Cagney, the rebel, who won screen fame so swiftly, is still, at this writing, "resting."

You, Ann Dvorak, are not yet important enough to get away with it. And when you are important enough, you won't want to. The motion picture industry is bigger than you are. It can get along without you, but you can't, excuse me, get along without it. Because no other profession in the world can give you so much. Granted that your salary of something like $250 a week isn't much for Hollywood, it was more than you'd ever made before—and it would be only the beginning for a bright girl like you. If you are really good you have a long career ahead of you—

it's not necessary to make big money fast. Give yourself a chance!

And don't forget how Paul Muni came to the studio at six o'clock some mornings to help you with your work in "Scarface." Muni, who has been an actor since he was a kid; who knows what it means to work hard over a period of years; who is only just now coming into the fame he so richly deserves. You can learn a lot from him.

You may wonder why, since I feel this way about you, I take the trouble and the space to spank you. It's because I think you have real stuff. That's why I say to you, Ann Dvorak, "Be a trouper!"

By GLADYS HALL

WHEN Director Frank Capra read James Hilton's prize-winning, world-read novel, *Lost Horizon* he wanted, then and there, to screen it. He said: "It held up a mirror to the thoughts of every human being on earth."

The other day, in his dressing-room bungalow on the Selznick International lot I talked with Ronald Colman who, in the magnificent picture, so magnificently portrays *Robert Conway* who goes to *Shangri-La*—and stays there.

And Ronnie said to me: "It does more than mirror the thoughts of every human being on earth. It mirrors the desire of every human being on earth. For all of us, famed or unsung, wealthy or impoverished, the successes as well as the failures, the frustrated or the reverse have a nostalgia, at the very roots of their beings, for going "back to the land," for a Castle in Spain, for some remote fastness, some Port of Peace. Whatever name we give it, it means the same thing. It means—a *Shangri-La*.

"In connection with which I can tell you an amusing incident, rather a revealing incident, too—and a sad commen-

RONALD COLMAN Gives
the Lowdown on Himself

Ronald Colman would like to find a real *Shangri-La*. In this new slant on himself he also sizes up the part of *Rhett Butler* in *Gone With The Wind*

tary on life as most of us live it. Over a year ago I was dining with a group of men, very sophisticated men, very successful men. Men who could have had no valid reason for wishing to shut the doors of the world in their own faces. Such men as Marc Connelly, Charlie MacArthur, Bob Sherwood, a few others. Mind you, I had not, then, the slightest idea that I was ever to make *Lost Horizon* nor, indeed, that it was to be made at all. My interest was simply that of a reader of the book, one who had felt the nostalgia it gave to all who read it.

"I had no personal interest in it at the time. But my atten-

tion was caught and held as I heard the name *Shangri-La* said over and over again. And I was interested and fascinated by the rapt intensity with which these men of the world were discussing it, by the earnestness and eagerness, the almost feverish light in their eyes when they said how they wished that they, too, might find a *Shangri-La*.

"*So do I*," said Ronnie.

Which statement left me unsurprised. For Ronald Colman, if any man, would wish to find a *Shangri-La*. Failing to find the physical location he has, I think, found his own *Shangri-La* in himself. Such a place of apartness from the turmoil and confusion of the world he lives in must be in his own heart. I knew that, as I watched him in *Lost Horizon*. I was not watching Ronald Colman play *Robert Conway* (initials the same) but Ronald Colman playing himself.

As he explained: "After all, what is *Shangri-La* but a place where a few men and one woman found what they most wanted, what all men most want, I should suppose—love, work to do, health and peace of mind. Wherever these elements are to be found is *Shangri-La*. The only thing that was lacking is the only thing that doesn't really matter — an audience, spotlight, limelight." Yes, Ronald Colman would wish to find *Shangri-La*.

He has been termed, variously and somewhat luridly, a "man of mystery," a hermit,

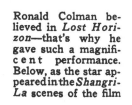

Ronald Colman believed in *Lost Horizon*—that's why he gave such a magnificent performance. Below, as the star appeared in the *Shangri-La* scenes of the film

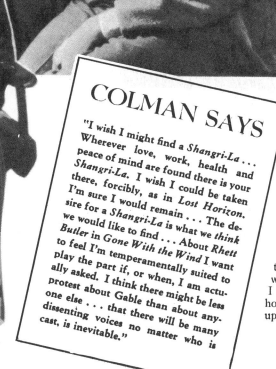

COLMAN SAYS

"I wish I might find a *Shangri-La* . . . Wherever love, work, health and peace of mind are found there is your *Shangri-La*. I wish I could be taken there, forcibly, as in *Lost Horizon*. I'm sure I would remain . . . The desire for a *Shangri-La* is what we *think* we would like to find . . . About Rhett Butler in *Gone With the Wind* I want to feel I'm temperamentally suited to play the part if, or when, I am actually asked. I think there might be less protest about Gable than about any-one else . . . that there will be many dissenting voices no matter who is cast, is inevitable."

an anchorite, a recluse, conservative, shy, withdrawn from the midway where other men, other actors, ballyhoo their wares—and themselves. He has been called a "woman-hater," an iconoclast. All of the terms with which men speak of a man they really envy but do not understand.

I spoke of these somewhat ridiculous titles the other day. Ronnie laughed. He has, by the way, the heartiest, most genial laugh of anyone I know. Nothing shy about it. As he laughed I thought of how Isabel Jewell once said to me: "Every man should have been born looking just like Ronald Colman." Ronnie has a delightful sense of humor, a superb sense of farce, a keen appreciation of how farcical are some of the rumors grapevined about him. He has a large hunk of the small-boy delight in "getting away with things." He chuckles over the fact that "sticks and stones may break my bones, but names can never hurt me." Names are all *they* can attach to Ronnie. The columnists collapse when they try to pin him down to romances. The things that he really does are his own business and he has managed, almost alone of the denizens of Hollywood, to keep his own business his own.

He always laughs loudly at the "man of mystery" idea, at the "woman hater" label. He said the other day: "Maybe I'm just clever, eh? Perhaps, when I do dine out with a lady, I dine out with the *wrong lady?* Or I may be deliberate about it. I may go deliberately, and with malice aforethought, to some public spot where it is so obvious that we will be seen that any columnist, gossiper, teller of tales is deceived.

"Hollywood can be fooled," laughed Ronnie, with manifest relish, "it's all in knowing how. People, generally, seem to have the idea that places like the Trocadero, the Derbys, the Vendome are the only places for people to go and that if we don't go to such places we don't go anywhere. But there are private parties, you know. Anyone who attends these parties would almost certainly see me there, too. Nothing is thought about it, said about it or printed about it because they are private parties given by private persons who are living their private lives. It's very simple, really. Besides," laughed Ronnie again, "I shall soon be dubbed the most brash, brazen and easily available actor in Hollywood, I'm sure. This is really amusing and one on me. A few days ago I was at David Selznick's house discussing with him some details on *The Prisoner of Zenda* which will be in production, under Mr. Selznick's banner, by the time your story is printed—some time before as a matter of fact. Anyway, David suggested that we go on to the studio together in his car. I told him that I would go down to my house first, get a coat and he could pick me up in his car in [*Continued on page 204*]

By Gladys Hall

Being a movie star sure has its drawbacks—and Ginger Rogers does not spare herself in telling what life has denied her

GINGER ROGERS *asks—*
"Did I Get What I Wanted from Life?"

"YES, I get what I want from life," said Miss Virginia Rogers to me, "except—except for one thing—*I want to go to college!*"

" 'College?' " I echoed stupidly, "you want to go to college?" I had expected anything but that. Some nostalgic reference, however reticent, to the recently divided home of young Mr. and Mrs. Lew Ayres. Some faintly spoken regret, perhaps, for the mortality of mortal love. . . .

But—"Yes," laughed Ginger, laughing at me, not herself, "yes—why not? Lots of professional women do go, you know. Maybe I will, some day. There are so many things I'd like to learn. And I would get so much out of college if I should go now—much more than I would have gotten a few years ago. I'd know now what I want to study, what courses I want to take. I've learned concentration—dancing teaches you that. I've learned patience, I think. I'd care more about learning than I would have cared a few years ago. I'd be able to choose what I want and to go after it.

"I really think that I only woke up four years ago. Before that I was asleep or numb, or something. Perhaps it's just that I've grown up. My ideas, like my face, are shaping differently, losing baby contours. I seem to see everything in sharper focus. I don't believe that I saw anything at all—not really—four years ago."

I had been watching Ginger and Fred

rehearsing. Tirelessly. Almost religiously—over and over and over, perfecting perfection. And watching Ginger, in pale yellow overalls, pale green polo shirt, red-gold hair flying . . . I'd thought: She has everything she or any other girl ever wanted from life. Yes, in spite of what may have grieved her and caused her separation from Lew. For she is young and famous and wounds heal swiftly for the young, and the rainbow is still arched and her dancing feet are only beginning the arc. . . . She has youth and beauty and fame and jewels. She has riches. She has a mother who adores her. She has cars and friends and fine feathers. And she has Fred Astaire for a dancing partner. She is the tops at the box office. There is nothing lacking—nothing that cannot be replaced or achieved.

And then we sat down to luncheon in the RKO commissary and Ginger sipped iced tea and nothing else—because she was rehearsing again after luncheon and one can't rehearse on a full tummy. And I told her what I had been thinking, or some of it. I said: "You have got everything you ever wanted from life, haven't you? In spite of—"

Ginger broke in, grinning, "But I never wanted very much. I never thought about it—"

"No, but—" I said, "all of your dreams have come true, haven't they? All young girls dream of having fame and riches and—and love. And so you must have dreamed. And even if some dreams never stay true, [*Continued on page 205*]

Ginger and Lew are separated

Can Hollywood Hold

ERROL FLYNN?

Errol wants to live a free
life, seeking new adventures

By James Reid

THE quickest way to find Errol Flynn in a mixed crowd is to study
the women. Consciously or unconsciously, they will be watching him.
I tried the test on a huge, crowded set of *The Charge of the Light
Brigade*—and spotted him in thirty seconds, at a distance of one hundred
feet. He stands six-feet-two, but if I had been looking simply for a tall
chap, I wouldn't have found him. He was seated—on some steps—talking
to an extra between scenes. Moreover, he didn't look as he had in *Captain
Blood*. His hair was trimmed; he was wearing a mustache; he was in military uniform. And every other man in the room was in similar uniform,
with a similar haircut, also wearing a mustache.

I would not have discovered him almost instantly if I had not sought the
focus of attention of the women on the set. There he was. Slender, handsome, finely-cut features. Boyish, restless-looking. Smiling. Apparently
unconscious—or was he?—of the feminine glances. It was hot on the sound
stage, under the arc lights. He had his close-fitting, heavy uniform coat
unbuttoned, fanning himself with the flaps. He was doing what every other
man on the set would have liked to do, if every other man hadn't been self-
conscious. Most men would have lighted *that* cigarette.

That one small incident is typical of Errol (Natural) Flynn. He has no
self-consciousness. He does what other men would *like* to do. Women
sense that—and can't help liking such a man. Neither can men. And Errol
Flynn is a man's man. Make no mistake about that.

The fact that he became a star in his first picture hasn't given him de-
lusions of grandeur. Neither has the fact that Warners are spending
another million on his second picture. Nor has the deluge of fan mail
changed him. Acting, to Errol, is just another adventure in an adventurous
life. And he's taking it in stride, just as he took pearl-fishing and shipwreck
in the South Seas, gold-hunting in New Guinea, policing cannibals in
tropical jungles. It's a pleasanter experience than some he has had, but that
isn't altering him any. He still stands with both feet on the ground.

For one thing, he isn't sure that acting—in some of its aspects—is a man's
job. Love scenes, particularly. Standing in front of a camera, pretending
undying love for a girl, speaking soft words to her, makes him uncomfortable. It isn't his idea of a he-man's way of earning a living. That's why
he's so convincingly reckless in physically   [*Continued on page 206*]

Deanna Durbin has found fame and has paid

fame's price—for no little girl can accept an

adult's world at fourteen without heartache

By KAY PROCTOR

It's Lonely

BEING A CHILD PRODIGY

A FEW weeks ago a little girl stood outside the stage entrance of a Hollywood theater. It was on a Sunday night and a wet rain had pelted down upon her, drenching her in the long minutes she had stood trying to get up courage to knock on that closed door. Finally, poised for flight she rapped timidly.

Inside the door stood another little girl, the center of admiring attention and flattery. She wore a pretty frock and was accepting compliments with a sweet but shy courtesy.

The doorman opened the door to the knock. The small waiting figure slid from the shadows into the beam of light.

"I would like to see Edna Mae Dur——I mean Deanna Durbin," she said, hesitantly.

"Are you expected?" the man asked, the routine gruffness in his voice tempered at the sight of the child's obvious timidity

"Er—a—no," she admitted, "but I think maybe she'll say it's all right. I'm Paula." She was told to wait a moment.

In a flash the door was flung wide. Two little girls ecstatically hugged each other while tears of happiness mingled on their faces.

Thus the paths of Deanna Durbin and Paula Jenkins her best friend, crossed for the first time in well over a year; Paula, the average little American girl who lives in an unpretentious bungalow in a middle-class part of Los Angeles, and Deanna, the fourteen-year-old sensation of Hollywood, star of "Three Smart Girls," and radio discovery of the year.

"And Mother," Deanna said, in relating the eventful meeting later, "just imagine, Paula said she and the other girls were all so proud of me! Isn't that wonderful?"

Only Mrs. Durbin knew why praise from that humble source meant so much to her suddenly famous daughter. Meant, in all truth far more than the lavish words and laudation heaped on her by important critics everywhere, knew with a catch in her heart.

DEANNA'S story begins back in 1923. Deanna, christened Edna Mae, then a baby one-year-old, came to Los Angeles with her mother, father, and older sister, Edith. The family home had been in Winnipeg, Canada, where Mr. Durbin was a moderately successful contractor. The boom in Southern California real estate drew them south.

From the day of their arrival [Continued on page 208]

No longer a joyous game of tennis with her particular chums after school. Instead—a serious study of music, with Leopold Stokowski, for her next picture and (opposite page) personal appearances with Jimmy Wallington and Eddie Cantor

the truth about the *Mysterious* Miss Loy

First part in the charming story of a plain freckle-faced Montana girl who became Hollywood's leading exotic lady

a little girl of thirteen stood alone in a strange room and said to herself, *"My Daddy is dead."*
And, as that thin, chill knife of dread certainty entered her heart, it cut her life right in half, as neat an incision as ever was made.

For on one side of the knife-cut stretched thirteen sunny, secure years for little Myrna Williams, daughter of David and Della Williams. Happy home life in the pleasant spacious house in Helena, Montana.

Helena was a wealthy community, for many of the Gold Rush families were still living luxuriously and gaily upon the wealth the Gulch had once given up to them. They were the comfortable custodians of the Gulch and life was lived spaciously there, substantially and well. And the Williams family, while not conspicuously wealthy, were comfortable, too.

The small Myrna's first thirteen years were lived in a peaceful, plentiful home of her own, with a room of her own and pretty clothes, books and toys plus good times with a young brother, David, to tease and be teased by. The Montana ranges were her playground and on those magnificent acres she grew robust, hardy and fit.

Myrna's grandparents were pioneers, stalwart men and sturdy, child-bearing women who had come over the plains in covered wagons, taking the day as they found it. From them, Myrna believes, she has inherited her belief that to live for the day is sufficient unto itself. As those hard-living pioneers laid them down to rest, giving thanks for a day of food and safety, so Myrna lives only for the day and does not reckon with tomorrow, and tomorrow. She takes good care of the present. She leaves the future to her Presbyterian God.

Once, when she was very small, a visitor teased her and said, "What nationality are you, Myrna?" And the child answered, soberly, "I am Presbyterian."

And she was. *Very* Presbyterian during her adolescent years. Given to reading the Bible for hours at a time and saying long and earnest prayers, very preoccupied with the rigors of observing the Ten Commandments.
Her father's people were Welsh, her mother's people came from Scotland and Sweden. Only last

By Gladys Hall

year her mother returned to Scotland to visit and brought back interesting tales of the eighteen sons and daughters of the maternal great-grandmother who are settled the length and breadth of the Scot domain.

MYRNA NEVER saw her father's mother but she is said to resemble her. From the paternal grandmother, she has been told, come those wide cheek bones and slightly Oriental eyes, that Celtic something in that calm provocative face. Strange and haunting are the tales told of Grandmother Williams, of her fascination and courage, her Welsh wit and wisdom, the aura of mystery that always hovered over her. The "Mystery Woman of Hollywood" must be legend derived direct from the "Mystery Woman of Wales!"

But it was Myrna's maternal grandmother who most influenced Myrna's childhood. Myrna's mother and father were gay and sociable people. They had a great many friends, a great zest for life and entertained and were entertained lavishly. And many a time Myrna and the small David were sent to Grandmother Annabelle's for the night or for a week at a time. And Grandmother Annabelle was a memory-making grandmother. The kind of a grandmother who had a storeroom full to overflowing with jams and pastries, and cookie jars full of ginger cookies and a reticule filled with pep'mint lozenges and a heart full of the old lore of the days when she had crossed the country in a covered wagon.

"She never took *anything* as a hardship," Myrna told me, "and I think that if I have any independence of spirit I owe a great deal of it to Grandmother Johnson. As a child she gave me to understand that there is something nasty about people who whimper and whine, even when those people have a real right to scream and cry. She had a lusty fearless joy in life and hardships were a part of life and you took them—standing up!"

Myrna's father was her pal, too. He was a gay person, Myrna told me, a man who made a lot of money in Montana lands and believed that

[*Continued on page 209*]

Above, Myrna as the daughter of Fu Manchu, one of the many oriental roles that first typed her. Below, as a dancer in an early picture—she expected to dance to fame.

Left, Myrna, the finished actress of today who will soon do a sequel to "The Thin Man." And below, Myrna Williams, as pretty a baby as ever opened her eyes in Montana!

With the first public acknowledgment of "my wife" the "great dictator" created a new enigma

The New Mystery of
MR. and MRS. CHAPLIN

BY RITA WILSON

OF all the muddled marital mix-ups of Hollywood's history, there has never been any that surpassed in excitement and mystery the one that is currently intriguing the town, the one in which Charlie Chaplin, Paulette Goddard and Anatole Litvak are the principal players.

The battles and the reconciliations of the fighting Flynns are kindergarten stuff compared to this. The Caliban and Ariel duet of John and Elaine Barry Barrymore is ten-cent fireworks; the Wayne Morris-Bubbles Schinasi tragedy is only a sad little saga; the heart trail of Lana Turner from Bautzer to Shaw to Mature to Martin is child's play when considered in the light of the major-league maneuvers of a great clown, a glamour girl and a charming, unattached director.

For, after all, in each of the above cases you knew to a certainty exactly what the marital status was. Lili and Errol, despite their partings, stay united. You always knew when John and Elaine were in marriages or in between them. You knew when the Morrises were in the courts and out of them. A dozen candid cameras an evening could constantly tell you right where Lana was and with whom. But Chaplin and Goddard and Litvak! Compared to them, Finnegan, the lad famed for being out again, in again, was as set in his ways as Queen Victoria.

If you had asked anybody in Hollywood's inner circles two weeks before "The Great Dictator" was released, they would have told you that Chaplin and Goddard were all "through." But all through what?

That was the question.

While no less an authority than Randolph Churchill, son of Britain's Prime Minister, Winston Churchill, has announced to the world that he knew definitely that Paulette and Charlie were married, no busy reporter—and how busy they have been on this trail—has ever been able to find a record of the marriage having been performed.

Hollywood generally believe that Paulette and Charlie were married. The most accepted date when the marriage is believed to have been performed was the morning of Paulette's birthday in June, 1934, and the place, supposedly, Charlie's palatial yacht. A wedding at sea does not have to be registered on land. Another report had them married in Canton, China.

One thing at least was positive. From the day of their first meeting in 1932 until well into the spring of 1940 Charlie and Paulette were never seen apart from one another. But come 1940 and things began to change. First, close on the heels of a rift rumor, Paulette went on a long vacation alone in Mexico. Secondly, she became a star in her own right in "The Ghost Breakers" and "North West Mounted Police." Thirdly, by late summer, she was constantly seen in clubs and at private parties in the company of Anatole Litvak, he who is the ex-husband of Miriam Hopkins and the ex-escort of such belles as Ann Sheridan, Olivia de Havilland and almost any beautiful girl about Hollywood that you can mention.

Things got so constant with Paulette and Tola, actually, that when Chaplin headed for New York for the Eastern debut of "The Great Dictator," the harassed press representatives of Warner Brothers, to whom Litvak is under contract, Paramount, to whom Paulette is under contract, and United Artists, who were releasing "The Great Dictator" were all in a desperate huddle trying to discover Paulette's whereabouts. Frantic phone calls went back and forth from studio to studio and from coast to coast. Frantic cables went back and forth from the mainland to a ship sailing toward Mexico, a ship on which Paulette was supposed to be and on which it was whispered Litvak was also present. For weeks before this crisis, the Hollywood press had run sly little items which said, "It looks as though Charlie Chaplin has released his long-awaited picture and Paulette Goddard simultaneously"... such veiled cracks, and that was only the half of it.

The other half was whispers that pointed out that something strange always happened to the careers of Chaplin's leading ladies after they were once a hit in his pictures. Mildred Harris and Lita Grey, both very young girls whom Charlie starred, married and by whom he was divorced (and these divorce costs to him were reported as $300,000 to Mildred Harris and $850,000 to Lita Grey); Edna Purviance, his first leading lady when he was a producer of his own films and could dictate all terms; Georgia Hale; Virginia Cherrill—all these girls had been raised from obscurity to fame by Chaplin and after appearing with him one or two times had oddly and immediately disappeared from things cinematic.

Thus it was that after her flash in Chaplin's "Modern Times" the movie colony asked, "Will Paulette Goddard disappear, too?"

Paulette said nothing. She said nothing when the first stories about Charlie's tiring of her were hissed. She said nothing when asked whether or not she was his wife. She most distinctly said nothing when she began appearing with Litvak. But she had already broken the Chaplin leading lady tradition by quietly appearing in "The Young in Heart" which she followed with five solid successes, ending up with the main feminine role in "The Great Dictator."

THE pert Miss Goddard, who is made of cleverer stuff than the other Chaplin wives and leading ladies, has what amounts to a genius for saying nothing and for getting ahead. When she and Charlie first met in 1932 she was only a New York chorus girl who had gotten a divorce from a boy millionaire and who drove to her Hollywood work as a bit player in an imported car that cost thousands. At that time Charlie said he had met in her the only woman who could equal him in talent and intelligence. His friends laughed then, but now they realize that he was a true prophet. The way Paulette has developed in talent, intelligence, beauty and acting ability is amazing and inspiring.

Therefore, it is not at all impossible that, hearing the tales of the other lost leading ladies, clever Paulette may have determined that if there was to be any leaving done, she would be the one who did it. Or it may have been only a quarrel between her and Charlie that led her to listen to the delightful language of Anatole Litvak. Or it may have been only a girl growing up, in her life and her art, and wanting to discuss it with fellow artists. Or it may have been the sum of all these things.

At any rate, there could be no doubt of the attraction there was between her and Litvak. Their dining and their [Continued on page 212]

"Modern Times" started the cycle: Paulette, Chaplin's leading lady, came to the premiere with him . . .

. . . was thereafter his constant companion, the hostess for the intimate parties at the Chaplin home

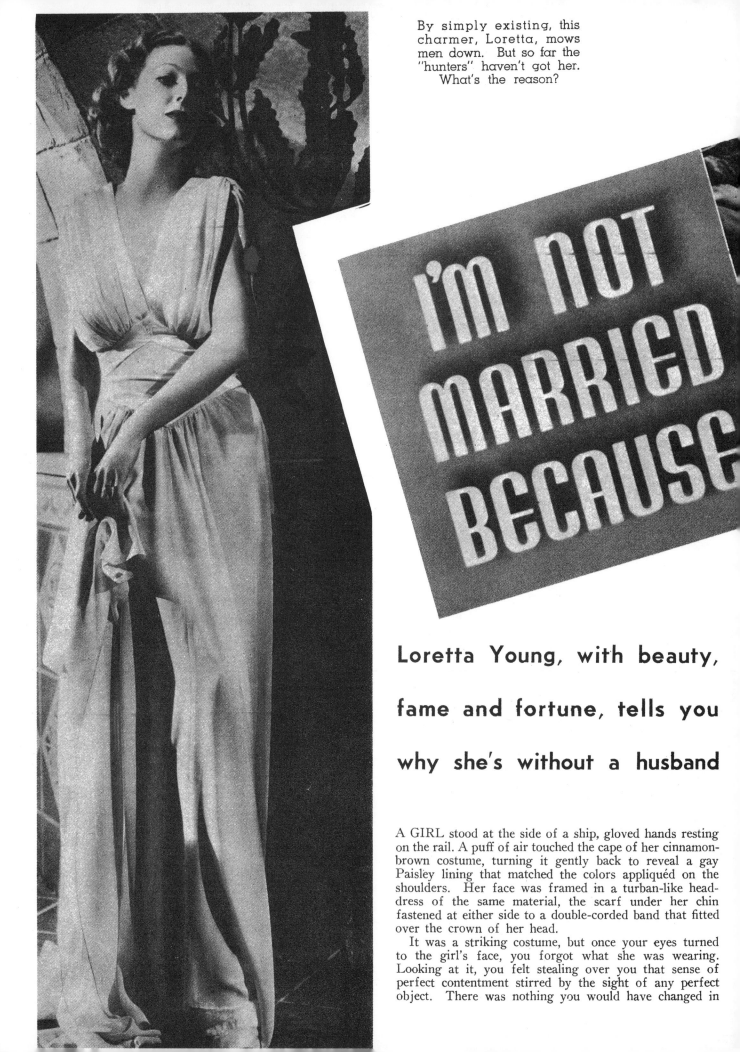

By simply existing, this charmer, Loretta, mows men down. But so far the "hunters" haven't got her. What's the reason?

I'M NOT MARRIED BECAUSE

Loretta Young, with beauty, fame and fortune, tells you why she's without a husband

A GIRL stood at the side of a ship, gloved hands resting on the rail. A puff of air touched the cape of her cinnamon-brown costume, turning it gently back to reveal a gay Paisley lining that matched the colors appliquéd on the shoulders. Her face was framed in a turban-like head-dress of the same material, the scarf under her chin fastened at either side to a double-corded band that fitted over the crown of her head.

It was a striking costume, but once your eyes turned to the girl's face, you forgot what she was wearing. Looking at it, you felt stealing over you that sense of perfect contentment stirred by the sight of any perfect object. There was nothing you would have changed in

A tense moment from "Love Under Fire," with Don Ameche, left. And right, a romantic scene with Tyrone Power, from "Cafe Metropole."

By

Caroline S. Hoyt

that cream-skinned oval with its straight nose and full, sweet mouth and wide-spaced, dreaming gray eyes that seemed to hold all the serenity of the sea she was supposed to be gazing at. But the sea wasn't there, and the ship was moored to a set, and the puff of air was stirred by a wind-machine. Only Loretta Young was real.

"Cut!" called the director, and her quiet face broke into laughter. Don Ameche and Borrah Minnevitch, romantic and comedy leads in "Love Under Fire," had placed themselves safely outside the camera's range but within Loretta's, and were cutting fantastic grimaces at each other in some remarkable game of their own.

"You idiots!" she cried. They faced about, approached at a smart trot and stood before her, features contorted. She considered them both. "Borrah gets the award," she decided. "Sorry, Don, but you shouldn't compete with your betters. He's got the funnier face, to begin with."

Gay or tranquil, she remained utterly lovely, utterly desirable. And the question I'd come to ask her took on a more personal significance. It was no longer just a job, but something I wanted explained to myself. Here was a girl who, by simply existing, must mow men down. Every turn of her head, every change of expression spelled enchantment to the senses. How had she escaped the hunters? Why wasn't she married?

It wasn't an easy question to ask, but once it was out, she made the rest easy. A moment's reflection, then she nodded her head. "Yes, I think I can talk about that." Having agreed, there was no backing and filling. What she wanted to say, she said in straightforward fashion, without flustered reserves or coy hesitations. What she didn't want to say she kept to herself. She made it easy, too, because she's intelligent. She doesn't babble. She

doesn't dish out hooey that she learned from a copy-book or thinks may sound well in a magazine. At one time and another she has searched her own mind, learned to know herself, to be honest with herself. She'll give you the honest fruit of that self-knowledge or she'll give you nothing.

"The whole thing can be summed up in a sentence," she said slowly. "I don't want to marry—I won't marry —till I meet the man I feel I can't live without.

"I'm a normal girl. I've fallen in love. If it were just a question of that, I'd have married long before now. But falling in love isn't the whole of marriage. And with me marriage has got to be for life. I can't say, 'I've made a mistake. Divorce!' My ethics, my religion, my whole outlook forbid it. When I marry, I've got to stay married. I have no choice."

With the headdress removed, her face looked lovelier than ever in its natural frame of soft brown hair. The eyes she lifted to mine had a little smile in them, but it wasn't a merry smile.

"I know what you're thinking, what anyone would be thinking at this point. About my first marriage. You see, I wasn't married to Grant Withers in the Church. It was a civil marriage and, therefore, to the Church, no marriage at all."

She paused for a moment, putting her thoughts in order; then she went on. "I don't want you to misunderstand what I'm going to tell you now. I wouldn't for the world say a word to hurt my former husband, and the whole thing isn't too easy to explain. But if I'd had to marry Grant within the Church, I might not have done it. Not that I didn't love him. I did. Not that he wasn't marvelous to me. He was. [Continued on page 212]

Round-Up of Romances

BY RUTH WATERBURY

You've heard eyebrow-raising rumors about these five couples; here are the facts

Lili Damita and Errol Flynn both claim the break is final. Is it?

MR. ED JUDSON was waxing philosophical at Ciro's. "What fun does she see in that?" he asked.

By "she" Mr. Judson meant the eye-beguiling Rita Hayworth, his young wife. By "that" he meant the new seriousness of Miss Hayworth regarding her career, a seriousness that makes her want to stay in at night studying, rather than going out to night clubs to see and to be seen.

Home to Mr. Judson is strictly a place for sleeping, making appointments and changing clothes, an accommodation, in other words, and not a retreat. But lately, since her triumphs in "The Strawberry Blonde" and "Blood and Sand," Rita has been retreating. Recently she has preferred to remain, night after night, curled up with a good script. Recently she has yearned for rest, rather than play. She has been given to sharp, driving thoughts about ambition, not to the easy ways of laughter and dancing.

"And what fun is that?" asks Mr. Judson, who is a big businessman, but who drops his business like a tweed coat at five P.M. when he goes home to don a dinner jacket for the later evening's dancing.

Well may Mr. Judson ask, but right there you get the fundamental difference toward careers between Hollywood's men and women. Hollywood's male stars can take their careers up until six o'clock and then let them alone for the evening. But once a girl gets really hit by stardom, it becomes like a jealous god to which she must, and will, sacrifice everything. When love gets mixed up in all this, it is just too bad for love.

It isn't that the course of true love —like the old ungrammatical proverb— doesn't run smooth in Hollywood. Love in this town sure does run, and is it

Half of Hollywood says Roz Russell is Mrs. Fred Brisson. She says . . .

140

smooth! Boy, and howdy. Love is terrific, wonderful, thrilling, glorious, deathless, until it lands up in front of a shooting schedule. One touch of production delay and love goes all to pieces —or to the divorce court.

Which is why Photoplay-Movie Mirror as your authentic guide to glitter, knows it is necessary to keep you posted periodically on who is playing Hollywood hearts with whom.

The five big heart headline couples at the moment are Rita Hayworth and Ed Judson; Lili Damita and Errol Flynn (again); Rosalind Russell and Fred Brisson; Ann Sothern and Roger Pryor (also again!); Cary Grant and Barbara Hutton; and this is Ruth Waterbury, the old feedbox, reporting.

There are rumors of possible trouble in the Judson-Hayworth household. Definitely things are not as blissful over there as they were and the cause can most certainly be traced to Miss Hayworth's increasingly busy acting schedule. Quarrels there have been between there two recently. Talk there has been about the attentions of a flirtatious actor-about-town to the charming Rita. But the quarrel—and the flirtatious gentleman—will probably be forgotten by the Judsons since actually Rita and Ed also have much in common.

Older, more poised, Ed Judson does understand the demands of Rita's career. He it is who originally counselled Rita to be always friendly and co-operative to publicity people, reporters and photographers. To Rita's credit be it said that she has lived up to this good advice. She is definitely one of the most gracious and sweet girls in the whole film colony. Personally I think she is smart enough to realize that she is primarily a publicity-made star just as Ann Sheridan is. Equally, however, if she wants now to pause in that publicity campaign of being dressed, photographed, interviewed and stay home to study singing, voice production, dramatic acting, which lessons she does take daily, that, too, is understandable. However, the trouble is Mr. Judson doesn't find that staying home any fun at all. *He* is not interested in an acting career and if Rita gets interested in hers to the extent of twenty-four hours a day it may get to be too much for both of them. I hope it doesn't, for they are two very nice people who, so far, have shared a lot of happiness.

On the subject of her possible elopement with Fred Brisson, Rosalind Russell gets violently emphatic, even emphatic for a girl who is even emphatic about the number of sugar cubes she will take in her coffe.

"I am not going to elope," Roz practically screamed at me in answer to my direct query. "You know the kind of family I come from, a rather old-fash-

It was common knowledge that all had not been so blissful as it once was in the Rita Hayworth-Ed Judson household. The cause of the complications can be easily traced

ioned family. When I get married; when I fall in love, I'll do it in an old-fashioned way. I'll send out announcements. If I ever get to the wedding stage, I'll have the photographers down while I sign the license. I'll want to invite everybody to my wedding. In other words, I'll be proud to be in love and I'll tell the world. As for Fred Brisson, he is my good friend and also my agent. Right now when I've decided to free-lance instead of being under contract to Metro, it has been necessary for me to see more of him in the last few weeks than I have seen of him for months before. Since I have been working for the past year without any kind of a break, the only time I've had to discuss business with Freddie has been over a dinner table, or possibly out in a night club, or maybe driving back and forth to the studio. But none of that dating means that I am eloping. We may have been observed a dozen times practically talking our heads off, but I assure you it has been business we've been discussing, not love, and most certainly not elopements. I'm not going to elope, no matter what the newspapers say."

WHEN it comes to the Ann Sothern-Roger Pryor whispered trouble, Ann offered Hollywood this explanation. She said she had been having house trouble, so Roger had moved out of the house and into a hotel. Ann insisted that was all there was to it, and one could only assume that this forthright girl who had always been utterly honest on all other occasions was still being utterly honest on this one.

Hollywood did know that Roger's ten-year-old daughter by his former marriage had been visiting them. Just prior to the little girl's arrival, Ann had had her bedroom newly decorated. The house only has two master bedrooms and no sooner did Ann get her bedroom done than it burned up. This is literally true, and a rather funny story. Ann was so crazy about the new decorations that she wouldn't even let her maid clean up the room. She did it herself each morning and locked the room when she went to the studio. One morning, apparently, she left a lighted cigarette behind her. When the frantic maid finally smelled the burning hangings, got Ann at the studio and Ann got home with the key, it was all too late.

Naturally no movie star can be expected to sleep in a gutted-out bedroom, so Annie had moved into the other bedroom with her stepdaughter and Roger had gone to a hotel.

That was the way things stood until not so many days ago there appeared in the newspapers this bombshell—a statement that she and her husband were separating. "Due to our widely divergent actions," she said, "problems have arisen which we felt might more easily be solved by a trial separation."

Ann and Roger, as you can see, are still fighting for their marriage. But at this point not even they can prophesy the outcome.

The break-up of the Errol (Fighting) Flynns so immediately after their first baby was born was really shocking to Hollywood. Despite the numerous separations and reconciliations of this pair, [Continued on page 200]

SO YOU'D LIKE TO BE A STAR?

By Faith Service

Myrna Loy shows you what is back of Hollywood's glamor front

MYRNA LOY was, ostensibly, talking to me. At least I was the only person in her suite at the hotel where she and her husband, Arthur Hornblow, were living while they awaited the completion of their new home in Cold Water Canyon, Beverly Hills.

Yes, Myrna seemed to be talking to me. Actually, she was talking to you, Mary, to you, Sue, to all of you little Marys and Sues and Sarahs who wish you could be movie stars, who see them through rainbow-colored glasses—immune from the pains and problems of the workaday world.

"If they only knew," sighed Myrna. She stood there, guileless of make-up, looking very unstarrish and young-wifely, serving me and herself bread with lime marmalade and tea.

"Girls write me," Myrna explained, "like this: 'Day after day I have to sit at my typewriter. I am a secretary. My boss is a hard taskmaster. I have to do everything perfectly, or else. All I can do is take orders and like it. But you lead a glamorous life. You're paid for being made love to. Do you wonder that I envy you, who can be your own boss?'

"I'd like to tell that girl," said Myrna emphatically, "I'd like to tell her in good plain English that I am not my own boss. I'd like to tell her that I serve not one boss but several million. For my boss is—the Public. My boss is that very girl who writes me herself and thousands like her. It is the Public that first hired me, and it is the Public that can fire me. The Public criticizes me, praises me, reprimands me. If you've got any sound sense and adaptability, you can manage to please one boss. But millions! And after the Public there is the producer, the supervisor, the director, the script writer, publicity department, cameramen, sound men. I am not my own boss, girls. I am top-heavy with bosses.

"Then there are the girls who write me like this: 'I work in a store, selling lingerie. I go to work at nine A. M. If I'm late, if I stay out a day with a cold, there is the deuce and all to pay. At five-thirty

"You go to such glorious parties. You're paid for being made love to. You don't have to punch a time-clock. Do you wonder that we envy you?" girls write to Myrna.

Above, Myrna Loy with Hubby Arthur Hornblow and, below, with Clark Gable in "Parnell."

I have to punch the clock and go home. How would you like a life like that—you who can loll in the sun, plunge into swimming pools, lunch at places like the Brown Derby, the Vendome and other spots I've read about?'

"I'd like to tell such young ladies," said Myrna grimly, "that my work is nine parts drudgery and one part thrill and glamor. There is nothing I know of that is quite so exhausting as working under hot lights. It is tiresome, undoubtedly, to stand behind a counter all day or sit at a typewriter pounding the keys, but at least these girls don't have millions of watts pouring into their faces.

"I'm going to tell Sue and Sarah just exactly what I have to do to earn the glamorous reward of being a

moom pitcher star. The behind-the-scenes facts, not fairy-tale publicity. Let's take 'Parnell,' my latest picture, and do a case history on that.

"Well, weeks before the actual shooting began, there were the preparations. I read twenty books on Parnell and his times. I conferred with the son of Kitty and Willie O'Shea. I wear fifteen costumes in the role of Kitty O'Shea. That meant the making of innumerable sketches by Adrian, over which he and I conferred for hours. Materials were tried and approved or rejected. There were one hundred and fifty fittings. There were the hats, hundreds of hats. There was the jewelry. That had to be just right, not only for the period, but also for me. There were the shoes. I had to practice standing

and walking. Kitty O'Shea didn't stand or walk as does the girl of today.

"When we began to work I got up at six every morning, as I always do when in production. It takes from two to three hours to dress, get to the studio, have my hair dampened and waved every single morning, get into make-up and costumes. I make myself up. I can't stand having anyone fussing over me. It took me twenty minutes to get into each gown I wore. And then the set and work. Comes lunch hour. But, my dear good women, no Vendoming, no Derbying for little Myrna. No. Lunch served in my dressing-room, eaten from a tray and, usually, an interview or a conference with the director or lines to be learned [Continued on page 214]

Perfect Wife's Marriage Failed

These are the things Myrna Loy might have told you about her breakup with Arthur Hornblow Jr. They are things that make you wonder if romance is, after all, the right basis for marriage

BY ELIZABETH OWENS

WHEN it was announced a few weeks ago that Myrna Loy was to go to court and file her action for divorce against Arthur Hornblow Jr., even Hollywood, bitterly accustomed to separations and partings, was hurt in its secret heart. The marriages of Lana Turner, Hedy Lamarr, Carole Landis—this year's crop of swift unions and swift dissolves—were all obviously madcap from start to fierce finish. Hollywood positively hoped that the Norma Shearer-George Raft romance would not last—and it didn't. Everybody knew, almost from the moment of the wedding, that Crawford and Tone would eventually part. But Myrna Loy and Arthur Hornblow Jr.! That was really a marriage, not just a flaming romance that had been solemnized with a ceremony.

Myrna announced that she would get the divorce because of incompatibility of temperament.

She let it go at that and, perforce, Hollywood had to let it go at that, too, for incompatibility is the cause of every divorce, if you want to put a fine point on it, and constitutes legal grounds in the state of California.

There were, however, a lot of things that Myrna might have told if she were not the kind of person she is. They were things that would have stirred people's hearts with tender sympathy. They were the things that make you wonder, sometimes, if romance is the right basis for marriage after all; that make you consider if perhaps it isn't smarter to base a marriage on practical reasons and to more or less count love out of it.

For Myrna could have told a story of a woman's love, if she had been willing to.

She could, for instance, have started back on the exciting, sun-drenched, exquisite day four years ago when she and Arthur Hornblow were wed. She could have told how they were so giddy and happy about the whole event that they completely forgot about ordering her a bouquet.

They had gone just across the Mexican border to Tia Juana for the ceremony and in the moment before the binding words were to be read by a sleepy Mexican justice, Arthur climbed over the fence into a field of wild flowers they saw growing there and gathered Myrna a colorful bunch of them.

The gesture delighted Myrna. That wild, sweetly foolish bouquet was like a symbol of the marriage she wanted for herself and Arthur. She wanted their entire life together to be like that, uncalculated, never stuffy, always charming.

THE start of their romance had not been too happy. Arthur had been married then, married to Julie Hornblow, though long estranged from her. Juliette Crosby Hornblow had been an actress, too.

Myrna could have told that Arthur wasn't the first man she had loved, but that he was so surely, so wonderfully, the first man she had wanted to marry and to live with forever after. Almost from the moment of their introduction, she was in love with him, stimulated by his colorful intelligence, fascinated by his ambitions, touched by his loneliness. She wavered, in fact, between ecstasy and anguish for a couple of years, the ecstasy of her love and the anguished fear that he might never attain his freedom.

So it was not alone because of her love but also because he had already known one marriage, and that an unhappy one, that made her determine on that day in Mexico, when he was finally free and they were able to wed, that she would be a perfect wife. She would create a perfect marriage. She and Arthur, she swore, would be no average man and wife. They would be sweethearts forever, playmates and partners in love forever. Theirs would be a romance that would never be allowed to die.

That, of course, would have been a wonderful start on Myrna Loy's love story. She could have made the story most thrilling if she had gone into how she and Arthur built their dream of a house. Its setting was a hollow hidden in the hills, an untamed spot that Myrna had discovered when she first arrived from Billings, Montana, and which she had loved ever since. The house they built was a white, rambling country affair. They put plain wire fences around it and surrounded themselves not with swimming pools and tennis courts and such show-off things but with the permanent natural things, fruit trees and massed flowers and tangled wildwoods where birds could safely sing.

It would have been sweet to have heard, too, about their first three years when they lived in that honeymoon house. They were rich, of course, rich with their combined salaries, rich in friendships, rich enough in every way to go in for a lot of things which are definitely chichi, but which are equally colorful and fun; wines at the right room temperature, exotic imported foods, flowers chosen to match the colors of Myrna's gowns and guests picked to match the mood of the host.

ARTHUR glowed over being lord of the manor and Myrna glowed over him in that role. Arthur was always a magnificent host and their parties were always correctly done, in terms of menu, wines and the like. They never gave big jamborees; they weren't apt to be formal, either, in the sense of everyone's dressing for dinner and all that. But the Hornblow parties were perfect in the aesthetic and gustatory sense.

As a result, about a year ago, Myrna was distinctly overweight. The studio murmured about it. Myrna smiled about [Continued on page 215]

145

My husband is my Best friend

By Adele Whitely Fletcher

THE really successful people in this world are those who waste neither time nor energy grousing over the conditions which exist in their lives but, instead, get busy and shape them into a happy pattern.

Which brings me to Irene Dunne. For Irene has taken her marriage, which circumstances projected into a pretty difficult pattern, and made something darn swell out of it. A husband and wife separated most of the time by three thousand miles might be expected to grow apart. But, after four years of this state of affairs, Irene Dunne and Doctor Francis D. Griffin are as close and as good friends as any two people you know. And far closer and much better friends than entirely too many married people you know.

The first evening Irene and Frank Griffin were in New York this last time, after their trip from California by boat, he took her to the theatre.

"Let's run over and see 'Personal Appearance'," he suggested at about eight o'clock when the last of the friends who had dropped in to see them had left. "Not

dress? Okeh. I'll call down and have them reserve seats." And he was on the telephone.

"Personal Appearance," one of Broadway's most successful comedies is, you know, the story of a movie star, a flamboyantly temperamental upstart who mushrooms to fame. There are many who feel there has been no star, like the lady Gladys George portrays in this play, since the talkies. Claiming, therefore, that the play is dated. Be that as it may, it remains good fun and no one laughs harder than the movie stars who go to see it.

The Griffins sat well down in front. But because they hadn't dressed and because they had come in quietly no one recognized them. They were as alone in that theatre as any other couple who moved closer and reached for each others' hands when the lights went down.

EVERY TIME there was a little jibe at the expense of the movie star, Frank Griffin would turn to Irene and she would feel his eyes bright with laughter.

"Must I do everything myself?" the movie star in that

Above left, Irene Dunne and her husband, Dr. Frank Griffin, in New York. Their first long trip together in four years. Irene says news pictures don't do Frank justice. Above, Irene in her great success, "Roberta." She will make "The Magnificent Obsession" and "Show Boat" on a loan to Universal.

Above, Irene and Randy Scott, her leading man in "Roberta." Irene deftly handles her life so that a brilliant career and a happy marriage dovetail despite enforced separations during work.

Often, Irene Dunne feels, we dwell too much on love and forget that husbands and wives can also be friends

play asks in an harassed moment while at least six people wait on her, hand and foot.

Irene felt a nudge in her side. And she remembered times, when her secretary had neglected to send a check for the telephone bill or her gardener had failed to tie up the chrysanthemums against the tugging wind, and when she had said something very similar.

She pretended, however, that she didn't know what that nudge meant. She continued to sit there very seriously for a second or two. Then, as usual, unable to resist his salty laughter, she began laughing, too. And when she couldn't find her handkerchief he had to give her one of the huge affairs she has made especially for him, since those sold in the shops rarely come large enough to please him.

As the final curtain fell they hurried out into a taxi and back to their hotel. Then, while Irene went in to change into something comfortable, Frank Griffin lit the electric grate fire. For the sake of cheer.

"You wouldn't have any good Irish reason for taking me to that particular play on our first night in New York?" Irene challenged him over their cheese sandwiches and beer.

HE SHOOK his head soberly. "Certainly not!" He was as innocent as Irishers can be when they've been up to tricks.

"That's what I thought," Irene said sweetly. It was a game two could play. "That's exactly what I thought!"

I lunched with her on one of her crowded days in New York. Her suite had the atmosphere it always has. New books were about. Music stood open on the piano which is moved into any suite she occupies, simultaneously with her trunks. Red tulips and purple lilacs were lovely against the pale green walls. And the jonquils which filled a silver bowl were no brighter yellow than the sweater Irene wore with a black tailored skirt.

She shuffled a batch of photographs which had arrived, photographs taken of her and Frank Griffin during their voyage from California—on [Continued on page 215]

By SONIA LEE

OLIVIA DE HAVILLAND sat in her box-like location dressing-room—in silver-cloth and chiffon trappings for her role in *Robin Hood*—a girl of another age! She looked untouched by life, exquisite —perfect replica of a woman of a past era.

But the problem she discussed was as modern as tomorrow. Her words and her thoughts mirrored the honesty of the girl of today.

"Women have always been afraid of being hurt," she commented. Her eyes are startlingly large in the face which might have been born of a poet's dream. Grave eyes. Intelligent eyes.

"But the woman of another day permitted hurts—particularly if they were of an emotional character—to subdue her, to subtract from her happiness, to paralyze her emotions," she continues. "Fortunately, women have come far. They are not afraid of broken hearts or broken loves.

"They take it as material to build into character and to give them wisdom and insight.

"I have invariably refused to discuss my personal life because I felt that an actress should be evaluated by what she does on the

The hurts suffered in Olivia's romances are healed. They've made her a better actress as in *Robin Hood* and *Gold is Where You Find It* —with George Brent

DON'T BE AFRAID OF A BROKEN HEART-- OLIVIA DeHAVILLAND

A BROKEN HEART NEED NOT BE A TRAGEDY SAYS

OLIVIA. PLEADING HER OWN CASE, IT HAS MADE

HER MORE UNDERSTANDING—A BETTER ACTRESS

screen rather by the dramatic incidents in her own life.

"But recently many letters have come to me from girls my own age who ask me for advice on very personal problems.

"I don't consider myself as having lived long enough or learned enough to give adequate counsel. And so I have usually hedged such questions—frankly replied that an older person might be more competent to advise them."

Then she turned to me—"If I thought something that once happened to me would help other girls—"

And she began telling this untold story, without undue emphasis or dramatics.

She is not a girl given to dissection of herself nor intimate revelation. With inherent dignity she shrinks from a public parade of her emotions. And so it is a difficult task. And yet she realizes that there might be profit in it for others.

"THERE was a time," she begins, "when my heart was broken. When I thought it would never mend. It was long before I had thought of a career—long before Max Reinhardt's production of *Midsummer Night's Dream* in the Hollywood Bowl proved the Open Sesame to a screen career for me—that I met the man who was to influence my heart so greatly!

"He was the personification of charm! He had ease, grace, assurance. People inevitably fell under his spell! And he had the gift of laughter! That appealed to me. As it does, I think, to all young girls. They put such value on the man who can amuse them.

"Then, like a revelation, I was in love!

"It had come upon me slowly. At first, there was a delightful companionship—pleasant, unemotional, friendly. With not even a suggestion of that desperation which usually precedes love.

"*Suddenly*, it was something far deeper. My world began to revolve around him. This, I said to myself, would last. It was the real thing. The sort of thing for which every woman waits. If I had been a bit older I would have realized that no woman can weigh emotion unless she has a standard of past experience and old knowledge. I was very young, and very impressionable.

"The inevitable happened, given the personality of the man. My love came in conflict with all the ideals bred into my bone. From childhood I had been taught that the basis of a man's character was integrity and honesty and sense of responsibility. This was a nice

person and I cared for him deeply, but he had none of these qualities.

"I told him I couldn't see him any more. But I did. And for another month my mind and my heart were at war. After days of indecision, I realized I had no choice. He had no place in my life. It was finally finished.

"This, I believed, was the end of my life—the most devastating thing that could possibly happen to me. My heart, I was confident, was completely shattered.

"I cried for three months. Until I had no more tears in my eyes or in my system. I would never love again!"

Olivia smiles in amused memory. "Curious how girls at eighteen jump to conclusions. How irrevocably they make every incident. With what desperation and youth they write 'Finis' to life! My heart was broken—and it would stay broken!

"There would be no mending cement for it!

"I think if I had been a little older, and a little wiser, some of the pain would have been tempered by the certain knowledge that nothing ever goes to waste—neither emotion, nor pain, nor disappointment. That everything contributes to our character and helps in the maturing process.

"A woman can't learn if she insulates herself. It is more true today than it has ever been, that experience is the one great teacher.

"At the moment, when I was baffled and perplexed and distressed by that gnawing pain which refused to go away for so long, I little realized how worthwhile this would prove to be later.

"Shortly after I was signed to my contract at Warner, I was introduced to a man who could easily have influenced my life and career—impaired both, I am certain—if I had not had the memory of three months of tears to guide and caution me.

"It would have been very easy for me to be dazzled by his importance. But now, *I could be objective*. I could measure him more casually. I said to myself, wait a minute, be cautious; it's easy to fall in love, but awfully hard to get over it. I had a standard set by experience, and now it served an excellent purpose.

"Frequently nothing makes a woman so sane as a remembered insanity. From the vantage point of three years, I realize how much that emotional upheaval has modified and formulated my attitudes.

"I HAVE never, for one moment, regretted that hurt—after the first three months.

"For an actress, an emotional dis-

appointment has peculiar and singular value. I don't believe that it is important for us to live every experience, or to know every emotion which we portray on the screen.

"But the camera is pitiless. It not only photographs your face and your figure; it has an X-ray eye which probes into your spirit. If there is nothing in your character, the camera will ruthlessly reveal it. Not *every* experience is necessary—but experience of some sort, *is!*

"And so it is my contention that anything which contributes to insight, to a sympathetic understanding of human ways and human errors, is a priceless contribution to character and to dramatic validity.

"Personally, I think that the modern woman prepares herself better for love and marriage than the girl of older times. We ask a lot *of* it, and we are willing to give a lot *to* it. It isn't a matter taken for granted—marriage is no longer the only accepted sphere for a woman. And so it has assumed a significance which it never has had before. At least, that is my impression.

"I sometimes wonder whether the fundamental reason for the many divorces we have today, isn't that we ask much more of our emotional relationships than women have ever before demanded. We are honest with ourselves. We want the best and expect it. We want everything out of love and marriage, or we will take none of it.

"WOMEN are still hurt today, as they've always been, as they always will be. Just because we are more independent doesn't imply a change in our sensibilities or in our makeup.

"But this is certain. Women take their hurts and make something worthwhile out of them. They enrich their lives with the lessons learned from them.

"*Now* of course, I know that what I called a broken heart three years ago, was nothing of the kind. I was merely going through emotional growing pains. It was a tempering process. I am inclined to think that it has made me a better person—more understanding and more human. And I like to believe that it has helped me as an actress."

There will come a time when love in all its splendor will come to Olivia de Havilland. For she does not isolate herself from real emotions—but does analyze them and separate the real from the dross.

A broken heart isn't a tragedy! It's good for woman and actress alike! It has been a splendid thing for Olivia!

The Final Fling

A Movie Fan's Crossword Puzzle

By Charlotte Herbert

WE ARE continually being reminded in letters which come to this desk that something ought to be done about the curse of the double-feature program at neighborhood movie theatres. Friends and acquaintances whom we meet occasionally at cocktail parties for visiting screen and literary celebrities whisper the same thing in our ear. "Can't something be done about it?" they cry.

Well, recently one enterprising manager of a theatre in a choice midtown section of New York City decided "to do something about it." As his theatre is situated in a neighborhood of smart apartment houses catering to small families, and smart apartment hotels whose principal clientele are well-to-do young couples, bachelors and career women, he thought he would give them the kind of entertainment they apparently wanted. That is, one "A" feature, a newsreel and several short subjects of the better grade.

However, in spite of the fact that children who demand a whole lot for their money do not make up more than a small percentage of his clientele, his plan failed after eight weeks' trial.

Which proves, perhaps, that we're all creatures of habit. For a number of years we've taken for granted the "B" picture served up inevitably as part of the diet in every neighborhood theatre. Even though we squawk while waiting for it to end and the feature picture to go on, we're evidently getting same small "kick" out of it. For it is generally unpretentious, straightforward story telling, minus the frills and furbelows allotted to the more extravagant "A" pictures.

As for us, we feel about the double program much as we felt about birthday parties when we were children. A certain amount of games had to be played before "the main event"—lemonade, cake and strawberry ice cream.

Like this lemonade, cake and ice cream, the "A" picture is something to be looked forward to with varying degrees of impatience, boredom or excitement, according to each member of the audience's own personal reactions.

So, what difference does it make if you have to sit through an orchestra rendering a classical symphonic selection, a swing fest, a blues singer lustily rendering torch songs through a microphone, as you do in the more showy picture palaces—or a "B" picture at the neighborhood movie emporium? If you came simply to see Don Ameche and Loretta Young in "Alexander Graham Bell" you're going to be annoyed with everything handed you, in the interests of choice entertainment, that blocks the way to seeing it.

As we analyze it at the moment, the only solution is a five cent telephone call, a convenience made possible by the unswerving genius of this same Alexander Graham Bell whose life story you wish to spend your money to see. The pretty girl at the box-office with the nice voice (we hope) will tell you the precise moment the feature is going on, and if your watch has been correctly set no precious time need be wasted.

LENORE SAMUELS

ACROSS

1-7 Stars of "Made For Each Other"
13 "Whip McCord" in "The Oklahoma Kid"
14 Umpire (slang)
16 German scientist in "Idiot's Delight"
18 Wander from the truth
19 Wool (Scot.)
20 By birth
21 Regarding
22 Beverage
23 Herb
25 The colonel in "Gunga Din"
28 Man's name (abbr.)
29 Near
30 Northern state (abbr.)
32 Manager of stagecoach line in "Stand Up and Fight"
33 Famous playwright (initials)
34 Our favorite ice skating champion (initials)
35 Either
36 Electrical Engineer (abbr.)
37 In "Only Angels Have Wings"
41 Doug's sweetheart in "Gunga Din"
45 Feminine first name
46 Always (poet.)
47 In "Disbarred"
48 Starred in "Let Freedom Ring"
49 With Jack Haley in "Thanks For Everything"
50 In "Cafe Society"
52 Hurry
53 Prima Donna
55 Whirlpool
57 The playboy in "Four Girls in White"
60 A head dress
63 Existent
66 Thoroughfare (abbr.)
67 Suffix
68 Little crippled brother in "One Third of a Nation"
71 Note of the scale
72 Mid-Western state (abbr.)
73 Intoxicated doctor in "Stagecoach"
76 Shirley's "jester" in "The Little Princess"
79 Identical
80 Mother of "Peer Gynt"
81 Forever
82 Periods of time

DOWN

1 One of the four sisters in "Alexander Graham Bell"
2 Cruel monster
3 Parent
4 Brother (abbr.)
5 Minute particle
6 Now at work in "Invitation to Happiness"
7 Long pointed weapon
8 Pale brownish color
9 Grief
10 Degree (abbr.)
11 Feminine name
12 Breach of allegiance
13 In "Son of Frankenstein"
15 Measure
17 School mistress in "The Little Princess"
24 In "Torchy Blane in Chinatown"
26 Prefix
27 Scientific instrument
28 Swindled
31 Humorous
33 Carlotta in "Juarez"
37 Listen
38 Japanese money (pl.)
39 Demolished
40 With Maureen O'Sullivan in "Let Us Live"
41 One of the Morgan Brothers
42 The truck driver in "Ambush"
43 An Indian tribe of Texas
44 Mrs. Charles Laughton
51 With Errol Flynn in "Dodge City"
54 "Scarlett O'Hara" herself
55 Every
56 Ravines
58 Vestibule
59 She was born in Vienna
60 Hats
61 In "Stand Up and Fight"
62 Morning (abbr.)
64 Ornamental dress trimming
65 Organs of hearing
69 Suffix
70 Greek letter of alphabet
74 Husband of Alice Faye (initials)
75 Munitions manufacturer in "Idiot's Delight" (initials)
77 Doctor in "A Man to Remember" (initials)
78 A call to excite attention

Answer To Last Month's Puzzle

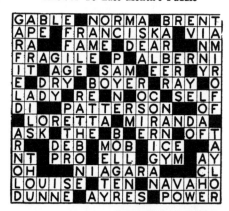

GABLE NORMA BRENT
APE FRANCISKA VIA
RA FAME DEAR NM
FRAGILE P ALBERNI
IT AGE SAM EER YR
E DRY BOYER RAY O
LADY RE N OC SELF
DI PATTERSON OF
LORETTA MIRANDA
ASK THE B ERN OFT
R DEB MOB ICE A
NT PRO ELL GYM AY
OH NIAGARA CL
LOUISE TEN NAVAHO
DUNNE AYRES POWER

AWARD

OF THE

SILVER

SCREEN

MEDAL

FOR

1935

The most popular player on the screen today. Shirley Temple, with her proud mother, Mrs. Gertrude Temple.

SHIRLEY TEMPLE WINS

THE great popularity of little Shirley Temple was one of the most remarkable developments of the last few months. Her charm puts over picture after picture and extends beyond that to many commercial enterprises. Dolls, dresses, books, magazines—all reach a tremendous sale so long as they carry the magic of Shirley Temple's name.

It all began in May, 1934, with the appearance of a gangster film, "Little Miss Marker," and like every popular success it was a complete surprise to the producers. Shirley Temple had been on the screen before but never had been given a real opportunity. "Little Miss Marker" introduced the bewitching Shirley that we have come to know in her later films. At that time Shirley was not quite six years old.

As everyone knows, she has two older brothers, and with them and her father and mother she lives a perfectly normal home life. Through the wisdom of her mother she has been kept from being spoiled.

It is interesting that the Temple family makes no claim of ancestors of brilliant stage tradition. Shirley is the first of their kin on both sides ever to have entered the theatrical profession. Her first appearance on the screen was in Educational Comedies, and it was the all-seeing eye of a Fox director—who came to the conclusion when viewing one of these comedies that here was a little girl with possibilities—which is responsible for her success. And how right he was!

Among the pictures that came out soon after "Little Miss Marker" was "Stand Up and Cheer!"—in which Shirley did her first cute little dance with James Dunn. This was followed by "Baby Take a Bow."

FINAL STANDING OF THE STARS IN THE VOTING

Shirley Temple
Jeanette MacDonald
Joan Crawford
Clark Gable
Ginger Rogers
Claudette Colbert
Dick Powell
Nelson Eddy
Greta Garbo
Bing Crosby
Ruby Keeler
Fredric March
Jean Harlow
Gary Cooper
Norma Shearer
Charles Boyer
James Cagney
William Powell
Robert Montgomery
Myrna Loy
Fred Astaire
Katharine Hepburn
George Raft
Gene Raymond
Janet Gaynor
Sir Cedric Hardwicke
Franchot Tone
Robert Taylor
Loretta Young
Carole Lombard

Writers in Hollywood were now enthusiastically interviewing the little star. SILVER SCREEN'S representative, Mr. Mook, asked Shirley, while she was making "Baby Take a Bow"—"Suppose the film is not a success?" "Then," said Shirley, "we'll call it 'Baby Take a Flop.'" This is a true story, as we can well believe from what we have since come to learn about the little player.

Shirley has had the trying experience of being cast in a poor picture, too, for "Bright Eyes" was not generally liked. But her popularity survived this setback and when the SILVER SCREEN readers were asked to vote for the Most Popular Star on the Screen for 1935, the ballots indicated, from the very first day, that to Shirley Temple belonged the greatly desired title—The Most Popular Star in Pictures.

The recent films in which Shirley has appeared have shown the little star in nineteenth century costumes, very quaint and pleasing. Every production, these days, has to have a dancing star and Shirley has tapped up stairways and down, and, thanks to Bill Robinson, has quite out-classed in dexterity any other child star.

In addition to playing her emotional parts Shirley sings—very sweetly and naturally. In fact she is at her best when singing or dancing. In "The Littlest Rebel" she gives a finer performance than ever before. The high spot is her duet with John Boles.

There is, at the present moment, a gold medal being prepared which will be sent to Shirley as soon as it is ready. SILVER SCREEN is very happy for Shirley and very proud to have helped to establish the little star in this unique position. We wish her many years of good pictures.

ANOTHER HOLLYWOOD

Find Out Which Glamour Girl Would Like You Best.

Jeanette MacDonald answers very definitely: 1—Yes, 2—Yes, 4—Yes, 6—Yes, 7—No, 8—Yes, 10—Yes, 16—Yes, 17—No, 18—Yes, 21—Yes.

AND now it's the men's turn! Have *you* the qualities one of the glamorous single girls of Hollywood is seeking in the man she'll marry?

Learn the answer by filling in the questionnaire on opposite page—read answers at end of the article and see which girl you'd suit, if any!

All the way from little Marie Wilson, she of the amazingly long eyelashes, to stars like Carole Lombard, Luise Rainer, and Jeanette MacDonald, the feminine beauties of Hollywood are demanding, particular, and very decided in their tastes.

Just as with the girls' questionnaire we published last month (and we hope everybody drew a bachelor successfully!), there *are* no right or wrong answers to this test. Almost any combinations of Yes and No will match one of the stars.

We'll warn you right now, however, to rush out and take up dancing if you don't shine in the ballroom. Practically all the girls are looking for beaux who can do them justice at the Troc or the Cocoanut Grove.

Luise Rainer was an exception; with her it's a love of nature that's most important, and let those who would rather dance, dance. "Men should be honest," Luise says firmly, meaning just as much as the word can. "Men should be strong willed. Men should not be stupid, affected, or dogmatic." Decidedly old-fashioned in her tastes was the little Rainer, despite the fact that Hollywood considers her a very modern member of the Bohemian set. Maybe that's why she hasn't married! When we asked if her ideal man must be handsome, she answered almost smugly, "Handsome in mind is more important."

None of the girls care much if you've been married before, but Olivia de Havilland, outlining her requirements very earnestly, said, "He must be trustworthy, discreet, and understanding." Unselfishly enough, she hopes that "he will feel a strong responsibility toward his profession or business, *and perhaps put that first in his life.*"

Olivia can't make up her mind about being independent after marriage. When asked if she intends to give up her career for domesticity, she gasped (very prettily, too), "Heaven knows!" She does insist that the lucky man be as important in his own sphere as she is in pictures—and remember she started right in as a full-fledged star!

A sense of humor is most important to Jean Harlow, who seeks, in a beau, the same steadfast qualities she would demand in a friend. In Hollywood it's generally conceded that Mr. William Powell fills the bill.

Pat Ellis, heartfree at the moment, wouldn't look twice at a lad who couldn't dance. "He must be taller than I," she adds definitely, "and his shoes must be shined at all times." She also wants a chap who can tend bar, if necessary, but he must *not* like premieres, he better not ask her to see *all* the football games, and he's sure to lose out if he talks for hours on the telephone.

Jeanette MacDonald, much more serious than you might imagine, is definitely against heavy drinking. In fact she's the only girl who thought to mention it. Gambling is out, too—and so are members of what Jeanette, with all the fervor of a girl who works for her living, calls "the idle rich."

Naturally, an appreciation of good music is especially important to this lovely singer, and you must like dogs. Otherwise you couldn't possibly be happy with la MacDonald, who always has a few sheepdogs parked around the house.

Marie Wilson, one of our own favorite girls, expects any prospective beau to be a good conversationalist. "I can never think of enough to say myself," she admits calmly. *Unbaggy pants* are another requirement with Marie, and if you want to step right up and make decisions for her after engagement or marriage it's O.K. "It will save a lot of wear and tear on me, don't you think?" says Marie.

Suddenly going serious, she added that he should have gentleness and strength of character, and be as much as possible "as George Brent appears on the screen. He'd never embarrass a girl even if she *didn't* look like Kay Francis!"

(We didn't even ask Miss Francis the sort of lad she likes, since Delmar Daves, the handsome scenario writer, is admitted to have the inside track against all other entries.)

Marian Marsh, one of Hollywood's most beautiful girls both on and off the screen, hedged a little on all our questions. Handsome? "If I liked him," Marion smiled, "he'd be handsome to me." Well-dressed? "But not a band-box effect!" Well-informed? "So long as he's not a walking encyclopedia on any one subject!"

Marion also wants a fellow who is a little jealous. "It's such a subtle form of flattery," she admitted. And he must be a good mixer

Olivia de Havilland will like you if your list checks with this: 2—Yes, 4—Yes, 15—Yes, 17—No, 20—Yes, 22—Yes.

Patricia Ellis' ideal man would answer thus: 2—Yes, 4—Yes, 6—Yes, 7—No, 9—No, 13—Yes, 15—No, 17—No, 19—No, 21—Yes, 22—Yes.

Marian Marsh's heart would go pit-a-pat if you answered this way: 2—Yes, 4—Yes, 6—Yes, 7—No, 8—Yes, 10—Yes, 17—No, 20—Yes.

"DATE TEST"

—not out of place anywhere. Do any of you men think you might qualify?

These are just a few of the fascinating facts we learned about Hollywood's bachelor girls as we plied them with questions about their "dream men."

Remember, the girls weren't allowed to read the questionnaire that accompanies this article. (It was written with the aid of a noted psychologist.) And if you come out one or two answers wrong with your favorite feminine star, you might still win her. Hollywood has never before boasted so many beautiful and glamorous unmarried ladies, and they're all waiting for the right man!

Where Player Fails To Answer Certain Questions, It Indicates She Takes No Definite Stand on Them

Marion Marsh: 2—Yes, 4—Yes, 6—Yes, 7—No, 8—Yes, 10—Yes, 17—No, 20—Yes.

Luise Rainer: 1—Yes, 3—Yes, 4—Yes, 8—Yes, 15—Yes, 16—Yes, 17—No.

Patricia Ellis: 2—Yes, 4—Yes, 6—Yes, 7—No, 9—No, 13—Yes, 15—No, 17—No, 19—No, 21—Yes, 22—Yes.

Gail Patrick: 1—Yes, 3—Yes, 4—Yes, 6—Yes, 7—No, 8—Yes, 9—No, 10—Yes, 14—Yes, 16—Yes, 17—No, 19—No, 20—Yes, 22—Yes.

Gertrude Michael: 1—Yes, 2—Yes, 3—Yes, 4—Yes, 7—No, 8—Yes, 12—No, 13—Yes, 16—Yes, 17—No, 19—No, 20—Yes, 21—Yes, 22—Yes.

Frances Drake: 1—Yes, 4—Yes, 6—Yes, 7—No, 10—Yes, 12—Yes, 14—Yes, 15—Yes, 16—Yes, 18—Yes, 19—No, 21—Yes, 22—Yes.

Ann Sothern: 1—Yes, 3—Yes, 4—Yes, 6—Yes, 7—No, 8—Yes, 9—No, 11—No, 13—Yes, 15—Yes, 16—Yes, 18—Yes, 19—No, 20—Yes.

Olivia de Havilland: 2—Yes, 4—Yes, 15—Yes, 17—No, 20—Yes, 22—Yes.

Isabel Jewell: 1—Yes, 2—Yes, 4—Yes, 6—

Yes, 8—Yes, 9—Yes, 13—Yes, 15—Yes, 17—No, 19—No.

Anne Shirley: 2—Yes, 3—Yes, 6—Yes, 17—No, 19—No, 20—Yes, 22—Yes.

Marie Wilson: 3—Yes, 4—Yes, 6—Yes, 7—No, 13—Yes, 14—Yes, 15—Yes, 16—Yes, 17—No, 18—Yes, 19—No.

Carole Lombard: 1—Yes, 3—No, 4—Yes, 6—Yes, 7—No, 9—No, 11—Yes, 13—Yes, 15—Yes, 17—No, 18—Yes, 21—Yes, 22—Yes.

Jean Harlow: 2—Yes, 3—Yes, 4—Yes, 6—Yes, 7—No, 10—Yes, 13—Yes, 15—Yes, 17—No, 22—Yes.

Paula Stone: 1—Yes, 3—Yes, 4—Yes, 9—No, 12—No, 13—Yes, 14—Yes, 15—Yes, 16—Yes, 17—No, 18—Yes, 19—No, 21—Yes, 22—Yes.

Jeanette MacDonald: 1—Yes, 2—Yes, 4—Yes, 6—Yes, 7—No, 8—Yes, 10—Yes, 16—Yes, 17—No, 18—Yes, 21—Yes.

Anita Louise: 1—Yes, 3—Yes, 4—Yes, 7—No, 8—Yes, 13—Yes, 14—Yes, 15—Yes, 16—Yes, 17—No, 18—Yes, 19—No, 20—Yes, 21—Yes.

Maureen O'Sullivan: 1—Yes, 4—Yes, 7—No, 10—Yes, 11—Yes, 12—Yes, 18—Yes, 19—No.

Luise Rainer favors a man with staid qualities: 1—Yes, 3—Yes, 4—Yes, 8—Yes, 15—Yes, 16—Yes, 17—No.

PERSONALITY QUESTIONNAIRE

(NOTE) *Answer the questions that interest you, either Yes or No, then refer to list of answers to see which Hollywood girl would be attracted to a bachelor of your type.*

	Yes	No
(1) Can you name two philosophers who have influenced modern thought, and one modern American composer of music?		
(2) Can you name the state where President Roosevelt's favorite health resort is located?		
(3) Should a young couple have children on an income of less than $5,000 a year?		
(4) Do you make friends with stray dogs?		
(5) Ever been married?		
(6) Do you dance well?		
(7) Would you wear a white tie with a mess jacket?		
(8) Do you dislike "jazzed-up" versions of classical music?		
(9) Should a man forbid his fiancée or wife to go out with other men?		
(10) Can you beat two or more friends at any popular sport?		
(11) Do friends ever say you look like one of Hollywood's romantic leading men?		
(12) Answer Yes if light-complexioned, No if dark-complexioned.		
(13) Do you know the difference between pate de foies gras and crepes suzette?		
(14) Were you a letter man at school or college, and have you a chest expansion of 3 inches or more?		
(15) At parties, can you lead the conversation into whatever channels you wish?		
(16) Do you ever think about an "ideal" girl?		
(17) Would you be angry if handed a "loaded" cigarette at a party—or any other practical joke?		
(18) Would it bother you if a girl wore satin slippers with sports clothes?		
(19) Would you forbid your fiancée or wife having a career?		
(20) Can you name the birth dates of your father and mother?		
(21) Would you allow your wife a separate bank account or regular allowance if she had no money of her own?		
(22) Are you an officer of your school, class or club, a captain of any team, or an executive of the company you work for?		

Jean Harlow could admire a man whose answers agree with hers: 2—Yes, 3—Yes, 4—Yes, 6—Yes, 7—No, 10—Yes, 13—Yes, 15—Yes, 17—No, 22—Yes.

WHAT HOLLYWOOD IS THINKING

The second in a series of the frankest answers film stars ever gave to a set of questions. Photoplay dared them to tell what is in their hearts. The dare was taken

BY MARIAN RHEA

...POLITICS...RELIGION...MARRIAGE...MOTHERHOOD

CAREER WOMAN

IS Hollywood so busy it does not have to consider the world outside studio gates? Is Hollywood so ambitious it will not stop to contemplate problems which have nothing to do with picture-making but everything to do with modern social welfare? Is Hollywood so egotistical it cannot look beyond self to a broader horizon of affairs political, economic and religious?

In the following article, the second of two setting forth the results of a remarkable dare which PHOTOPLAY made to Hollywood, are to be found answers to each of these questions.

"We dare you, Hollywood," PHOTOPLAY said, "to forget motion pictures and tell us what you think about the fundamental problems of life as it is being lived today!"

Hollywood accepted the challenge. Last month, through means of a questionnaire circulated by PHOTOPLAY among a large and important percentage of the four hundred stars and other players under contract to the various studios, and upon the promise of anonymity, it told frankly and honestly what it thought about such problems as romance after marriage, chastity before marriage, love adjustments of all kinds.

This month, through the same means, it speaks its mind with equal forthrightness concerning child rearing, sterilization, social theories, world affairs and religion. And, as you shall see, Hollywood neither is so busy, so ambitious nor so egotistical that it cannot use its head actively and for the most part, wisely. . . .

PHOTOPLAY'S first question in this second phase of its inquiry was: "*Do you, or will you, refuse to have children because of an unstable future?*"

In answer to this, fifty-one per cent of the women said no—several of them a vehement no, their decision definitely colored by their religious scruples against birth control for any reason.

"This is just an excuse to practice birth control," one actress wrote, flatly. "I believe that parents with children usually can find ways to provide for and take care of them."

"I should take a chance on the Lord providing for my children—aided, of course, by myself and my husband," said another young matron.

"If everyone waited for conditions to improve before having children, the human race would die out. There always has been something wrong with the world!" said a third feminine star in support of having children regardless of political and economic hazards.

On the other hand, "Yes, I believe it is unfair to bring children into the world unless there is a better prospect than at present that they shall survive. Poor little things, they don't ask to be born!" declared one of the feminine advocates of birth control because of a doubtful future.

And, "I refuse to produce cannon fodder!" wrote another, an important star, married but childless.

Of the women refusing to have children under these circumstances, two-thirds were married. Of those in favor of having children, regardless, two-thirds were unmarried.

A considerably larger per cent of the men—eighty-four per cent—believed this modern world safe for children.

One wrote: "Our ancestors didn't worry about every little thing!"

"We are getting too picayunish about this and that, these days. I say go ahead, have your families, do the best you can by 'em and let nature take its course!" declared another. A large majority of men belonging to this school of thought were unmarried.

Of the sixteen per cent refusing to have children because of unsettled conditions, all were married and many of them gave danger of future wars as the reason for their stand.

"I was a soldier. I wouldn't raise a kid to be the same for all the tea in China!" announced one, vehemently.

PHOTOPLAY'S second question was: *"Do you advocate sterilization of mentally unfit persons?"*

To this, eighty-seven and one-half per cent of the women and ninety-four per cent of the men said yes.

"Certainly I believe in it!" wrote one feminine starlet, still in her 'teens. "My father was a disabled American War veteran and most of my life has been spent near army hospitals, where the need for stopping perpetuation of hereditary disease of body and mind cries out on every side!"

"Emphatically, yes!" said another. "This talk about violation of personal rights is a narrow and selfish attitude which should have gone out with witchcraft and snake doctors."

One feminine dissenter said, however, that such is the miracle of modern medicine that the unfit person of today may be cured tomorrow.

While endorsing sterilization in greater majority than the women, the male supporters were, in the main, pretty cautious about it.

"Yes, but with strong legal safeguards," said one young star.

"Yes, but only when there is absolutely no chance for improvement," was the vote of another.

Most of the small percentage of men who declared themselves against such a measure said they thought it too final and irrevocable to be arbitrarily enforced upon society. "Why not examination before marriage, instead, and prevention of marriage among the physically and mentally unfit?" several suggested.

Turning, then, to a question which was once upon a time the center of considerable controversy, PHOTOPLAY asked: *"Will you let your daughter earn her living?"*

To which all of the women and ninety per cent of the men said a hearty yes.

"Why not? I've always earned mine!" wrote one woman star, the mother of two small daughters.

"Certainly. This is a new world. A woman who cannot take care of herself gets kicked around," said a second mother.

"Yes, although not until she is over eighteen," said a third actress, unmarried but betrothed.

And a fourth: "Yes, if she has sense enough. Kids, these days, seem much more addlepated and irresponsible than I was in my 'teens." This star is, herself, not yet thirty-five, but she was earning her own living at fourteen.

While most of the men declared themselves in favor of a career for their daughters, they were a little more conservative in their answers.

"Yes, but not as a fad," said one father. "If she starts, she must see her job through."

Among the dissenters, one young father wrote: "At risk of appearing 'horse and buggy,' I think woman's place is in the home. We wouldn't have a depression today if so many women weren't competing with men for jobs!"

"IF married, what is the subject you and your husband, or wife, most frequently discuss?"

To this query, twenty-six per cent of the women said the future; thirteen per cent money; thirteen per cent, motion pictures; ten per cent politics and six per cent world affairs, with other answers mentioning children, sports, music, books, art, the "isms."

"Building toward the future is a vital thing in marriage. Naturally my husband and I talk of it most," said one young star.

"We talk about our future. This means in our case, our careers, because we are both in pictures," wrote another.

"Money," wrote a third. "After all, you can say what you will, it is money that makes a marriage go 'round!"

One good wife wrote, commendably: "Sports. I don't know a baseball from a football, but my husband is crazy about all kinds of sports and I try to be a good wife."

A fair-sized group—sixteen per cent, to be exact—of the married men also said they discussed the future oftener than anything else, but thirty-two per cent said that money and finances held first place in their marital conversations.

"A good many of our discussions and, I am sad to relate, all of our quarrels are about money," one male star wrote, somewhat disconsolately.

"The thing is," he added, "we are trying to save it to forestall a precarious future and the present is too expensive to make that project successful."

"Money and what we will do with it is our favorite topic," said another, confiding, also, that: "My wife is non-professional and I never made very much until so recently that it still is a very pleasant novelty."

Other favorite topics of discussion, according to masculine players questioned, were world affairs (sixteen per cent listed this topic), home building, music, pictures, children and social theories.

Disregarding these, however, one bridegroom said, with refreshing honesty: "We discuss ourselves. Nothing else seems quite as important two months from your wedding day!"

IN answering PHOTOPLAY's fifth question, the difference in point of view between the average Hollywoodite and Mr. and Mrs. America, concerning finances, became apparent.

"What do you consider an adequate income for marriage?" PHOTOPLAY asked.

"At least $100.00 a week!" said fifty-seven per cent of the women and fifty-five and one-half per cent of the men!

A pretty high figure, you protest? Certainly. But incomes are high in the picture business compared to those of other industries. And so $100.00 a week looks to the average screen player about the same as $35.00 to anybody else. Moreover, when you consider the extra expenses anyone in the movies has—photographs to fans, fine clothes to be "seen" in, the countless expenses of "keeping up appearances"—$100.00 a week *is* about the same as $35.00 a week, or perhaps less.

Sliding down the scale, thiry-three per cent of the women chose $50.00 a week as an adequate income for marriage, while only nine per cent selected $75.00 a week. Three per cent selected between $25.00 and $35.00. A few more said: "It depends upon station in life and demands from outside interests"; still others, that anywhere between $25.00 and $50.00 would be fine for a childless couple, but that for each child there should be from $10.00 to $20.00 more, weekly.

In the majority of cases, the $100.00-a-weekers" mentioned this sum because it would allow a margin for saving. "The future is precarious, especially for a movie actress," announced one, frankly.

One of the "$75.00-a-weekers" pointed out that she thought she and her husband could get along on less, but that this much money meant "freedom from

[Continued on page 216]

155

HE WANTS TO BE ALONE

Bill Powell, eligible bachelor, becomes Hollywood hermit!

DEAR BILL POWELL:

Won't you please stop being a hermit for one evening and come to the party that we're giving on the fifth? It will be informal, and you will know everyone there. We have invited Jean. Couldn't both of you arrange to arrive at seven, before the others appear? It's been ages since we've seen you socially!

Love from———

That was the note the producer's wife penned. This was the reply she received:

Dear ———

I am flattered, as usual, to be asked to one of your festive gatherings. But, as usual, I must extend my regrets—and for the same old reason. I am afraid to accept.

If I should attend, I should be running the risk of alienating the affections of a number of other people whose invitations I have not accepted. Having persisted so long in being a hermit, it looks as if I am fated to continue.

Sincerely,
Bill

The producer's wife, reading Bill's note aloud to her husband, said, "This is the third time in a year that Bill Powell has dodged one of my parties. He's the most disillusioning man I've ever known! A man-about-town who always stays home. What's the matter with him, anyway? He wasn't always like this. What's changed him? Is he trying to become a man of mystery? Is he tired of seeing people? Is he bored with life?"

"Why," asked her husband, "don't you ask him?"

The lady lacked the courage. So I asked him for her. A reporter dares enter territory where producers' wives fear to tread.

I found Bill on the sidelines of "The Emperor's Candlesticks" set, regaling Luise Rainer with a story. It hardly looked as if, on the set, Bill persisted in being a hermit.

Luise was called off the set. Bill was left alone, alone and vulnerable. Before he could escape, I was upon him. He was taken unawares. But did he show it? Not Bill! With all the cordiality at his command, and that's considerable, he shook hands. He insisted on my having a chair, while he insisted on standing.

"I can think of answers faster on my feet," he said. "An old carry-over from my school days. 'Twas a rare teacher who could pin a crime on me, if I had a chance to scramble to my feet before she reached for my ear."

I TOLD him that I had searched him out to solve a mystery even more baffling than anything Nick Charles was ever called on to explain.

On the screen, he is the epitome of the man who gets out and around. Off the screen, he is the Invisible Man. Why is this so?

"I want," he said, with elaborate airiness, "to be alone."

"Absolutely alone?"

"Well, reasonably alone."

"You have no ambitions to be aloof?"

"None whatsoever. Just alone. That's all."

"You aren't bored with life?"

"No."

"Or tired of seeing people?"

"No."

"Your arteries aren't hardening prematurely?"

"They're as soft as jelly."

Bill sighed, beginning to wear under my restless grilling. "You're sure you want my story?"

My answer was the one you would have given.

"I'm not sure I can tell it as it should be told," he said. "I haven't interviewed W. Powell on this particular subject yet, myself. I haven't exactly *thought* myself into privacy. It's just grown on me, like hair.

"I suppose it could be traced, indirectly, to the roles I've played. It's been my fortune, the past few years, to play a succession of clever fellows, all a bit on the smooth side. Nick Charles, for example.

"Now, there was an amusing fellow, the kind of fellow you'd like to have around. I enjoyed being around him, myself. He was eccentric, but witty and debonair. Or,

By James Reid

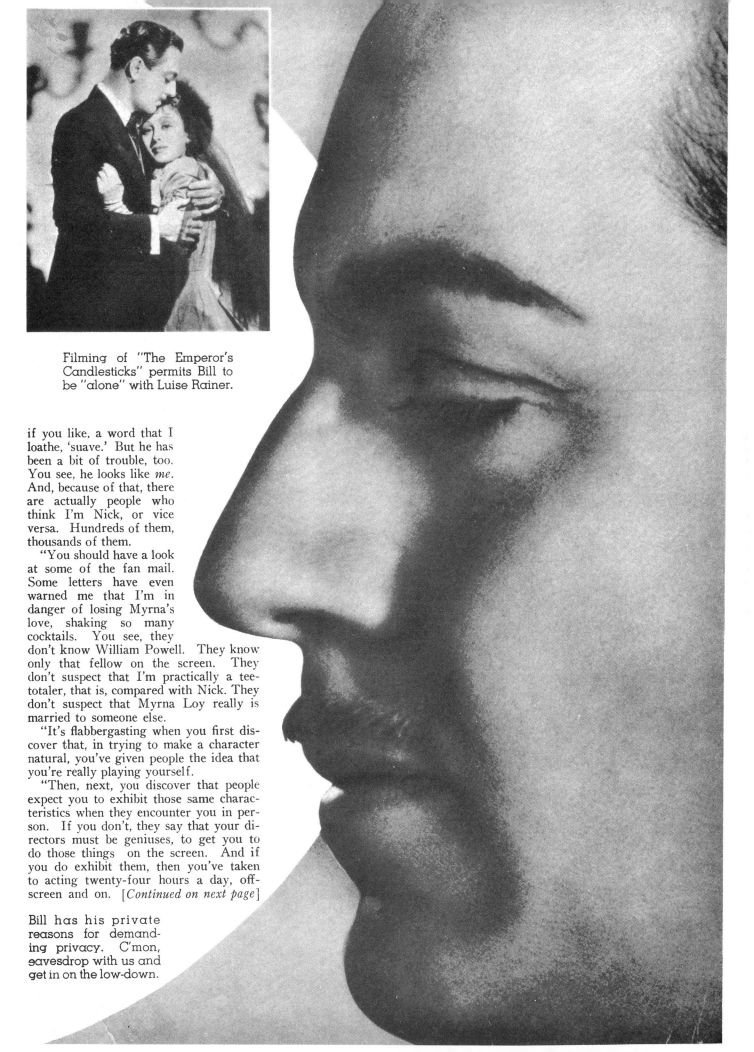

Filming of "The Emperor's Candlesticks" permits Bill to be "alone" with Luise Rainer.

if you like, a word that I loathe, 'suave.' But he has been a bit of trouble, too. You see, he looks like *me*. And, because of that, there are actually people who think I'm Nick, or vice versa. Hundreds of them, thousands of them.

"You should have a look at some of the fan mail. Some letters have even warned me that I'm in danger of losing Myrna's love, shaking so many cocktails. You see, they don't know William Powell. They know only that fellow on the screen. They don't suspect that I'm practically a tee-totaler, that is, compared with Nick. They don't suspect that Myrna Loy really is married to someone else.

"It's flabbergasting when you first discover that, in trying to make a character natural, you've given people the idea that you're really playing yourself.

"Then, next, you discover that people expect you to exhibit those same characteristics when they encounter you in person. If you don't, they say that your directors must be geniuses, to get you to do those things on the screen. And if you do exhibit them, then you've taken to acting twenty-four hours a day, off-screen and on. [*Continued on next page*]

Bill has his private reasons for demanding privacy. C'mon, eavesdrop with us and get in on the low-down.

"One time I was invited to a 'small dinner party.' Only a horde of fifty people finally showed up. During the course of the party, the hostess said coyly, 'When are you going to say something funny, Mr. Powell?' Then she turned to the rest of the table and said in her quaint falsetto scream, 'I've heard that Mr. Powell saves all his bon mots for the screen; but who believes such a thing?'

"That," Bill cocked one eyebrow eloquently, "goes to show you what can happen, if you try to be yourself and go out in public, too."

BILL paused, considered a moment. Then he continued: "Of course, if you don't go out, you run another kind of risk. People misunderstand your motives.

"Cultivate solitude and quiet and a few sincere friends, rather than mob merriment, noise and thousands of nodding acquaintances, and you're called a hermit. They suspect you of having a grudge against the world, or going high-hat, or being afraid your 'art' will be contaminated by contact with the common herd.

"So far as I know, I haven't been accused of that yet. That's where Nick Charles and 'My Man Godfrey' and some of the other boys have done me a good turn. No one would accuse *them* of being stuck-up. So I'm not accused.

"But people do wonder why I spend so much time by myself. They can't understand it. Here you are, wondering yourself.

"It's all very simple. Painfully simple. It all comes down to this: More actors have been ruined by the cry, 'For he's a jolly good fellow,' than by all the poor roles in the world. The charity lists are full of them.

"You can live on hey-hey for awhile, but it's a diet that tears you down, instead of building you up. I know; I've had a try at it. We all have a try at it when we first feel our oats and are showing off a bit.

"On one of those 'mornings after,' you awake with a cracking head and an ache to get away from it all. It's inevitable. You ask yourself how many real friends you have among all the good-time Charlies. You wonder if you haven't had a one-sided education, concentrating on parties and night-clubs. You wonder if you aren't missing something. You wonder if there isn't something in books, fine music, outdoor life, travel.

"In short, you grow up. You go into solitary confinement, just for a change and find it the least confining life you've ever known."

Bill paused, grinned, said, "A serious guy, this Powell!" His mood changed, and again he was light.

"Then there's another thing. I have an uncontrollable urge for old clothes. That's what wearing so many dress suits has done to me. 'Comfort at any price' has become my private-life motto.

"Some tailoring connoisseurs, again confusing me with my screen characters, have nominated me as 'one of the best-dressed men in Hollywood.' It only proves they don't know me. A 'best-dressed man' should be sartorially perfect every hour of the twenty-four—which I'm not.

"My favorite evening garb, alone at home, is attire that looks like something out of the Salvation Army's old-clothes bins, or else a dressing gown and shorts. That's one reason, too, why I never eat in the studio commissary, never give luncheon interviews. Eating in my dressing-room, I can take off my clothes and be comfortable. And have another look at the script."

VISITORS to sets, watching William Powell at work, invariably comment on his delivery of lines, his sureness, his naturalness, his perfect timing. There is an explanaton for that, too, which is tied up directly with his hermit existence.

"As an actor, I'm no genius," he told me. "I can't glance over some lines just before going into a scene and then say them smoothly, with every nuance of inflection they ought to have. No. I have to work for my living.

"I have to memorize my lines the night before, when I have time to try out how they should be delivered. I try 'em one way, then another, until I hit upon the most effective way. Maybe I'm too damned conscientious; but that's the way I have to work.

"Doing that takes a large part of any evening. But it has its compensations the next day. I'm not tense when I get on a set, all tied up in knots, worried about my lines. I know 'em. I'm sure of the way to say 'em. I can relax. I can be effortless, natural. Maybe I'm wrong, but I don't think that can help showing in the finished picture."

He's far from wrong. But still you wonder why he lives so completely alone. Why doesn't he live with Bill, Jr., his fast-growing son by his long-ago first wife? They're famous pals.

"Every other week-end, I spend with Bill, Jr.," he said. "My father and mother are usually along. It's a regular family reunion.

"He's a great boy—and all-boy. He goes to a private school here on the Coast and spends his summers at camp and rates high with the other fellows for what he is, not for what his father may be. I want to keep things that way.

"I'd like to have him with me. But I can't do that and expect him to have a normal life. The spotlight would be on him. And the spotlight isn't good for any growing boy, no matter whose son he is."

ASK Bill what truth there is in the persistent rumors of a near-future marriage, and he shrugs his shoulders noncommittally.

A few years ago, he built one of the show-places of Southern California. Into it went every known comfort device and glamorous decoration. In fact, he had the help of Jean Harlow in the decoration, a circumstance that provoked surmises that he and Jean were about to marry and that Bill was about to forsake forever his non-party existence. But, to the best of anyone's knowledge, both still are single. Bill still is dodging parties. And the house is no longer his.

"I'll never own property again," he told me. "There's too much grief connected with it.

"I didn't build that house for myself. Heaven forfend! I couldn't have used all those rooms in fifty years. The real reason I built it was because I didn't know what else to do with my money. If you remember, the dollar was sinking to nothing, banks were closing, even gilt-edged bonds were a gamble. So I put what I had into this house, in the hope of retrieving it, maybe even making something when things picked up.

"When I finally got rid of it a few months ago, I took another big house in part-payment. Now I'm rid of that, too, and leasing a smaller place in Bel-Air. My worries as a man of property are over."

He won't talk about Jean, or about women in general. He won't talk about any of his close friends. The reason: "Back in the early days, I gave an interview in which I made some remark about actors in general. A friend of mine took it as a personal affront. He hasn't spoken to me since."

Neither will Jean talk about Bill. But intimate friends of both, not so reticent, say, "The're very fond of each other. Very. There probably isn't a more companionable couple in Hollywood today. They're both lonely people who have discovered that, together, they aren't lonely; they have a million laughs together. But it's companionship, not love. That breathless, eager note just isn't there—yet."

That may explain Bill's persistent bachelorhood.

Before he started "The Emperor's Candlesticks," there were rumors that he not only wanted to be alone, but wanted a fight with his studio. A widely read columnist hinted that he was hiding out in the desert, rebelling against the role of Barton Volenski.

Bill laughed about that. "Somebody
[*Continued on page 218*]

DIETRICH
Is Still
Selling Glamour

By WILLIAM BOEHNEL

ALTHOUGH Hollywood's Number 1 Glamour Girl, Marlene Dietrich, likes America enough to become a citizen—she has already taken out her first papers—she is peeved at American newspapermen in general, and, in particular, at ship news reporters. The boys and girls who cover the waterfront— a hardboiled and enterprising crew who usually get the news they are after—displayed altogether too much ingenuity to suit Miss Dietrich's plans on her arrival from England, recently, and the questions they asked and the information they obtained on their own got on her nerves.

The reason for Magnetic Marlene's irritation was that the shipnews reporters upset her story about her twelve-year-old daughter, Maria Sieber. Miss Dietrich didn't want anyone to know that the child was with her and kept insisting that she was in school in Europe. When the reporters dug up proof that the girl was on board, there was nothing left for Miss Dietrich to do but brazen her story through to the end.

The shipnews reporters, incidentally, weren't the only ones to feel Miss Dietrich's displeasure over the questions they asked. Less inquisitive interviewers found it difficult to get the star to talk about things which in their opinion needed clarifying and were news about which the large movie public wanted to be informed. At interviews she granted, the best they could get was a polite silence when [Continued on page 218]

Marlene's legs had considerable to do in building up her glamour. Here she gives them the sun. Left, as she appears in British film, *Knight Without Armour*

selling glamour arlene's in a class herself. She's be- ming an American tizen but prefers live in England

An open letter from

"I've dyed my hair a copper-gold and I like it"

Transcribed by Gladys Hall

I think it was Oscar Wilde who once quipped that it's better to be talked about, no matter how, than not to be talked about at all. But somehow, I just can't feel that way. I can't help caring how people feel about me. That's why I'm taking the opportunity Modern Screen has offered to answer some of your questions and at the same time get things off my chest.

"Why don't you tell us more about your children?" you write me. I don't because, in the first place, I feel it is unfair to bring them into the limelight of publicity before they have any choice in the matter. How do I know they are going to like publicity when they are old enough to judge? After all, there are those who don't. Too, though I adore my children and love to talk about them, I don't feel that "child-talk" should be forced on the fans who, for the most part, regard me more as an actress than a mother. Don't you agree? I'd really like to know.

Then there's the question of money. Although I have been asked many times about my finances, I've always felt that was something that shouldn't be discussed. I

think it's poor taste to parade one's bankbook in public, and this feeling has often led me into trouble. On one occasion, I tried to pass off a direct question and succeeded only in creating a wrong impression. It happened in New York, when an interviewer asked me, point blank, how rich I was. I remember saying that I didn't want to discuss it, but he stuck to his guns and I tried to compromise with half-answers.

By the time all expenses were paid, I said finally, my income was really only about $25,000 a year and, by way of explanation, added that the net was naturally much less than the gross income.

When the interview was published, I found myself quoted as saying I couldn't live on $25,000 a year! What a ridiculous thing for anyone to say! As a matter of fact, I enjoy an extremely good income and, though it does not leave me enormously rich, I consider myself one of the world's luckiest persons.

Now, I believe that that kind of story about income and expenses hurts us and also annoys you, our fans. Am I right? I know that frequently we're at fault, but when something like that is printed about us, there it is, and we never have a chance to tell you whether or not it's true. That's why I am so eager to make the most of this chance and speak without reserve. We can't make retractions because they always sound weak and silly. And the minute you make a retraction you're not believed anyway. Isn't that so?

As another example of what I mean, take my operations—or the ones I'm supposed to have had. Why, every time I've gone to New York in the past three or four years I've been startled to hear, while lunching at the Colony or dancing at 21, that "Norma Shearer is in

Here's a personal reply—friendly as a handclasp—to all those

Norma Shearer

"I can't relax between takes—I keep living the part"

"My friendship with George has made me very happy"

the hospital, following a major operation," and if not at death's door, preparing to rap on it! I can't very well take the floor and announce that I'm not having an operation! It's really rather funny, this rumor that keeps popping up. I wouldn't object to it at all except that, actually, I'm one of the healthiest persons in the world and, of course, glad of it. The real reason for the story is this: A few years ago I arrived in New York with some badly impacted wisdom teeth. I found a very fine surgeon who corrected the condition and now every time I come to New York I go to him for a check-up. There you have it!

Another question frequently asked me has to do with my so-called power and influence at the studio. It always embarrasses me, and I can only answer by saying that I don't think anyone has ever behaved more like an employee than myself. You can ask any of my associates. They'll testify to that, I'm sure. Just because of my marriage to Mr. Thalberg and, as a consequence, my friendship with other executives, there have been any number of times when I did not put up as stiff a fight as another actor or actress would have under similar circumstances. I didn't want to appear to be taking advantage of my association. For instance, I didn't want to make "The Women." I did make it, for the reason I've just explained and also partly because I was taught by Mr. Thalberg to think of what is good for a picture as a whole rather than what is good for me as an individual. I've really tried to refrain from ever being temperamental. I've never attempted to use any influence which I, as Irving's wife, might have had —and all because I feared I would be accused of wielding a power I do not wish to have. [*Continued on page 219*]

"It was such fun working with Bob Taylor in 'Escape'"

questions you want answered

161

Francis Lederer arrived with a trunk full of lofty ideas and ideals, but he wasn't able to keep them unpacked for long.

Hollywood exacts penalties, to be sure—but how those penalties pay!

By

Jerry Asher

THERE are one or two things left in Hollywood that money can't buy. All right, I *will* name one of them! Take ideals, for instance. And if you can take 'em to Hollywood, sooner or later they take you. They are truly Hollywood's greatest luxury. Their price comes high and cannot be valued in terms of dollars and cents.

Hollywood heroes who cling tenaciously to ideals, eventually discover they are wrong for Hollywood—although right for themselves. Through bitter experience they learn that they must change. Some are forced through necessity. Others recognize the futility and wisely make the adjustment before it is too late. In the long run they find it better to bend to the rule, than be broken by it.

Better to

Bend than to Break

[Continued on page 220]

A little bundle from heaven wrought the miracle in George Murphy's somewhat static career.

Francis Lederer and George Murphy are two who lived to learn that they were wrong, according to the rules and regulations of the Hollywood game. Even in his brief stellar moment, John Garfield has already come to the realization that there is only one way to follow the pattern of Hollywood success. Lew Ayres finally gave in (with certain reservations) and is once more at the top. John Beal quit the film city cold, because he retained his beliefs. But John will be back and so will Franchot Tone, who affected a charming compromise.

Louis Hayward discovered he could be the idol today, idle tomorrow. And he was powerless to put up a fight. After years of standing firm, George Brent opened his heart and mind and decided to allow himself the treatment of a star. David Niven and Sam Goldwyn have called off their feud. No longer will David refuse to play certain parts. Cesar Romero sacrificed his rights to a private life, when the studio decreed that he would be the glamour girl's delight.

Of the many examples where Hollywood stars were right for their ideals and wrong for the executive's money, Francis Lederer paid the hard way. How simple it would have been if someone had taken Francis quietly aside and explained that in Hollywood movie stars were only supposed to look handsome and crusade for the box office. But Francis had to discover this and many other painful things, before he realized how wrong he was and how much damage had been done.

Bubbling over with genuine enthusiasm, Francis arrived in Hollywood with two great dreams in his heart. One was to *make fine pictures,* to *give fine performances.* Through the medium of Hollywood

channels, Francis also saw the possibility of carrying on with an ideal that will live with him forever. He hoped his reputation as a star would make it possible for him to talk on radios, speak on stages, give out interviews on his plan to establish world peace.

Granted that it might have been an impossible, impractical task. There isn't a mother, sister or wife who sees Francis on the screen today, who shouldn't revere him for at least trying to avert a tragedy that is threatening the world today. Francis saw [Continued on page 220]

Why GIRLS say

"Mere beauty is nothing" says Marian Marsh. "Talent sells the tickets."

DOES it pay to say *NO* in Hollywood?

Let's ask the girls who say it!

I mean our bachelor maidens, of course—those who see the other actresses marrying into influential studio circles, throwing impressive parties, playing the social and political games for all they are worth.

It has long been a legend that the public prefers its heroines single. When you know there are husbands and children just out of camera range, the fair lady is not quite so romantic.

Or *is* she?

Today a strange new situation prevails. Most of our feminine stars are married and getting away with it. In fact, it looks as though they are getting away with the better breaks, too—thanks to their husbands' pull and their skill at the social racket.

Is a husband a help or a hindrance? And are the married stars in the best spot?

Every unmarried actress has her own opinions. So I started out to learn the facts as they appear to some of our charmers who have so far said *No* to all altar calls.

Sylvia Sidney invited me down to her Malibu house for lunch. (I invariably say *yes* to such proposals!) I burned up the road to her husbandless, seashore abode.

"Hollywood girls marry for love!" Sylvia declared. "That's shown by the failure of most of their marriages. They don't think carefully about husbands. They are not designing. They marry the men they love without thinking of the consequences.

"I know of no actress who has married primarily to advance herself. Most fine actresses marry inferior men. Just as brilliant men usually choose inferior women. Why? I don't know. Maybe there is less strain with a commonplace mate.

"Norma Shearer is the one star who has married an influential man with personal charm and ability. But Norma married for love. Remember, she was a big star before her marriage and I am sure she would have been just as big even though she had not married Irving Thalberg. Marriage has nothing to do with a girl's career!"

The rapid rise which Sylvia herself has made lends authority to her viewpoint, doesn't it?

"But, being a conventional soul," Sylvia went on, "I think every woman should marry.

"Social contacts? Going to parties and meeting influential people? I don't think that's important at all! Ability counts more than luck now. I do not think that an actress has to have love affairs to portray heavy emotions convincingly, either. At fifteen I was playing very emotional roles on the stage, and heaven knows I knew nothing about love!

"Gossips," added Sylvia for good measure, "are the main cause for unsuccessful marriages in Hollywood."

She then walked me out to my car and started me home. I had lunch with Karen Morley out at M-G-M next. (Always eating with lovely ladies. But why not? Everyone should do what he likes best!)

"Most actresses *do* marry for the resultant advantages!" Karen flashed at me. "I could name several who have done so. Being a lady, I shan't!

"Hollywood girls are necessarily very ambitious and sophisticated. And I am certain that a girl who has enough fight in her to rise to stardom, also has enough brains to pick a husband who will be an asset. Not all, but most Hollywood girls say *yes* because they think it will help them. They either want to further their careers or acquire financial security.

"So far as the public goes," Karen reasoned, "it doesn't make any difference whether a feminine star is married or not so long as she is interesting. A colorful wife is better than a single—and, perhaps, dull girl.

"Personally I hate to play politics and I abstain from social contacts. Some women love to entertain and they get roles that way. I don't want to be dependent upon favors. I know then, when I'm chosen for a role, it is because of merit.

"From my own observations, I should say that an actress gets along better without a husband and family. However, when I fall in love I'll marry. If I stopped to worry about the outcome, it would no doubt mean that I wasn't seriously in love."

Inasmuch as Karen and Sylvia didn't agree on the subject, I accepted Anita Page's invitation to dinner in her Manhattan Beach home. (Crazy over food, or, er—blondes?)

"Yes!"

Can A Single Girl Get The Breaks In Pictures?

By
Ben Maddox

"Ambitious girls," says Karen Morley, "pick husbands who will be assets."

"Love will come first," says Sidney Fox.

Sylvia Sidney thinks a fine actress should say "yes" to an inferior man.

"Most Hollywood girls marry for 'this thing called love!'" Anita told me. "They don't marry to advance themselves, or for real love, but for what, in their haste, looks like the real thing. The many divorces in the picture colony illustrate how few find the true 'once in a lifetime' love.

"Audiences are becoming more sophisticated all the time, and care less about whether the heroines are already spoken for off-screen. But I think the fans have a subconscious hope that the stars will stay single. This enables one to dream that someday one may meet and win the beautiful creature or handsome hero."

(Why, Anita, what a mind-reader you turned out to be!)

"Do married stars get the breaks? I don't think that is true in every case. I really don't believe marriage has any effect upon one's career. Perhaps it helps, because it is *supposed* to develop one emotionally. I'm not in love myself, so I can't say for sure.

"Social contacts? *Yes*, they count a lot. If you are seen you

are discussed. If you are a recluse (unless you're Garbo) you are very apt to be forgotten!"

Whereupon I trundled home and endeavored to reconcile the gorgeous Anita's theories with the previous ones. The next morning I decided to get Sidney Fox's answers. I found her busy on a set at Universal.

"I like to believe that Hollywood girls get ahead strictly on their merit," said Sidney, an adorable half-pint of femininity. "Screen girls marry for advantage? No! ! I have never seen so many happy marriages as there are in Hollywood. Never heard so much talk about babies as here.

"To me acting is a job. A very pleasant and remunerative one. When I fall in love and want to marry I shan't let my career stand in the way. Why should your job [Continued on page 221]

No More Divorces!

THE NEW-FASHIONED LOVE AFFAIR OF LANA TURNER AND TONY MARTIN

This experienced columnist knows a scoop when he sees it.

This is it—the strange story he uncovered behind

Lana and Tony's sudden headline friendship

"THE NEXT time I marry, I'll take plenty of time beforehand to think it over. There will be no more spur-of-the-moment marriages for me."

Lana Turner seemed as sure of that as we are of breathing. In fact, everything about Lana these days radiates calm, certainty and a new assurance. People in and out of the studio who have known the emotional redhead for years are talking of the change that has transpired in Hollywood's playgirl. They say it's as though she had grown up overnight. Well, that is exactly what she did.

We'll tell you about this transformation of the "sweater girl" a bit later, exactly how and why and when it happened and the part men played in the rather cruel and sudden metamorphosis.

Then we'll come to the new Lana and the strange romance (strange for Lana, that is) with Tony Martin.

BY CAL YORK

Perhaps some part of this has happened to you, too. Perhaps you, too, were forced to give up suddenly by circumstances that seemed unbearable at the time. If so, you'll appreciate the story of this inexperienced girl in her teens who came down from San Francisco to Los Angeles, enrolled at Hollywood High School and then was literally hurled into a dream world beyond her wildest imagination —the movies.

Lana just wasn't equipped, either by temperament or experience, to take it. And she has taken it, you may rest assured, has suffered, has grown and broadened her emotional scope so that it can include a grand companionship with one of Hollywood's nicest people —Tony Martin.

A year ago Lana wouldn't have understood or appreciated Tony Martin;

wouldn't have found pleasure in the simple pastimes, the love of sports and easy laughter that are a part of Tony. In fact, Lana and Tony had met several times in the past and then had promptly forgotten each other. Nothing clicked, as it did with Lana and Artie Shaw, as it did with Lana and Greg Bautzer. Nothing could click then, for much had to happen to Lana before she and Tony were to laugh their way through to romance.

You might say the whole keynote of the romance of these two people is laughter. Seldom have they been seen when they weren't enjoying a joke; when Lana, with head thrown back, wasn't laughing. Several times on Vine Street we've encountered them lost in laughter, swinging hands or coming out of previews animatedly discussing the picture.

We'd seen Lana with Greg Bautzer. We'd seen her with her former husband Artie

No More Divorces!

Shaw. There was little laughter, little exchange of gay banter with either man. Lana hadn't yet taken out insurance against break of heart that can be acquired, oddly enough, only through break of heart. That gift of the gods is hers now; we doubt if she'll ever lose it.

Night clubs, clothes, excitement, love and glamour once meant more than anything in the world—yes, even career—to Lana. But last week we encountered Tony and Lana on a typical date and we aren't over the shock of it yet. On a Saturday night, too!

PASSING down Beverly Boulevard, we had halted our car to watch the miniature golfers when something about a laugh, a familiar, contagious laugh, drew our attention. There on the links, whanging balls through impossible tunnels, were Lana and Tony and a girl friend of Lana's.

"We were all set for Ciro's," the friend said later, "for Lana only goes to a night spot on Saturday nights now, so as not to interfere with her work. In fact, Lana says it proves just what a small-town girl she really is to go stepping only on Saturday nights. Anyway, Lana spied the golf course and nothing would do but we must play golf. Not only that, but we played every nickel machine on the place and spent hours at the shooting galleries. It was one o'clock in the morning when we finally left the place and went home. I never saw two people in all my life more companionable, two people who could have more fun at simple things, than Tony and Lana."

"You mean to tell us," we interrupted, "that Lana, on a Saturday night, preferred a golf course to Ciro's?"

"I know," the girl shrugged, "seems incredible, but you have to know the 'new' Lana to understand. . . ."

The "new" Lana came about just a few months ago; when M-G-M's little redhead boarded a boat for Honolulu.

"All my life," Lana once said, "I had dreamed of marriage. The wonderful day when, in a white veil and satin dress, I'd walk down the church aisle to become a wife. I'd pictured it over and over in my mind. . . ."

On the day she sailed all she had left of that dream was a sense of bewilderment at what had happened, the tragic memories of the months before that had so completely changed her life.

For in a short time, too much had happened to Lana—the violent romance with Greg Bautzer that had torn her so emotionally; his demands that she leave the screen if they were to marry; the constant quarreling, the indecisions.

Then, out of a clear sky, there had been that sudden strange, unexplainable elopement with Artie Shaw.

He had painted a pretty picture for Lana, Artie had, and one he undoubtedly believed himself; of home and children and work and fireside. He hadn't demanded Lana give up her work. He had simply offered a haven for her torn heart.

Her happiness those first few weeks was something to turn the eyes from, for it was almost out of this world. That's why it hurt so dreadfully when the marriage ended so abruptly. That's why it became so necessary for Lana to get away, to untangle the webs that had enmeshed her. That's why Lana had sailed away to Honolulu.

She never came back. The Lana who loved clothes and excitement and good times above all else disappeared in Honolulu. A new Lana returned, a Lana who had found herself.

"I just know everything in my life has changed," she said. "I've got back everything I'd lost. I harbor no bitter feeling toward Artie. It just wasn't the right time for marriage for either of us."

In Hollywood she began work in earnest. Instead of the usual Sunday cocktail parties that she had loved, she would spend the entire day studying her role for "Ziegfeld Girl" with coach Lillian Burns. Down at the studio they began to refer to her as A. H. Turner—After-Honolulu Turner. That was how marked the change was.

FOR a few brief weeks she tried out the old whirl with Victor Mature. Then she gave it up. Parties and night spots had lost their fascination.

At that moment came laughing, brown-eyed Tony Martin with his talk of football, of baseball, of golf, of music, of fun. Now, at last, Lana was ready to understand and appreciate a companionship such as this.

It was in San Francisco, where Lana had gone to be matron of honor at a friend's wedding, that she ran into Tony He suggested that they go dancing; they walked into the Palace Hotel only to find Artie Shaw playing there. It was a second-act real-life drama, but Tony's easy charm and poise smoothed over the situation. From then on, Lana and Tony were friends.

She went to football games with him on Saturday afternoons, dressed in one of the conservative suits she always wears now, and shouted her head off. She listened to his talk of baseball, learned the players' names and grew excited over the World Series. She took up golf and spent hours with Tony on the golf courses. She sold her violent red car and bought a subdued gray one. Occasionally—but only occasionally—she went to dinner with Tony at Ciro's. She bowled over director and cast by bouncing onto the set early every morning, eager to begin her work.

Her whole personality has undergone a change to the point where acquaintances scarcely recognize the calm, the sure, the happy Lana.

Tony Martin gave Lana laughter and happiness at a time when she needed it most. Thus it is that she has accepted his counsel and advice.

Recently Lana was scheduled to do a benefit. Dozens of other stars were to be present and several times Lana, who loves clothes, had gone to the closet and looked at the beautiful new dress that she could scarcely wait to wear. But when the day came she was feeling desperately tired from her work at the studio. She consulted Tony.

"Don't go," he advised. "You've got to think of your health and your work."

"Can you imagine me?" Lana said afterwards, "eating milk toast in bed and going to sleep at nine o'clock with a new dress hanging in the closet?"

No man has ever given the tender solicitude, the understanding and friendship that Tony Martin has given Lana. He has brought her to a new maturity, given her a new idea of what companionship between a man and a woman may mean. Most of all, he has shown her how to work out her problems.

Hollywood therefore, was not surprised when it was rumored that Lana Turner might be reconciled with Artie Shaw. They remembered what she had said just recently: "I have no illusions now about marriage. I've learned a lot. I'll profit by my mistakes."

For the wisdom of that statement made by the new Lana, credit goes to Tony Martin. Perhaps Lana will go back to Artie Shaw; perhaps she will go on to a new romance; or perhaps she will continue as she is, a girl to whom work is foremost in mind and heart.

Whatever comes to pass, Tony Martin will remain an important milestone in Lana's life; for even greater than love right now is the new Lana Turner, the girl who has found herself.

HOLLYWOOD'S UNMARRIE

BY KIRTLEY BASKETTE

"Just friends" to the world at large—yet nowhere has domesticity taken on so unique a character as in this unconventional fold

The romance of Clark Gable and Carole Lombard is an interesting manifestation of how famous untied twosomes take to one another's hobbies. But calling the case of Paulette Goddard and Charlie Chaplin (top) is something else again. Did they take the vows on Charlie's yacht? Even Hollywood wonders

EVERY afternoon, for the past three years, a little market on Larchmont Avenue, near Paramount studios in Hollywood, has received a telephone call from a woman ordering a choice New York Cut steak.

Sometimes she orders it sent to the Brown Derby, sometimes to an apartment penthouse on Rossmore Street, sometimes to the studio.

Wherever George Raft happens to be dining.

The woman who sees that George Raft has his favorite evening meal, no matter where he may be, is Virginia Pine. She is not George's wife, although there's little doubt that she would be if George's long-estranged wife would give him a divorce.

Carole Lombard is not Clark Gable's wife, either. Still she has remodeled her whole Hollywood life for him. She calls him "Pappy," goes hunting with him, copies his hobbies, makes his interests dominate hers.

Barbara Stanwyck is not Mrs. Robert Taylor. But she and Bob have built

ranch homes next to each other. Regularly, once a week, they visit Bob's mother, Mrs. Brugh, for dinner. Regularly, once a week too, Barbara freezes homemade ice cream for Bob from a recipe his mother gave her.

Nowhere has domesticity, outside the marital state, reached such a full flower as in Hollywood. Nowhere are there so many famous unmarried husbands and wives.

To the outside world Clark Gable and Carole Lombard might as well be married. So might Bob Taylor and Barbara. Or George Raft and Virginia Pine, Charlie Chaplin and Paulette Goddard. Unwed couples they might be termed. But they go everywhere together; do everything in pairs. No hostess would think of inviting them separately, or pairing them with another. They solve one another's problems, handle each other's business af-

fairs.

The build houses near each other, buy land in bunches, take up each other's hobbies, father or mother each other's children—even correct each other's clothes—each other's personalities! Yet, to the world, their official status is "just friends." No more.

Yet George Raft, a one-woman man if there ever was one, is as true to Virginia Pine as a model husband would be. He has been, for three years. He has just bought her an expensive home in Beverly Hills. Recently, when they had a slight tiff, George took out some other girls, but was plainly so torch-burdened he could hardly stand it. He has never seriously looked at anyone else. Nor has Virginia.

Consider the results—strictly out of wedlock.

Before they met and fell in love, George was the easiest touch" in Holly-

HUSBANDS AND WIVES

Gilbert Roland (top) has been Connie Bennett's devoted slave for years, while Connie's titled husband remains in Europe. Just "going together" are Virginia Pine and George Raft—but she orders his meals and he fathers her little daughter, Joan

Another "almost perfect" domestic picture—Barbara Stanwyck (top, with her son Dion) and Robert Taylor. Interests—deep, expensive, permanent—merged when Bob bought the knoll adjoining Barbara's Northridge ranch. Marriage couldn't have worked more of a change

wood. He made big and easy money and just so easily did it slip through his fingers and into the outstretched palms of his myriad down-and-out friends. George, who came up the hard way, still has a heart as big as a casaba melon and as soft inside. But he is more careful with his money now. He invests it—and well.

Before he met Virginia, George's civic interests ventured little further than Hollywood and Vine, the fights, and a few of the better night spots. Now George Raft has his finger in a dozen Los Angeles business ventures and community interests. He is a solid citizen.

Before George and Virginia teamed up as a tight little twosome, George gloried in flashy, extremely-cut clothes. His suits, always immaculately knife-edge creased, had trousers with the highest waistlines in town. His coats were tight across the shoulders, narrowed extremely at the waist. His shoes were narrow, pointed and Cuban-heeled.

[Continued on page 221]

Hollywood

America's ace columnist gives the lowdown

New role: Winchell as a Lieutenant Commander in the Naval Reserve

BY WALTER

Wayne Morris traded his dinner coat for the khaki of a naval aviator, works as a reserve Ensign at the Long Beach, Cal., Base. Giving the greatest performance of his career is Robert Montgomery, a naval attaché at the American Embassy in London

GOOD evening, Mr. and Mrs. America, and all the ships at sea . . . especially the ships of the United States Navy.

In honor of Navy Day, October 27, the editor of PHOTOPLAY-MOVIE MIRROR has dedicated this issue of the magazine to the hundreds of thousands of film fans, ashore and afloat, now wearing the uniform of the United States Navy or Marine Corps. And because I have just finished serving a month of training duty as a Lieutenant Commander in the U. S. Naval Reserve, he has asked me to report on the new and closer tie that exists between Hollywood and the sea arm of the service.

The Navy's interest in the movies has always been keen. On shipboard, and at shore training stations, the frequent showings of films have been one of the most important items on the program of recreation and morale for the enlisted men. Hollywood has gained the further high regard of the Navy, over the years, with such fine pictures of service life as "Hell Divers," "Submarine" and, more recently, "Flight Command" and "Dive Bomber."

Now Hollywood has won a new salute from the service. More than a dozen of the top figures in the film business, while others were sitting around talking about it, have taken off their coats and personally gone to work to help the Navy.

Just a few weeks before he joined the Army, Jimmy Stewart was handed an "Oscar" by the Academy of Motion Picture Arts and Sciences, Hollywood's highest honor to an actor. When the Academy meets again this year, I have a proposal for its members.

How about awarding "Oscars," or

Joins the Navy

on the higher-ups of Hollywood who are now wearing the Navy blue

WINCHELL

at least some sort of recognition to the other movie men who have traded their make-up kits and megaphones for duffle bags?

Take Robert Montgomery, for example.

Right now Bob Montgomery is giving the greatest performance of his life in the most dramatic show the world has ever known. Deserting the screen at the very moment when he was climbing back to the peak of popularity, Bob applied for a commission as a Lieutenant in the U. S. Naval Reserve, flew the Atlantic by bomber and is now stationed in London as one of the naval attachés in the American Embassy.

Originally granted a fourteen-week leave of absence from his contract with M-G-M, Montgomery recently cabled a request that his leave be extended indefinitely and will probably stay in the service for the duration of the emergency.

As one of the naval attachés of the American Embassy in London, a diplomatic post requiring a talent for tact and a capacity for shrewd observation. Bob daily is being called on to exert the same winning manner which has marked his screen performances There is one great difference, though, between his new and his old career

There'll be none of the ballyhoo about Bob's dealings with the British Lion that once colored his association with M-G-M's Leo. His billing, once splashed on billboards the size of a house, will be confined to initials at the bottom of official reports.

Just before he left America, Bob was quoted in a garbled news story as saying he was "washed up" in the movies. We doubt Bob said this. We know it isn't so.

There isn't [Continued on page 223]

Personal emissary of Mr. Roosevelt to South America was Douglas Fairbanks Jr., now a Lieutenant in the Reserve. Lieutenant Commander Wallace Beery is one of Hollywood's best pilots

HOW STARS SPEND THEIR FORTUNES

[*Continued from page 13*]

other odds and ends. She spends between $15,000 and $20,000 a year on clothes—a very modest sum in view of the position she is forced to maintain before the public. In her Beverly Hills home she has a housekeeper, nurse, cook, second cook, maid and two gardeners. For the beach house she employs a secretary. It costs her about $12,000 a year to take care of her fan mail and she pays the Equitable Investment Corporation approximately $5,000 annually for handling her financial affairs.

Her intimates report that her charities are enormous. She gives heavily to the Community Chest and pays one-half of one per cent of her salary to the Motion Picture Relief Fund. It is known that she supports four needy families.

Although most screen stars dislike talking about their charities the fact remains that no class of people in the world gives so lavishly to help the poor. Nine players out of every ten have felt the sting of poverty and are anxious to do their bit.

Marion Davies' donations to charity are almost incredible. She supports a clinic for children in Sawtelle, California, and a large foundling home in New York. She gives generously to many established philanthropic organizations which solicit her aid.

On the other hand, her personal expenses are fabulous. One can only gasp at the lavishness with which she entertains. To attempt fixing the cost of one of her parties would be an utterly impossible task. Her jewels are insured for $500,000.

ANN HARDING, on the contrary, entertains but rarely and then in an ultra-modest fashion for her small clique of tried and proven friends.

Ann's salary is in the neighborhood of $5,000 a week. She owns her home, valued at approximately $125,000, and keeps a staff of four servants, a cook, houseboy, maid and nurse. In addition she employs a secretary and three guards for her baby, Jane Bannister. The guards earn a combined salary of $450 monthly. At present, fifteen workmen, recruited from the army of unemployed, are constructing an elaborate playground for Baby Jane.

She gives generously to many charities, but refuses to discuss her donations. She carries considerably more than $100,000 life insurance, which demands large premiums. The taxes on her property must be in the neighborhood of seven or eight thousand dollars a year and her income tax, according to creditable reports, will amount this year to nearly $100,000. She spends very little for clothes in comparison to many

cinema luminaries. Wallace Beery spends lavishly. Even the series of bank crashes and stock market losses which have wiped out the bulk of his fortune seem unable to slow up his open-handed way of living.

He pays out a goodly sum every month in insurance premiums. Besides his airplane policy, he carries $7,500 on his fine hunting dogs, $5,000 on his gun collection and $250,000 on his life.

He owns his home, worth about $60,-000, and a hunting lodge at Lake Hughes, worth at least as much. He has a Lincoln and a Ford, but does not employ a chauffeur. Four servants, a gardener, cook, nurse and housemaid, care for his home and receive a combined salary of approximately $360 a month. The family clothing bill is in the neighborhood of $600 a month and the grocery bill averages about $300 for the same period. Of course, the biggest deductions from his salary are for income tax and commission to his agent, who receives ten per cent of Wally's pay check each week for negotiating his contract with Metro-Goldwyn-Mayer.

CLARK GABLE, having tasted poverty for many years and not liking its flavor, is industriously saving most of his income. He lived, until recently, in a modest, unfurnished apartment which he rented for about $150 a month. He does no entertaining, spends little for clothes and employs only two servants, a maid and a cook.

Norma Shearer, with a screen income of approximately one-half million a year, spends very little of her own money, according to studio reports. Her husband Irving Thalberg, insists on being the provider. Perhaps her largest expense, excepting the inevitable income tax, is her life insurance, said to be a $1,000,000 policy.

JOHN GILBERT lost heavily in the stock market and since then has been a canny investor. He owns a magnificent Beverly Hills estate but for several years has been living during the summer months at Malibu Beach, where he rents a house for approximately $2,000 a month. He does very little entertaining, dresses modestly and employs only two servants and a business manager. He carries a $1,000,000 life insurance policy. His salary in the last three years has totaled $1,000,000.

Joan Crawford, with a salary estimated to be in the neighborhood of $4,500 a week, is carefully investing the bulk of her income. She owns the home in which she and Doug Jr. live, but he, in common with most other male members to a co-star marriage, pays all the household bills. Joan dresses well, but not lavishly, and manages to hold her modiste bills down to about $15,000 a

year. She employs a studio maid and a driver for her Cadillac and shares a secretary and business manager with Doug. Her voice is insured for $100,000 and her feet for $50,000. She gives generously to charities, entertains frequently, but not extravagantly, and considers her yearly vacation trip to New York, costing about $2,000, her one luxury.

Any article of this kind must necessarily be very incomplete, since to list all of the luminaries of the screen and report in any semblance of detail each one's mode of living would require a book-length manuscript. Many stars whose living expenses are almost incalculable—for instance, Douglas Fairbanks, Mary Pickford, Gloria Swanson and John Barrymore—I have not attempted to include.

A few statements apply to every person in the picture colony. One and all, they give with exceeding generosity to charity; one and all, they realize their good fortune and spend freely to the general betterment of business. There is not a hoarder or a radical in the whole lot.

If that Chamber of Commerce billboard—"Spend Now and Keep Business Alive!"—offers a cure for the world-wide depression, then the rest of the world might well profit by the example of Hollywood.

THE FIRST TRUE STORY OF GARBO'S CHILDHOOD

[*Continued from page 15*]

MRS. LONN, short, heavy-set, was nursing a sick husband, and she was distraught about his condition, but her kind blue eyes lighted up at the mention of Garbo.

"Yes, I remember her well."

I asked some questions about Garbo's childhood.

Mrs. Lönn sighed as she let her mind wander back.

"She was always so happy and full of life. She spent many hours here in my apartment and I liked her very much. Everybody liked her. They couldn't help it."

Mrs. Lönn sighed again.

"I'm not surprised that she has become so successful. It was in her to be an actress. You couldn't help but know that when she was young. . . ."

Mrs. Lönn pointed toward the little courtyard, serene in the morning sun.

"She used to get all the children together out there. And how the children liked her! That was when she was a little older. They came from all around to have Greta teach them how to play games. And you could tell then that she was a born actress.

"She knew then, I think, that she wanted to be an actress. She mentioned it to me many times. She was so fond of pretending in her games, and she was always so happy and gay. You couldn't help but love her. And she was so pretty. . . ."

Here, too, was honest sentiment, delivered in the Swedish language in the hallway of the quaint, romantic old house that was Garbo's first home. A few feet from the door that for a number of years was the entrance to Garbo's home. By a stairway with stone steps, which resounded many times to the echo of Garbo's footsteps as she came and went on her way to school or play.

Mrs. Lönn was busy, and she had many things to think of, with her husband ill. But it cheered her to even think and talk about Garbo; to discuss the little girl who tasted her cookies on baking day. I got the impression that Garbo would have left an indelible impression on the people who knew her as a child, regardless of whether she had become famous as an actress.

For the people here in Stockholm who knew Garbo as a child, as a young girl, do not begrudge her the place she has attained as one of Sweden's national figures. The sentiment among such people is genuine, inspiringly honest.

The house at 32 Blekingegatan is interesting. Through high wood doors you proceed into a hallway, from which steps lead off to the right and left. The hallway then carries through into the courtyard. The stairs have banisters worn smooth by many hands. The various apartments have shiny brass nameplates on the doors.

Leaving Mrs. Lönn, I paused to watch three children playing in that little courtyard, all concerned as ever in the grand game of make-believe. I turned away and walked down Blekingegatan. In the window of a tiny shop, where Garbo once might have bought things, I paused to look at a picture of her, a recent photograph; much different from the mental impression that one gets of a young girl who stood in the center of an admiring group of children in that courtyard, and fascinated them by her innate knowledge of ways to pretend.

But the impression that stays the longest, most purposeful, is that Garbo did not stumble into a career. Chance may have played some part, to be sure, but more fundamental was a certain force within her, that would not be denied. A force that made people believe in her.

For whatever place Garbo has attained in the vaulted and resplendent cathedral of fame was due, it would seem, to a wish. And they say that you get what you wish for if you wish hard enough. That, after all, may be construed as destiny. And Garbo, as one learns to understand her here in Stockholm, is most assuredly a woman of destiny, say what you will to the contrary.

WHAT ABOUT CLARK GABLE NOW?
[Continued from page 21]
ture alone," he went on to explain as we talked at the studio. "In 'China Seas' it's entirely up to me to deliver the goods. I've always been featured with a prominent woman star before. I don't know whether I'm really popular or not." (Oh, Clark!) "Every hit in which I've acted has had a big feminine star of undoubted drawing power.

"You ask how I feel now that I've reached the climax of my career? Good Lord, don't say I have! To me stardom is the real beginning. The chance at last to show what I can do!"

Though he no longer claims that he is a balloon, liable to be popped back to the ranks of the unemployed any moment, he finds success still too new to be accepted casually.

Half a dozen times Clark has been absolutely stranded. With no money and no one to wire for help. He got himself out of the jams as best he could. Don't believe those occasions are forgotten.

Divorce?

Nine out of ten great stars let Hollywood spoil their home life. Clark Gable won't. So here's one marriage I think we can depend upon.

This is his second marital attempt, you'll recall. His first wife was Josephine Dillon, a graduate of Stanford University, class of 1908. An instructor of voice, she did much to train and encourage Clark when he was struggling for a foothold on the stage. Today she lives modestly in Hollywood, teaching other aspiring actors. She and her now famous husband never meet.

In his early thirties, Clark is married to a cultured, charming woman who has the knack of completely satisfying him in every way. Like the first Mrs. Gable, she is older than he. Her two grown children by a previous marriage attend private schools in the East and spend their vacations in California.

"Mrs. Gable and I are thrilled with our new home," he told me with an enthusiasm that belied the trouble-making gossips. "We have always lived in apartments, but I've wanted a house all along. When we came West we stored our furniture in New York. Mrs. Gable went East and had it shipped out. We've had to shop for more to fill the house. And has that been fun!"

The new place in which they just got settled last month is in Beverly Hills. They are renting. The report that they had bought a lot in Benedict Canyon near the Harold Lloyd estate and would build there is wrong.

Suppose you hadn't had a home since you were sixteen and had been on the move the following seventeen years. Then you'd understand what this place means to Clark. He has tenanted all sorts of boardinghouses and apartments ever since he left Cadiz, Ohio, as a youth.

Margaret Livingston's Colonial House, in which the Gables had an apartment last Winter, was luxurious. But it wasn't the same as a home of their own. Besides, Clark loves to putter around a yard. He hopes the neighbors won't raise their lorgnettes when he waters the lawn or digs in the garden on his free days.

I asked him what he intended to do with his movie money.

"Travel!" he immediately replied. "I've covered a good deal of the United States while working at different kinds of jobs. I want to be able to go anywhere the spirit wills, and in comfort. Right now I'm saving as much as I can to guarantee a steady income in the future. We aren't going in for the traditionally lavish Beverly manner! After I get enough salted away to take care of rainy days, we'll start to see the world in style."

His salary is said to be $1,500 a week with bonuses on each film. It obviously isn't nearly so large as his popularity warrants—in comparison with the other stars. It will be gradually upped, though.

Today's Gable is not the man who worked as a glorified extra in several plays which starred Lionel Barrymore on the Los Angeles stage.

"The movies have taught me many things," he says. "I had never had a really nice home, for instance. The idea didn't appeal to me. I didn't particularly care to settle down in one place. Mine was a case of ignorance being bliss! Now I want a home, permanence. I have learned to appreciate the comforts which money buys.

"In another way I'm happier, too. I have the time to get outdoors and take up sports." Husky ever since he worked as a lumberjack, Clark was so busy keeping the wolf from walking in his door that he never had a chance to play tennis and golf. The direct, determined method in which he quickly became proficient in these two games is a tip-off to his character.

The average star would be instructed with all the quietness of a Hollywood first night. But Clark didn't go to a high-toned club where his advent would be a signal for a crowd to rally 'round. He found that the one-armed janitor of his apartment house had once been a fine tennis player. And he and the janitor went daily to the public courts in a Beverly park!

He decided that he ought to be adept at golf. The other afternoon a friend of mine chanced to see him patiently taking a lesson at an inconspicuous little course near the Beverly High School. No flourishes for him!

"If I can't do it well, I won't do it!" This is one of his pet remarks. He has enough Dutch stubbornness in him to mean it. You read that the studio wouldn't allow him to play polo because it was too dangerous? The real truth is that Clark tried it and it was apparent that he wasn't cut out to shine in that sport. He refused to be mediocre, so he quit.

His grace on a horse was acquired for his first talkie. Clark was so anxious to get started in pictures that he gladly accepted the rôle of a hard-riding cowboy in "The Painted Desert"—when he'd never ridden a horse in his life! By the time production began he was cantering about with the aplomb of one to the saddle born.

How do you think he learned to ride? By going to a stylish academy? Not Clark Gable! He hired an old veteran of the range to teach him.

At M-G-M they tell me that Gable is not in the least conceited. Stellar skyrockets are quite apt to acquire superiority complexes. Probably Clark keeps his feet on the ground because he worked so long and so hard before his big break came. He wasn't just a pretty boy, inexperienced and callow. He played in third-rate stock companies and on Broadway, was an extra in silent films.

When he was an unknown actor he covered the walls of his bedroom with photographs of his favorite stars. He idolized them. Now he is at the top of the theatrical ladder himself. If imitation is the sincerest form of flattery, it looks like he's bound to stay up. Every rival studio has unearthed a second Gable. Hollywood has concluded that even brunettes and men—as well as blondes—prefer his type! About his imitators, Clark gallantly maintains a discreet silence.

Will he last? I think so. He isn't temperamental and high-strung like John Gilbert. Not sheikish like Valentino. Not complex like Phil Holmes. He has a depth and virility which the juveniles lack.

What if he plays "nice" rôles? His hit was made as a dangerous he-man. When he has portrayed straight leads he hasn't been as effective. Much has been written about his appeal being purely elemental. If he goes Beverly Hills, will he lose that necessary vigor?

They don't expect to do a lot of entertaining in their new home. Clark already feels the strain which Hollywood puts on its celebrities. He loves to go away between pictures. The Gables are fond of Hotel Del Monte and of the desert. Which reveals Clark's varying dress moods. He likes to dress up and yet he also enjoys turtle-necked sweaters

and old pants! He never goes to Malibu.

Did the mustache he grew for "Strange Interlude" please you? To grow—or not to grow one again—that's what he and the missus debate these evenings!

Soon he will be loaned to Paramount to co-star with Miriam Hopkins in a fiery number entitled "No Bed of Her Own." Imagine Clark and Miriam, who packs an elemental wallop herself, in a torch story like this!

"They won't rubber-stamp me if I can help it," he declares. "I have played a wide variety of parts so far, and I anticipate continued versatility. While they're guessing, they're interested. That's the way I figure.

"I'm in such a peculiar business," he concluded our talk, "that I can't put my finger on anything definite. It's based on public opinion, studio breaks, and downright hard work. I've noticed that the fellow who is given responsibility usually works more seriously than ever. Stardom? I'm satisfied that it's a real job that will keep me out of mischief. Please hope with me that the fans and the breaks will be kind!"

This man comes from the class of people who assume that they have to struggle and fight for what they get. He doesn't think the prizes of the world are handed out on a silver platter. Hard knocks have prepared him to stand the gaff of movie fame.

"Hollywood no longer awes me," he says. "If worse came to worse I could go back to slinging hash!"

He deserves his pre-eminent place on the screen because he's earned it by years of apprenticeship. And because there's no one else exactly like him. To the women he's brought a new brand of love. To us men a masculine and intelligent movie hero whom we can respect.

"I'M NO GIGOLO," SAYS GEORGE RAFT
[Continued from page 23]
he was a taxi-dancer. He learned to grit his teeth and maintain an expressionless face while hefty females promenaded on his toes. He acquired the taciturnity that marks his work in the motion picture "Scarface." If you have not seen that screen drama, by all means do, for it will introduce you to Raft as mere words can not.

Many of the women he danced with were married. They were middle-aged wives who thought themselves wicked when they sneaked away for an afternoon of dancing. No doubt their husbands were trotting younger females elsewhere. But as many more of the women were not married, and from many of these Raft received insinuating invitations to become a gigolo. Some promised fine homes, servants, all the money he could spend; in short, the

same promises that wealthy old men sometimes proffer pretty young girls. In both cases, the older ideas are similar.

Some young girls accept old men's invitations; others do not. Some taxidancers yield to the promises of old women; Raft did not. As far as fat old dowagers were concerned, he retained his youthful innocence. Young ladies? Well, er—let us return to our subject. *The idea!*

Raft refused all such vicious propositions because he possesses an inborn respect for himself. In all fairness to him, it is unjust to term him a gigolo today. In his own words, spoken somewhat bitterly, "I have been given the ill repute without the reward that might have been mine had I done something to deserve the name." It is not right to call a man a thief until the proof is irrefutable. Raft would as soon be described a thief as a gigolo!

"I could never be a gigolo, even if my personal dislike for the vocation permitted," he says. "During the few hours I spent daily in my guise of taxi-dancer, I was sickened by the innuendoes of absurd old women, who were as silly as spinsters playing post-office, and no more serious than a gin marriage. The one or two times during my life when I was tempted to chance a gigolo career, the thought of dwelling constantly in the company of an old hen with chickenish ideas restrained me.

"But sex really has little to do with my antipathy. Sex has its importance in life, and forever will have. My own tastes do not include women in the *roaring forties,* but I can conceive that other men's animi may differ from my own. My principal objection to gigolos is that they abuse masculinity. Man was placed on earth to work and provide for woman. When he shirks his duty and leans on woman for support, he misuses his purpose and his self-respect goes into the discard. I like my self-respect.

"Call me rough-neck! Call me taxi-dancer! Call me ham actor, if you wish.

"But listen, friend: *Don't call me a gigolo!*"

THE ONE STAR WHO HAS NO ENEMIES
[Continued from page 25]
"What about social activities? What is your viewpoint on this aspect of Hollywood?"

She smiled. "I don't play bridge, or go to many parties," she answered. "Actually, Hollywood night life isn't as black as it's painted. In the first place, we have to get up too early when we're working; secondly, most of us are athletically inclined. No wonder visitors dub us provincial!

"The old, old line about burning the candle at both ends still is a very true one. The camera is inexorable. Makeup can cover a few sins, but it can't hide those haggard, late-hour circles which will creep under tired eyes! When I am working, unless I've a night call for more scenes, I am in bed and ready to sleep at nine o'clock. No matter if I've been late getting home and haven't had dinner, or if I should be learning my script for the next day—nothing interferes! Lights go out at nine!

"Maybe," she mused, "it's the climate that causes me to be so crazy about the outdoors. I can't wait to get into the sun. If I woke in the morning and had to moan. 'Oh, another day!' . . . well, I wouldn't call that living!"

An excellent way to waste energy in Hollywood, Jean contends, is to fall for the "being seen" routine. "The truth is that if you are seen in the social spots too much, people will assume that if you have unlimited time to play around you can't be serious about your work. One must conscientiously build a reputation for reliability. The method for that is to stay home, little girl, stay home!"

Common sense from this siren was undermining my armor of doubt. I feebly rallied with the comment that she evidently lived expensively.

"I don't, and it's silly to throw money away. My home is comfortable, yes. But I've always lived so. The house in which I was raised in Kansas City had eighteen rooms! That certainly dwarfs this. And I drive a three year old Cadillac!

"I'm *home*-conscious, if there's a phrase like that. I'd rather have a lovely home than any amount of jewels."

Golf, I was informed, is her passion. "I'm the world's worst golfer!" she exclaimed. "But you ought to watch me pounding the green. You'd think I was training for the championship!"

I ASKED her—in a final endeavor to be stern—what advice she had for newcomers, in view of mistakes she might have made herself.

"So far as the business end is concerned, I'd suggest they not sign a contract for more than a year. If a company wants you badly, they'll take you on that basis. Then, if you click, you can profit on your rise. I got into a mess, myself. For *Hell's Angels* I signed a long contract. Howard Hughes had nothing for me to do for months afterwards, and I was loaned for some of the worst pictures ever made. It's a miracle to me my career wasn't completely ruined by them! . . . As to accepting advice—a normal person has native good judgment, I'd say. When in doubt, consult a clever agent or attorney. Otherwise, be yourself!"

Before leaving I asked Jean if there was any one particular principle she followed in her constant, every-day battle with Hollywood.

"Yes," she immediately responded, "one word sums up my theories as to

the right away to live. It is *gratitude*. Battle? I don't waste my precious hours in fighting, and I have no enemies because I have only friends!

"Gratitude, I am convinced, is a good foundation for progress and success. The law of appreciation has worked marvelously for me. When I played my very first rôle at seventeen, I realized that my career would depend upon whether folks liked me. I make every effort to reciprocate any interest shown in me."

Jean went on, recounting incidents where mutual appreciation has built bonds of friendship between people and herself. She has *faith*. It is this trust in the elemental goodness of people that has freed her from the petty entanglements of a movie career—which has, indeed, enabled her to survive tragedy. Why, she even had faith in *me*—and that chip fell off my shoulder long before I left her house. I can resist anything but sincerity!

JOAN GRABS THE BENNETT SPOTLIGHT
[*Continued from page 27*]
person to find worthy love in Joan's heart.

When their engagement was first announced, one of Gene's closest friends wrote him in sincere opposition. It is characteristic of Gene that he was deeply hurt. He could not understand—cannot believe—this first wife shall not always be his.

Joan, who has never concerned herself much with matters religious, although brought up in convents, has embraced the belief of her husband, and to climax the domestic scene the three-and-a-half-year-old Adrienne is an adore and adoring third in this newest triangle!

Let no one be deceived, Gene as a husband, talented, well-bred fits admirably into the Bennett picture: that of Richard Bennett, the father, and his second wife; of Adrienne Morrison, the mother, now Mrs. Eric Pinker; of Constance and her Marquis; of Barbara, the brunette Bennett, and her radio-famed husband, Morton Downey. But Joan, the darling of the gods, and the certain despair of all men, will, in the future, be a somebody to reckon with. At twenty-one, on the very threshold of life, she has already crowded two normal lifetimes. Will she be satisfied to bask in her continued screen success, in matrimony, motherhood and abundant money? It is certain, as a Bennett, the limelight will be hers, probably the Bennett spotlight. One hopes that Gene will share its glamor. One can but speculate. Joan is very young, beautiful, self-willed. What, after you have seen the new Joan, a deeper, more womanly Joan in "Salomy Jane," do *you* think?

THE BENNETTS ANSWER
[*Continued from page 28*]
tongue of the cat's two-legged sister in Hollywood.

I think, however, that to broadcast those rumors in print revealed remarkably poor editorial taste, as well as a rather uncomplimentary estimate of the public's intelligence.

It is difficult for me to excuse the publication of certain other rumors which were used to garnish and sensationalize the article in this magazine. They were vicious and absurdly untrue. I resent them bitterly, and I want to answer them once and for all.

It was insinuated that I married the Marquis de la Falaise because I wanted to "spite Gloria Swanson" and because I wanted a title for the sake of "social prestige."

I did not meet Henri de la Falaise until after he had separated from Gloria Swanson—and I have never met Miss Swanson! I do not care one iota for social prestige and I have only the heartiest contempt for social climbers. Under the circumstances, please do not charge me with snobbishness if I point out the fact that I do not need, and never have needed, a title to give me social entree.

A still more vicious insinuation was that my husband married me for money. If only the author of the article had paused in her joyous work of vivisection long enough to make the most casual investigation, she would have discovered the asininity of that charge. Without being a Croesus, the Marquis de la Falaise had no need of a marriage dowry.

THE rumor that before our marriage, I forced my husband to sign a legal paper, relinquishing all claim to my property, is too ridiculous to warrant an answer. Really, it never occurred to me —but since the press is now rushing me into the divorce courts, and since a divorce rumor is invariably succeeded by "another marriage" rumor, and that, in turn, by another "newspaper divorce," and so on, *ad infinitum,* I should keep the trick in mind.

Seriously, I wonder if the person, or persons, who edited that article actually believed that it contained some element of truth. The most charitable supposition is that he did, but, if so, it seems strange that he should take such infinite pains to accredit every libelous statement to poor old Dame Rumor! How often, in the history of Hollywood, has that much-maligned lady been "put-on-the-spot" by a reporter who was willing living.

ONE day, a friend calling on her in an effort to cheer her up, brought along a friend of his, whom he introduced as "Gene Markey, the writer." Gene entertained her; she liked him. He more than reciprocated.

to override the limitations of good taste, truth and good judgment for the sake of sensation!

[*Continued from page 29*]

Months ago, Joan was guest of honor at an Assistance League luncheon. Now the Assistance League of Hollywood, as you may know, is a charitable organization which turns all its profits on meals or sale of art goods to charity. Motion picture stars consider it a privilege to help the Assistance League in its worthy work, having their pictures taken lunching at the League.

On this particular occasion, a news photographer asked Joan if she would pose with a young leading man lunching there. Joan graciously consented. She knew the young man because they had made a picture together. Her acquaintanceship with him, however, was only business.

A CAPTION writer for the news photographer's office, whom I would call not only stupid but spiteful minded, sent the picture out all over the country with the title "Another Hollywood Romance —are Joan and Gene breaking up?"

The Assistance League, the occasion for taking the picture, was not mentioned. Just the statement, the two were lunching together—which was not true, and the question asked, where is Gene Markey?

It was malicious, horrid action. Because he couldn't think of anything bright to write, the caption writer had made up a divorce rumor. And that, I have an idea, is the way many of the rumors about Hollywood picture people start—in somebody's low but fertile imagination.

In due time, the picture arrived upon the desk of the magazine editor and that's how he got the idea for the story which was printed in this magazine and which has so outraged Joan, a vast circle of friends and members of her family.

What has Joan to say?

She says: "I think it is time that something is done to stop malicious and spiteful rumors that are disseminated by people who apparently enjoy scurrilous gossip and untruths.

"I have never been more furious than when I read this story about Gene and me—never!

"I didn't know the writer of the article. I had never met her, never made any of the statements attributed to me, and could not understand, and cannot now, why anybody would be permitted to circulate untruths, viciously false, printed insinuations about me, just because I happen to be in motion pictures.

"I was particularly upset because of the untruths and nasty things said about my husband. He was grand about the article, tried to console me, said that it

didn't matter. But it does matter to read horrible things about you and your wife.

"I welcome this opportunity to condemn the whole vicious circle of Hollywood gossip and rumor and to say that whenever the opportunity arises, I for one, propose to nail on the head any or every untruth that is spoken or written about me."

I think Joan is right. I've been reading stories for years which put happily married couples of Hollywood "on the spot," and attacked their right to happiness.

Maybe she and this magazine can start a "new deal."

THE INSIDE STORY OF JOAN'S DIVORCE

[*Continued from page 31*]

uneventful, self-conscious childhood. From the cradle forward, she had led a wallflower existence, subdued by the glamor of two older sisters. At long last, she had been sent away to school. And there, she had ceased to be neglected on the sidelines. People noticed her, liked her. One boy—his name was John Fox—said that he loved her.

All of her life she had had one recurring daydream of an escape from loneliness. A daydream of meeting someone who would understand her instinctively, without words—love her—want to be always with her.

With all the headlong impetuousness of sixteen, she told herself that John Fox was that someone. He told her that he loved her and would always love her. She told herself that the attraction that he had for her was not girlish infatuation; it was love. They eloped.

HER surprised family talked of an annulment action; after all, Joan was under age. Her mother finally decided against any interference. Joan's life was her own, and Adrienne Morrison Bennett trusted her to make the most of it. Perhaps the marriage would last; perhaps it wouldn't. But Joan had the right, her mother decided, to find out for herself.

Joan soon discovered that what she had thought was love was, instead, a delusion. She hoped that the coming of a baby might change all that. Countless babies, countless times before, had brought happiness to couples who had not been particularly happy. That was another self-delusion. Motherhood gave Joan only mother-love.

By the time she was eighteen, she had been a wife, a mother and a divorcee. She had made a mistake which could be charged off to youthful inexperience. All right, she had admitted her mistake, but she would not ask anyone else to pay for it. She wanted no alimony for herself. And she would not ask her own family to support her.

Joan had not been trained for any

career except that of a society girl. But acting was in her blood. That was one thing at which she might be able to earn a living and insure small Diana's future, if she tried hard enough.

"Trying hard enough" absorbed her completely for the next three years. Her life revolved around her career and her child.

She established herself as an actress. Her income passed the point where worry about Diana's future was necessary. Joan relaxed. She began to notice the life about her. She began to go out, meet people, join in parties. Then the unexpected happened. She fell in love. Head over heels in love.

All except those who knew Joan in those days have forgotten that—or never heard of it. Yet, more than anything else, it explains why the Markey-Bennett marriage was destined, eventually, to founder—even if no one else ever happened along.

This love was not a case of self-hypnosis. It was the real thing. Joan had never known before what love was like. Now she learned, for the first time, how quickly and quietly and surely it can pick you up, lift you to the clouds, dazzle you with the shining brightness of the world, then shake you into a forgetfulness of self so completely that you are conscious only of your heart, which alternately aches with loneliness and pounds with joy.

And Joan Bennett found that kind of love, only to lose it.

She became one side of a dramatic triangle. The other two sides were John Considine, forging ahead as a young producer, and Carmen Pantages, beautiful brunette daughter of the theatre magnate, Alexander Pantages.

It was no secret to those close to Joan that she was unmistakably in love. It was no secret to those close to Carmen that she was just as unmistakably in love. No one knew which Considine favored. He was attentive to both. No one had dared to prophesy which girl he might marry—when his engagement to Carmen was announced.

Joan took it very hard—so hard that friends worried about her health. Then, suddenly, she had reason again to be happy. The Considine-Pantages engagement was broken. John was attentive to Joan again. But only briefly. Only a few weeks after their public cancellation of all wedding plans, John and Carmen were quietly married.

At the time, Joan was in a hospital with a broken hip—an injury incurred in a fall from a horse during the making of a movie scene. There were rumors that her screen career was over, that she would never walk again. And her friends were convinced that Joan cared little whether the rumors might be true or not. Life hardly seemed worth the

The next day, she received a little note from him, which read, "Dear Miss Bennett—When you are feeling better, I hope you will allow me to call."

She laid it away with other get-well notes and might have forgotten about it completely, if she had not received constant memoranda in the form of flowers. And when she was finally discharged from the hospital, he was one of the first to call on her. He became one of her constant callers. He was unmistakably in love.

When she could walk well enough again to get about a little, Joan wanted to do just one thing: go away, take a long trip, escape from the scene of her heartache.

She sailed for New York. Gene saw her to the boat—to give her a going-away message that he loved her.

During the long, lonely voyage to New York, she was deluged with radiograms from Gene. When she arrived in New York, she received daily phone calls from him, amusing wires, flowers. He wanted Joan to marry him.

She married Gene on the rebound from a broken romance.

Joan had not known, when she married the first time, what love was. She did know when she married the second time. So perhaps she deserves condemnation for marrying a second time, with that knowledge; perhaps not. You or I might have done as she did, in her place. Joan, after all, was honestly convinced that if she ever could fall in love again, Gene Markey was likely to be the man.

The ironic part of it was that Joan, who had loved someone who did not love her in return, was now in the position of being more loved than loving. The tragic part of it was that, to Gene, their union was not an affectionate companionship which might become something greater. To him, it was already love.

Joan tried to repay him for his devotion. She hoped, as in her first marriage, that the coming of a baby might give her something that was lacking in her life. Something intangible, indescribable, important. She interrupted her career to bear Gene a child.

The years passed. Joan knew fame and wealth and popularity. She had a beautiful home. She had two lovely children. She had a husband who was brilliant, fascinating, devoted. She had every outward reason to be happy. But always, despite all that she said in her interviews and tried to believe herself, something was missing from her happiness. In her heart of hearts, she did not have the love that every women lives to have.

The day Joan Bennett admitted that to herself, that day she knew that her marriage would not endure. It could not.

THE Markeys have moved in one of the most exclusive social Hollywood circles. And so, the Markey-Bennett divorce will split that tight little circle wide apart. For, two of the members of that little group have discovered that they should be married to each other. They are in love. It is late for them to make such a discovery. But, perhaps, not too late. The pity of it is that, in clearing the way to their own happiness, they have to hurt someone else.

But—if they cannot be happy except with each other—what other recourse is there? They have tried to convince themselves that this is not love; that their futures are with their present mates. The efforts have failed. The announcement of Joan's divorce has been on the way for at least six months. Those close to the inner circle have seen it coming.

Gene has taken it very hard. Last Valentine's Day, he sent Joan a heartbreaking Valentine, written by himself, and saying that once she had loved him, and now she didn't and why couldn't they be happy as they had once been happy?

That Valentine arrived too late. Joan's efforts to be happy except with the man she loved had already failed.

What brought the actual announcement of Joan's divorce plans? There was no final dramatic scene. There was only an accumulation of small irritations on both sides—irritations extending over a period of months, mounting to a point where "incompatibility" did describe their disharmony. Until finally Joan—always a realist—asked herself, "What's the use of our even pretending to be happy any longer"? She called her lawyer and told her press-agent to release the news to the papers.

That is the inside story of Joan Bennett's divorce.

READY FOR LOVE
[Continued from page 33]
she admitted, "that I'd be completely willing to devote the rest of my life to my husband and forget, entirely, that present important something known as my career! That is, important only to myself. If I retired tomorrow there would be five hundred others to take my place. One must be practical!"

That word again! Somehow I think it is a litany which she has learned against disaster, against disappointment.

"What do you think of it all?"

"It has been a miracle," she answered simply.

"Do miracles last?" I meditated, more to myself than for her consideration. "Can one forever be the darling of the gods?"

And, half to herself, she answered:

"One must take what comes, with

laughter. So far only the good has come, but one shouldnt expect too much, just hope. . . ." Olivia, you can see, has assimilated some of the serene fatefulness of the land of Buddha, of the Orient which gave her birth. "Besides," she added, "anyone can entertain people— the really important thing is doing good —and being happy."

Happiness? Be assured she will find it, for her future is bright with promise and just beyond the studio gates rides a knight in shining armor. It is he who, eventually, will play the leading rôle in Olivia's true life story, and in his own way coin the phrase "Call it a day!"

JEAN HARLOW—FROM EXTRA TO STAR
[Continued from page 44]
her broken promise was not in vain.

She played a few small bits, appeared in several Christie comedies, and then her great chance came. She met Ben Lyon and Jimmy Hall who told her that Howard Hughes, the oil millionaire from Texas, was re-making his spectacular Hell's Angels as a talkie. He was searching for a leading lady who could put over as frank a love scene as any camera had ever recorded. At their insistence she went to see Mr. Hughes, and after several tests she was notified that she had been given the rôle.

Hell's Angels was released and Jean Harlow became a sensational controversy overnight. She entered the consciousness of a nation, set vogues, and made "Platinum Blonde" a part of the American vocabulary.

When she was a little girl her grandfather had told her that everything had a price. Jean Harlow now found that the price of fame was misunderstanding. As happens frequently, the screen personality and the off-stage personality became confused. To her horror, she found herself handicapped by a ready-made reputation which followed the pattern of the siren in Hell's Angels. No one attempted to understand or know Jean Harlow.

If the studios considered her a showpiece, they certainly did not consider her an actress. However, they clamored to borrow her from Mr. Hughes who flatly refused to loan her. Instead, he sent her off on a personal appearance tour.

But on her return, at her demand that she be put to work, he finally consented to loan her to Metro-Goldwyn-Mayer for The Secret Six.

In the following year she made seven pictures, whose schedule was interrupted only by her appearance at the Chicago première of Hell's Angels. But not one of those pictures cast Jean Harlow as anything but the Platinum Menace—heartless, shrewd, flippant, completely contemptible.

Jean was tired of playing hussies, yet no one cared to discover whether she could really act.

Hollywood had given her fame, but it had not given her satisfaction in her career, so she determined to leave pictures entirely. She and her mother and Marino Bello left for New York one day, and the girl felt that she was saying goodbye to Hollywood forever.

In the East she signed a contract for personal appearances, and that tour lasted a year and a half. When she did return to Hollywood it was to step into the rôle of the coveted *Red Headed Woman*—a picture which was to reveal her not only as an exquisite beauty, but also as a sparkling comédienne. Jean had the courage to play the relentlessly unsympathetic rôle for all it was worth, but audiences liked her because she brought humor to her interpretation. Jean proved to Hollywood that she had something more than physical appeal—a definite talent.

RECURRENTLY in these years when Jean was battling for a solid career, she had proven her capacity for friendship. Men who knew her admired her, not so much as a woman is admired, but rather because she had a logical, scintillating mind, and a nature which never stooped to pettiness.

It was this ability, this near-genius for friendship which had brought her into close relationship with Paul Bern, the producer. Frankly, I think Jean Harlow never really loved Paul Bern. I believe that Jean again made the error of mistaking a great admiration and a community of interest for love. The same thing happened when she married Hal Rosson. Hal was a friend whom she needed desperately in the month following Paul's tragic suicide.

Jean never has been able to understand suspicion. She never has been able to understand why there should be dislike, why there should be lack of faith in any human contact. The storm that broke about her platinum head, following that tragic Labor Day morning when Paul's body was found with his unrevealing goodbye note—was eased for her by Hal Rosson's mute sympathy. Jean again met a man who was a splendid companion. And Jean again married friendship.

Love is selfish. Friendship never is. Jean couldn't understand the transmutation of a friend into a jealous husband, but that change had come equally in Paul and Hal. Needless to say, a marriage based on friendship only has neither the glamour nor the excitement nor the ecstasy of a marriage for love. It is difficult to admit that friendship is insufficient for marriage—that it can only be a small part of marriage.

But Jean found that to be true twice in her life. Whether she will make that mistake again depends largely on the next year. Unquestionably, she is changing. She is like a little girl who has just discovered that there is no Santa Claus. Not that she is disillusioned—for Jean

If it may be said of any woman in is much too sane for that.

Hollywood that she has been tried by fire, it may be said of Jean Harlow. She hasn't been spared ever—anything. And now Jean is learning caution. It is conceivable that from now on she will be a happier person—and less often hurt!

MARLENE DIETRICH ANSWERS HER CRITICS
[*Continued from page 47*]

Trousers Not A "Gag"

I FOUND another one when I spoke of her humor and charged her with perpetrating a joke upon the American public by donning her famous male attire.

"That is not fair," she replied, "to think I dress in trousers to get publicity. I have never done anything to start publicity about myself. I would be afraid to do so because who can control publicity once it is started?

"I wore trousers long before I came to America. In fact, I used to dress up in boy's clothes when I was a little girl. I have always liked the freedom of men's garments.

"It is a career in itself for any woman to be well-dressed. Do you know how much time it takes? Shopping, fittings, advanced styles and unduplicated models to worry you night and day. Why even the accessories—gloves and bags and other things—are too much for me.

"I like old things better. This coat I am wearing is seven years old.

"I have not a single dress for morning or afternoon wear in my personal wardrobe. Only evening gowns. I like them to dance—when I dance."

Another quick smile and another quick change of mood.

Dietrich Is Lonely

"HOLLYWOOD is the loneliest place I have ever lived in. Never in my life have I been so lonely nor stayed home so much. When I first came, I did not think I could stand it—I would not have stood it if I had not had my work.

"Hollywood is more like a country town than a city. It has magnificent distances and no metropolitan life. That electric something that is in the air in big cities is not here. In Paris I can get intoxicated on just the air and the excitement of being in Paris.

"Here I go home quietly. I am

leisurely in everything I do. The home I rent is protected and no noise disturbs me. I have peace, I have security. I have grown not to miss the excitement."

Von Sternberg Explained

"BUT," I interposed, "the general opinion is that you hate America."

"That is something else that is not true. At least, not now. I did not like it at first. The language, the people, the customs were strange to me.

'I came to Hollywood for one reason—to work with von Sternberg. You were about to say something? Something perhaps about Trilby and Svengali? Maybe I should confess.

"I started this talk about my being a Trilby to von Sternberg's Svengali—started it by my frankness about why I had come to Hollywood. It amused me when people thought they were annoying me with the report I had begun, so I did nothing ever to destroy that story.

"I work with von Sternberg because he is touched with genius. He dares to be different. Not always does a picture turn out as he wanted it to but he keeps trying something new.

"They say von Sternberg is ruining me. I say let him ruin me. I would rather have a small part in one of his good pictures than a big part in a bad one made by anyone else. After all, I have the final say in the selection of my story and director. If I prefer to work for von Sternberg that is my business.

"Maybe in saying this for publication, I will give greater conviction to the Trilby-Svengali fantasy. Maybe I will be further misunderstood as to my motive. But don't forget I don't mind being misunderstood."

I can practically guarantee Marlene Dietrich that she will be. Hollywood can't understand a relationship between a man and a woman based upon mutual respect. Hollywood must get a love interest in it somewhere. And nothing anyone can say will change matters.

It seems surprising that this Trilby-Svengali hoax gained any credulence whatsoever. If you recall, Trilby was *not* a strong-minded girl.

But there I go trying to solve the riddle that is Marlene Dietrich. Not that I ever will, for she has no ambition to rectify false impressions nor to explain herself.

"BOGIE"
[*Continued from page 49*]
early days when sometimes he didn't know where his next meal was coming from, he worked just as hard and sincerely as he works now, and even then he didn't like playing straight young juveniles. The parts often enough were sympathetically written and even made

heroes of him, and Bogie played them conscientiously and got good notices. His performance in "Saturday's Children" was full of charm and humor. But none of it was Bogie's stuff. Being just a nice young man in light youthful comedies wasn't good enough for him, and after a while he got a little sick of the parts for which he was always cast, and a little discouraged. And at the same time the jobs became a little rarer and sometimes there were long lean stretches when the pockets were close to being empty.

Because he had made a great hit in the same sort of role in "Saturday's Children" and "Cradle Snatchers," nobody would give him a chance at any other sort of role until Arthur Hopkins cast him in a role as far removed from that of a young juvenile as is possible.

THE play was "The Petrified Forest" and the opening night, although I had nothing whatever to do with it, was for me an exciting occasion and one which I will always remember. Concerned with the play were four good friends, Leslie Howard and Humphrey Bogart, actors, Robert Sherwood, author, and Arthur Hopkins, producer. Gilbert Miller, another friend, had an interest in the play, but the production was Arthur Hopkins'.

Bob Sherwood and Leslie Howard were doing all right for themselves but Hopkins had had a lot of bad luck and three or four failures in a row and I loved Arthur. Also, I knew that for Bogie that opening night meant everything. Not only was he down to his last nickel and beyond that, but he was so discouraged that if the play flopped and he made no impression he was ready to give up acting forever. I knew that he liked the part and that for days before the opening night he had sacrificed his good looks by cropping his hair so short that his head appeared to be shaven. He was putting everything into this chance of showing that he was the excellent actor he knew that he was, and not just an insipid young juvenile. I knew what first night audiences could be for I had suffered from them. That night I could not have been more nervous if the play had been my own.

Well, everybody knows about that night. The play was a great success not only as a play but as a comment on American life. And on the opening night the audience remained to cheer long after the curtain came down. The whole cast came out again and again and from the cast the audience singled out Humphrey Bogart, the boy who had always played pleasant young juveniles, for its greatest cheering. Now Humphrey Bogart was playing a gun man, a cold brutal killer, and he gave one of the best performances ever seen on the American stage.

Back stage that night the dressing rooms were filled with happy people but happiest of all were, I think, Humphrey Bogart and Arthur Hopkins. Even so, I doubt that they were any happier than myself. That night we celebrated until the morning papers appeared and then we celebrated some more, for the papers thought that Humphrey Bogart was as fine an actor as the audience thought him. And those of us who were celebrating knew that not only was he a fine actor but a swell guy as well, because that night Bogie was very humble.

From then on there are few incidents in Bogie's career which most picturegoers do not know. After "The Petrified Forest" Hollywood wanted him. He had been out there two or three years earlier when picture companies paid very little attention to him. I was there at the same time, working and trying to understand, without much success, how Hollywood figured. Only to me it didn't make so much difference because I was never dependent on Hollywood or the theater for a living. But Bogie was an actor and that was different. Nevertheless, during the first attempt to get a break I never heard him complain or turn bitter.

After "The Petrified Forest" things changed. Hollywood wanted him and he gave Hollywood in return all he had, which is still worth more than Hollywood is paying him.

When Paul Muni differed with Warner Brothers on "High Sierra," Muni walked out and Humphrey Bogart stepped in. I think Warner Brothers were lucky because I am sure that in the role in question Bogie's performance is better than Muni's would have been.

BEFORE "High Sierra" Bogie played

Were Mary Astor's parent's justified in demanding support from her in court?

While we don't know full details, we do know that Mary has always lived sensibly herself and that she's one of the sweetest girls in Hollywood. There may, however, be some very good reason her family had to maintain a lavish establishment and gigantic swimming pool; if so, we feel certain Mary would have been reasonable without taking the situation to court.

in a picture made from one of my own stories, "It All Came True." It was a difficult part—not the conventional gangster role into which Bogie had been forced again and again, but that of a gangster with a grim sense of humor who is kidded throughout by the story itself. And there were other complications, because at one point the writers attempted to turn the character into one of unrelieved menace. The picture was partly shot before the producers discovered that this was a mistake and attempted to remedy the error by retakes and rewriting. However, the character still remained a little muddled. Nevertheless, Bogie turned in one of the best comedy performances I have ever seen and audiences took him to their hearts wherever the picture was shown.

In Hollywood Bogie ran into the same danger to a career which had confronted him years earlier in Hollywood. There because he was so good as a young juvenile they never wanted to let him play anything else; in Hollywood because he was a magnificent gangster they have insisted on his being a gangster forever. I, myself, believe Humphrey Bogart is a good enough actor to play any role you give him and make it vivid and real.

Few people in pictures have played so many parts exactly the opposite of their own characters. Bogie is about as far from being a cold, inhuman gangster as it is possible to be. He is intelligent and kind and even sentimental and generous. He has a great love and understanding for animals and in his house a half dozen dogs live in peace and comfort.

Few people have known such violent ups and downs. It's all right now. He's arrived. And I know no one out of a pretty big acquaintance embracing most of the world who deserves great success more than Bogie. He's a swell guy.

LET ME GROW UP
[Continued from page 53]
BETTE made personal appearances in the East and when I asked her whether she liked it her answer surprised me.

"I didn't want to do it. I was afraid people would say, 'Who is she?' Personal appearances always give me the fear that the audience is going to be terrifically disappointed in me when compared with what they see on the screen. But it rained as the train pulled out of the Los Angeles station."

She is very superstitious about rain. She believes it always brings her good luck. This belief goes back to the time when she appeared on the stage. If it rained on the opening evening of a play, the show had a good run. If the weather was clear, the play was sure to be a flop.

Bette is extremely modest about her work. She never views the rushes after a day's work. This is because she saw the rushes of her first picture and disliked her screen likeness so much that it was two days before she regained enough confidence to do her best work.

"I never would be where I am if it weren't for Mother," Bette says. "That sounds trite, but in this case it is true. She seems to have a sixth sense. Even before I was on the stage I remember distinctly one night when I was at a dance and Mother was attending a play. She got the feeling that something was going to happen to me. A friend of ours was sitting back of her. She asked him to take me home immediately. He did. And the car in which I would have returned had an accident. Two people were killed. Do you wonder that I pay attention to her intuition?

"When I decided to become an actress Mother was very happy. It was doing the thing she had wanted to do, for when she was a girl she was ambitious to go on the stage. She encouraged me at every turn. When I was discouraged, it was she who advised and helped me over the rough spots. Without her help I would be lost."

WHY I STAY MARRIED
[Continued from page 55]
hands. When I come home at night and am too tired to talk about the studio or what I've been doing I don't have to. Ria doesn't care. There are dozens of other things, vitally important, to talk about. On the other hand, if I do feel like talking about what has been going on, she is as keen about it as I am, and knows as much. If I want advice, I get it.

"I could not, I would not, be married to an actress. In the first place, one professional ego is enough in any home. Two egos of the same stamp would blow the roof off Buckingham Palace. If I were married to an actress, and I never will be, here is what would happen: We would have had a bad day, each of us. We would come home with nerves frayed and teeth on edge and we would want to talk about it; we would want peace and comfort and sympathy. We wouldn't get it, either one of us. And all hell would break loose. In the course of many times like this one or both of us would look for comfort and sympathy elsewhere. Or we would have had a good day in the studio and would be full of it, wanting an admiring and appreciative audience, eager to do a little strutting, a bit of boasting. We would both want the floor, in other words.

"I don't have to combat that situation. If I'm tired and fed up, Ria has other things to talk about; other things to do. And because she is a mature woman

and knows men and how to handle them, she does just that. If I'm keen about something, want to blow off steam over some scene I think I've done especially well, I can do it without having the nervous fear that she will want to break in with some similar bragging of her own.

AND just as I wouldn't be married to an actress neither would I be married to some sweet young thing, many years my junior, even though she were a non-professional and stayed at home. A younger girl could not know what it is all about. She would not be able to cope with the difficult and trying life of an actor's wife in Hollywood. Because wives in Hollywood *are* on a spot and don't you forget it. A young girl would be jealous. She would be suspicious. She would be resentful. Resentful of all the limelight flattery shown me. She would, at least subconsciously, crave the same flattery, the same attention for herself. She would be an easy victim of all the well-meaning 'friends' who would come to her and say, 'My dear, I think you ought to know, Clark and that So-and-So, etc., etc.

"Things like that do happen. Ria had a lot of it to put up with during our first year in Hollywood. Any number of people came to her with little tales calculated to prove that I was stepping high, wide and handsome with this one or that. I was going here, I was going there, I was having an affair with a certain star . . . did she know . . . what did she intend to do? It was rather hard for her, just at first. It takes a good deal of adjusting. And only because my wife is a balanced, sane and wise woman did she survive.

"And also because she believes me. No actor should marry a woman to whom he cannot tell the truth and be believed. Ria knows that I always have and always shall tell her the truth. And so, when people came to her with trouble-making tales they got no reaction. Which is one reason, no doubt, why they have about given it up of late. It's no fun to try to stir up trouble where it can't be stirred. Ria always came to me and said, 'I've heard this or that about you and so-and-so, Clark, is it so?' And I would say, 'It is not so.' And that would be the end of it. I would never hear about it again. No nagging. No subterfuges in an effort to find out. I'd told her the simple truth and she knew it.

"Because Ria is a woman who has been about, who knows the world and life, she is intelligent. She knows how to handle life and how to handle men. I have none of the uneasy fears and compulsions under which many actors have to labor. If I forget to phone her during lunch hour, I do not have to spend the rest of the day with the uneasy knowledge that when I get home that night I shall be greeted with tears and reproaches, martyred looks or suspicious sniffs. I do not have to work on half a cylinder because I fear I'll get the devil all evening. If I do not call at noon, that's that. Ria doesn't even expect me to. She'd probably be out somewhere if I did.

"My wife has never been on the set with me since we've been in Hollywood. *Not once.* Once or twice, when I've had to work late, she has come to the studio to have dinner with me and has left immediately after dinner.

MARRIAGE is a see-saw. If the balance is an uneven one, one or the other crashes down. Our marriage balances evenly and one side is equally as important as the other.

"Ria enters into every one of my interests. She makes them hers—or she makes me believe that they are hers. Who has said that many a good actress is a good wife, but more good wives are good actresses? Whoever did, spoke the truth. Between you and me, I've a pretty good idea that Ria does a lot of things with me she wouldn't do if it were not for me. Hunting, for instance. I don't honestly believe she gets a big kick out of that. But she plays the part with such realism you'd never suspect.

"For my part, I share her interest in the children, in their plans and interests, in what they like to do. For a time the girl thought she would like to be in pictures. Louis B. Mayer saw a picture of her and offered to have a test made. I said that I'd make it with her and I did. Clarence Brown directed us. It wasn't so good and she gave the idea up, then and there. Now she is interested in one particular boy and I imagine she'll marry before long and settle down. Personally, I'm rather relieved. I think it is a better life for her, better chances for happiness, and so does Ria.

"Allen is absolutely anti-movies, or rather, he's simply not interested at all. He never asks to come to the studio. He takes no interest whatever in me as a movie star. I think he forgets most of the time that I *am* one. I take him on hunting trips with me. We play ball together and swim and ride. Their friends are in and out of the house so much, both girls and boys, that they accept me, too, not as a man in pictures but just as a man. Allen is really funny. The other night he and Ria and I went to a movie together. As we came out Scotty, MODERN SCREEN's photographer, was there and wanted to take some snaps of Ria and Allen and me. The boy wouldn't do it. He edged away. He said, 'Aw, I can't be bothered. You and Mother do it.' We did."

WHAT'S THE MATTER WITH LOMBARD?

[Continued from page 57]

mathematics, then, to figure that some of the places she doesn't go, some of the things she doesn't do. Carole will, Fieldsie told me, forget and neglect the doing of things which may be of some advantage to her. She never neglects doing those things which are of advantage only to others.

This, by the way, is a matter Lombard never discusses. She has the quaint and lovable idea that if you do good you negate it by talking about it. For it is a fact that Carole does a great deal of good. Not by the simple, customary star-formula of writing out checks. She takes bowls of soup, made in her own kitchen, to the poor, to tuberculars, to places and persons that endanger her own health. She always finds time to comfort those whose lives are not lived among the stars.

THEN, Carole takes her work very seriously. This is something few of us, even here in Hollywood, have ever fully realized. For Lombard seemingly touches Life with light, laughter-tipped fingers. But this antic attitude, I know now, is only seeming. For Fieldsie told me that when Carole is playing a character on the screen, she *is* that character all the time, at home as well as on the sets. When Carole was playing the squirrelly dame in "My Man Godfrey" and the others, Fieldsie nearly went nuts. Because Carole was being squirrelly all over the place, laughing her lunatic laughter as she poured the breakfast coffee, knocking over the furniture. You couldn't get a word of sense out of her.

And then, when she again went dramatic in "Made For Each Other," playing the part of a life-saddened woman, she would come home from the studio every night and sit down and cry. She would cry for hours. She couldn't talk to anyone without choking up. Having a child in the picture, she would go all quivery at sight of a child in the streets. So that, when Carole is in production, she is either too wild to know what is going on or too depressed to care.

Carole's whole life, it should be remembered, is predicated upon the twin sources of laughter and tears. As a small child, with her father so desperately ill, in such constant pain that he could only live at all with the help of drugs, she knew the dark shadows of hovering death.

And there is the gallant tale of that automobile accident in 1925—that Sunday afternoon when the young Carole went driving with the son of a prominent Hollywood banker. They were driving through Beverly Hills. The car struck a bump. The catch of the removable seat unhinged and Carole was catapulted, face forward, into the windshield. The wind-shield shattered and the beauty which was Carole's became a long, blood-masked gash from her upper lip to the middle of her left cheek.

No anaesthetic could be administered when that mangled face was sewn together. The surgeon did not want the facial muscles to relax while he sewed up the wounds. Only a slight scar now remains of what was once wrecked beauty. But certainly there must be an inner scar, not so slight, the result of those nine months when Carole moped about the house, sick at heart, believing that she must go through all her youth, all her life, unsightly in the eyes of men, her career ended before it had fairly begun. Surely something pretty strong was forged out of that frightful ordeal.

It was from that holocaust that she went to Mack Sennett. "Get her over to Sennett's," a friend advised her mother. "They care more for figures than for faces over there, anyway, and she'll forget herself in the middle of that mad bunch. She'll find her stride again." She did. She hit the stride of laughter, of doing the Charleston at the Hotel Ambassador on merry-making evenings, of cutting capers, playing jokes. There's nothing the matter with a girl who can take disaster with a custard-pie caper, is there now?

THEN, too, Lombard is a fuss-budget. It takes time to be fussy. When she travels, for instance, Fieldsie says that "she is so neat about everything that it's just like being at home." When on a train, for instance, she always spreads dainty, crêpe de chine blanket covers over the Pullman berths, "so the place will look homey and attractive," she says. That's all right. That's fastidious and charming.

But that isn't all. Oh, by no means. For Carole also has every article of wearing apparel packed (she does her own packing) in the most painfully systematic fashion. At any hour of the day or night she can "lay hands" to anything she may happen to want. If a travelling companion has a migraine, a tummy ache, a fit, Doc Lombard is right there with the proper remedy. On a recent trip by plane two of the passengers got air-sick. Before the hostess could get to them, Lombard was there with the proper first aid. There is the gypsy in Lombard, too, of course. But it's a nice, capable gypsy who keeps her earrings, bandanna and stiletto in apple-pie order.

She's the same about everything. When she plays tennis, she not only wears the proper tennis dress and shoes, but she also has the right-weight coat handy to fling over her shoulders when the game is done. She always has an extra pair of shoes along so that, if her feet hurt, she can change.

When she goes duck-shooting with Clark and the Andy Devines—this duck-shooting quartette is now so familiar to the ducks that they call them by their first names before they die—Carole is equipped. Not in "what-the-well-dressed-duck-shooter-will-wear" type of thing, but in old cords and a shapeless sweater. For Carole doesn't ride, shoot ducks and hunt quail in order to be Gable's shadow—when Gable can't go, Carole goes alone. She has her own shot, and plenty of it. She has her bags for her own ducks. She is equipped with all the first aid remedies which might be required in case of any casualty.

When she goes hunting with Gable, Carole is no delicate doll lopping on Gable's broad shoulder. Not if he knows it, or she, either. She draws a bead on her own bird—and what a shot she is! She even wades hip-high into the marshes to retrieve her own birds. Gable has made it plain to her that he will not act as retriever for her birds, not he. And Lombard, you can be sure, would not have it otherwise.

When she and Gable shoot at the same bird there is a rough and tumble brawl as to whose bird it is, whose shot brought it down. And Gable admits that he doesn't always get the best of the scrimmage. And then, when the day's shooting is done, it's Lombard who is on hand with steaming coffee, drinks, hot food, whatever the hunters require. Carole is the one who comes prepared with extra blankets, cords and shirts for those not so far-sighted as she.

Lombard, her friends tell me, has a splendid sense of balance about everything. Furiously energetic, she always rises at seven. No breakfast trays in bed for Mrs. Gable. But she also goes to bed early nights. Neither she nor Gable care for night life and so don't have any to speak of. Their tastes, their likes and dislikes are so genuinely mutual that it's like something made to order, the mating of these two.

SHE doesn't diet, not Lombard. She doesn't have to 'cause she "eats right," her friends will tell you. For instance, if she has a heavy dinner one night, she will eat a light breakfast the next morning. If she goes to bed on a light dinner, she will have bacon, eggs, toast, all the fixin's the next morning. This balance prevails in everything she does. If she hasn't played tennis for some time, she is careful to play only one or two sets when she begins again. She doesn't overdo anything. Under her seeming levity and lightness there is a substratum of common sense as hard and dependable as the Rock of Gibraltar.

She is, further, a punctilious house-keeper. The Gables live well but, when eight pounds of butter are used one week as against seven pounds the week before, she finds out why. She can spot dust a mile away. She does her own ordering and planning of meals and, when possible, her own marketing. Often she will call her friends and say, "Darling, I found the most divine new butcher in the Valley. His lamb is two cents a pound cheaper than I've found it anywhere else. Better meat, too. Try him." She is, herself, a superb cook. I'm sure that she didn't reach Gable's heart via his tummy but she could have.

She is economical in almost every way. She buys fewer clothes than any other star in Hollywood. And she isn't the least bit stuffy about them. If she buys something she especially likes, she tells her friends where she got it and says, "Go and see if it looks well on you and have it copied." This, in a town where one lady-star swoons if another lady-star enters a room, wearing a duplicate model of her gown!

NO, THERE is nothing remotely snobbish about Lombard. She certainly hasn't that excuse for being as evasive as she has been of late. She is, Fieldsie told me, wonderful with her servants. She has had the same cook, Jessie, for years. And Jessie is one of the family. When Carole comes in from the studio and says, "It's been a tough day, Jessie," Jessie just doesn't talk. She listens for the running of the bath water, she serves dinner quietly. When Carole says, "It's been a good day, Jess, everything swell," Jessie does talk, relates all the little household happenings of the day. Carole never gives orders. She always says, "Jessie, what do you think about duck and wild rice for dinner tonight, huh, tell me?" Well, they say that you can tell a lady by the way she handles her servants.

Carole still drives herself around in her old car, because she likes to drive herself. She could have a couple of town cars if she wanted them, but she figures that, apart from the initial purchase price, town cars cost money to run, to fuel, to re-tire. When they are out of cigarettes, Clark and Carole will hop in the car, drive down to the corner drug store and buy a package of smokes. Neither of them wants any part of the show-offiness of stardom. Both of them care for the outdors, old clothes, horses, guns, tinkering with cars and having fun.

So now you have it. Now you know what's the matter with Lombard. What can you do about a gal like this? Lord love her, you've got me!

KAY'S DREAM OF ROMANCE
[Continued from page 58]
cis announced that she was finishing her contract in as short a time possible in order to take a year off, was that she had plans for a baby. But Kay denied it —the bunnies will do for a while. Then there was another report—that she was going to Europe, but that, too, was blasted. Then what?

KAY FRANCIS, in this breathless, non-stop race from one picture to another, has just one goal in mind—an overwhelming longing that has gone unfulfilled for three years.

"Ever since my entrance into films in 1929," she told me, "I have hoped against hope that the studio program would afford me sufficient leisure to make a hurried trip to Havana. Contrary to any reports, I do not plan to retire from the screen. Nor do I intend to take a full year for the trip; it will be three months at the most.

"I know I need a rest, and no doubt it is the Spanish blood of my grandmother stirring in me, which suggests Havana. I have been there once, but I must go again. It is something entirely different from the ordinary tourist's curiosity. Really, I have had what amounts to a hunger for it ever since I went there for the first time.

"I couldn't afford to return then. Besides, my theatrical ambitions overshadowed everything else, and for the next few years I thought of nothing but succeeding on the stage. By the time I was able to consider the trip financially, I was never able to get away at the right season. Winter is the season in the East Indies, you know, and winter is a star's busiest season in the studios.

"But now I'm beginning to see my way clear to go. I am ploughing ahead as swiftly as studio schedules will permit. I'm going to complete as many pictures as they'll let me in the least possible time—and then, for that long vacation—Havana—my honeymoon."

OUT OF TRAGEDY TO HAPPINESS
[Continued from page 59]
and went about the business of making their marriage a happy one. Frank discarded his real estate business and took over the management of Helen's affairs.

And then Helen learned that she was to be a mother. Her cup was overflowing. They went East, to Brooklyn for the happy event and in October, 1932, the baby arrived. Returning to Hollywood, Helen signed a long term contract with Paramount and *A Bedtime Story*, with Chevalier, was her first assignment.

"I was surprised at myself when I saw the first rushes," she admits, "I knew that I was far more happy than ever before, but I was astounded that it should reflect to such a degree from the screen."

Helen believes that one of the greatest mistakes that a girl can make is to marry too young.

"At the age when I first married, no girl can possibly know her own mind. The hero of her dreams at that age would be a man she wouldn't look at five years later. She thinks of romance and none of the practical business of marriage and of course, except in exceptional cases, it doesn't work.

"Frank has made me happy where Clark failed because he is a man I can admire and respect, as well as love. He is kind, considerate and patient and he is not a boy."

No movie household in all Hollywood lives more quietly than that of the Frank Woody's. Anna, the nurse who took care of Helen as a baby, is both nurse, manager and major domo.

"We almost never go out in the evenings," said Helen, "because we enjoy being at home too well."

"I DON'T see anything unusual about our marriage or our happiness," said Frank Woody to me as we sat in his office in a Hollywood office building. "Making pictures is a job just like any other job. It's when both husband and wife lose themselves so completely in the movie atmosphere that they can find no other interests, that marriage out here fails. Helen and I don't allow ourselves to do that.

"I take care of her affairs and at home we seldom mention pictures. When we go vacationing, we pack into the mountains and never go to Caliente or the places where picture people congregate. Helen had a terrible experience for a young girl and I'm glad that I can make her happy, that's all."

Those who remember Helen in her older pictures, *Her Man and Millie*, watch her the next time she is on the screen and see if you don't agree with me that her happiness is evident. In *Heartbreak Town* where so many find only disillusionment and sorrow, Helen Twelvetrees has found her happiness.

WHAT'S WRONG WITH HOLLYWOOD LOVE?

[*Continued from page 62*]
most of the Peggy Hopkins Joyce romances. She has sought so much publicity (she, too, was reported interested in Jack LaRue) via the romance route. All the world loves a lover—but certainly not a lover who is using love as an excuse to get her name in the paper.

Thus there is around Hollywood love a cloud of cynicism you could cut with a knife. The question is asked over and over again. "Is this romance on the level or is it just for publicity?"

THERE'S another way in which ro-

mance is put to political use. Remember that in Hollywood there are many more women than men and every man is able to do something to further a girl's career. Once Bill Boyd said to me, "Dorothy and I don't go to parties because we're apt to quarrel if we do. Foolish little girls make a play for me not because they like me, not because they even know me, not because of anything but that there might be a chance for them to play a lead in one of my pictures. And men make a play for Dorothy because she is attractive and beauful. But no matter how much in love you are the aftermath of this is bad and a doubt stands between the two people in love. Dorothy and I had rather stay away from parties." Thus you can see how it is possible for a scheming woman to step between two real sweethearts. That's been done before in other towns, but in Hollywood the women scheme in a more deadly fashion than anywhere else—since the stakes are so much higher. And if they win they win so big.

Yes, every man in Hollywood can do a favor, so when a girl is interested in the man is doubtful, doesn't know whether it's real interest or "good business." That's why nice boys like Joel McCrea play the field.

One of the loveliest romances in Hollywood at the present time is that between Myrna Loy and Ramon Novarro. Those who saw the meeting said it was love at first sight. Of course there were "those who saw the meeting." It happened on the set and there are plenty of witnesses to every Hollywood love encounter and it's not only the 150 reporters who report it. It's the people of Hollywood who do the gossiping. So, instantly, the Loy-Novarro romance was broadcast.

Thus far it has thrived. It is in its early stages and is very genuine. Ramon has never been "the ladies' man" type. There have been very few romance rumors about him bcause he has led a rather cloistered life, but now these two seem to be in love. The list of their mutual interests is long—both enjoy music, both love quiet and composure better than the usual round of Hollywood revelry. They differ in religious beliefs but Ramon is a liberal Catholic and Myrna has a religion of her own. While Ramon is in Europe, Myrna has leased his beautiful modernistic house.

So it would seem, somehow, that this was a romance that would endure. Everything, apparently, is for it—nothing against it except the fact that the scene is played in Hollywood. It will be interesting to watch what happens. I do not want to put a printed blight upon it, but we have seen that Hollywood is a bad town for romance.

Now here's another important obsta-

cle that stands in love's way. All of the people in this amazing town have careers—and a careerist is selfish. He thinks first of himself. He must in order to have a career, but love should learn the meaning of sacrifice and there have been only a few girls in pictures who, when it was necessary, gave up their careers for love. Ann Dvorak is one of the very few. But, ninety-nine times out of a hundred that career comes first.

I'M going to tell about Hollywood's latest romances and then let you—in the next few months—watch and see for yourself what happens. There are Wera Engels and Ivan Lebedeff. Their coming together was one of those strange Hollywood tangles.

It seems that Gary Cooper liked Wera and was taking her out places when the Countess de Frasso returned unexpectedly. Gary was taken up with Wera so the Countess began to be seen places with Ivan Lebedeff. One day the four of them met in the Brown Derby. Wera and Ivan were introduced. Then Gary began being the Countess' escort again and Wera and Ivan—perhaps to console each other—began being seen everywhere.

Other romances for you to keep your eye on are those of George Raft and Marjorie King; that handsome Randolph Scott and Virginia Gaye (she's Sari Maritza's manager); Phillips Holmes and Florence Rice, Grantland Rice's daughter (and they say they are secretly married. That's what Hollywood says); Helen Mack and William Janney; Ralph Forbes and Martha Sleeper; Douglas Fairbanks, Jr., and Benita Hume.

Hollywood has already watched and commented upon Jean Harlow as she went around with Howard Hughes, Jay Widden, Jesse Lasky, Jr.; then Gary Cooper with Evelyn Brent, Lupe Velez, the Countess, and now—his new flame —Lilian Harvey; Clara Bow going with Gilbert Roland, Victor Fleming, Gary Cooper, Harry Richman and, at last, marrying Rex Bell which, so far, has been grand; Norma Talmadge in love with Gilbert Roland and now George Jessel.

So love comes and goes in Hollywood because love isn't given a chance. If you're seen three times with the same man in Hollywood you're rumored engaged. But there's more than that— there's the political jealousy. When anybody is close to an important and famous star there are always dozens of others who are trying to oust the favorite to become close themselves. When Alice White was a big star and Cy Bartlett was the steady boy friend dozens of people were trying to influence her against him, telling her he gave her bad advice, that he was a handicap to her career, that he was not working for her best interests, etc., etc., etc. Some of these people who told her these things might have been sincere but most were trying to oust Cy in order to stand in well with a famous star. Does it remind you a little of old-time court intrigue? That's just what it is like. Incidentally, Cy and Alice have split and now Alice is going around with John Warburton.

A few people have found real and lasting romance in Hollywood in spite of all of these menaces. A few couples have remained in love both before and after they were married, but they are people who have definitely set out to beat the game. And for the most part Hollywood is no place for the steady flame of love.

You may envy the stars their beauty, their money, their fame if you want to —but don't envy them their romances. True love just doesn't have a chance!

PHOTOPLAY-MOVIE MIRROR DANCING SCHOOL
[Continued from page 67]
stand perfectly still in one square-foot area on the floor and do the step. When this happens, you've got it.

SLOW Lindy Hop and Variation: The Lindy Hop (see diagram on page 71 for basic step), a blood-brother to the shag, covers four counts, except the first two are a sliding skip. We'll call it one-and-two—on the "and" you slide your off foot up and that makes the skip. Then it's just steps: three, four. On a crowded dance floor the step can be done on a dime, but we'll walk you through it to show you the rhythm. One way to understand the diagram is to pretend your index and middle fingers are legs and put the tips of them on the footmarks. Then watch what your fingers do as they dance along.

Jackie and Bunny show you their favorite Lindy Hop variation in Photos 3 and 4 on page 50. For the two steps that cover counts five and six, seven and eight, they face each other and kick forward, first with the left foot, then with the right. You'll notice from the picture that the right kick goes between the feet of the partner and the left kick on the outside. Then, for the quick one-two-three count, Jackie takes Bonita's left hand with his right and they back away from each other with long steps, getting all the way back on the "two" count. He pulls her to him for the third step and they go right into a repeat.

That backing-away business needs some description, by the way. The steps are done in a swing slide-shuffle, with the derrière out and knees very straight. You swing your ankles out a little as you used to do in the Charleston. It's

all kind of sedate jitterbug stuff and fun if you're with a young crowd.

THE Balboa: Remember that sway-shuffle step some tap dancers break into sooner or later, when they look as if an invisible hand is holding them a quarter-inch off the floor and slowly waving their limp bodies back and forth so that their feet just brush the wood? That's the basis of the Balboa, which is done to the catch-time fox-trot we described at the beginning of this month's lesson. The distinguishing feature of the Balboa is that while you are doing it you cross one foot over the other for one or two steps; and further, that practically anything you want to do with your feet is okay, so long as it's a light, fast shuffle.

Jackie and Bunny have their own version, as you can see. (Photos 5, 6 and 7, page 67). They stand side by side, holding hands, and (1) kick forward with the right foot; then (2) they cross the right foot over the left, shifting the weight to it, and (3) bring the left foot over to the left. Then they just walk out of it to the right, turn to face each other and repeat, starting on the left foot this time instead of the right.

When you do this next turn you're just being fancy, although it's no trouble at all for the boy. The girl has to know how to whirl like a dervish and end up facing the right way, on the right foot, and not dizzy. You can break into it at any time, on any step you like; Jackie and Bunny chose a favorite of their (see picture, lower left) in which he turns to one side and she to the other, alternating each step, for two or three steps. Then Bonita puts her right arm behind her back so that her hand reaches Jackie's right hand as he leads her. He takes it and swings her away, stepping back himself.

Whirling to her right, Bunny takes one full turn away from him, pauses for a beat; then, whirling this time to her left, she does two full turns on the way back, taking smaller steps, of course, and ends up on her right foot close to Jackie and facing him, ready to continue dancing. In the picture at the right, below, she's just completing her final turn.

Naturally you'll go on learning from here, watching other people and copying their steps. But if you use in combination the three simple steps and variations Jackie and Bunny have shown you, you'll more than get by on any floor.

FIGURING THE STARS' SALARIES
[Continued from page 69]
Further evidence that big salaries aren't absolute essentials for stellar happiness and artistic progress is given by wise and enduring favorites such as

Douglas Fairbanks, Mary Pickford, Richard Barthelmess, and several others. Their huge incomes for years have gone more or less automatically into investments and trust funds, via reliable financial agents. This leaves the stars with relatively small incomes for current use —their actual living scale would average well under $1,000 weekly.

Many another star, while drawing over $1,000 per week, has voluntarily lived on what the average American professional man of any sort—doctor, lawyer, preacher, engineer—would consider a very modest budget. The rest, week after week, went into savings accounts, to repose there untouched. Those I happen to recall who have done this for a year or more without interruption include Ruth Chatterton, Clara Bow, and Florence Vidor.

Miriam Hopkins told me recently that she has only $25 weekly for her personal needs, and that her household is maintained on an equally modest budget. The rest of her salary is banked, thus sparing the wise little star all distraction that business problems might cause. She scarcely knows at a given time what salary she's drawing! And she assured me that she would be perfectly satisfied to live on a weekly sum of between $50 and $100.

SOME startling salaries are paid popular "free-lancers." ZaSu Pitts, once getting nearly $5,000 per week, was often in such demand that she had to "lap" pictures (work in one film in the daytime, and in another at night), drawing full salary in each! So did Betty Compson, a few years ago, while drawing about $3,500.

Edmund Lowe and Vic McLaglen, popular free-lancers, draw about $5,000 weekly. Wheeler and Woolsey individually get the same as each of the Marx Brothers, it is said —$100,000 per picture for the comedy pair, and $200,000 per picture for the fraternal quartette! Gloria Swanson probably refused the largest long-term offer ever made— $20,000 weekly. That was when she went into her own productions—saddling herself with business worries that, of course, sapped even her strength and talent. Tom Mix topped all cowboy salaries on record with the $10,000 weekly of his hey-day.

There are some oddities, too, about *small* salaries received by popular players. Adrienne Ames is said to get only $100 weekly; Buster Crabbe got $50 during most of his work on *King of the Jungle,* and finally was raised to $100. Johnny Weissmuller got $250 per week while making his hit in *Tarzan.* And for years Richard Arlen worked uncomplainingly—and to the decided profit of his employers—for $500 weekly. And Kay Francis got the same amount for an almost equal period, while enjoying a popularity probably as great as at present.

The one star in the movies whose talents for business and actual liking for the game seem to go hand in hand with her artistic ability is Mae West—and she is one of the few who is getting a *top* salary at the *height* of her screen popularity!

"Oh, yes, I got only $5,000 a week for *Night After Night*. My new contract with Paramount, however, provides for a big increase," Mae declares with obvious relish. "No, movie money doesn't seem so awful big to me. When I produced my own plays, my percentage was often $10,000 a week."

And at this writing Mae is wondering whether she should do thirteen radio broadcasts for the paltry sum of $60,000.

CHARLIE CHAPLIN'S KIDS

[Continued from page 72]

"The chauffeur served and drived," Charlie persists. "And his name was Albert—he was the chauffeur." For some reason Albert has made a lasting impression on Charlie.

"In France," says Tommy, "we lived at the *Pension Etoile*. That's a French name." He pauses courteously, to make sure I have it. "It isn't so nice as America. There aren't very many lights. There are almost not any lights in France."

Charlie has been eyeing me thoughtfully. "Parlez vous Français?" he asks suddenly.

I admit to a slight knowledge of the language—which I discover instantly was a great mistake. For they break into a rapid patter of French that's completely beyond me. They talk with astonishing ease—considering that they were abroad only nine months—and, to my inexperienced ear, with a perfect accent.

Tommy has caught my comment to that effect and, cocking an impish eye at me he clambers over the back of his grandmother's chair, he proclaims in what is intended to be a deep bass: "Je p-r-r-r-ononce mes r-r-r-s beaucoup." (I pronounce my r's very distinctly.)

Meantime Charlie has burst into song. "Au clair de la lune," he carols.

"Mon ami Pierrot," growls Tommy.

And so they go through the charming French nursery rhyme, Charlie singing in a high, sweet, serious voice—Tommy tumbling and laughing and clowning, to amuse himself primarily, and if his audience is also amused, so much the better.

He picks up a long stick—the stick on which his broken bird had once flown —and hands it to his brother.

"Do a Charlie Chaplin!" he commands

Charlie hangs back bashfully for a moment, but is finally persuaded. With an adorably shy half-smile on his face, he starts toward us from the back of the room, his hands turned slightly outward, twirling the stick between his small fingers, and aping so perfectly that world-renowned trot that for one hysterical moment I almost expect to see the stubby feet swallowed up before my eyes in a pair of familiar, flat-footed shoes.

"Shall I do the monkey now? Shall I do the Chinaman?" Tommy clamors.

"Le singe! Le singe!" (The monkey! The monkey) Charlie claps his hands. He hasn't yet learned that no actor should willingly relinquish the center of the stage to another actor.

But if Charlie is good, Tommy is uncanny. He hunches his shoulders slightly and his mouth takes on the protruding, bony structure of an ape's, as he starts pattering around what must be a cage, one hand plucking rapidly at his side, the other circling incessantly about his mouth.

He stops and laughs and is a little boy again. Then, with his fingers, he draws the corners of his eyes upward. Next second, all the life has died out of them. They're gray—old—tired. His mouth sags. His face is drawn. He shuffles slowly down the room—an age-weary, haunted Oriental. It's a little masterpiece. It must be seen to be believed.

It's evident that Tommy has created an impression. But his wise Nana takes a look at Charlie and smiles. "Tommy can't walk like his daddy at all, though," she says.

"No," Tommy concedes amiably. He thinks it over for a moment. "Because I'm a little pigeon-toed," he decides

Charlie's tired now. He climbs into Conchita's ample lap—Conchita is the Spanish nurse the children had in Bronxville "years and years and years ago." She begins rocking him and singing a gay Spanish tune.

Tommy, sparring the empty air, stands listening for a second and his eyes begin to sparkle. One arm rises in a graceful curve over his head, the other hand is poised seductively against his hip, and a señorita in boxing gloves pirouettes about the room to Conchita's melody. But make no mistake. Tommy isn't showing off. His response to that music was as spontaneous and lovely as a flower's response to the sun.

The children talk readily of their father. It doesn't seem strange to them that they see little of him, and almost as little of their mother, who has been touring in vaudeville for several years. They accept the fact, as children do, and are still too young to ask questions that can't be easily answered. They carry their father's photograph about

with them; they know he's a great movie actor, and they've seen "City Lights."

"I liked the part where he ran all around the boxing man," Charlie crows.

"And I liked the part where he had a bell tied around his neck, and every time the man did punch him, the bell used to ring."

The New York newspapers featured the story that Mr. Reilly, Director of Safety for Fox, who had been sent by the film company to watch the Chaplin children, was guarding them against possible kidnapping by their father—a story which distressed Mrs. Grey painfully. "It's ridiculous and untrue," she protested, almost in tears. "There's no sense in such things. Please tell people that, won't you? Mr. Chaplin sees the children. They're very proud and very fond of their father. We're all proud of him."

And I couldn't help thinking of that earlier moment, when she had said to me with such fervor that there was no doubting her sincerity: "In the old days —when we lived with him—I loved and adored the ground he walked on."

How their father feels about this screen venture is, I suppose, nobody's business. The only report to have reached my eager ears from any reliable source is that he commented somewhat cryptically: "They don't have to do it."

On my way out Tommy escorts me to the telephone to call up the editor. I get the office and wait for her to come on the line, and I note a glint of wickedness in his eye as he raises his angelic face to mine, and I see his hand stealing out toward the receiver hook.

"If you jiggle it," I warn, "I'll have to get my number all over again."

He ponders that for a second. "But you *could* get it again, couldn't you?" he asks anxiously.

"Yes, I could," I admit, "but it would mean a little more trouble."

A hurt look steals into his eyes. "A little more trouble doesn't matter. If you couldn't get it again," he assures me earnestly, "I wouldn't do it. But anyone can take a little more trouble." And so guilty does he make me feel that I all but beg him to please jiggle the hook.

In September they're to start work on a picture for Fox, in which their mother will play the lead—a film version of the play, "The Little Teacher." What waits for them on the screen it would be foolish to try to predict—the children of that other little boy who walked the London streets, ragged and half-starved, looking for something to do so he could eat—and of the dark-eyed girl he found years later, playing in front of her door —the girl whom he made an angel in "The Kid," and then his wife. But if the director succeeds in capturing one-tenth of the natural charm which is theirs and which turned me all but maudlin, then the Fox Company will find themselves with a sensation on their hands.

Watch for them, anyway. They're well worth watching for—Tommy, the gay one, and Charlie, the wistful one.

JANET'S FINEST INTERVIEW
[*Continued from page 73*]
yearns to be a siren, to play the type of thing that Garbo does.

"I really don't mind so very much," Janet said, "what people write *about* me but I do object to being quoted as a fool. I do *not* want to play siren rôles. I know that I could never do the sort of thing that Gargo does, not if I live to be ninety. I also know that I can never again play the 'Seventh Heaven' sort of thing. You see, I know, now, that there is no 'Seventh Heaven' and my knowing it would show through.

I BELIEVE that I have made a pretty exact chart of what I can do and what I cannot do. Even when I was a child and used to give imitations of girls on the screen I'd always imitate Mary Pickford or, at my most daring, Norma Talmadge. Gloria Swanson was always a great favorite of mine, still is, but I always knew that she was too exotic for me to copy.

"I know that I shall have to find stories that will keep pace with the growth of a woman. *You mustn't outgrow stories.* No one remains forever young and *no one should want to.* The trouble with staying always a 'Size Sixteen' as a magazine recently called it, is that you remain a size sixteen mentally and emotionally, too. There is nothing more pathetic than a woman who has felt and suffered and thought trying to *be* a girl who has never felt or suffered or thought anything. She never fools anyone. *I'm not going to try to.* And this is the real reason why I was so anxious to have Henry Garat play opposite me in 'Adorable'. I wanted a man of a certain sophistication, a certain grown-upness to sort of bring me up!"

Janet's childhood has been described as "touching."

Janet said: "Every childhood is touching because it is untouched. But mine held many sterner things than school plays and girl friends. Sickness, and worry about money and the necessity of growing up and doing something."

Janet's love for Jonesey, her stepfather, has also been described as "touching." One pictured a desolate child weeping because a beloved playmate had gone on a journey.

Janet said: "Death is an adult experience. It makes an adult out of you.

It did out of me. You can't touch the hand of death and be just a weeping child any longer—"

Her supposed romance with Charlie Farrell was touched with mysticism and evasion, a thing of starlight and song. Janet doesn't mention names when she talks. She is too wise, too shrewd, too grown-up for that.

But she did say: "There are two kinds of love, I believe. There is first love and that comes to you only through the emotions. It is a dream, a song heard far away. There is no *thought* to it, thinking doesn't enter into it at all. There is no conscious planning about it. Marriage doesn't seem to be the natural culmination of it, because marriage is planning and thinking ahead. And then it leaves you, eventually, because it has never been quite real. You never really touch it with your hands. And it leaves you without bitterness *until you grow old enough to realize that first things never come again.*

THERE is second love, or I hope there is. There are probably several kinds of love, really. I am not one of those who believe that there is only one love in a lifetime.

"We all have many different friends, for instance, and we give them different things of ourselves. Each friend evokes a different reaction. Loves are like that, too—we may love one man one way and another man quite another way—second love is apt to last longer, I believe. It is more apt to be based on sound, substantial things. Common tastes and interests, common friends and plans and ambitions. It is durable. It is not—a dream."

Janet lives, now, with her mother, in a rented house in West Hollywood. She keeps a cook and a chauffeur and, when she works, a studio maid. She has a large library and reads, mostly, the classics, books of travel and biography and metaphysical subjects. She has, too, a fine musical library and when she is working she spends an hour or so every evening with these two libraries. Janet doesn't look into the future. She says that most of us live too much in plans that may never come true.

She said, "Of course I want, rather vaguely, happiness. But what is happiness today is unhappiness tomorrow, very often. Once I thought that success, stardom, an assured income was happiness. I find that the struggle is not in attaining a success but in *staying there.* And for what success gives you with one hand it takes away with the other.

"I have no personal life at all, for instance. There isn't any use in my trying to have a personal life while I am working. I really should not have a home of any kind, at all. I should go from the studio every night to a pro-

fessional trained nurse to be massaged and soothed and put to sleep. That is all I am good for, all I want.

"In between pictures I like to go away, to Palm Springs, on little trips, wherever I feel like going at the moment. You can't have a home, you can't have marriage, you can't have any shared life on such terms as these. I've found that out.

"Of course I hope to marry again, some day. *I hope I have a baby.* No woman should go through all of life without that supreme experience. But, on the other hand, I am not really domestic. I may as well admit it. I could never be satisfied to lead a purely domestic life, managing servants, talking about the baby's diet, playing bridge afternoons, going to matinées, things like that.

"I don't *know* what I want—that's the honestest truth I can tell."

* * *

Then, again, I said to Janet "All of this you have been through—what has it done—has it broken your heart?"

And Janet smiled and said, "I don't believe hearts *break* any more, do you? They are too elastic . . . perhaps they bruise a little . . . or a great deal . . . So that they never quite heal again and always give out fragrances that are stronger . . . and warmer . . ."

WHY GARBO HAS NEVER MARRIED
[*Continued from page 75*]
Garbo did not marry Gilbert, although the world felt positive that she had been deeply in love with him. Subsequently, John married Ina Claire and Garbo withdrew into herself a little more, if that were possible. The marriage of Jack and Ina didn't last long and Hollywood has always felt that the Swedish siren retained her place in his heart.

With the exception of Gilbert, all the men for whom Garbo ever cared have been foreigners. Gilbert was the only American in her life. Nils Asther figured prominently in her private life but only in a Platonic way. Their friendship lasted longer than most, due to the fact that Nils never attempted to make love.

With William Sorensen comes another picture. She met him several years ago when she visited her native Sweden right after the death of Stiller. He followed her to Hollywood, where the romance that had its inception abroad, was renewed. Disillusionment followed, only to see Garbo retire even further into her shell of solitude.

Stiller was the great kindly soul in her life. Sorensen was an episode, an interlude that may have seen her heart conquered, but terminated in aggravation. Gilbert was gay, gregarious, completely bowling over the enigmatic Circe.

In every way possible Gilbert sought to take Garbo into his social world. It was for him that she bought evening clothes. It was for him alone that Garbo made a valiant attempt to go to parties. It was one of the most difficult things she ever undertook. With Mauritz Stiller, Garbo had the love and companionship of a man who desired solitude as much as she did.

The two used to go into the mountains far away from any town or city after a picture was finished. They would stay there for two or three weeks, completely happy in the stillness. They rarely talked, but the beauty of the mountains held them more closely than anything else in the world. Stiller not only spoke Garbo's language of the tongue, but of the heart.

The answer to the riddle of why Garbo never married is to be found in that faraway grave in Sweden. It is to be found in the disillusionment of her episodic romance with a fellow-countryman who followed her to Hollywood. It is to be found in her determination to forego the love of a great screen lover rather than to heed the dictates of her heart.

It is to be found in a statement once made by Garbo, herself—one of the few times that the Sphinx of the Screen has spoken:

"I shall never marry anyone! I am completely absorbed in my work. I have time for nothing else.

"My friendship with Mr. Gilbert? It was only a friendship; nothing more. I was very happy in pictures with Mr. Gilbert. He inspires me. With him I do not act. I live! But that is not love."

But the real reason, the most potent reason, why Garbo has never taken a mate, is that she is too honest!

Her innate honesty will not permit her to marry without love. She must give as well as receive, according to her code of life. She cannot love any man as she feels a wife should love. For that reason marriage would soon prove a disillusionment to her.

Perhaps Garbo knows that it is not for her to last in anyone's life!

THE STAR WHO IS MORE MYSTERIOUS THAN GARBO

[Continued from page 76]
owned any illusions of grandeur, or felt it would be good publicity, but because she is naturally reticent. As a child, she kept her own counsel . . . and in those younger days she formed the habit that now is one of her most pronounced traits.

I have known Fay personally for ten years, yet by no flight of the imagination can I say I really know her. I

helped make her a Wampas Baby Star the same year that Herbert Moulton was responsible for Janet Gaynor's ascension to that same dignity. I took her to the theater, to dinners and to parties. I spent much time in her company . . . and while we have been good friends ever since she is almost an unknown quantity to me.

I met Fay while visiting on the Hal Roach lot. Fay worked occasionally then as an extra and the publicity man who introduced me took us out to the Roach ranch, to see Rex, the wild horse. "Don't point at him," the publicist cautioned us. "Don't even look directly at him. If you do and he sees the motion he'll charge. He's killed three men already."

Fay looked so enchanting in a white linen riding habit that I rather thought I *would* deliberately point at Rex, just for the pleasurable sensation of saving her life. But when we reached the huge paddock, and entered—there was no other way of seeing Rex except by going into the enclosure, an area about forty-five feet in length—I changed my mind . . . and Fay and I devoted most of our time to holding our breath and inwardly praying that Rex wouldn't look our way. He was acting up in a savage manner at the other end of the arena.

FAY was very young then . . . but I still remember the remarkable courage she displayed on that perilous occasion. Once, Rex did turn suddenly, and saw us staring at him. Immediately, he charged, like a thunderbolt. Instead of fainting, however, or running, terrified, before the onrushing animal, she didn't bat an eye. Only by a miracle did the horse miss us. In all my years as a newspaperman, I have never witnessed such *sangfroid* as Fay exhibited when almost certain death stared her in the face.

Nothing ever disturbs her. This was given further proof only recently, when she flew from New York to Hollywood under formidable weather conditions.

In one of the worst thunderstorms New York had ever seen, Fay arrived at the airport, to take her place in the huge plane. Every other reservation had been cancelled . . . and even the pilot was skeptical about letting her fly with him.

The sky was dark as night. Through great mountains of inky black clouds, lighting flashed and cracked dangerously near. Rain fell in torrents and the air was so charged with electricity that Heaven and earth seemed on the verge of a disastrous explosion.

Without even a word to airport officials, inquiring if it would be safe for her to take off, the actress seated herself in the cabin and waited, as calm and

collected as the proverbial cucumber.

I asked her why she, too, hadn't cancelled her trip west. "Why should I?" she answered, almost in surprise. "I'm a fatalist, you know . . . and if God had meant for me to die I would have died, whether I was in the air or on the ground." There is no arguing with that kind of faith.

SHE lives in a large and beautiful mansion on a shady street bordering Beverly Hills. The house once belonged to Florence Vidor. Even though people are aware she resides there, no one knows anything about her home life. Except when she goes to the studio, Fay is seldom seen outside her home and gardens. She rarely attends parties or social functions.

While she is acquainted with many people, she has no intimate friends. Of confidantes there are none . . . and only very infrequently are guests invited within the portals of her dwelling. Fay and John Monk Saunders, the Rhodes scholarship writer whose persuasions led to his becoming her husband, live in quiet luxury . . . but not even her press agent, that glorifier of stars whose business it is to see-all, know-all, has the remotest idea how Fay conducts her private affairs.

In the studios, she is well-liked . . . although she seldom carries on unnecessary conversations with members of the cast. People unconsciously keep their distance, not because of any hauteur or up-staginess on her part, but by virtue of the fact that her reputation has preceded her, that she is hard to know.

One day, some months ago, a distressed studio publicity man besieged and begged me almost on bended knees to tell him about Fay Wray. "You've know her for years," he said, "you must know *something* I can use in a story about her. I haven't a single item I can include . . . and I've known her for several years myself."

SCANDAL never has attached itself to Fay, and even before her marriage to Saunders local columnists rarely mentioned her name. The reason was that they had never heard anything, good or bad, about her . . . and that, to a Hollywood chatter writer, spells calamity.

Yet, as I say, it is not Garbo, Dietrich or Sten, Hepburn or Mae West who puzzles Hollywood . . . it is this actress who more nearly resembles an ultra-aristocrat than any other person in the colony. Fay Wray is Hollywood's enigma woman.

NORMA TAKES A DARE

[Continued from page 77]
No breath of scandal has ever touched her. That she and Irving Thalberg are

well mated and happy, cannot be gain-said. Certainly, she has never had the opportunity to acquire personal experience to guide her in her daring rôles.

"How do I account for it? Because it is silly to contend that an actress must have *lived* and actually acquired a past, before she is capable of portraying that type of woman on the screen or stage. Of course, there must be intelligent observation; most of all, it requires imagination.

"If the contrary were true, then members of the demi-monde would make the best actresses, wouldn't they?"

"NORMA is the most perfect wife and mother I know," said a friend recently. "She separates her two worlds sharply. When she leaves the studio, after completing a picture, she likewise leaves it mentally. Until the script of her next picture is ready for her to read, she seemingly doesn't know that pictures exist."

"But the influence of your pictures on impressionable girls?" I asked Miss Shearer. "Don't you think many girls might be encouraged to emulate your tactics?"

"I wouldn't advise them to," she laughed merrily, "for it couldn't be done. Not that I mean it would be impossible, but because in a picture things are *made* to work out. That has been attended to by the skill of the author before the picture begins. No matter how clever and attractive a woman might be, it could never be enough to bring things out her way in real life as we do on the screen."

Miss Shearer feels no apprehension about the daring of her part in *Strange Interlude*. She faces it with the same serene confidence that she confronted each picture after *The Divorcée,* when it was said by many that no reputation of the screen could survive the increasing sophistication of her rôles. She has a way of accomplishing things, has Norma Shearer.

4 RULES OF MARRIED LOVE

[Continued from page 80]
take anything for granted, it loses its charm and you lose your perspective."

"Nothing is sure. In marriage you ought to live with the constant knowledge before you that if you do not work at marriage you may lose the one you love."

"Wouldn't that make marriage more insecure than it is?"

"No, it would make it more secure. If you had a job and knew you might lose it, you would work all the harder to keep it. But if you thought you had it cinched and that anything you did would get by, the chances are you'd slacken.

"Marriage is a career in itself. To succeed in any career you have to keep on working at it. The same thing is true of marriage. You must keep right on building it up just as you built its foundations. The minute you think your marriage is sure, that minute your marriage becomes most insecure."

"Do you think marriage is a career for a man as well as for a woman?" I asked. "Many people still hold to the old Byronic philosophy:

" 'Man's love is of man's life a thing apart,

" ' 'Tis woman's whole existence.' "

"If that is true, that does not necessarily mean it is right," said young Doug thoughtfully. "It is simply the line of least resistance for man.

"It is not an honest or equitable philosophy. To keep a marriage from going on the rocks, it is necessary first of all to be honest with yourself, next to preserve the essence of comradeship."

I asked Douglas Fairbanks, Jr. whether he thought marriage was more likely to succeed where those concerned had other careers.

"That depends," he replied. "It is a matter that is adjustable to personal temperament. Some couples are happier when the woman devotes all her attention to the home; other marriages are most likely to succeed where the marital partners both have other careers in addition to marriage. The thing to do, is to find out in which category you belong and then to do what you want to do and what you feel is right, so long as it does not hurt the other person's feelings.

"The greatest sin in the world is hurting somebody. When that person is the one you have married, that sin is especially black. Love, kindness and comradeship can all begin at home."

These then are Doug's rules for a happy marriage.

Be honest with yourself.

Preserve the essence of comradeship.

Never hurt the person you love. For that matter, never hurt anybody.

Never take anything for granted.

It should be easy for Doug to follow the last rule where such a glamorous, witching person as Joan is concerned. They move in an enchanted circle in Hollywood. They have the same friends. Among them are Ann Harding, Harry Bannister, the Gleasons, Billy Haines, Marion Davies, Gloria Swanson.

They have both struggled hard for their success. The story of how Joan worked as a slavey in a boarding school is well known.

Things should have come more easily for Douglas Fairbanks, Jr. But after his father's divorce from Beth Sully, the family money was scattered through unwise investments (a sore point this and one not too long to be dwelt on). Doug and his mother went to Paris to live because living there was cheaper. They had so little money that often they had to live on one meal a day.

Douglas Fairbanks, Sr. was all unknowing of their plight, Doug Jr. too proud to say a word.

Then suddenly out of a clear sky stardom was handed to young Doug because he was the famous son a famous father. But the picture he made, "Stephen Steps Out," was a total failure, and Paramount didn't take up its option.

He returned to Paris and lived for a year on what he had made in four weeks. Then he began to build the foundations of his career slowly, playing bit parts in Hollywood, taking a flyer on the stage, making "quickies" on Poverty Row.

He won through hard work the stardom that had been given to him prematurely. But a career in Hollywood is uncertain. There came a few flops. First National decided that young Doug was washed up. His swan song was going to be a part as John Barrymore's brother in "Moby Dick." He wasn't in a position to refuse, but he knew that if he were given a part in a picture like "The Dawn Patrol" he could win back his following. The company hated to give him the part, but Howard Hawks and Richard Barthelmess pleaded for him. At their insistence he was given his big opportunity and you all know what he made of it.

Young Fairbanks regards "The Dawn Patrol" as the best picture he has made so far as his own part in it is concerned. But though he does not consider his own rôle in "Outward Bound" an important one, he feels that as a picture that is the finest one in which he has played.

Though he can write, paint and sculp, he has no intention of giving up the screen for any of these activities. They require too much concentration. He does hope to work up to some sort of executive position in movie work. He would like to direct, act and have a hand in the producing of a picture. That would give him a chance to find an outlet for various types of energy, mental and physical.

I asked him why he and Joan have not played together since "Our Modern Maidens."

"If we were to play together," he replied, "people would not lose themselves in the characters we representd but would be conscious of our real identities. If the picture called for me to make love to Joan, they would say, 'Oh, that's the way he makes love to his wife at home.' If the script called for me to beat the heroine, they'd say, 'That's his own wife he's beating.' "

I rose to say goodby, but before doing so I asked curiously how old Doug was.

"What do you think?" he parried.

"I can't guess."

"Well, I was born in 1907."

But as I took out my little pencil to put down that date, Doug, Jr. said laughingly, "Sometimes I say 1903, sometimes 1908, sometimes 1905 and sometimes 1910, so that when I get to be fifty or sixty, people will be so confused that I can tell them I was born in 1916."

"But is 1907 correct?"

"Oh, within a year or so.'

Now I know how Douglas Fairbanks, Jr. is going to keep the home fires burning.

He'll keep Joan guessing.

THE INTIMATE LIFE OF A GENTLEMAN REBEL

[Continued from page 84]

Royce up the main drag.

It was while appearing with Jane Cowl that M-G-M signed him to a contract for motion picture work in Hollywood—"Although it didn't happen as suddenly as that might sound," he added humorously. "From the moment I got my name in a Broadway cast, I had been making motion picture 'tests' for one company and then another. I suppose if the tests I made were strung end-to-end, they'd make at least a twelve-reel feature. They weren't bad, either. I remember being quite surprised that they were as good as they were, considering that I didn't think I had either a screen face or personality. But for some reason (or many of them) nothing had come of my very persistent testing until M-G-M offered me a contract beginning at the same salary I was then getting on the stage, to try my luck in Hollywood.

"Frankly, it was the year-around salary that tempted me. I decided to make as much money as possible for a year and then return to the stage. So I asked for a trick clause in my contract to the effect that after I'd served my year of financial sentence, I (not the studio) should have the option of re-signing for another term."

In the beginning, Franchot did not like Hollywood. Even now, I'm not quite sure it is his favorite environment. At the very start, his whole life and scheme of living seemed turned bottom side up.

He had few friends and his original impression was that he was marooned in a completely mournful place, and to add to the gloom, he had rented a place at the beach and was thus enveloped in fog for the first month or two of his stay.

But day after day Franchot reported hopefully to the studio, only to be told to "wait." When, after five dreary weeks, he was advised that he was to go into the cast of Joan Crawford's "Today We Live," he refused to believe it until he was actually in make-up and on the set. Even then he remained skeptical until he began his first scene with the star.

Joan was a revelation to the by now discontented actor from New York. She was the most vivid and intensely magnetic person he had encountered in Hollywood. He liked her immediately. And he was delighted when she went out of her way to be kind to him—talking of the stage, books and music. They found a mutual fund of interests, and if he became a bit more interested in Joan as a beautiful and charming girl than as a student of the art, it was an emotion he kept carefully to himself. For Joan was married to Douglas Fairbanks, Jr. at the time and, as far as Franchot and the world knew, very happily married, too.

It wasn't until the following spring, when they appeared together in "Dancing Lady," that their friendship blossomed into something more than "Hello" as they passed each other on the lot. This, then, was the very beginning of their romance for, by now, Joan had filed divorce papers against young Doug.

In the meantime, Franchot's career had gone ahead with such pictures as "Gabriel Over The White House," "Stranger's Return," and "Moulin Rouge." (His favorite picture by the way, is "Bengal Lancers" which he made some time later.) His "trial year" in the movies was almost at an end as he appeared for "Dancing Lady" and when he began the picture he had every intention in the world of returning to Broadway as he originally had planned.

By the time the picture was completed, wild horses couldn't have dragged him away from Hollywood. Franchot and Joan were, by then, deeply and sincerely in love.

He doesn't talk about the romance that led to his marriage with the glamorous Joan because Franchot steadfastly refuses to make publicity fodder of anything so intimate and personal in his life. But I happen to know, nonetheless, that the early stages of their love story were not happy for Tone despite the eventual happy ending. Not that Joan didn't return his love, but she had been hurt and bewildered by the crashing of her marriage to young Fairbanks. She needed time to adjust her life. In addition, it was slow agony for him to be dragged through the Hollywood gossip mills as the suitor Joan "might" or "might not" marry. Franchot had been able to maintain a private life on the stage; in Hollywood, and sincerely in love with a girl whose very name spelled headlines, it was indeed another story.

During the year that an old love died and a new love was born, Franchot was devotion itself to Joan. She has said more than once that he brought new values, new ambition and new aspirations into her life. Less has been said about Joan's influence on Franchot but it was definite from the beginning. Joan loves Hollywood and her career. She respects her profession. In time, she showed Franchot that Hollywood—with all its outward glitter and glamour—was not a mere money mill to be condescendingly embraced by Broadwayites who deigned to come to the movie town. They had many long discussions, even arguments, concerning the relative merits of his world and hers. Gradually those two worlds came closer and closer together; finally, they found them mysteriously blended.

ON the 11th day of October, 1935, Joan and Franchot were married in Englewood Cliffs, New Jersey—after one of the most denied, affirmed and re-denied romances Hollywood had ever witnessed.

They went East to be married for two reasons: First to escape the ballyhoo of a Hollywood ceremony and secondly for Joan to meet Franchot's family. The wedding, however, couldn't have been more hectic if it had been staged in Hollywood.

"Nicholas Schenck, M-G-M's New York executive, helped us with our secret wedding plans," says Franchot, "by having one of his close friends—the Mayor of Englewood Cliffs, New Jersey —fix it up with the license clerk to bring a license to the Mayor's home and we were married there. Immediately after we got back to New York, Joan began worrying about the story leaking out. Walter Winchell had her promise for the story and she finally told him— asking him to wait until his Sunday broadcast (this was Friday) to break it. Winchell later told us that he never went through two such days in his life. He bought every edition of every paper, scared to death to look at the front page for fear of seeing the story. After his broadcast, he told us that he was through holding stories; too many gray hairs were the result.

"During those two days while we were secretly married, we had a grand time. We danced until dawn and did a lot of silly things we'd always wanted to do. I remember going home from our Saturday night's revelry; it was just breaking daylight and we stopped the taxi on Sixth Avenue and waltzed with an ancient newsboy. The old gent had no idea who his partners-in-gaiety were, I'm sure, but he joined in the fun and stepped pretty lively, too, for an old codger."

Then, in the white glare of national publicity, Joan and Franchot returned to Hollywood and a newly-decorated home in Brentwood two dachshunds, a few close and chosen friends and their mutual love for music, the stage and motion pictures. It is hardly necessary to detail their activities, either socal or professional, since that time—as practically every word that can be printed concerning them has been printed a dozen times over.

That Hollywood has chosen to misconstrue their musical ambitions, their singing lessons, the little theater they have added to their home and many other of their mutual interests as being "highbrow," has bothered Franchot not the slightest. That Hollywood continues to interpret his refusal to be a backslapper and a proverbial hail-fellow-well-met as an indication of snobbery, bothers him even less.

And so he stands where he is today, one of the finest and certainly one of the most sincere actors on the screen. There is no gainsaying that he is one of the most independent personalities off the screen. Perhaps, at heart, he is as much a rebel to the traditions of the glamour game as he was to the rules at The Hill or the social conventions of his fraternity at Cornell. The real difference lies in the fact that he no longer seeks converts to his creed. His code is individual. All he asks is the privilege of adhering to it himself.

I doubt that Hollywood will ever change him or mould him to the standard, accepted patterns.

We must accept him for his fine work, his sincere portrayals, and credit his lack of the usual Hollywood social conscience to his determination to avoid hypocrisy—leaving him a stranger within the gates.

CAREER COMES FIRST WITH LORETTA

[Continued from page 85]
well know. But, besides that, it looks pretty much as though Eddie's going to be the guy who's going to make Hollywood's Law of Three's come true once more. For I'm betting plenty, right now, that before long, Eddie's going to marry Loretta—and then she, too, will move out of the big, white house. (And probably follow sisterly precept by having a baby!) And then the house'll be empty, and the wood-knockers and ladder-dodgers can sagely say: "See? We told you so! The Law of Three's *never fails . . . !*"

The Loretta-Eddie marriage won't surprise Hollywood any, when it happens. It's almost a sure-thing bet. The only real uncertainty is "when?" Loretta can't quite make up her mind.

Up to recently, there *was* an obstacle to the marriage. Loretta, you see, is churchly enough to respect the laws of her religion. And, divorced as she is from Grant Withers, there were certain bans against remarriage. But that obstacle has been cleared away. The

church, surveying the situation, absolved Loretta, granted full dispensation for her remarriage. And so, today, the only factor that stands between Loretta and rematrimony is Loretta's own hesitancy . . .

IT'S not that she doesn't love Eddie Sutherland. She makes no secret of that, with her friends. But she is not sure, just yet, whether she can again try to mix career and marriage. It failed once. She loves Eddie so much that she doesn't want to fail again.

"I want, first, to prove my merit as a true actress," she says, "and then, maybe, a home—with a husband, children. But then I feel I should retire from the screen."

However, as a veteran Hollywood observer, let me stick in my own two-cents'-worth of comment, please? I've heard stars say that before. And I've seen them change their mind. After all, one's public doesn't let one easily quit the screen. And on the other hand, love demands fulfilment. A star can't, off-hand, choose one or the other. They have to take the middle course. And I'm betting that Loretta, seeing the inevitable, will both marry Eddie Sutherland, and continue her screen work. And soon, too . . . !

There are straws in the wind—"the big house," she says, now and then, when she's with intimate friends, "is lovely, but now that Polly and Sally have left, it's—well—kind of lonely." And then, too, you only have to see how Loretta goes simply mad over her 13-year-old step-sister, Georgiana, to realize the child-hunger in her heart. Besides, I know that she told a friend, not long ago, that her one dominant regret over the outcome of her romance with Grant Withers was this:

"My only regret is that I didn't have a baby!" And she adds: "I could have so much fun—now—playing with my son, or daughter . . ."

She takes that out on Georgiana. Nothing's too much for the child. Loretta spends much money, more time, making Georgiana happy. Buying her things, playing with her, hours on end. Loretta even loves to sew clothes, for Georgiana.

SHE'S a "homey" gal, this movie-star Loretta. Oh, I know that's been said, with a press-agent wink, about lots of other glamour-girls of the screen. But with Loretta, it's really true. Why, she hasn't even a personal maid . . . ! She keeps her own room in order—even to making her own bed, taking care of her own clothes, keeping her room tidied. She loves to do it. And besides, she says, "I'd feel as if I were losing some of the freedom of my own privacy if I had a maid." She can cook like a

wizard, and when Eddie marries her, Loretta will probably kick the cook out of the kitchen, more often than not, and fix her man's dinner herself . . .

Does that sort of thing sound a bit too—er—stodgy and kitchen-smelly to you? I mean, does it make Loretta look too dumpy and not romantically-glamourous enough? Well, then, let me set you straight. Behind her practicality, there's a streak of romanticism in Loretta that's as naive and as sweet as a schoolgirl's first awakening. She daydreams about the man—well, *The* Man. Once, on the set, between takes, she spent long periods, earnestly writing, writing, writing. At last, somebody picked it up, snoopy-like, to see what Loretta was so engrossed in. And found that Loretta had been writing a letter to "Dear Phantom"—"the person with whom I expect to build my life," she added. And in that letter, she described the man of her dreams—

". . . you're kind," she wrote. "—have the gentleness of a strong person who scorns to capitalize his strength—you wear your strength so slightly it is almost hidden—sparing of the weaknesses of others because you have never spared your own—

"—you are essentially serious, because at bottom, life is serious. You're bound by a *noblesse oblige* that will not tolerate flippancy—that isn't to say you haven't your own dry, gentle humor, but you have no flair for wisecracking for wisecracking's sake. You'd never trade someone's discomfort for a laugh.

"—you've learned that most nastiness is a bad retaliation of the sick and wounded and weak. Your tolerance is that of a mature intellect . . .

"—you dance just well enough. I couldn't stand it if you were a polished rhumba artist . . . you send flowers, not just to flatter me, but because you love flowers . . . when you send me books, they're about the things *you're* interested in, and thereby you pay me a compliment . . . you don't speak sharply to waiters . . . your tennis is cagey and competitive . . . you're brown, and your hands are medium-sized and well made, and they look more at home resting on a tiller than shuffling a deck of cards . . . you like music, but don't give long monologues about it—with all your strength, you're a fall guy for anyone under six, and they adore you . . . you like dogs (some dogs, not those shrill little ones) and you're quite comfortable when there's a cat around . . . you own a dozen revolting old pipes but you smoke cigarettes around me; not cigars, thank heaven . . . you wear the kind of clothes and shoes that look best when they're several years old . . . your nails are short and clean, and they aren't polished . . . you usually smell deliciously of soap and your face shines like a well-scrubbed boy's . . .

"—and you are, to me, something more than all the sharp nervous affairs of girlhood combined. You are the one person I can't think of living without, this year, or twenty years from now, or any time in between. We belong together, you and I . . ."

YES, Loretta wrote that. Don't ask me if she was thinking of Eddie Sutherland when she wrote it. Don't ask Loretta, either. She won't tell you. I just quoted her, you see, to show you that sheer romance runs riot in the girl's makeup, as well as that practically that is another side of her. Besides that, what can I tell you, to make you know her better—

I can tell you that discipline is one of her basic rules of life. She learned it in the convent where she spent years of her childhood—a Catholic convent, where discipline was drilled into her, day in and day out. Today, she's glad of that, because she has realized that that very discipline is essential to the life of a motion picture actress whose very existence must be rigidly disciplined as part of the price of success.

And she's independent. That came of living with two older sisters—those same two, Polly and Sally—and not ever being willing to grant that they could do anything that she herself couldn't do.

She's acquisitive. Mentally, I mean. She is hungry for knowledge. On the set, she scorns her dressing-room, pokes around where the technicians are working, picking up new bits of knowledge about the profession of which she's a part. Loretta Young knows more about the behind-the-camera side of moviemaking than ninety-nine out of a hundred other stars. She takes home scripts of not alone the pictures she's working in, but others as well, and she studies them, and writes out analyses of each of them. Her reading runs to historical novels, and with a hang-over of childhood's hero-worship, she still is fascinated by Mary, Queen of Scots, and Joan of Arc, and day-dreams herself playing those characters.

She's an inveterate movie fan, for two reasons. One reason is because she feels that part of her own work is to keep up with the new pictures. Second reason is because she loves them! She is a Garbo fan. Hepburn and Elisabeth Bergner are runners-up.

She is not especially gregarious. She hasn't a huge circle of friends—not as many as you'd expect a movie star, to have. But the ones she has are the sort of friends to whom the much-abused word *friend* can be properly applied. She believes that a few true friends are worth a thousand fair-weather acquaintances.

YOU'VE heard much talk, recently, about her poor health. That's all over now. And she's living a strenuous life, to keep her health good. Horseback rides, swims, table tennis, sunbathing—these are her daily routine. But above them all, she likes dancing, and she spends hours on the floor. She's often said that if she weren't a film actress, she'd be a professional dancer.

She's not particularly "sold" on herself. For instance, she's quite sure her legs are too thin. So she doesn't like to go swimming in public—does it at friends' pools. And all the ravings of studio photographers about her figure don't change her mind. She wants to put on weight, and works hard to do so. She gorges on steak and French-fried potatoes and turkey dinners and all the fattening things other stars'd like to eat, but don't dare. And then, when she gets on the scales, she finds the needle still quivering at the 107-mark!

About her, there's none of the self-importance and self-adulation that characterizes some stars. She's avid for criticism, and actually takes it on the chin and doesn't get mad at the people who offer it. There is, for instance, Lucille . . . Lucille de Antoine is her full name. For nine years, Lucille has worked with Loretta as the star's hairdresser. And Lucille is not star-shy, nor afraid. She doesn't mince words. When Loretta does anything of which Lucille doesn't approve, Lucille sounds off.

"Lucille is my best critic," Loretta says, when anyone asks her why she lets Lucille get away with it. "When I'm 'lousy' before the camera, she tells me that I'm just that. She doesn't try to flatter my vanity, like others do, by telling me I did okeh. And so, by letting Lucille tell me, and by listening to her I am often able to do better the next time."

DOMINANT trait in Loretta, probably, is her kindness. She cannot bear to hurt anyone. She cannot bear to hear of anyone's hurt. Illness of others dismays her deeply. She spends much of her off-screen time in charitable work, but says nothing of it, and resents it being mentioned. Never forgetful of what treasures she derived from her convent training, Loretta has always remembered the Sisters and what they did for her. Every yuletide, she turns over her automobile and her chauffeur, for weeks, to the Sisters of Nazareth at San Diego, to work their good.

Never the "big star" on the set or at home or among friends or strangers, Loretta amazes shopgirls by offering to wait while others are being served.

And significant, too, is this—at home, to Georgiana, the 13-year-old, and to Loretta's own mother, who lives there with her, she's just "Gretchen." You

see, that's her real name—and its her real character. They can't call her "Loretta"—she's Gretchen, and a gretchen, to them, always . . .

And that's the picture of Loretta Young—movie star who works at it, and who's as practical as any other expert in working at her profession; the sort of woman who, trying to make up her mind on marriage, is willing to thrust everything else aside but her love, as she says:

"I don't feel that I could ever ask my husband to share me with the public. I want to belong to him alone . . ."

WHO'S WHOSE IN HOLLYWOOD

[Continued from page 88]

DIX, RICHARD—Gave up "perennial bachelor" title for socialite Winifred Coe, October 20, 1931. Daughter born, January, 1933. Divorced, June 29, 1933. One year later, to the day, he married his secretary, Virginia Webster. They have six sons.

DIXON, LEE—Learned to dance to win girl he loved, but before he completed his lessons, she eloped with a rival. Claims he hasn't recovered yet.

DODD, CLAIRE—Newspapers first learned she had married J. Milton Strauss, broker, in Mexico in 1932 when she invited reporters to her home in January, 1937, to meet her son, Jon Michael, born October, 1936.

DONLEVY, BRIAN—Celebrated his freedom from Wife No. 1 by marrying Marjorie Lane, actress-singer, December, 1936.

DOUGLAS, MELVYN—Twice married. Son by first marriage, Melvyn, now 11. Son by second, Pierre, now 3. Present wife (since 1931): Helen Gahagan.

DOWNS, JOHNNY—Still intermittently pursuing Eleanore Whitney.

DRAKE, FRANCES—Popular with the boys, but elusive.

DUNN, JAMES—His first marriage ended, pre-Hollywood, in 1925—in Denver. Recently married again. Beautiful Frances Gifford is the bride.

DUNNE, IRENE—Married Dr. Francis Griffin, New York dentist, in 1930, little anticipating she would have the world's most famous long-distance marriage. Adopted baby, Mary Frances, November 1936.

DURANTE, JIMMY—Married to singer Jeanne Olson since World War days. Jimmy, the kidder, once said, "It don't seem no longer ago than the Civil War to me."

DVORAK, ANN—Met Leslie Fenton in January 1932, flew to Yuma with him March 17, 1932, gave up career for year to go to Europe with him. "And would do it again," she says.

EBSEN, BUDDY—Easygoing, married to energetic Ruth Cambridge, Winchell's former "Girl Friday."

EDDY, NELSON—M-G-M still is looking for a romance for Nelson. How about the ex-Mrs. Sidney Franklin? She's his favorite audience.

EILERS, SALLY—Unsmilingly divorced Hoot Gibson, August 1933. Smilingly married Director Harry Joe Brown, September 1933. Son born, August 1934. Still smiling.

ELLIS, PATRICIA—Of all the suitors rather favors Fred Keating.

ELLISON, JAMES—Eloped to Yuma with actress Gertrude Durkin, April 1937. Said: "Hollywood will be startled. You see, we knew each other only four years, and our marriage is very sudden."

ERIKSON, LEIF—Married to Frances Farmer two years now.

ERWIN, STUART—Persuaded pretty June Collyer to give up her career for him. They have two children, William and Judith.

EVANS, MADGE—Still living a quiet life—and a single one.

FAIRBANKS, DOUGLAS—No. 1: Beth Sully (mother of Doug, Jr.)—married, 1907; divorced, 1918. No. 2: Mary Pickford—married, March 1920; divorced, January 1935. No. 3: Lady Sylvia Ashley—married, March 1936.

FAIRBANKS, DOUGLAS, JR.—Divorced Joan Crawford nearly five years ago. "Engaged" to Gertrude Lawrence for a time, but that blew up. Currently attentive to Marlene Dietrich. And others.

FARMER, FRANCES—It's still love with the Leif Eriksons—who discovered each other before anyone else did.

FARRELL, CHARLES—Millions still wonder why he and Janet Gaynor didn't marry each other. Yet he has been married since 1931 to Virginia Valli. Recently derided a new crop of divorce rumors.

FARRELL, GLENDA—Married and divorced, early in life and has a son, Tommy, in his teens. Claims she won't marry again. But many not mean it. With writer Robert Riskin out of picture, has been going with Drew Eberson.

FAYE, ALICE—Honeymooning in Hollywood since September 4, 1937, when she finally said "Yes" to patient, persistent Tony Martin.

FAZENDA, LOUISE—Married ten years last Thanksgiving to producer Hal Wallis. Son born April, 1933.

FIELD, VIRGINIA—The newest "most-dated girl in Hollywood."

FIELDS, W. C.—Unhappily married once, and only once. Under pressure, he has also admitted to a grown son.

FLYNN, ERROL—Despite their battles—or, perhaps, because of them—Errol and Lili Damita still like matrimony, after two years. Gossipers have them calling it "quits" every other day.

FONDA, HENRY—Married Margaret Sullavan when both were unknown. Divorced in 1933. During trip abroad, Summer 1936, met and married Frances Brokaw, pretty socialite widow. Child born December 1937.

FONTAINE, JOAN—At 20, intent on career, discouraging willing suitors.

FORAN, DICK—Married Ruth Piper Hollingsworth, socialite divorcee, secretly in Mexico June 6, 1937. Now blessed-eventing.

FORBES, RALPH—After 3-week courtship, eloped to Yuma with Heather Angel, August 29, 1934. Previously wed to Ruth Chatterton—for eight years.

FOSTER, PRESTON—Married for years to schoolday sweetheart, Gertrude Warren.

FRANCIS, KAY—No. 1: Dwight Francis (div.). No. 2: William Gaston (div.). No. 3: Kenneth MacKenna (div. 1934). The leading candidate for No. 4 (if they aren't already secretly married) is writer Delmar Daves.

FURNESS, BETTY—Stepped to the altar with Johnny Green, orchestra leader, November 26, 1937. Her first trip, his second.

GAAL, FRANCISKA—In 1934 became the Budapest bride of Dr. Francis Dajkovich. He is in Hollywood with her.

GABLE, CLARK—He learned about acting from his first wife, Josephine Dillon, now, Hollywood's best-known dramatic coach. Soon after breaks came his way, married Ria Langham, wealthy divorcee with two children. They separated in 1935, are not yet divorced. When free, expected to marry Carole Lombard.

GARBO, GRETA—Once started to elope with John Gilbert, but changed her mind on the way. Has denied all romance rumors since, including the newest (Stokowski) one.

GARGAN, WILLIAM—Married since his Brooklyn days to Mary Kenny.

GAYNOR, JANET—Disappointed millions of moviegoers by not marrying Charles Farrell. On September 11, 1929, married Lydell Peck, San Francisco lawyer, instead. Divorced, April 7, 1933. Now the constant companion of Tyrone Power—and it looks serious.

GEORGE, GLADYS—Ex-husbands: Ben Erway and Edward Fowler. Present husband: Leonard Penn, who has given up factory management for acting, to be with her.

GLEASON, JAMES—Married to the same woman—Lucille Webster—since August 1906. It's a Hollywood record. They have one son, Russell.

GLEASON, RUSSELL—Engaged to Cynthia Howard, society girl, November, 1937.

GODDARD, PAULETTE—Divorced from E. J. Goddard, wealthy lumberman, in 1932. Reporter secretly married to Charlie Chaplin for past three years.

GRABLE, BETTY—See Jackie Coogan.

GRAHAME, MARGOT—Before Hollywood married Francis Lister, English actor. Have seen each other seldom since, but are not divorced—yet.

GRANT, CARY—Strenuously a bachelor since his 1935 divorce from Virginia Cherrill (they were wed a year). Now serious again—about Phyllis Brooks.

GRAVET, FERNAND—Has a pretty wife—

Jean Renouardt, French actress.

GURIE, SIGRID—So beautiful, but oh, so retiring. Romance rumors haven't touched her yet. Denies any pre-Hollywood marriage.

HALEY, JACK—Even his vaudeville partner, Florence McFadden, liked his sense of humor. She married him. They have two children.

HALL, JON—Playing the field till he gets acquainted.

HAMILTON, NEIL—Once took full-page ad in Hollywood paper to deny divorce rumors about self and Elsa Whitmer. Married about 15 years, and a father.

HARDING, ANN—Married actor Harry Bannister in 1926. Daughter Jane born in 1929. Divorced May, 1932, because of unhappiness over public calling Bannister "Mr. Ann Harding." Married Werner Janssen, world-famous orchestra conductor, in London, January 17, 1937. Has been "Mrs. Janssen" since.

HARDY, OLIVER—Tentatively divorced by Myrtle Lee, 1933. He divorced her May, 1937, following one near-divorce, one reconciliation and a separate maintenance suit.

HAYWARD, LOUIS—Still courting Ida Lupino, as he has been for two years.

HENIE, SONJA—Those romance rumors (with Tyrone Power, Cesar Romero, James Stewart, et al) have been just publicity. There's somebody in Norway. His name is Carl Carlson, insiders say.

HEPBURN, KATHARINE—Long denied having a husband. Then divorced Ludlow Smith of New York "400," May 8, 1934. Since then has looked at only one man twice—ace aviator Howard Hughes. A romance is suspected.

HERBERT, HUGH—He woo-wooed and won Rose Epstein, 'way back in 1916.

HERSHOLT, JEAN—Nearly 25 years ago, in Montreal, married Via Anderson. Like his great friend, Dr. Dafoe, has a grown son named Allan.

HERVEY, IRENE—Her first husband's name was Fenderson. Had a daughter, Gail, legally adopted by her second husband, Allan Jones. They were married July 26, 1936. Nursery first occupied December, 1937.

HILLIARD, HARRIET—Married briefly and unhappily, very young. Happy since late 1935, when she married Ozzie Nelson, orchestra leader, on eve of movie contract. After first picture, gave up career for year to have a baby.

HOLDEN, GLORIA—Married H. C. Winston, theatrical man, in 1932. Divorced, late 1937.

HOLM, ELEANOR—Became Mrs. Arthur Jarrett in 1933. Surprised him November 11, 1937, by announcing she and Billy Rose (husband of Fanny Brice) would marry as soon as both achieved divorces. Jarrett sued her for divorce month later.

HOLT, JACK—Divorced from Margaret Wood in 1933. Father of Tim Holt.

HOMOLKA, OSCAR—When starring in Berlin, married German stage star, Greta Mosheim. Clash of temperaments soon drove them to divorce.

HOPKINS, MIRIAM—First married to Brandon Peters. Then to writer Austin Parker, whose divorce was one of Hollywood's friendliest. Adopted baby, Michael, May 4, 1932. Eloped to Yuma with Director Anatole Litvak, September 4, 1937. They plan to live in separate houses on same estate.

HORTON, EDWARD EVERETT—The perennial bachelor.

HOVICK, LOUISE—Twice married to Robert Mizzy, manufacturer, Summer 1937—first in water taxi, then on land. Honeymooned in trailer.

HOWARD, JOHN—Still eligible. Current interest: newcomer Kay Griffith.

HOWARD, LESLIE—During a World War leave married Ruth Evelyn Martin. They have a son Ronald, a daughter Leslie.

HUDSON, ROCHELLE—Still collecting proposals.

HULL, WARREN—First revealed publicly, late in 1936, that he had not only a wife, but three sons. And his fan mail promptly tripled.

HUME, BENITA—Married briefly, some years ago, to one Eric Siepman. Often rumored romantic since. Popular with Ronald Colman.

HUNT, MARSHA—It's a romance between Marsha and Jerry Hopper, film cutter.

HUNTER, IAN—Married Casha Pringle, English actress, in 1932. Children; Jolyon George and Robin Fan.

HUSTON, WALTER—Twice married and divorced before marriage to actress Nan Sunderland in November, 1931. Has a writer-son, John.

HUTCHINSON, JOSEPHINE—Her married name now is Mrs. James Townsend. In her early stage days it was Mrs. Robert Bell.

Next month's installment picks up those stars who surnames begin with the letter "I"—and concludes with the letter "Z." You'll be surprised over what these romantic and marital statistics reveal. So don't fail to get next month's copy of MOTION PICTURE—and learn the complete lowdown.

I WANT TO TALK ABOUT MY BABY
[Continued from page 89]
back at him. Imagine a baby laughing at five months, three days, and five hours old! It's almost unprecedented. And he says, 'Ma-ma' and 'Da-da,' too! Of course that's all he *can* say yet, but he says that all day long. Starting at about five in the morning. . . .

"Oh, of course he wakes us at five in the morning. And we love it! It used to be that we most often were going to sleep at five—whereas we now wake up at five. Oh, *no!* We never argue about who's going in to see if he's all right. We both get up and go in. Why, I wouldn't miss a minute of my baby—not those I don't have to miss. It's bad enough being away from him at the studio all day long. When I'm working, I always play with him from five to six in the morning. Then I have to get dressed and have breakfast, to be at the studio by seven-thirty. Then, when I get home at five-thirty in the evening, I have a half hour more with him before he goes to bed.

"WHEN I brought him home from the hospital, we put him in the downstairs nursery which we had fixed up for him. But we didn't like being so far away from him, so George and I slept downstairs on the couch for a while. But that was a bit inconvenient, because our things still had to be kept upstairs. Now we're having the house remodeled so that the nursery can be right near us.

"Wait till I tell you about the room we are fixing for him now! It's a regular college boy's room, only on a small scale. I've ordered a miniature desk for him, with a miniature world globe on it. On the wall there will be college pennants, only scaled down, of course. And you know those silly signs that college boys always collect and hang on their walls. Well, we're having some of those made now, in miniature. One is a 'Don't Disturb!' sign. Another says, 'Men at Work.' You know . . . crazy things like that. Everything is going to be exactly like a college boy's room, only in baby size . . . even down to the pictures of girls that are always pasted around. Only I've cut out the grown-up girls' faces, and pasted little-girl faces in, instead!"

Husband George Barnes joined us at that moment, and, putting in his two cents, worth, said, "Yes, and when he grows up he probably won't even want to go to college!"

"It won't matter. He's going to do and be just what he wants. We're not going to run his life for him. We agreed on that, didn't we, George?"

"Yes, only it would be a shame for him to become a plumber or something like that, since we gave him a middle name."

"Yes," Joan explained. "He's not just to be Norman Barnes. It's Norman *Scott* Barnes. I think three names always sound so much more important—like George *Jean* Nathan, you know."

In case you haven't heard . . . little Norman was named after Norman Foster (Claudette Colbert's ex-husband). Norman has always been one of Joan's and George's very best friends. And he is their baby's godfather.

"George didn't want the baby to be named after himself, because George is a Junior, and to have three George Scott Barnes would really be too much for any family tree. Besides I think it's a good idea to give a baby a fresh start in life by giving him a new name.

"Even if Norman had been a girl, we were only going to give her my name as a middle name. The first name would have been Georgia. Georgia Joan Barnes."

Before the baby was born, Mr. Barnes presented his wife with a beautiful bassinet for the baby. On it was a card which read, "To my baby, from your baby, for our baby!" Darn clever, these cameramen.

"And I've been getting presents ever since," Joan went on. "Having a baby really has other inducements, in addition to the baby itself. Look what George gave me the day the baby arrived!" Proudly she showed me the bracelet she was wearing on her arm.

IT was a charm bracelet (a fad which has become quite popular in Hollywood). But, instead of having odd and incidental charms hanging on it, the charms on this bracelet tell the complete story of the Blondell-Barnes romance. First, there are two tiny, diamond-studded hearts, welded together, that hang from the bracelet. Next, there is a miniature engagement ring. Then a diamond wedding circlet. Then a diminutive house. And last, but not least, a stork on the wing. The whole happy story in a bracelet! (Of course, there's nothing sentimental about these two.)

Then—the latest present—is a set of two beautiful bracelets which George had given her only that day. "Because I've been such a good girl," said Joan beaming.

"No," said George, "because you let me photograph your new picture." (It's "Broadway Gondolier," by the way.)

"Oh well, it doesn't matter what for, only I think you're foolish to give me presents in between times, when we have so many more things to celebrate, now that the baby is here. There's Mother's Day—I can hardly wait for that—and Father's Day, and all the baby's birthdays, besides. It doesn't seem like enough!

"Did George tell you about the toy train apparatus that he's building for the baby? At least he *claims* it's for the baby . . . but I have my doubts. It's laid out in the cellar, miles and miles of tracks, it seems, and real trestles and bridges, and tunnels, and what not. And one of the most beautiful engines that you have ever seen. The same people who built the toy train exhibition at the World's Fair last year, are building ours. Of course it's a bit difficult on my nerves . . . the whistles shrieking and the house shaking as the train goes around the curves and all that. But the worst thing is that George spends half his time in the cellar now. I have to yell down the drain pipe to get him to come up to dinner.

"Oh, and the play yard! Wait till you see it! We're putting in a miniature tennis court, a small handball court—everything like a real gymnasium. Of course, he won't be able to play those games for a little while, though, at the rate he's going, it won't be long now."

WE haven't taken any movies of Normie yet . . . though we take snapshots of him every Sunday. They're all pasted into his baby book. And speaking of books, you have no idea how many there are, written on child psychology. I'm studying it as thoroughly as I can, and read every book I can lay my hands on . . .

"You know, there's a school at the University of Southern California where they take children as young as two and three years. They don't teach them anything, of course, except how to play . . . which is important, in itself. And they teach them good sportsmanship, and unselfishness.

"One of the things they do, for example, is to give a child a toy he likes very much, and then, just as he is about to start playing with it, the teacher says, 'Now dear, why don't you give that to Mary? I'm sure she would like to have it.' Great idea, I think. When Normie gets a little older we may enter him there—though I'm trying to practice some of their methods at home, right now."

At last I did get a word in edgewise. "All these books and modern theories on bringing up children, say something about *not* talking baby-talk to children, don't they?"

Joan tried awfully hard to hide a smile.

I dared to go on. "They say you shouldn't talk baby-talk to babies, or that is the first language they'll learn—thereby delaying their instruction in proper English. *You* don't talk baby-talk to *your* baby, do you?"

Now Joan was really grinning. "Oh, you can't help it, once in a while!" she admitted!

THE TRUTH ABOUT WILLIAM POWELL
[*Continued from page 97*]
caused by others. A sentimental thread ran through the letter. In fear, he nevertheless mailed the masterpiece.

A month passed. No answer came.

He had told his aunt in the letter that seven hundred dollars would take care of him for a year at the Academy. He had even offered to pay it back at a high rate of interest.

More unhappy days passed. His work at the telephone company desk grew more monotonous. When, not hearing from his aunt, he decided to get to New York in some manner and work his way through the Academy.

Then one day, long after weeds had grown high on the grave of his hope, a letter came. It was postmarked from the town in Pennsylvania where his aunt lived.

She had long considered her nephew's letter. Many paragraphs followed in a cramped and ancient female hand. She thought the letter was well-written, almost intelligent. She told him that she considered his ambition, though dubious, almost worthy. She had instructed her attorney to advance him seven hundred dollars.

ONE brought back to life could have been no more elated than was the young telephone clerk. The world was now his oyster, and his aunt had furnished a knife with which to open it.

He studied at the Academy for a year. It ended all too quickly for him. No further advance came from his aunt.

Powell went from one theatrical agency to another, and found indifference instead of work. So many battles in the economic war were lost by the young invader that the sweetheart in Kansas City was at times forgotten. He was rapidly learning one thing, that absence does not make the heart grow fonder.

It was the low ebb of his life. Still at that dangerous stage between boyhood and manhood, he seriously considered jumping into the East River.

By an odd stroke of irony, he might have been a suicide had not another young fellow from Kansas City joined him at this time. The new comrade cheered Powell in his moments of despair. He convinced him that no-one had asked him to be an actor, and that he needed humor more than self-pity. "If you carry the thoughts of suicide and failure in your heart, other people will feel them."

He had done some drawing in high school and had come to the same conclusion as his fellow townsman that he would make a career in New York. He went far among the masters of his craft, and though he saved Bill Powell, he himself died a suicide at the zenith of his fame. He had made the mistake of pursuing the shadows of futility and beauty. When they eluded him, he died. His name was Ralph Barton.

They rented a cheap room together; then walked the streets in destitution, looking for work.

They pawned their belongings until everything had seemingly disappeared. In the lowest depths of despair young Barton discovered a small air rifle and several boxes of tiny bullets in the room. Together they started for the pawnbroker's. A thought came to them to shoot the cockroaches in the room before the gun was sold. They returned and began shooting.

The landlady rushed to the door, thinking that war had been declared. Whether in pity for the cockroaches, or irritated because the walls and floor of her room were perforated with bullets, history does not record. It does record, however, that a future cinema actor and a famous illustrator were ejected from their room.

The pawnbroker gave them a dollar and a half for the gun. They lived on this sum for three days. Then a humorous weekly paid Barton thirty-three dollars for a drawing. Joy came to earth again.

IN THIS desultory manner the two youths lived for another year. It might have cheered them could they have seen the golden road that stretched ahead for both. But these things are not given to mortals, else, perhaps, they would see the dark road also.

Powell was soon given work in *The Ne'er Do Well* at forty dollars a week. This was in 1912. He appeared in three different small rôles in this play. In spite of high hopes and hard work, the play died early and Powell was soon destitute again. From the Fall of 1912 until the following Spring he was often hungry, as was Barton.

Then the clouds of misery parted. He was given a fairly important rôle in *Within the Law*. The play ran two years. When it closed he "went into stock" and acted in plays in Pittsburgh, Boston, Detroit, and Buffalo. Barton remained in New York and began to go to far places, while Powell next played forty weeks of one night stands "on the road." During this time he learned much of America.

Five heart-breaking years followed. Powell alternated between musical comedy, farce, and melodrama. He played one season in Portland, Oregon, another in Buffalo, and other seasons on the road.

It was now 1920.

Ralph Barton was becoming famous. Bill Powell was still in the ranks of the unknown.

While debating his future, he received an invitation from Ralph Barton to have dinner at the Lambs Club.

Whether or not it had been pre-arranged, Barton would never tell.

A director shook hands with Ralph shortly after they entered the club. Barton introduced him to Powell.

After glancing casually at Powell's profile for some time, he asked, "How would you like to work in a picture?"

Powell's answer was, "When do we start?"

"Right away," said the director.

Thus the master detective of the screen made his bow to an indifferent world as a "heavy" opposite John Barrymore in *Sherlock Holmes*. That Powell was later to surpass Barrymore in the portrayal of such rôles was not yet written in the faraway cinema sky.

He went from one picture to another and patiently waited for the lightning to strike.

At last it came.

HE FIRST attracted attention on the screen with Marion Davies in *When Knighthood Was in Flower*. He had not been originally cast for the rôle. An actor had been injured, and the director had to get a man to take his place. Someone had remembered Powell's work in another film. It was sheer accident, as the man who remembered was a visitor on the set. He told the director of Powell. A frantic search was made for him.

They rushed him to the studio and tried to fit the injured actor's costume upon him. Finding it impossible, they threw another costume on him and Powell played one of his biggest rôles —that of Francis I, the heavy.

Powell says calmly, "I really made my motion picture début through another man's misfortune."

B. P. Schulberg was the first to see big possibilities in the former telephone clerk. He brought him to Hollywood and watched him become world famous.

IT WAS upon Schulberg's advice that Powell made a sudden change in *Sea Horses*. It was from heavy to lover. His enormous fan mail indicated that he was popular in the latter rôle. In *Philo Vance* he was soon to reach another high pinnacle of popularity.

He next signed a long term contract with Warner Brothers as a star. His salary was a thousand dollars a day.

He is now under contract to M-G-M Studios, and is scheduled to play *The Great Ziegfeld* for Universal.

His parents joined him in Hollywood. His sweetheart of the early Kansas City days is now married—to another man. She sends the suave ex-telephone clerk a Christmas card each year. And Powell, remembering, says, "She was a fine girl." He does not say for whom.

His aunt learned to love one relative. Proudly she watched her brilliant nephew become an honor to her name. She first collected; then went to heaven.

William Powell was thirteen years in returning the seven hundred dollars to his aunt. He is a conservative man—and honest. This item, more than anything else, indicates how precarious is an actor's life, and how hard the struggle.

The effort to pay the money gave Bill much.

It made him a first-rate man.

DANGER SIGNALS!

[*Continued from page 103*]

AND so, Fredric March stopped work. Somewhere in the heart of Southern California's vast, golden desert is a little ranch. There went Freddie March, trying to forget the most vital thing in his existence—his art. Studios are wearisome factories. Physically he enjoyed such peace and quiet as he hasn't known in years. Mentally, it was the battle of his life.

But Freddie has the indomitable will of genius. He'll *get there*. Big obstacles have always seemed little in his way. He was a go-getter, a nervous dynamo of almost limitless power, 'way back in 1920 at the University of Wisconsin, when he was a track star, senior class president, active in *Haresfoot*, the men's dramatic association, partook in Union Vodvil, and at the same time managed to maintain an enviable scholastic record.

Freddie is a bundle of nerves—but not of the "nervous wreck" variety. If anything, he is over-fired with nervous energy, a sort of human motor that has no *off* switch.

It's worth the price of a good show to watch him rehearse or work before the cameras. His is true temperament. He gets so wrapped up in his part that you begin to think he has worked himself into some sort of trance that succeeds in obliterating the world of reality. You actually can *see* him throwing himself deeper and deeper into the thing he is doing. You have a mad desire to rush onto the set and throw a pail of ice water over him, or give him a brisk shaking before it is too late and Mr. Hyde—or whomever he is portraying—consumes him!

In *The Royal Family*, he portrayed an impetuous, high-strung, and erratic young thespian. Freddie may not like this, but—allowing for a little exaggeration—his off-stage manner is strikingly suggestive of that character.

Once satisfied with his lines, he rushes onto the set, taking his place before the cameras with the other characters. And, until the cameras are ready to go, he continues to mutter his lines and shake his fist, squinting at the actor whom he is to address, but not seeing him.

He studies every movement and every line religiously to the veriest detail. Often he will stop the cameras in the midst of an apparently perfect "take" to say that he feels a certain bit of action has been timed awkwardly, and ask the director to tell him how he can make the sequence move more naturally.

FREDRIC MARCH is, in spite of his keen sense of humor, not a comedian. He was a riot in *The Royal Family* because he was impersonating a famous comedian. His interest while making that picture was to give as pat an impersonation as he could—in the meantime, if he made you laugh, it was all right with him.

That is why many critics referred to John Barrymore's *Dr. Jekyll and Mr. Hyde* as "John Barrymore doing a black-face;" whereas, they refer to March's version as ". . . gruesome, but by far Fredric March's most artistic triumph. . . ." Freddie put everything he had into making Mr. Hyde a beast, and bringing out everything weak and everything fine in Dr. Jekyll.

"I conceived Mr. Hyde as more than just Dr. Jekyll's inhibited evil nature," Freddie told me, when I commented on the fact that—in contrast to the John Barrymore version—the two characters looked nothing alike. "I saw the beast as a separate entity—one who could, and almost did, little by little, overpower and annihilate Dr. Jekyll. And I tried to show the devastating results in Dr. Jekyll as well. To me, those repeated appearances of the beast within him were more than just a mental strain on Jekyll—they crushed him physically as well. I tried to bring this out by increasing lines and shadows of Jekyll's makeup as the picture progressed, until, in the last scenes, he looked as though he already had one foot in the grave. Hyde was killing Jekyll physically as well as mentally."

The making of that picture, with its tiresome changes of makeup—makeup that was, at the least, *uncomfortable,* with its extreme demands for every drop of emotional and physical effort that Freddie could wring from himself —was one of the great moments in his thirty-four years of existence.

Fortunately, it was enough of a strain to make his nervous system raise an objection. A rest in the desert brought him back to the studios, physically able to give his best to the powerful part that awaited him in *Merrily We Go To Hell.* Had the stomach disorder not occurred when it did our Freddie undoubtedly would have prematurely plunged himself, body and soul, into this picture, and, unable and unwilling to elude the compelling force of his tempestuous genius, would have come out of it with his health seriously—if not permanently impaired.

Providing his pictures continue to have the power deserving of his ability, Fredric March's path leads straight to glory. *Still waters run deep*—Freddie doesn't look the genius—but its flame is all but consuming him!

MARLENE ANSWERS ALL YOUR QUESTIONS
[Continued from page 105]

"There are too many stars for one to be a novelty. Nor do they try to disturb my home life. No one ever attempts to climb over my walls, to break into my house. A few children come and ask for autographs, but that is no nuisance. I think all this talk of lack of privacy is odd. I notice it only when I am *away* from Hollywood. Then everyone stares and I am scared. I am eager to get back here where it is quiet and peaceful."

Rudolph Sieber, Marlene's director husband, has decided to stay in Hollywood permanently. That is, as long as his wife is fated to remain. Their four-year separation, which was punctuated by twice-a-year visits, is thus over.

"I was only away from my little girl for the first six months I was here. I didn't bring her from Germany because I was very uncertain. I didn't know whether I was to succeed here. It was for her own good that she stayed at home until I learned. Now she is growing up to be very American. I think that personality is determined when one is very young. I was never allowed to express any emotion in my face, to show dislike for anything. That is why I couldn't act all over the set. I would be ashamed to be unrestrained. But Maria is being raised to have freedom."

Hollywood plays such jokes on ambitious women. Marlene has escaped the town's capricious whims. She has had no terrific disillusionment because she never was lured into a worship for fame.

"I always had an admiration for the screen. But I never dreamed of becoming a star," she said. "Even when I first came to Hollywood it was not the fame and the money which attracted me. I came to work with Mr. Von Sternberg."

"But doesn't the money mean a lot to you?" I probed.

"No. Half of what I earn goes for income tax. I could accumulate more in Europe. Or I could go on the radio here and make enough in a year so I should never need to work again."

"The applause, the flattery, do they please you?"

"NO," she replied. "I am not proud of being a film star! I see no reason to be. Compared to important professions this, that I am doing, is so unimportant. Even in comparison to the stage this work of mine falls far short. On the stage you must struggle for years before you can advance to a lead. In pictures, stars are made overnight because of their beauty. There is a haste and a lack of dignity to film stardom. I do not mean to criticize. There are many stars here who have great talent. I merely say that from my own standpoint I am not at all proud because I have become a film star."

Such modesty had never come my way from a Hollywood lady. So I asked:

"But what makes all this worth while to you then?"

"The sheer joy of acting, of creating a characterization, of being associated with Mr. Von Sternberg."

"And," I reiterated, "have you no desire to stand on your own feet, to work with another director? A fine actress should be as fine under any guidance, shouldn't she?"

"Certainly she should. But I do not understand why I must prove I am not an automaton. As I said, if I find an interesting story I will do it with someone else. Then I shall return to Mr. Von Sternberg's direction."

"And the stage . . . ?"

"No. I haven't command enough of English to act on the stage in this country. Perhaps some day again in Europe. As for the screen, when there are no more plots which are appealing, then I will stop.

"I have never been the kind who could mix with many people, so I have few close acquaintances in Hollywood. In Berlin I had three or four friends. Does anyone really have more? Here I go straight home from the studio. I am perfectly content to have just a few friends. I do not want any more. There isn't time. Between my home and my work I am kept busy.

"But how can you develop your personality if you don't notice what others are doing and adapt yourself in various ways to suit those others?"

"I said I thought one's personality was determined when young. I don't believe in making one's self over. I have never tried to please everyone. If it is someone I respect highly I pay attention. But I don't want to make other people over, either. And as for developing, I have never endeavored to consciously improve myself. That is confusing. I mean, of course, that I do my best to be my best. But I simply trust to life my mold my personality."

I was becoming more and more intrigued with this amazing woman. So feminine is she, and yet so thoroughly brave in her convictions. Every article about her has been an attempt to reveal how she has been changed by Hollywood. They've missed the point. Marlene has been perfectly poised. It's the rest who have been doing the flustering.

But if her replies to my pertinent questions have astonished you, wait until you hear her sum up these four film years in America. I asked her what she considers her accomplishments to date.

"I have a child," she said, without a second's pause. There was no mention of Hollywood peaks! I must have looked startled for she then added, "And I have made a few people happy. That is all."

"But your career!" I exclaimed, so used to listening to the cinema stars chatter on and on endlessly, egotistically.

"Ah," she declared, "there is so much more in life for me. Earning the respect of the people I love, carrying out my duties to them, bringing up my child . . ."

You have read numberless tales about Marlene. No one had ever gone to her and frankly asked for her own explanations. I'm glad I did because now she seems not a high-hat mystery, but a normal, eager, and loyal woman. Four years have brought overwhelming changes to Hollywood. But none to the tranquil, tantalizing Dietrich.

Even if she hadn't behaved so intelligently during my twenty minutes with her, I'd have approved of her. She is so marvelously beautiful.

Do you suppose she has ever delved into Lord Chesterfield's tomes? Remember, he advised, "address yourself to the senses if you would please; dazzle the eyes, sooth and flatter the ears of mankind, engage their hearts and let their reason do its worst against you."

I am sure of few things in this perplexing world, but one of my certainties now is that none of the slams on Marlene could have been written by a man who has met her!

TARZAN SEEKS A NEW MATE
[Continued from page 106]
almost frantic with grief. Bravely she concealed her breaking heart from the world and when they went to see a lawyer, it was she who wise-cracked and smiled while Johnny looked on, hurt and sorry that things had to be as they were.

"HE IS such a big baby," smiled Bobbe, "and so unbelievably naïve. Poor

Tarzan, he couldn't understand why we had to see a lawyer. He seemed to think that if he wanted a divorce, that was all the formality necessary, to tell me about it. When I asked him to move his things from my apartment, as was fitting under the circumstances, he said, 'What's the matter, haven't you got room for them?' Poor Johnny, he is a wonderful boy but I wonder who is going to take care of him."

If ever a man owed his success to a woman, Johnny Weissmuller owes his place on the screen to Bobbe Arnst. When they were married he was already a world's champion swimmer but he was content to do exhibition work for a bathing suit company and rest on his laurels. It was Bobbe who brought him to Hollywood. Bobbe who haunted the casting offices pleading for a chance for him. It was Bobbe who made life unbearable for M-G-M's casting director until he agreed to test Johnny for *Tarzan* and Bobbe who saw to it that Johnny made his calls on time and who drove him on. Tiny mite that she is, she has been the mainspring which drove the mightly bulk of *Tarzan* to success.

"When I saw the preview of *Tarzan,*" she admits, "I knew that Johnny would be besieged by a million women, women who wanted him. I thought that the best way to hold him against them was to give him free rein. I wanted to go to New York with him but I knew I should not, so I stayed at home. I thought I could beat this game which Hollywood plays but now I must admit that I have lost."

Johnny Weissmuller and Lupe met in New York. The stalwart *Tarzan* and the fiery little Mexican were drawn together as the magnet draws the steel. Accused of having a romance, they both laughingly denied it. When Johnny returned to Hollywood, their friendship was resumed. They were seen places together but their denial of any heart interest persisted.

"Eet is not true," cried Lupe over the phone when confronted with the accusation of Bobbe Arnst that Johnny was divorcing her for love of Lupe, "Eef I am in luf I will say eet is true. I like thees Johnny ver' much but that ees all."

"I have nothing against Lupe," says Bobbe. "She was very kind to me once, when I was ill in New York. I do not know if she even cares for Johnny in a big way but I am sure that he is infatuated, at least, with her."

Bobbe Arnst believed with all her heart that she could hold her husband even against the onslaughts of Hollywood. When she told reporters that nothing could tear them apart, she spoke in good faith. It was soon after Johnny's spectacular success in *Tarzan* that Hollywood began to see the hand-

writing on the wall but Bobbe, her belief in the man she loved unshaken, refused to accept the truth. She fought a gallant fight, believing that she could win but like many another Hollywood wife, she underestimated the potency of the virus which creeps into the blood of those whom the cinema gods select as their favorites.

And so Bobbe Arnst sits alone in the apartment she once shared with *Tarzan,* wondering if after all their marriage is definitely on the rocks or if they have only hit a snag from which they will soon pull away and once more be the happy lovers.

"All I want is to get away from Hollywood," she told me. "My plans are not yet complete but I shall return to the stage. If we had never come here, Johnny and I would still be happy. I do not blame him, for after all he is just a big, lovable boy."

Johnny Weissmuller was Bobbe's first love. She will learn to laugh again but I doubt if the wound which Hollywood has dealt her ever will be quite healed. Her place on the stage is secure and no doubt she will go on to greater triumphs, but what of the boy she leaves behind? Without her guiding hand Johnny Weissmuller may find Hollywood a jungle more devouring than any conceived in the brain of Edgar Rice Burroughs!

I'M NEVER GOING BACK!
[Continued from page 107]
can say is thees. *Lupe never broke up any home.* I don't want anybody's husband. I deedn't even know Johnny liked me. Then one day he said, 'Lupe I luf you. I jus' want to look at you.'"

Lupe was charging around her dressing room. Her hair was standing on end. She looked like Salome about to behead John the Baptist.

"I yell at Johnny. I say, 'Go away and don't let me hear your voice. I never want to see you again.' Besides, Winnie Sheehan ees my boy friend.

"Let that Johnny Weissmuller go back to hees wife. I don't want anything to do with heem. Believe Lupe, she can't help eet eef handsome men say they luf her, can she?"

FAY WRAY'S DESIGN FOR MARRIAGE
[Continued from page 108]
and comedies, Fay married a man whose education and schooling were so beautifully complete that they dazzled. To a girl who has an admitted sense of inferiority, it was a terrific handicap. Especially when she loved the man. She had beauty, poise, acting ability. She was hailed in cinema circles as an Eric von Stroheim "find," having made a memorable appearance in his *Wedding March.* The picture really made Fay.

The young Saunders had common interests—films and their love. Beyond that, not much meeting ground. However, Fay had an instinctive feeling for the "better things." John was quick to understand her desire to develop those tastes. Thus, Fay set about making herself into the person she wanted to be. She didn't try to bring herself to the level of John Saunder's intellectual accomplishments. She knew that she was years behind him in that score. She knew, too, what every thinking woman knows, that a man usually marries because he wants a loving, amusing companion, not an intellectual duelist. But, still, Fay wanted to be able to talk John's talk. Quietly, she commenced with the better fiction, biographies, classics, reading twice as much as she had previously read.

"Poor John," says Fay, today, with her crimson-lipped smile, so strangely like that of Gloria Swanson's. "In those days, he barely had a chance to see the new books that came into the house. I always got them first, and read them so that I would know about them as he went through their pages later."

Reading everything except the modish books on psychology that were then the vogue (she did not like them), Fay Saunders soon found that she and John could discuss subjects that ranged from Wedgewood to weevils, and she did not bother him with housewifely dissertations on drains and the new maid. Too, Fay soon found herself a part of the swift, live patter of the young married set in which she and her husband moved.

Nothing pleased her more than to have one of her husband's friends ask if she remembered the little cafe in back of Paris' Notre Dame where the *bouillabaisse* was enchanting. Fay liked the accepted thought that she was traveled, had been abroad. At that time her itinerary had been Wrayland, Alberta, Canada (her birthplace); Bingham, Utah; Hollywood, California. Despite this, she looked and talked like a cosmopolite. The past two years have changed her travel status. Thrice she has been to England for picture-making, appearing in four films, including *The Clairvoyant, Come Out of the Pantry* and *Alias Bull-Dog Drummond*. She has toured the continent, including Scandinavia vacationed in Nassau, flown to New York City for radio programs. Her familiarity with a menu card (largely in French) is awe-inspiring. In other words, Fay has matured.

THIS fruitfulness has taken time. French, Italian, Spanish lessons. Voice and piano lessons. Hard practice at tennis and ping-pong. Attention to clothes. Things like line and color tones and harmony. When I interviewed Fay in 1927 (it was her first interview) she

wore a red hat, a black velvet bodiced dress, with black and white taffeta skirt. The effect was gay, and pitiful. The brightness of the costume overshadowed her natural beauty. The other day, Fay wore black and white, too, but what black and white! A *chic* small white felt hat with tiny veil. A black dress with white *decor,* punctuated by five tiny metal stars. Fay has learned well her lessons in selecting her garments. And she has the good taste to give much of the credit to her husband for this added knowledge.

Strange, then, you may think, that out of this indebtedness to John Monk Saunders has come Fay's joint marriage rule: "freedom of thought and interdependence." But Fay, in mentioning "freedom," at all, is thinking of their two separate careers. A film assignment took Fay to London. When Saunders followed to spend the Christmas holidays with her, he found a directorial opportunity awaiting him. It meant he would have a chance to direct instead of only write for the films. It was a chance he could not forego. And Fay would not permit him to pass it up because her film work called her back to Hollywood.

Thus, by their complete understanding of each other, they have established a bond that separation cannot sever. Today, when three films a year for Columbia bring her back to Hollywood (*Roaming Lady* is her latest), she manages to meet her husband between continents, at Nassau, for example, and they have exciting re-unions. Then he returns to England, and she to Hollywood. How long they will be busy on separate continents, neither knows. But they do know that this does not lessen, but strengthens their dependence upon each other.

Although her allegiance is stretched between England and the United States (Fay was born in Canada, became a naturalized American citizen; her American-born husband enjoyed a fine schooling through Oxford by means of a Rhodes scholarship. He had his first directing opportunity in Britain), there isn't much chance that the Saunders will pack up the family belongings and move to England. They feel "rooted" in Hollywood. In Hollywood are their friends, and friendship is something very important to this young couple.

IN analyzing the "interdependence" of her marriage, it is easy to see that Fay's attitude is that of the old-fashioned wife who has assumed the added burden of a career. She runs the English house in Hollywood with a precision that would please her Scotch-Irish-English forebears, discussing menus with the cook, draperies with the draper, carpets with the rug-maker.

From the moment she leaves the

studio at night until she enters her dressing-room the next morning, Fay is Mrs. John Monk Saunders. At home she is the efficient young wife who runs her house smoothly. She is independently equipped, too, with her own thoughts, her own pre-occupations (her career, her garden, her athletics, her studies), but when John comes home it is to an eager young person whose personal preoccupation has vanished in an unfeigned and undivided interest in her husband's pleasure match or playing "Monopoly," she is ready to do the same, her thoughts entirely divorced from the kitchen or the studio.

Thus the marital status of the Saunders is that of two intimate strangers, eagerly enjoying life and adventures together, sharing an enthusiasm for work, laughter, and the future. That is the kind of "interdependence," as Fay calls it, that makes for happy marriages.

BETTE FROM BOSTON
[*Continued from page 109*]
Academy there. During her years in school, it wasn't the easiest thing in the world to realize that there were to be no long stretches of idle time and fun. Because she was so ambitious and so anxious to learn, she had to figure out for herself some way of attaining her desires.

So Bette put her pride in her pocket and got herself a job. During the last year or so of her education, Bette waited on tables at the Academy to pay for part of her tuition. And not a word of complaint was ever heard about it, either.

And it certainly didn't make any difference to Harmon O. Nelson, Jr., who sat right across the aisle from her in school. The minute he laid his two eyes on Bette, he'd made up his mind about certain things. Most of them had to do with a little cottage with a white fence around it and a girl with a big blue eyes and the "swellest" disposition! And he kept right on thinking these thoughts until his dream came true.

As far as Bette was concerned, she'd made up her mind about a few things, too. One of them was Harmon, but the other was something quite remote. Bette had decided to be an actress. Every chance she got, she applied for a rôle in the school theatricals. It was a bit difficult, at times, to keep up with her studies and her part-time job, but she managed it all somehow.

It was as a result of this hard work and natural ability that Bette was finally given a scholarship by John Murray Anderson to his dramatic school in New York, where James Light, director of the school, began to sit up and take notice of this blue-eyed girl. She was finally given a rôle by Blanche Yurka in Ibsen's "Wild Duck," when it played in Boston. As a consequence, she then was cast in "Broken Dishes" and "Solid South."

Just about this time, thoughts of Hollywood and the movies began to bother Bette. So she packed her bag one fine day and landed in the town of opportunities. Because of her extremely youthful appearance, Bette was doomed to disappointment. No one could fancy her as anything but a little girl. For a whole year, Bette waited, until there seemed no possible chance for a screen career. She was ready to give up and go back to New York. And then came the "Big Opportunity." She was offered a rôle in "The Man Who Played God," with George Arliss. And what is more, Mr. Arliss himself had asked for her! She was thrilled beyond all words.

For this picture, Bette was obliged to bleach her hair. This, she feels, is the most fortunate thing that has ever happened to her, outside of meeting George Arliss. The honey-colored hair set off perfectly her fair skin and blue eyes, to such an extent that the studio officials rushed around madly to prepare a long-term contract for her to sign. That was four years ago and she is still going strong.

Of course, Bette was delighted at the opportunity to play with Leslie Howard once again—in "The Petrified Forest" —because of their tremendous joint success in "Of Human Bondage." It seemed like a good omen to be associated again with someone who helped give her the biggest break of her career.

Directly after this rôle, Bette had to pull herself together and transform her personality from the simple, uneducated but overwhelmingly ambitious "Gaby" of "The Petrified Forest" to the sophisticated woman of the world which she plays in "Men on Her Mind," a Dashiell Hammett mystery originally titled "The Man in the Black Hat." Warren William has the male lead in this. After that you may look for her in a little opus called "The Golden Arrow," unless the title gets changed all of a sudden.

There is one small room in Bette's little cottage that has been devoted to a strange but exceedingly sensible purpose. Bette calls it her "Deflation Room." It is entirely bare of pictures or furbelows and contains just one easy chair. The chair is placed facing the garden.

"Whenever I feel particularly proud of myself," says Bette, "I go into that room and have a long talk with myself, 'Bette,' I tell myself firmly, 'you're really not so much, you know. You mustn't lose your perspective and begin to think you're a big shot. Just stop and think of all the marvelous actors and actresses you know—remember how much better they are than you. You've

got a long way to go before you become a great actress, so you just calm yourself down and don't go getting any queer notions.'

"Invariably, that treatment will set me straight. It may sound a bit childish, but I think we all need to really make a business out of analyzing ourselves occasionally. A good old-fashioned session of self-criticism is the only cure for an attack of self-satisfaction."

More and more, I think people should be grateful for girls like Bette Davis. Nice, wholesome, sane people, who are willing to work for what they get out of life. The world is too full of women —and men, too—who figure somehow that it owes them a living and who are quite willing to sit back and wait for success to "just happen."

I, for one, am glad to have known her. She's delightfully refreshing, somehow.

THAT MARITAL VACATION

[Continued from page 112]
and "Ham" had a remedy for misunderstandings of any size. She called it "running away with my husband."

If one of them started getting on the other's nerves, if any sign of maladjustment popped up, if either of them began feeling restless, or wondered if the other was, if they got tangled up in the details of everyday life and their separate worries; well, they just went away somewhere, alone together. Some place they had never visited before. They'd see new things, have new experiences, meet new people, talk on new subjects —together. They'd come back refreshed, with new viewpoints, their disagreements forgotten. Bette said that, even when life was being perfectly serene, she and "Ham" were sold on the idea of running away with each other if only for short weekends.

She even went so far as to add, "If I ever thought my marriage was heading toward the rocks, I hope I'd run away with my husband first. In fact, I know I would." Yet, when a crisis approached, Bette didn't run away with her husband. She ran away with her sister.

What happened that "another honeymoon" couldn't cure? What problem came up that didn't seem capable of solution by a trip somewhere together? It was something sudden. That much seems certain.

Bette isn't talking about it. Neither is "Ham." And, here's an odd thing, neither are their friends. In the past, their friends have never been so reticent about the Nelsons' marital life. And now, just when you would expect their tongues to be wagging most, they turn into clams.

What is behind the conspiracy of silence? What brought about the "mar-

ital vacation" that can't be discussed?

Well, if Bette had fallen in love with someone else, or if "Ham" had fallen in love with someone else, that would explain this pall of silence now. Twice, before she married "Ham," Bette fell in love with other men. One threw her over, and she threw over the other. But the fact remains that she twice found it possible, years ago, to fall in love with someone else besides "Ham." It might be possible for such a thing to happen a third time. Stranger things than that have happened in Hollywood.

However, Bette has never gone looking for a new romance. If anything, she has gone out of her way to be circumspect in her private life. When "Ham" was away so much, early in their marriage, and she attended social functions with a variety of escorts, and Hollywood said "Uh-huh," the rumors were so silly that Bette made the silliest possible retort to them. She appeared at one party with eight escorts. With that New England conscience of hers, she had never been addicted to fast company. Her friends have been quiet people, intellectuals, contentedly married.

She has encountered no dashing Don Juans in her small social circle. And she has encountered few in her pictures. Most of the men she has had opposite her have been known for their dramatic appeal.

Bette is very attractive to men. Any number of men could have fallen in love with her, if she had given them the slightest encouragement. But she hasn't been tempted. She just hasn't met any with whom she could even think of falling in love. That is, until recently.

Then, for the first time, she met a certain man to whom any girl, even a happily married Bette Davis, might well be attracted. Tall, dashingly handsome, charming, intellectual, witty, gaily alive. She seemed to find him attractive. And he seemed to reciprocate. Nobody was looking for a romance, even though, during the next few weeks, they were often together and always very gay. He was married—none too happily—according to reports. But it was a foregone conclusion Bette was Mrs. Harmon Nelson for keeps.

Then a strange coincidence happened. About the same time that Bette got a vacation, he also got one. She went off to a Nevada ranch without her husband. And this chap's wife, who has made a point of vacationing with him in the past, just as "Ham" has made a point of vacationing with Bette, suddenly left for the East without him.

A few days later, the news of the Nelsons' "marital vacation" came out. About the same time, this chap fell seriously ill. Word was sent to his wife. She was expected to rush back immediately. But she didn't. She stayed in the East.

This all may be just a strange coincidence. It may not be a prelude to two divorces. It may signify nothing. But, until Bette, herself, tells all, it offers one possible explanation for the Harmon Nelsons taking a "marital vacation" to test their ability to live without each other after six years together.

SCOOP! THE MAN BETTE DAVIS MARRIED

[Continued from page 113]
first by private tutors and then, after a term or two at high school in Rutland, had attended a school for boys at Hoosick, New York. He had decided first on a business career, but music, the common love that united his entire family, eventually won out. Arthur left for New York to study the violin. Concerts all over the East followed with his sister Barbara, a concert singer, and brother Dan, a cellist.

A second interest was flying. Arthur became active in aviation through his first wife, Betty Jane Aydelotte, designer and aviatrix of Boston and Barnstable, Massachusetts, before their divorce two years ago. He became a skillful pilot, winning ratings of one S—land and two S—land and his plane was a familiar figure at the East Boston airport, where he flew for a private company.

AT the Lodge Bette and Arthur rode, played golf, tennis and went swimming, Bette's favorite sport. In the evenings, Arthur played and sang for her.

In Boston, Arthur's close friends, among whom are the Cushings (especially Betty Cushing, ex-wife of James Roosevelt), began to hear of the happy twosome. So did the reporters, and in no time Boston papers were printing rumors of a romance—rumors promptly denied by both Bette and Arthur.

One evening, as Bette sat on the porch of the hotel with its owner, Robert Peckett, he said very quietly, "Bette, I've lived here nearly fifty years, yet I never look out over those forests and fields of mine without feeling a thrill to the core of me when I think that these are my trees and this is my own land."

In Hollywood Bette had never cared to own or possess for long a home or land. The town seemed too restless, too uncertain for her.

And then, far up there in New Hampshire, Arthur Farnsworth and Bette one day walked up a roadway lined on either side with colorful butternut trees to see an old home Arthur had purchased as an investment. The minute Bette Davis saw the house she knew so many answers to things that had puzzled her before. Here, before her, was *her* home.

She bought the house, of course, and called it "Butternut Lodge" because of the trees around it. Instantly she plunged into plans for redecorating, plans in which Arthur shared intimately. A furniture connoisseur, he spent many hours with Mrs. Davis touring New England buying the antiques Bette wanted.

But soon, all too soon, she had to return to Hollywood for "All This and Heaven, Too."

She said good-by to her friends and neighbors—and to Arthur Farnsworth. As yet, not one word of love had been spoken between them, but something even deeper—a feeling of friendship born from a sharing of land and home —had grown in their hearts, something even they didn't understand at the time.

The first Hollywood evidence of a new element in Bette's life came when the word spread that a handsome stranger named Arthur Farnsworth and his sister were house guests of Bette Davis in her River Bottom home in Glendale.

On a motor trip they took to Death Valley with Mrs. Davis, Barbara Farnsworth and a party of friends, Arthur's devotion to Bette was observed by all. It was plain that he worshipped her.

Not too unnaturally, the romance rumors began. Bette, in the midst of work, nervous, upset and embarrassed, denied the rumors vehemently. So strongly, in fact, did she speak that Arthur Farnsworth, sharing her feelings, left Hollywood for home before even Bette's friends had a chance to know him. Several close friends had met him at the christening of Bette's sister's baby and once photographers had snapped the couple at the Grove. But that was all Hollywood knew of him.

"Anyway, it's ridiculous," several people close to Bette said. "No one has ever been in Bette's heart but Ham." And friends, returning from New York, brought word that Harmon Nelson, Bette's ex-husband, who had been popular and successful in New York had confided, "I'll never marry anyone but Bette."

So almost at once, Hollywood forgot that a man named Arthur Farnsworth ever existed. Bette went on from success to success—until the summer of 1940 when she went back East. Again she and Ham met in New York and were seen everywhere together; again rumors were revived.

But from New York Bette telephoned close friends in Boston, "I'll be there soon," she said. "Give my love to Arthur." (Arthur, at that time, was living in Brookline, a Boston suburb.)

"I knew," said Mrs. Robert Peckett, wife of the owner of the lodge, "that Bette and Arthur were in love." And I think Bette knew it, too, when she again returned to Franconia.

THEN came last Christmas in Hollywood. Bette sat among us at Ciro's, and presented the Red Book Award to Martha Scott for "Our Town," the award she herself had won the year previous for "Dark Victory."

Not one of us with whom she laughed and talked guessed her secret. Oh, there had been a bit of whispering, of course, for the papers had announced Harmon Nelson would be in Hollywood to spend Christmas with Bette; and he hadn't come. We all wondered silently at that.

But the following Tuesday morning, Bette and her friend Ruth Garland, her brother-in-law and her sister, Mr. and Mrs. Pelgram, her mother and several friends set out to attend what everyone, except Bette, supposed was a New Year's Eve party at Jane Bryan Dart's ranch home in Arizona.

Bette, at the wheel, kept her eyes fastened to the road ahead as a blizzard swept in over the desert. Then, just before they finally reached their destination, Bette said quietly, "This is not a New Year's Eve party. Farny has flown out from Boston to meet me here. I am going to marry him this evening."

It was the first intimation they had. They arrived at the Darts two hours late and as Bette, beautiful in her white jersey evening dress, and wearing lilies of the valley, stood before the bank of flowers in Janey's living room to repeat the vows that made her Mrs. Farnsworth, they still couldn't believe it. But Bette knew her own heart and mind.

The Farnsworth family are "very happy" about the marriage. Extremely fond of Bette, they realize that Arthur's love for her is worth the sacrifice he is making in giving up his Boston work in order to live with Bette in Hollywood. His great pride in her career has prompted him to put her before any selfish interests of his own.

Hollywood, who loves Bette Davis for her realness, her loyalty and kindness, wishes them both all of the best—forever and ever.

THIS YEAR'S LOVE MARKET

[Continued from page 115]
Bidding for the favors of the young British star sent his stock soaring to remarkable new highs for the year.

July: The Hearts' Exchange held its gains this month, in spite of a rapid turnover as reflected in the Franchot Tone and Richard Arlen separation reports. The latter was unexpected and caused gloom among Heart Throb dealers.

A general optimistic tone, however, prevailed. Trading in Matrimonial shares was brisk, with the Claire Trevor-Clark Andrews marriage leading the movement. The rise was reflected in the Lee Tracy wedding. Lita Grey Chaplin's recovery was marked, with announcement of her participation in Matrimony, Preferred. The Mary Lou Lender-Delmer Daves nuptials attracted the attention of traders and insiders considered the marriage of Carole Lombard's secretary, "Fieldsie," to Director Walter Lang significant.

Foreign holdings were depressed by reiterated attention to the affairs of Sigrid Gurie, hailed as deriving from Norway but actually originating in Brooklyn. Her divorce from Thomas W. Stewart and the Zita Johann-John McCormick split caused Foreign Hearts to lag, but they recovered during the session.

Romances shared in the month's recovery, along with Matrimonial shares, on a broad front. Hepburn stock broke through the old high, with rumored association with Howard Hughes. The Michael Whalen-Ilona Massey participation caused a flurry and much out-of-town interest was reflected by the rise in Romances, based on the Simone Simon-Gene Markey rumor. The Loretta Young status continued to interest Exchange heads: her adoption of the George Brent directorate was said, though not authenticated, to be distressing to the Tyrone Power interests.

August: The market held its gains, in spite of considerable speculation on the downside. Bears' raids were reflected in the precipitate decline of the Jack Oakies' Matrimonial listing. The suspension of Velez Weissmuller Maritals had been predicted by all the insiders and caught few gossip-traders short. Foreign shares were easier, with Michael Brooke (the Earl of Warwick) splitting, two for one, with his former Countess. Other declines were shown in the Ann Sheridan-Edward Norris marital status; the Vera Steadman-Martin Padway listing dropped the symbol Mrs. on the tape.

The Blue Chips, however, firmed after their recent sharp rise and, in some cases, continued their advance. Marriages rebounded when Humphrey Bogart, twice divorced, and Mayo Methot, once divorced, were merged in a new corporation. The Sylvia Sidney-Luther Adler amalgamation sent Marriage shares to a month's high and caught many oldtimers unprepared. Marital Tangles reflected the rumor that Dorothy Lamour, wife of Herbie Kay, seemed somewhat interested in a new merger with Randy Scott. At least, the two were seen here and there at the different dine and dance spots.

Pivotal stars showed revived interest. The Ronald Colman-Benita Hume stock soared on the rumor that consolidation of their interests had already been quietly arranged. The Janet Gaynor-

Adrian situation was regarded as very bullish by experts downtown. Incorporation papers were said to have been drawn up between Arleen Whelan and Richard Greene, whose stock had been one of the most actively traded on the board in recent months. Hints that he had been managed by a pool were discounted by authoritative sources on the Exchange.

The rise in Hearts and Marriages was reflected on the Stork front. The Morton Downeys (Barbara Bennett) profited when their stock rose 1 baby girl during the month. At the close of business Stork was still firm, with the Melvyn Douglas-Helen Gahagan firm reporting a new and important member.

September: Romances were easier, with many participants taking profits after the recent upswing, and news scarce. Year-end reports are said to be gratifying, but the interest was not yet reflected in the street. The Margot Grahame-Francis Lister divorce caused a slight decline in the Marriage Stability Index, but the Hearts Exchange went up a few days later with Margot's marriage to Canadian Allen McMartin.

The renewed rumor of a merger between Gaynor and designer Adrian helped maintain the list, while definite announcement that Marie Wilson and Director Nick Grinde would merge was considered good news by the traders.

A setback was caused by a hinted Reno visit by Bette Davis. The Tyrone Power issue, which had been very volatile in recent months, again rallied sharply with much widespread participation. The Norma Shearer firm was rumored to have the largest commitments in T. P. Preferred.

Three events of major importance brought renewed activity into the market in the last two weeks of the month. Marriage stocks jumped three points upon the definite announcement of a consolidation between Ronald Colman and Benita Hume, Genevieve Tobin and Director William Keighley and Shirley Ross and Ken Dolan. The list sagged a little at increasingly serious rumors of divorce between Bette Davis and Harmon Nelson, picked up later at the notice that Frances Drake and Cecil Howard (brother of the Earl of Suffolk) would amalgamate their American-British interests some time in the near future.

October, November, December: Despite the jitterbug quality of Love stocks due to the War scare in Europe, the list took a slight turn for the better with the merger of Martha Raye, once divorced, and Dave Rose and these two major mergers: Margaret Tallichet and Director William Wyler; Doris Kenyon, former wife of the late Milton Sills, and Albert Lasker.

Stork went to a new high with issues made by the following firms: the Ernst Lubitschs, the Jules Garfields, the Anthony Quinns.

Straws in the wind indicate also that the English glamour bonds soon will rise again with the long-waited combine of Ida Lupino and Louis Hayward. American glamour bonds rose sharply with the Odets' and Oakies' reconciliations.

ROUND-UP OF ROMANCES

[Continued from page 141]

Hollywood had maintained the belief that theirs was really a love match, no matter how stormy. Therefore, where on all other occasions Hollywood has always laughed and said Lili and Errol would be back together again soon, this time it says just the opposite. Lili and Errol both say it is all over. Perhaps it is, but you can't be certain.

You can't be certain, either, in the case of Lana Turner and Tony Martin.

THE STANWYCK COURT CASE

[Continued from page 117]

her gravely. "You forgot all about me, mummy!" . . . *Forgot him!* . . . "You forgot to leave the note!"

That is the first thing he hunts for under his pillow every morning Her little note for him to read during the day while she is at work. It's one of the little things that bind them together so closely.

WHY FIFTH AVENUE LAUGHS AT HOLLYWOOD SOCIETY

[Continued from page 122]

chipped in whatever the studio had apportioned as their "share" of the fund which went down on the records as the individual contributions of the studio's big-shot executives.

The cheapness, the flimsiness, the gaudiness, the racket of the Hollywood social game paramounts anything anywhere else in the land. True, certain biggies are bigger than others; but the general run are pretty small potatoes when it comes to the bigger things in life. Each dollar earned goes out for so much nonsense that a Barbara Hutton or a Doris Duke must laugh herself silly when glancing in life's reflector before slithering into bed.

At least the Fifth Avenue set, as worthless as it may be in other things, has learned the true worth of spending the dollars it amasses. Fun is fun when you share your fun; but fun is folly when you don't give your money's worth to those who gather about it.

There is a passage in Henry VI which reads: "Beggars mounted run their horses to death." Did you ever see it to fail?

COME to Hollywood and get an invite to a typical party, and see what I mean. Sudden riches to many people are worse than none at all. Dozens of swell people go through the Hollywood mill yearly on the crest of a typhoon which crashes them to little pieces before they reach the shore. Tens of hundreds of pretty girls and swell young fellows get the braggadocian buncombe bumped out of them after it's too late.

Maybe it's the system that's wrong. Perhaps it's the associations they make. I don't even profess to know. But take any of them to Fifth Avenue for a few months observation and training and you'll turn out a cat of a different color.

Much of that pretense and pretentious pompousness will disappear. The heavy goo and over-made-up cheeks and hair will be more normal. The men will retain their masculinity without the use of perfume and loud coats. They'll talk in less harsh accents, both of them, and neither will strain the Oxonian which some Hollywood linguist has told them is the way the Four Hundred speak.

They'll be surprised to find out how thoroughly the correct New York hostess checks her guests. They'll be amazed to see how hard she works over her dinner or theater party. They'll be ashamed at their own lack of knowledge of how to drink, and how much. They'll admire and praise her selection of the press, and the way she handles those uninvited who print the bare facts about her party, without giving it so much as a splinter of scandal on which to start an idle rumor. They'll praise her trained staff of men and women servants constantly "in service" who know what to do at all times.

Some of them may find the parties, Fifth Avenue brand, dull and foolish, but most formal parties are. Did you ever hear of a Garden Party at Buckingham Palace, or a Supreme Court Affair at the White House smacking of jazz and jubilation? Formal parties are supposed to be formal. If you expect anything else go start a picnic of your own; but certainly don't try to mix the two.

And when greeting your hostess in her home or elsewhere, don't clasp her endearingly and use that old, threadbare gap: "How are you darling," for everyone from the pastry cook up will instantly know you've forgotten her name.

Back east it's become a sort of fad to visit the big wigs in Hollywood to learn what *not* to do later on. Then also it's become a lark to come to Hollywood to play around with the braggadocian set, a sort of a once-in-a-lifetime experience.

Many are the "Hollywood parties" given by the Inner Circle from time to time, in an effective take-off of the habits and customs of each individual star and director in the colony. Much refined laughter is enjoyed at some bull-in-the-pampas youth's expense 3,500 miles away.

Last summer in Newport, members of that ultra-umpity-umph group gave a very select party, in which each member had to come as some famous star and imitate them.

Now all of this is a bit unfair, to say the least. Jealousy may prompt it; for certain it is that there isn't a single deb on Fifth or Park Avenue that has half the personality of most of the younger movie stars in the film capital, and though there be many men in New York making larger incomes than some of those in Hollywood, nevertheless it's true that not one out of fifty of them could command the audience that the Hollywoodian gets. Regardless, it just goes to show that the way to spend money graciously at parties is not made usually but born.

I RECALL when Harry Richman was paying marked attention to a certain wealthy dowager some years ago, the crowd treated him as if he were some freak from Ripley's show.

"Oh, do bring him to tea," they would urge her. "I just want to see if he knows how to handle his refreshments," and other foolish twaddle.

Back in the early Twenties when Doug and Mary were putting on the dog you may recall that Edwina Mountbatten and other well-born Britishers often visited Hollywood. Back in New York I would hear them tell my family with actual astonishment: "Why do you know they really knew which fork to use"

Last fall young Junior Laemmle gave a large cocktail party at the Waldorf-Astoria. For weeks afterwards the Fifth Avenue set seriously discussed the fact that he mixed "all kinds of people."

Howard Hughes has often taken out dancing, debbies from the Park Avenue group, and gotten away with it. Yet when Walter Futter thought he'd cut a wide swath through the Golden Horseshoe he was merely coldly lorgnetted and asked "Who *is* this man?"

Fred Astaire married the ward of Henry Bull, the President of the Turf and Field Club; and Marjorie Oelrichs up and married Eddy Duchin, the orchestra leader. Gary Cooper ploughed through the dowager circle and picked himself a peach. And Connie Bennett once had herself young Phil Plant. Ellen Mackay had intestinal fortitude enough to marry Irving Berlin. But how long were any of them greeted by the dames and sires of the Backbone of American Society?

Maybe they don't care about any of it; but if they don't then why aren't they creating as sensible a system in Hollywood?

Jock Whitney lost caste on Fifth Avenue the moment he took Hollywood seriously; and no longer is he asked by the Inner Circle of America's uncrowned nobility. Even "Laddie" Sanford was given the cold shoulder when he took unto himself the charming and attractive Mary Duncan. My young cousin Alfred Gwynne Vanderbilt was cleft into the same shelf that I have reposed in for so many years when he paid marked attention to Ginger Rogers, and, what is more unhappy for him, was "cut" off the list of many Fifth Avenue hostesses' spring parties this year. And even young Winthrop Rockefeller was given stern parental coal rakings when he returned to New York after toying in movieland in March.

Fifth Avenue may be amused and amazed at Hollywood. It may be jealous of it. But in more ways than one, it has definitely intimated it will have nothing to do with it until Hollywood learns to conduct itself as the arbiters of American Social Customs believes it ought. Until then "East is East, and West is West; and never the twain shall meet."

WHY GIRLS FALL IN LOVE WITH ROBERT TAYLOR
[Continued from page 123]
any ladies down. He's not that type of man.

And audiences wouldn't believe him if he did. He is handsome in a matinee idol way. He typifies the good old moonlight-and-roses brand of romance. And if you'll ask any dozen girls of your acquaintance what they think of him, at least eight—and perhaps the entire dozen—will say: *"I'm crazy about him."*

WHY? Is it merely because he has the sort of good looks girls can't resist? Or is the taste of the female of the species changing again? I put that question to several Taylor fans. Their replies are interesting as an indication of his appeal.

"I like Bob Taylor because he's so strictly American," said an Eagle Rock High School girl. "He doesn't try to put on any foreign airs. He's natural and charming. There's nothing of that boastful, tongue-in-the-cheek wise-cracking about him. Personally, I think he represents everything that the ideal young American should be."

Said Claudine, the cute little blonde who does my hair: "Sure, I'm crazy about Robert Taylor. Who isn't?" When pressed for a reason, she replied: "Well, I guess every girl has a mental picture of the sort of boy who'd be a perfect date. So far as I'm concerned, he's it. It isn't so much because he's good-looking, although of course he is terribly handsome. What I like about him is that he has such grand manners. A girl likes to be proud of the man who takes her out. When he takes a girl out I'll bet he treats her like she was a princess—

no matter who she is."

"I like him because he looks like he'd be such fun," said a co-ed from U.S.C. "Usually, I don't go for handsome men. They're too likely to be conceited. Bob Taylor never gives the impression of being the least bit conceited. And when he makes love he does it so easily and naturally. He's romantic without being gooey—if you know what I mean."

None of these girls had ever seen Robert Taylor in person. The fact that they, instinctively, hit upon his basic qualities in giving their reasons for being crazy about him would seem to prove that an actor cannot really hide his true personality behind grease-paint, make-up or art.

THE Robert Taylor you meet in real life is very much as you would expect him to be—cordial, natural, likable. In talking with him you have the feeling that his charm of manner is something that he was born with—not something which he takes out on Sundays or for special occasions or something which he had to "learn."

I suspect that Bob has always been popular with girls though he would be the first to deny this. He's extremely modest about things like that which is, of course, another reason why girls like him. If there had ever been anything of the I'm-God's-gift-to-women attitude about him an event like the following could never have happened, that's sure.

Soon after he enrolled at Pomona University Bob went to a college dance —alone. I can imagine how the co-eds' temperatures skyrocketed when they spotted Bob in the stag line and with their eyes they, doubtless, begged him to cut in. But Bob didn't do any cutting in and the reason was, that back in Nebraska, where he came from, they didn't dance in that nonchalant, collegiate way that the Pomona dancers indulged in and he didn't have nerve enough to ask a girl to dance *his* way.

"What's the matter, Taylor? Why aren't you dancing?" A friend inquired.

"This trick dancing is new to me," Bob explained. "I'm afraid to try it."

"Tell you what," said the friend. "Get yourself a girl from Sacramento. They're kinda old-fashioned up there. She'll probably dance the way you do."

"But how'll I know whether a girl comes from Sacramento or not?"

"Ask her, you dope!"

So Bob started in asking girls whether they hailed from Sacramento. If they said "No, Hollywood," or "Pomona," he passed them up and went on to the next. Finally, he found a Sacramento girl and sure enough her step matched his.

BOB is thoroughly American in his tastes. He likes good substantial American food, fast motor cars, and radios.

In fact, wherever Bob is, there's usually a radio going full blast. He's crazy about tennis and he likes to dance. He hates to be alone and especially to dine alone. When it comes to dogs and women—he's a bit choosey. With dogs, personality comes first. With girls— the first specification is that she be wholesome and natural.

"I like a girl who isn't always thinking about her hair or her make-up," he told me. "I like a girl who doesn't mind riding in an open car and letting the wind blow her hair about her face.

He likes a girl with natural eyebrows. Brows that have been plucked to a hairline economy have no appeal for him. And he could never be keen about a girl who is constantly taking out her make-up kit and painting on a new mouth. Neither does he like the girl who is always trying to create an impression or show off.

"That's one thing I like about Barbara Stanwyck," he said. "She's so completely natural. I've seen her run her hand through her hair or push it behind her ears without any thought whatever about the way it made her look. She's real."

But the girl who really upsets Bob's equilibrium is the one who is always late. "If a girl makes a date for eight o'clock I can't for the life of me see why she can't be ready at eight," he said. "If I have to wait around for an hour while a girl gets dressed, the evening's spoiled so far as I'm concerned."

"Did you ever try walking out on a girl like that" I asked, "just to teach her a lesson?"

"Yes, I've tried that a couple of times," he confessed. "And then the next day I'd feel ashamed of myself and send her flowers as a sort of apology."

HEREDITY and background explain every man to a certain extent and it seems to me they go a long way toward explaining Robert Taylor. He comes of strictly American stock. He was born in Filley, Nebraska. He is the only son of cultured parents who considered such things as an appreciation of good music and good literature an important part of a boy's education. His father was a doctor, the sort of doctor who is an influence for good in the community in which he lives. Bob's first ambition was to follow in his father's footsteps with the idea, eventually, of specializing in psychiatry. But college, of course, came first.

He selected Pomona University (which is about forty miles from Hollywood) because of its high rating and also because of its excellent music department. He had fallen heir to a very fine old cello and he wished to study with the best instructors. The idea of becoming an actor had never once entered his head. He joined the college

dramatic club because he thought it would be fun. During his senior year he was chosen for the leading rôle in *Journey's End* which the dramatic club presented at the school.

Following the performance a stranger came up to Bob and offered his card and asked if he would come to the MGM Studio the following Saturday for a screen test. Bob wasn't particularly impressed with the idea of making a screen test. But the members of the dramatic club thought it would make a grand news item for the college weekly paper and urged him to do it. So he agreed. As soon as the film of the test was developed, studio heads took one look at it and offered Bob a contract. That's how well he screened.

"But I couldn't sign a contract," he told them. "I haven't finished school."

They suggested that if he could arrange to come to the studio twice a week and study under their dramatic instructor, Oliver Hinsdell, until his graduation the following June, they would hold their offer open. They wanted this young man.

Bob agreed to do this. But he soon found that the long trek to Culver City each week greatly interfered with his school work and he finally gave it up. Apparently, however, the studio sensed just what a good bet Bob was, and were unwilling to let him slip through their fingers. They promised to hold their offer open until he got around to allowing them to put his name on the payroll. It was almost a year later that he was in a position to accept their offer.

HE WAS not terribly enthusiastic about pictures at first. Like most American boys, however, he is enthusiastic about making money. And, as he explained to me: "Suddenly it dawned upon me that if I went in for medicine I would have to spend years getting my training. That I couldn't hope to make a sizable income in less than ten years, whereas in the picture business, if I was lucky enough to click, it wouldn't take me long to become financially independent. Also, after I got used to working before the camera I discovered that I really liked it. There's something fascinating about it."

It would have been so easy for a boy as young as Bob is—he's twenty-three, I believe—whose success came so swiftly and so unsought as his did, to have lost his head a bit; to have done a little plain and fancy swaggering. The fact that he has remained modest and unassuming in spite of the adulation that has been showered upon him is evidence of his stability and level-headedness. He is mentally well-disciplined. And that is, to a large extent I think, the result of heredity and background.

He is well aware that the lap of fame

is fickle. "And I realize that even though I may have gone up in a hurry," he says, "I could toboggan just as fast."

And there you have Robert Taylor—the young man of the hour. And after having spent several hours talking to him, I'll have to confess that I'm sort of crazy about him, too! Aren't you?

WHY DID I SLIP?

[Continued from page 125]

pretensions at being Booths or Barrymores and yet are very popular. On the other hand, I know one of the finest actors of the stage and screen who can't get a job in pictures today. He has everything in his favor, seemingly, and yet you fans won't go to see him.

Take someone like one of our outstanding feminine stars of the theatre who can act but isn't pretty. She can't get a job in pictures. Take someone who is pretty but can't act. She can't get a job in the movies. But it's a combination of the two, you say—acting *and* looks. But that doesn't answer the question either, because the Hollywood "graveyard" is studded with the headstones of men who were handsome and talented, and girls who were pretty and gifted. Somehow, they didn't have that "thing."

Maybe sex appeal is the common denominator? Well, maybe, but one of the most consistently popular men on the screen is Wally Beery, and Wally would be the last to stake his claim to box office favor on his sex appeal! On the other hand, there are the Lamarrs, Gables, Boyers and Crawfords who have sex appeal plus, and they're doing right smart for themselves, too.

It's all very confusing, you see. You may slip if you aren't a fine actor, but you may also slip if you are. You may slip if you have sex appeal; you may be signally successful if you haven't.

WAY back when I made "Broadway Melody of 1937" Barbara said to me, "It's coming, young man, and you won't like it. It's coming, but it will pass." What she meant was that it comes to all of us, in some measure, sooner or later. Public favor, asking your pardons, is fickle.

Often, the reasons for our slipping are none of our doing. Some crack-pot will sue a star on some false charge. Or some critic will lampoon us with a poisoned barb directed at our appearance for which, after all, we are not responsible. We can't help our looks. I certainly never thought my looks would be any problem to me. I worried about my stories, my parts and my acting. If I thought about my looks at all, it was that maybe I'd better have my nose straightened or my ears pinned back. It simply didn't occur to me that something for which I was not respon-

sible could be used as a weapon against me.

Now, how much, I'd like to know, does publicity like that affect a player in the estimation of you, his fans? When he gets blasts like that, do you think he should ignore them or do you think he should do something about them? For myself, I did nothing. It seems to me that the actor who is the target for personal criticism can do nothing. A man can't very well stand up and protest "I'm *not* a Pretty Boy!" without making a pretty fool of himself. So, I skipped it. I never went out of my way to muss myself up, break my nose, make myself look worse than necessary. Was that a mistake or wasn't it?

I don't know what your answer will be but personally, I really don't think looks have anything to do with it, one way or the other. Rudolph Valentino was certainly an extraordinarily handsome man, but it didn't seem to hurt him any. Wallace Reid was a handsome chap and was tops till the day he died. Ty Power has all the looks he can do with, and he's a regular Fourth of July conflagration at the box office; he's that "hot." On the other hand, a very good-looking boy went down to defeat a few years ago just because he was branded as "too good-looking." Wally Beery, again, is no Greek god, and yet he's as big box office as he ever was. So, for my money, appearance one way or the other, is not the answer I'm seeking.

Perhaps it's that bad publicity can only do you harm in proportion to how much people are ready to believe. Maybe it's not so much what you have that's good as how little you have that's wrong. Take Tracy and Gable, for instance. I don't believe anything could be said about them that would affect their popularity. People believe what they want to believe, and they want to believe only the best of Tracy and Gable. I like to think that maybe people were inclined to believe all that twaddle handed out about me before I went to England, because they didn't know me very well then. They were on the fence as far as I was concerned and so were ready to believe anything. I like to hope that, with the passing of time, they've come to know me better and to accept me as a friend.

But even the premise that, when you slip as a human being, you slip as a star is open to question. Because, regular fellows though Gable and Tracy are, there are other regular fellows in this business of whom people are ready to believe the worst at the drop of a poisonous paragraph. And, too, there are some men and women in this business, as in any other, who are not regular at all and yet occupy choice sites on the Movie Milky Way. Why? *You* tell me.

YES, my personal guess is that a

player's private life has little or nothing to do with his popularity. Not anymore. It used to be said that marriage hurt young players of both sexes. Well, most of the ranking stars of today are married and it hasn't affected their box office. When Barbara and I married, we didn't get any unfavorable reaction. Or if we did, we didn't know about it. Clark and Carole married and are bigger than ever. Ty Power married, and it certainly hasn't hurt him. Boyer's marriage hasn't destroyed his attraction in any way.

Some of the actors have scandals break over their heads. But their heads and their box office value remain intact. In fact, I rather believe that the public likes a dash of scandal with its stars now and then. Though it may be a sad commentary on us humans, it's true that most of us get more of a kick out of hearing that Mr. X eloped with his stenographer or that Mrs. X murdered her paramour than that Mr. and Mrs. X sit quietly at home playing pinochle.

Then I ask myself how much temperament has to do with it? Maybe temperament is the trick that captures the public imagination. Should an actor be erratic and difficult, or should he be business-like, stable and quiet? That's a tangled question, too. Because it seems if you're too "colorful," people resent you; if you're too tame, they're bored.

Me, I haven't much of the stuff. I've been criticized at times for being "too dignified, too reserved." It's been said that I never let myself go, never seem to show any emotion over things. Maybe I should put on an act. Yet I can't quite believe that. Gable and Tracy are not temperamental, and they do all right. Ronald Colman is a monument of reserve, and the same goes for Bill Powell.

Some say it's a matter of how hard you work, how seriously you take your work. Muni would seem to prove that this is so. Yet one of the biggest, longest established stars in this business say, openly, that he considers his work a "racket," that he never even reads his script until ten minutes before he steps on a set. And I must say that in spite of the nice things said about me in "Waterloo Bridge," I didn't work any harder, didn't take the part any more seriously than I did in, say "Lucky Night" which was, for me, a flop-pola.

Some people say that when you're "tops" too long, you wear out your welcome. That when your name is on everybody's tongue, you're like a book fans hear too much about and so don't bother to read. But that doesn't satisfy me, either, because men like Gable, Boyer, Tracy and girls like Bette Davis and Vivien Leigh confound that argument.

It's been said that it's a matter of "cycles." Then when comedy pictures are having a run, you're out of the race, at least temporarily, unless you're doing crazy comedies. But, during a comedy cycle, I've seen a tasty tragedy come along and be a big hit!

SPENCER TRACY, more than anyone or anything else, confuses me when I try to answer the question I'm passing on to you. There's nothing about Tracy that anyone can pick on. He's not too good-looking, he isn't "difficult," he never gives a bad performance. Yet, before he came to Metro-Goldwyn-Mayer, *he* was skidding! And not because he hadn't had good pictures.

Don't think that an actor doesn't worry about this matter of slipping. He worries just as much as the little grocery clerk who fears for his job. And for much the same reasons. Money, for instance. If I get fired, I can't maintain my present standard of living. "So what!" do I hear? "You'd still be living cushy on the street called Easy, wouldn't you?" The answer is "Yes." But everything is comparative. Every man gets geared to a certain way of life, and it hurts when that way of life is no more.

But it's not so much the money angle that makes a star dread a skid; it's pride. It's the fear of having so big an audience witness his debacle. When the little grocery clerk loses his job, his fellow-workers know about it, his family, his personal friends—that's all. But when a star gets fired, the whole world knows it.

There is another thing the grocery clerk has over the picture star. If he loses his job, he can, reasonably enough, hope for a better job. If a star slips, he may get another job, but you can bet it won't be a better one. A "dead" star is the deadest thing on this earth—and least liable to resurrection.

What brings some stars to this tragedy of early entombment? What gives other stars comparative immortality? What makes them slip? What made *me* slip? That's what I want you fans to tell me.

RONALD COLMAN GIVES THE LOWDOWN ON HIMSELF

[*Continued from page 129*]
half an hour. I got home, found my coat, slung it over the garden wall and did a little gardening, of which I do a great deal, while I waited. I was digging away, coatless, sleeves rolled up, hair mussed up, perspiring, when I heard, down my driveway, the honk-honk of a car. I waved both arms, yelled 'Coming—hold everything!' or something similar, grabbed my coat in my hand and went galloping down the drive, landed on the running-board of the car and was confronted by, not Selznick as I had naturally thought, but —*five strange ladies from Michigan!*"

I laughed then. I said: "That's what you get for trying to escape the common fate of actors."

"It was really very funny," Ronnie said, "especially my opening remark. I had to say something as they were stunned into complete silence. So I said, 'Er—did you want to see me?' That broke the ice and we all laughed. But they were still so taken aback that, for once, I had to do all the talking. And I did. I chatted away in the most verbose manner. They were really very sweet. There was one dear old lady in the party. They had been driving around, sight-seeing, had been told this was my house but had not imagined I could be the coatless laborer in the vineyard. They took me for the gardener and honked their horns intending to ask him whether it was really my house or not. And so, they were more taken aback than I when I leapt upon their running-board. They did NOT ask for autographs. They were very charming and it was all very nice."

I thought of what a gay summer some little town in Michigan will have when the five ladies, on various verandas and over how many chatty cups of tea, tell of their meeting with the great star, Ronald Colman—the star who, next only to Garbo, is least often seen, talked with or talked about.

"If contacts with the public were all like that," Ronnie was saying, "I should not mind, ever. I don't mind, really. I don't invite it, certainly, public recognition, but certainly I do my share of autographing when I have to. One must. Nor have I the slightest objection to talking to the Press. There are times, when I am traveling, when I could wish the Press would forget about me for at least two to three days after my arrival. Not because of the men and women of the Press themselves but because, immediately it is printed that a picture actor is in town, all of the car salesmen, curiosity seekers, real estate purveyors for miles around are on the trail. I sometimes wish, too, that interviews done with me some ten years ago were not matters of public record. So often the things we say, even the things we say intentionally or the things we do ten years ago are ridiculous and embarrassing ten years later. Yet there they are, seemingly indelible, raising their mocking little heads when you least expect them.

"But to go back to *Shangri-La*—I wish that I could be taken there, forcibly, as in the picture *Robert Conway* was taken there. Then, I am sure, I would remain even as he did, would be content to remain, would choose to remain. Especially if," smiled the man who is much too innately nice and open of mind and spirit to be a "mystery" at all, "especially if I could find a *Shangri-La*

like that—with love waiting and work to do waiting for me, with the chance to satisfy the dictator complex as *Robert Conway* was able to do, you know, being appointed ruler over all of *Shangri-La* and the inhabitants thereof. There a man found everything the earth can hold for the feeding of the heart, the substance of the spirit, the health of the body, the energies and ambitions.

"It has been said to me, it has also occurred to me that if such a life is what we most desire why don't we, some of us, have it? For there are those among us who have accumulated enough money, or could, to build ourselves a *Shangri-La*. Perhaps not so opulently beautiful as the lamasery and its gardens in the picture but, at least, a place remote from the world's intrusion.

"I have, at various times, contemplated a farm, a ranch, somewhere away from all traffic with mankind. I have thought of a life of laboring with my hands, the self-sufficing life, drawing sustenance from the soil and spiritual satisfaction from the only place it can come—within. I have thought of an island, isolated in wild seas, from any mainland. I have only thought about them—thus far.

"But, yes, given sufficient money and the real desire, it could be done. *But it isn't done.* So far as I know the priest-hoods, the good Fathers, the monks are the only men who ever seek and find complete retirement from the world.

"Voltaire once wrote," said Ronnie, "that 'Man is free the moment he wishes to be.' And so he is. There is nothing tangible stopping any one of us from stepping this moment out of the life we live today. If we really want to. We don't really want to—not enough. And so I believe that the desire for a *Shangri-La* is what we *think* we would like to find. Between the thought and the deed there is often a gulf so wide and deep that Death jumps in before we have time to bridge it."

"It's like retiring from the screen in a way," I said, rather apologetically for making so superficial an analogy, "I have never, in all my years of interviewing, talked to an actor or an actress who has not said to me 'at such and such a time I shall retire.' No one ever has, Ronnie. Not even you."

"No," agreed Ronnie. "No. But I could. I know it. I was away for a year, you know, away from pictures, away from Hollywood. And it was as if it had never been. A sense of shadows which had passed, leaving no mark. No, if I were told today that I could never make another film, was through, washed up, I should not greatly mind. There might be a stab of hurt pride at first. The pangs would pass. And there is an analogy in what you say, too, because as with men who would not seek a

Shangri-La of their own volitions but would be content to remain there if kidnaped and taken there by force, so it would be true, of me at least, that if I were forced out of pictures I would go—contentedly. To renounce your own world is almost more difficult than to be renounced by it.

"After all, and in my own defense, I make a very small percentage of the pictures I could make, should make, perhaps, if my career were all-important to me. Right now I will not even listen to offers. I not only will not listen to long-term contract offers, now or ever, but I will not even listen to a one-picture offer.

"When I have finished *The Prisoner of Zenda*, with its dual role, its heavy costuming, the details of a rather tremendous production I shall be studio-stale. And I shall go away and remain away."

"What if," I said, "they should get down on their knees to you and plead with you to play *Rhett Butler* in *Gone With the Wind?* Would you refuse the plum?"

"I don't know," Ronnie said, "I'm not sure. It would depend, in the first place on when the picture is to be made. I shall not do anything for at least three months after we are through shooting *Zenda*. Besides, I shall want it to be clear in my own mind that I am temperamentally suited to play the part of *Rhett* if, or when, I am actually asked. It is more important for the man who plays *Rhett Butler* to be temperamentally suited to the part than it is for him to look the part, even if that were possible. And whether I would play it or not, given the chance, would depend to a great extent on studio agreement as to the concept of the character. My own concept of *Rhett Butler* may vary from others. I believe that he was, fundamentally, not cruel but very kind. And he was always so *right*," laughed Ronnie, "in everything he did, so right.

"If the book were to be made into a stage play, done in London or in New York or both, then yes, I should like very much to do it. But to play the main character—for to me, *Rhett* is a more interesting character than *Scarlett*—to play the main character in the most overwhelmingly popular book in ten years and to play it to a screen audience, a world audience every individual of which has a pre-conceived idea of what the character should be, look like, talk like—I don't know. There is the Southern accent to be got around. That is important. Robert Montgomery played *Rhett* on the air, you know, and I have heard several Southerners say that his accent was remarkably right. One of the major difficulties in casting is, of course, that the actor who may be temperamentally suited to the role doesn't look

the part even remotely and vice versa.

"I should say that, on the whole, the casting of Clark Gable as *Rhett* might meet with the approval of the greatest number of people. I think there might be less protest about Gable than about anyone else. That there will be many dissenting voices, no matter who is cast, is inevitable. Gary Cooper has been suggested, Basil Rathbone's name has come up and Preston Foster's in private discussions in the all-Hollywood game called Casting *Gone With The Wind*.

"And so, it all depends so far as I am concerned, on when the picture is made and how the concept of the character works out in the script. If I feel that I am temperamentally suited to it then yes, I should certainly want to do it—and no kneeling would be necessary!

"But before then," said Ronnie, "I shall go away, as I have done before. And perhaps each time I go I shall stay longer . . . and then longer . . . I don't know."

There was a brief silence, rather strange, in which I seemed, fantastically, to hear the hum of a giant plane winging its recessional . . and then we said goodbye.

GINGER ROGERS ASKS: "DID I GET WHAT I WANTED FROM LIFE?"

[Continued from page 130]
forever, you've *had* them all, haven't you?"

And Ginger's pale young face, guiltless of any make-up, framed by that tawny silk hair sobered as she said: "Of course, I haven't got everything. No. Wait—I haven't got everything only because *there is no such thing*. I mean, there is no such thing as having everything. We are all mortal and being mortal means being limited, and so none of us has the capacity for everything. No one can have everything. Because for every dream dreamed there arises another dream. For every hope hoped there emerges another hope." I found myself thinking "And for every love does there arise another love to take the old love's place?" And Ginger replied: "It is an old saying and a true one— that the more we have the more we want. It's like eating—the more you eat the more you can eat! 'Everything' is limitless, don't you see? There is no end to it.

"NO, NO, for anyone to make the boast that he or she has everything is like going to school and graduating and then saying: 'Well, now, I know all there is to know. I never need to read another book or hear another lecture or study another subject.' So stupid, that attitude. Because the thrill and the glory and the whole come-on of living is just because

there are no limits. There is no saturation point. For every goal is, when you have reached it, only a sign-post pointing the way to the next goal. The end is never reached.

"I can't even say" smiled Ginger, "that all my dreams have come true. Because, you see, I never did dream very grand dreams. I never made very lavish demands on life. I can't honestly say that I spent my childhood in daydreaming of fame and riches and glory for me. Because I didn't. I never thought about such things at all. I always lived for the day, the hour. I still do. I live for the present.

"I certainly never dreamed about being an actress, of all things! I never thought above having a lot of money. Mother earned what would be called a sensible amount of money as a newspaper woman—enough to make us comfortable. The people I knew then all lived nicely, but modestly. I never thought about movie stars and their fabulous lives at all . . . but, if I had thought about them, I would probably have put them in the same fantastic category as *Alice In Wonderland* or something like that.

"I never thought about having a lot of money because I really need so little. If I cared about the things that money can buy I wouldn't go about as you see me now, dressed in cotton overalls and a dollar sweat-shirt. Oh, I like to get all tricked out now and then and go out with a crowd and have fun. But I can live without expensive clothes and be just as happy. I don't give a darn for jewels. My first ermine coat didn't make a different girl of me!

"When I was a little girl I only had one ambition that I can remember—I wanted to be a school-teacher. I think that was because I adored my English teacher. She lived at home with us for a term or two and I used to think that anyone so pretty and gentle and wise would be the perfect one to copy. I wanted to be just like her.

"NO, honestly, you can't have everything in a world so 'full of a number of things.' I'd like to go to college, as I've said. I'd like to try to write. I don't know whether I could write or not, but I'd love to have the time to try. I'd like to compose music, too. I don't say that I could do that, either—though I have written a song or two!—but I'd like to have the time to work at it. I'd like to have time to be a little bit domestic. I think I really am a housewife at heart. Most girls are, if you strip off the cellophane wrappings of their professional lives, whatever they may be. . . ." (And I found myself wondering whether this might be the Why Of It . . . whether the little housewife-at-heart who hasn't time to be a housewife might

205

be the explanation of the little wife who doesn't, perhaps, have time to be a wife? For Ginger is, I think, essentially whole-hearted. And where she couldn't give her whole heart and her whole time and her whole devotion she would rather not give at all. . . .)

"You know," Ginger was saying, "I have to live in my own house as I would live in a hotel. I never get time even to plan a menu. I never have the least idea what I'll have to eat from one meal to the next. I never have time to count the linens, to arrange flowers, to fuss over things—and *I'd love to*. When the maid tells me that we need three new table-cloths I phone a shop and tell them to send me three new tablecloths and then I never see them until they are on the table.

"I'd like to have time to work in the garden, to pick flowers and arrange them for the house. I'd like to be able to plan luncheons and dinners, to change drapes, to make little things. I do manage a certain amount of knitting and crocheting and hookings rugs and doing petit point and things like that . . . in between times, if ever. A stitch now and then.

"I'd like to be able to go out more—to do silly, on-the-spur-of-the-moment things, like going on picnics and down to Venice to do the chute-the-chutes and things. But I'm usually too tired when I come home from the studio to do anything except fall into bed and to sleep. When I'm rehearsing I do go out now and then just to keep in step with life. But when we're in production it swallows us whole and we're seen and heard no more—save on the sound stages."

AND how would that go, I thought, with marriage . . . ? A star too tired to do anything but go home, and so to bed and to sleep. A star swallowed up in production to be seen and heard no more. . . . Marriage and its multiple demands. The studio and its slavery. Alien bedfellows, I am afraid.

"So, you see," said Ginger, "all of the many things I have—this 'every-thing' you speak of—*I can't use*. I remind myself of *Midas*—everything he touched turned to gold but what good did it do him? He couldn't eat gold. He couldn't inhale any fragrance from golden flowers. And when he turned to the one object he loved more than anything or any person in the world, his little daughter, he could get no warmth or affection from her—for she, too, had turned to gold!"

(Perhaps, I thought, perhaps Ginger was saying more than she knew, revealing more than she thought . . . for may it not be that, here in Hollywood, under the greedy grasp of the Great God Studio . . . young, ardent, hopeful marriages, like *Midas'* daughter, also

turn to gold?)

"I have *things*" said Ginger, "and more than just things, I know. I have clothes, but I have no chance to wear them. I'd like to do some personal shopping now and then. I'd like to window-shop and hunt for bargains and try things on, the way girls like to do. I can't. When I need new clothes I phone again. I call a shop and tell them to send me three or four dresses and then I choose the most likely one and let it go at that. I have three or four new dresses at home right now and I can't wear them because I haven't been able to shop for the right accessories for them. . . ."

Ginger paused for a moment and looked out of the window . . . spread before her Irish blue eyes were the mammoth sound stages, the machine shops, the offices, the gardens, the whole vast body of the studio where she reigns supreme—a star . . . and I wondered what she was thinking, what values she was weighing in her mind. She didn't say. I knew that she wouldn't say. For if she talked to one she would have to talk to all—and there are some matters even a star cannot be expected to discuss with all!

SHE said, finally, "I'd love to have a baby. Of course, I would, naturally. I shall adopt one some day. It seems to me," said Ginger, her bright blue eyes wistful, as if asking a question, "that it's just as fine to adopt a baby as it is to have one of your own. Don't you think? To choose a baby because of all the babies you have seen that baby is the one you want the most? I sort of agree with Kathleen Norris when she said recently, that real motherhood is to love every baby born and not only the babies born to you. . . .

"Movie babies certainly cost a lot, too," Ginger laughed, her eyes coming back from the Neverland. "I read in a recent article somewhere that a certain very big star's last baby cost her exactly $150,000—because of her having to be out of production for so long. Time is very valuable to a movie star.

"You see, I am emphasizing the fact, now, that there is no such thing as having everything. I know that I have everything that meets the eye. I know that other girls must wonder what there is left for me to want. That's what I'm trying to tell them. And I'm not disparaging the things I have. I'm not making light nor little of the fun of fame, so-called, of money and success and all that. Not for one minute. I'm happy. I wouldn't change places with little Susie Glutz who works in an office for anything. Even though Susie is probably just as happy as I and with just as good reasons. Even though Susie is certainly normal and I am not. Be-

cause we are not *really* normal, not when we are 'movie stars.' We can't be. It is very much, I think, like running a temperature all of the time. And, after awhile, we get so used to being keyed up that we couldn't live any other way. We would feel depressed and weak if we didn't live at high pressure every instant. I know that I work better, the harder the pressure. It is literally true that the less time I have, the more I can accomplish.

"I ENJOY 'fame'. I really love it. I get a kick out of being recognized and praised and spoiled. There are times when it is tiresome, of course. But there are times when everything is tiresome. There are also times, most times, when it is thrilling and satisfying to find my name in electric lights. I enjoy the fan letters and the compliments and the consideration of being a star. I wouldn't be honest if I didn't admit it.

"But just because I do love it and value it, there is a drawback. I think it must be something like having a very beautiful and successful child for whom you have worked night and day, whom you have watched grow and for whom you feel a great love, a great pride of possession. And just because you love it so much, that love is shot through with fear. For *supposing anything should happen to it?* Supposing that you *should lose it?*

"That's the way I feel about my work. Supposing something should happen—to the industry or to my part in it? Of course I'd be hurt. Terribly hurt. I'd hate it. I'd be miserable. So that even when you do have everything, presumably, in the work you are doing, at any rate—even that is marred by the fear of loss, of accident, of fate. . . ."

In the doorway the assistant director was beckoning. Ginger waved a hand. "Time to go," she said to me. "I can't be five minutes late. I'm always late for everything, except my work. They've got me trained in the studio. So . . . I guess we can about sum it up like this: I get everything I want from Life except—TIME. Time to go to college, time to be a housewife, time to shop and play and experiment, time to have a baby, time to be normal. . . ."

Can you read between these lines? I can.

CAN HOLLYWOOD HOLD ERROL FLYNN?
[*Continued from page 131*]
difficult scenes. He's putting twice as much into them, getting twice as much he-man enjoyment out of them. Fortunately for him, he has more adventure scenes than love scenes. And that's all right with the women in the audience, too. Here is one hero who could give them thrills even if he *never* made love

on the screen . . .

The scene about to be filmed as I stepped on the set was of *"The Lancers' Quadrille"* in Government House, Calcutta, in the year 1850. Errol, reluctantly, buttoned his coat again, stepped into position, entered into the dance—in rehearsal. To amused onlookers on the sideline, it was obvious that he was cussing under his breath. But when the scene was "shot," his face betrayed none of his rebellion of the previous moments. He was, to all intents and purposes, a young English officer of the year 1850, having a good time for himself, doing a complicated, foppish dance with his sweetheart (Olivia de Havilland), just out from England.

As he came off the set, again with his coat unbuttoned, he asked if anyone had seen the sun—which had disappeared in a haze a couple of days before. The sun's return would mean a return to location, for outdoor shots; release from shots like these.

HE was drying his forehead, ringed with perspiration, when I asked him how long Hollywood would be able to hold him. He looked at me quizzically. Was I joking or serious? "I'm likely to decide to quite Hollywood any day," he said, simply and succinctly. He hasn't worked the wanderlust—or the fever for new adventures—out of his system. "I won't be content," he replied firmly, "until I can live a free life—do the things I want to do, when I want to do them—preferably in the South Seas."

I had read that he was a direct descendant of Fletcher Christian, of *Mutiny-on-the-Bounty* fame. Did heredity, then, explain that South Seas yearning? "I'm a descendant of Christian's family in Cumberland. That's how that story started. Or somebody twisted the fact that I *met* Fletcher Chrisian, his direct descendant, in Sydney." Errol (he pronounces it "Airl") discovered the attractions of the South Seas for himself. I asked him to tell me about it. He doesn't like to talk about himself. The story was pulled from him piece-meal.

"I was born in a little town near Belfast, Ireland. By the time I was through school, I was as tall as I am now—and filled out in proportion. In school, I had developed into a pretty fair boxer, so I entered the 1928 Olympic tryouts as a member of the English team. I was nineteen that summer. Just after I got back, my father, a college professor, set out for Tasmania, and took me with him. That was my first taste of life. He was going out to try to bring back the platypus alive. . . . What's a platypus? An amazing thing. It's amphibious, lives in the water or on top of it, has fur, and a beak like a duck. Yes, he brought one back—but wasn't able to keep it very long.

"Father left me in Sydney, Australia, to get on with my schooling. I stood it a few months. Then I boarded a boat for the South Sea Islands, borrowing the fare to get there. The one unknown place in the world was the interior of New Guinea. I wanted to see it—and I did.

"I did a host of things to make a living. First I went into government service as a jungle policeman. The uniform was shorts, shirt and helmet. Cool by comparison with the uniforms in this picture. All the natives a few days inland, on my 'beat,' were cannibals. I was in service about a year. Then I made a gold strike—of alluvial gold. I sold out after a while and tried pearl-fishing. Then I had a schooner. I never knew how to sail before I had it. I saw China, Japan, India, and most of the Islands in it before it bumped against a coral reef. Some day I'll have another boat like it.

"I was in the South Seas about five years, then went home to England—and the stage. Homesickness didn't drive me back. I went up to New Guinea with a good friend, a government official. The last straw was when he died of the dreaded black-water fever. Later, three more friends died. I said, 'Goodbye to *this* country! I may be the next one!'"

HE KNOWS all of the dangers of the tropics, as well as its attractions, but still he wants to go back. Is that explained by he fact that he deliberately sees the romantic side of life? Life isn't necessarily what you make it, Errol has found. You can be, just as easily, what life has made *you*. "I'm a great believer in luck," he explained. "The whole thing is purely a matter of luck." That's another reason why he isn't taking his screen success big.

Those South Sea adventures of Errol's still are the dominating influence of his life. Not only does a desire to continue them underlie his screen ambitions; but they have given him another ambition—the urge to write. He has just completed a book about his experiences in sailing a small boat from Australia to New Guinea, calling the story, *Beam's End;* a publisher is reading it now. More important, he has just written (in collaboration with William Ulman, magazine writer) a scenario entitled *The White Rajah;* moreover, he has sold it—and will star in it. The story, founded on fact, brought the highest price ever paid by Warners for an original screen story.

Today, Flynn is saving his money. Yesterday, he didn't. He made and lost two fortunes in the South Seas. One was in gold. He sold out his claim for $10,000 in cash and $40,000 in stock in a syndicate. The cash was soon gone, and the syndicate soon failed. . . . The other fortune came from the schooner that he plied in trade all over the Far East, and it went down with the schooner (which was uninsured) in a collision with a coral reef. If you are a potential collector of Flynniana, look up pawn shops in the out-of-the-way corners of the world—he deposited belongings in most of them. Some of them are very precious.

He is tight-mouthed today. That traces back to two years of keeping his own counsel in the bush of New Guinea—two years in which he saw a white man only twice. He is a light sleeper, also from old habit. Sleeping in the jungle, a man learns to waken at the trembling of a leaf.

HE WILL let no one double for him in dangerous scenes. That, too, traces back to the South Seas—to one time when he knew and conquered fear. It was during his pearl-fishing days. He had a native boy who did most of the diving for the pearls. The boy was able to hold his breath for five or six minutes under water. He would dive down to the ocean floor, walk along it to a rock, twist the oysters loose from the rock, collect several in a bag, then rise to the surface. The boy did not want to dive in this particular spot—where the water was dark, octopus-infected. Flynn at first was going to force him to dive, then said, "No, I'll make no one else do anything that I wouldn't do, myself." He dove overboard, walked along the dark ocean bottom, found pearl-oysters on a rock ledge, twisted them loose, every moment imagining the long tendrils of an octopus oozing toward him out of the water-cave nearby. After that experience, no movie stunt looks too dangerous.

Once, when he was in a tough port cafe in the Islands, he saw a big, brutish man beating another half his size. Flynn interfered, with the result that the giant went for him—with a knife. Flynn dodged his lunge, wrested the knife from him, and they fought it out hand to hand. It ended with Errol scoring a knockout. The other man, when he regained consciousness, swore that he would round up a gang and come back and "get" Flynn. Errol was so mad—why, he could have killed the ingrate, instead of giving him only a beating!—that he stayed in the cafe for two days and nights, waiting. The bully never came back. After that bruising battle, no screen fight looks tough to Errol. He can take it.

In the picture, Errol plays an officer of a company of Lancers. And, as in *Lives of a Bengal Lancer,* the hero has two companions for contrast. One, who dies an early, heroic death, is played by David Niven. The other is played by a tall, handsome, Irish newcomer,

Patrick Knowles. Errol and Pat are great friends away from the camera, though in the picture they are rivals for the same girl. (Olivia de Havilland). She loves Knowles but is engaged to Flynn and intends to carry out the bargain—until tragedy overtakes him in the suicidal Charge of the Light Brigade. So this time, in the end, "the other fellow" gets the girl. (P. S. Flynn gets the sympathy—which will be plenty.)

At the head of the 649, into the Valley of Death, he rides—to slay, and to be slain. In this battle scene, one of the most vivid ever filmed, he hurls a lance with deadly aim. No easy trick, but one he picked up immediately. A daredevil on horseback, he would race down the field in rehearsal, heaving the lance at a stuffed dummy—and he never missed.

ERROL, the realist, takes everything as it comes. If a scene is difficult, okay; if it's easy, okay. It doesn't matter to him. Everything is a new experience. And grist for the writer's mill. He wears very little make-up—so little that he can put it on himself. (And does.) His hair, his sideburns, his mustache are his own. His features are camera-perfect. He will be all right in color. (And does this picture—which is in black and white—cry for color!)

At the Fan Mail Department on the Warner lot, they told me that Dick Powell receives the most mail, with Errol a close second. I was present while a batch of the Flynn mail was opened. It was from all over the world, from people of all types, all ages. Requests for photographs, autographs, swords, cutlasses. Appreciations of his acting. Pleas for jobs, for money for adventure expeditions. Leap Year proposals, along side "best wishes" for himself and Lili. Actors, old troupers, named him as "the only man who can take Valentino's place." Ardent fans asked his permission to start fan clubs. Old friends, "so glad he's getting along," wrote of So-and-So, whom he remembers. People sent story suggestions. People hoped he and Olivia will continue as a team. None—and this was "very funny"—complimented him on his new mustache. (He still wears it).

After years of jungle life, he has an appraising eye for pretty girls—and admits it. He drives his car, himself, and drives it fast. His pals are mostly studio co-workers, except for members of the British colony. Warren William and Patrick Knowles are his closest actor-friends. When he first arrived in Hollywood, he was a stayer-up-late—because he had heard that Hollywood expected every young actor to be a night-club neurotic. He soon discovered that Hollywood expects no such thing. Now he lives a quiet life, seldom going

out, and then only to formal parties— the kind that can't be dodged. Clothes fetter him. ("But, after all, in civilized society, one must observe the amenities.")

He dislikes dentists and spiders. He won't listen to publicity stunts. He has very little English accent. (The dialogue director has to groom him, as well as Olivia, in English intonations.) He is awed by the man who saw *Captain Blood* fourteen times. He likes horse races—and bets on them. Between scenes, he is a great kidder. He lives on top of Lookout Mountain, which towers over Hollywood. On a clear day, he has a fifty-mile view in every direction.

"I'm renting now, but I'll build very soon," he told me. "I've bought eight acres—also on a mountain. We're landscaping already. The motif of the place will be orderly disarrangement. The house—a French farmhouse. A mixture of a house I once lived in, and American conveniences." I told him that didn't sound as if he is "likely to quit Hollywood any day."

The King of Present-Day Vagabonds readjusted the tight-fitting collar of his uniform. The fulfilment of dreams, my friend, requires money—at least to a realist. And while he *is* here, he wants to live as he would like to live.

IT'S LONELY BEING A CHILD PRODIGY
[*Continued from page 133*]
until Deanna signed her first motion picture contract with M-G-M when she was thirteen, they lived in a modest three-room cottage near Broadway and 86th Street in Los Angeles, a district of simple homes owned or rented by wage earners. While not in want, their means were far from affluent.

As is the case with any girl who is growing up, Deanna made her circle of friends and girl-fashion, had her "special best friends"—those intimates between whom grows a strangely close and precious bond. In Deanna's case, the "specials" were Paula and Jane Rawhut, who lived close by in the same neighborhood.

All three were members of the glee club of the Manchester Avenue grammar school and later students at the Bret Harte Junior High. Deanna was taking singing lessons by that time. Her exquisite voice had begun to manifest itself when she was three. Even then she could hear a song and sing it in clear, true pitch. By the time she was eleven, her extraordinary talent was obvious. However, Mr. Durbin could not afford to give her singing lessons and, generously, her sister, Edith, paid for weekly lessons with an inexpensive teacher from her own meager earnings.

In the school glee club, Deanna sang as a member of the chorus. Not once did she admit, or even hint, that her voice qualified her for solo work.

"I was afraid the other girls might think I was getting stuck-up," Deanna told me. "I was afraid it might make a difference between us, and we were so happy as things were."

Golden, glorious days. Deanna, Paula and Janie, complete unto themselves. Sharing secrets, confiding hopes and dreams, three girls on the threshold of young womanhood, a perfect trinity. Then it happened. Separation.

It was the inevitable, of course. If her latent talent escaped notice at school, it did not in the community church. Regular members and visitors alike were startled, then thrilled with the music that poured forth from the throat of the child singing hymns and anthems. They all knew that some day some person would hear that voice who would bring it to the attention of millions.

Jack Sherrill, now Deanna's manager, ultimately became that person.

METRO-GOLDWYN-MAYER about this time was searching for a child with some semblance of a voice to play the rôle of Madame Ernestine Schumann-Heink as a girl in the proposed starring vehicle for the great diva, "Gram." Sherrill brought Deanna to Metro's attention and promptly they signed her to a term contract with the usual six months option.

Los Angeles being spread out as it is, it became imperative that the Durbins move, since Deanna must be at the studio daily for lessons and training..

Weeping, Paula, Janie and Deanna said good-by.

"But never mind," they consoled themselves. "We'll see each other all the time. Promise."

They promised, in solemn good faith. But it wasn't distance, as such, that was to keep them separated for a whole year, although that too played its part. It was that Deanna found herself plunged into a new and strange life. Her days were spent at the studio learning the bewildering business of making movies. Even her schooling was conducted on the lot, as it still is at Universal. Replacing her former teacher of voice was Andre de Segurola, former coach of the Metropolitan Opera who today guides many of the greatest voices in the world of music.

Thus the days were filled. There was no time to see Paula and Janie. No time, really, for anything but work, work, work towards this new goal.

No new little friends were substituted for the former ones. Nor could fathers be blamed if it seemed unimportant to them, after a hard day's work, to drive Deanna or Paula across the length of the city, through heavy traffic, to visit each other.

THEN Schumann-Heink died. With her died the studio's plans for "Gram" and the brilliant opportunity for Deanna.

She made one musical "short" with Judy Garland, a none too successful affair. The six months elapsed and Deanna's contract was not renewed.

Now she had neither friends nor absorbing activity.

Sherrill's faith in her next brought her to Universal. A new contract was forthcoming. Again the Durbin family moved to be closer to the studio. This time the home was farther than ever from the beloved 86th Street—and Paula.

Once more Deanna was enrolled in a studio school, among strange classmates—a freckle-faced boy of seven, a chubby little girl of nine, and two sophisticated blondes of about fourteen.

Came the making of "Three Smart Girls." The original plans for "Three Smart Girls" called for an inexpensive and relatively unimportant "B" or second-class picture. In it Deanna was given a minor rôle. Her work in the first two weeks of shooting, however, proved so startling production heads called a halt.

Thereupon the studio was said to have been divided into two camps—pro and anti-Durbin. After a bitter fight, in which a number of resignations allegedly were threatened if Deanna was made the star of the picture, and *if she were not,* the showdown came. The pro-Durbins won. The budget was increased to "A" or first-class rating, the story rewritten to feature Deanna.

Box-office records everywhere proved how justified the change was.

Deanna emerged a top flight star in one picture. Immediately plans were made for her second starring picture with no less a distinguished personage than the conductor Leopold Stokowski, and ninety-nine other men playing second to this little girl's beauty, charm and ability. This picture is called "One Hundred Men and One Girl," and means just that.

It was during the making of "Three Smart Girls," and hence before her success was certain, that Deanna made her radio debut. Sherrill persuaded Eddie Cantor to give her an audition for a guest star spot on his Sunday night broadcast.

She's been the feature of the program ever since.

Thus brilliant success, fame, and growing wealth have come to Deanna. Such fame, in fact, that Al Levy, oldest restaurateur of Hollywood, remarked the other day that not since fans by the thousands came to his restaurant to watch Charlie Chaplin eat dinner has a Hollywood star created so much interest and furor in his establishment.

BUT—that success, fame and wealth was just what was estranging and losing to Deanna the things she held most dear—her little girl friendships. Glad as she and Paula were to see each other again, cry as they did with happiness, both knew when they went to their separate homes that night that another year might very well pass before they would see each other again.

Both knew, too, that things were not, and cannot be, as they were before.

It has cost her more than Paula's friendship. It has cost her every girl's natural inheritance of carefree youth, something she did not value until she had lost it.

Her days—and nights—now are a successsion of crammed schooling, fittings, make-up tests, music lessons, practice hours, film and radio rehearsals, radio appearances and actual work before the cameras.

She happened to mention to me she had celebrated her fourteenth birthday recently on her first trip to New York City.

"Did you have a party?" I asked

"Oh yes," she answered carefully. "In fact, I had *five* parties in one day!"

The Waldorf-Astoria, biggest hotel in the world, was host at one of those parties. Universal Studios' New York offices gave a second party, Jack Sherrill the third, Eddie Cantor a fourth, and Abe Blumberg, a big dress manufacturer, the fifth.

True, they were very elaborate parties, with expensive food and such, and more expensive presents for Deanna. But—not one girl friend of her own age was there. What is happy about that kind of a birthday?

DEANNA went roller skating at a public rink in Los Angeles not long ago. She loves to skate and it had been a long time since she had had a chance, since her days were filled and you can't skate on the busy streets here at night. So what happened?

She arrived at eight p.m. At five minutes after, before she had a chance to fasten her skates, a crowd of autograph seekers had surrounded her.

Still others stood and stared. By the time the last autograph book had been signed, it was time for Deanna to go home.

Still another night loomed big in anticipation to Deanna. That night, she said she 'had more fun than in a year.' The event was a fudge party.

The usual preliminaries went off in fine style for Deanna. There was the buying of the extras needed for the candy, the cracking and chopping of the nuts, watching the fudge boil, testing for the soft ball in cold water that means it is time to take it from the fire. Then waiting the long, long time until the confection was cool enough to beat.

There's nothing more fun than to make fudge with the right people. It is an exciting, tantalizing adventure. But waiting with Deanna for the fudge to cool that night, patronizingly amused at her breathless impatience were her mother and father, her manager, her singing teacher and heaven knows who else. All adults living in another world, a world a girl of fourteen is not yet ready to enter or understand!

Maybe Paula and Janie made fudge in one of their homes that same night. If so, they had something Deanna did not for all her fame and money.

They had a good time.

THE TRUTH ABOUT THE MYSTERIOUS MISS LOY

[*Continued from page 134*]
money was made to be spent—and spent it. He read books with Myrna and rode over the ranges with her and laughed at her early ambition to become a dancer.

This ambition was born, Myrna believes when, at the age of six, her mother took her to see Maeterlinck's "Blue Bird." The children who danced in that pageant danced straight into Myrna's heart and with their unconscious grace moulded an ambition.

BUT Father Williams didn't really sympathize with his small daughter's avowed career. He was of the school who thinks the theatre no place for a daughter of his. Not that he worried about it. He didn't have time . . .

And so, for those first thirteen years Myrna went to public school and played games in the afternoon. She made fudge with girl friends and read Louisa M. Alcott, "Lorna Doone," "The Wide, Wide World," and Tennyson's poems—and dreamed. She studied hard and successfully only the things she wanted to study. And the things she wanted to study were the subjects she thought would be of use to her when the world should applaud her as a premiere danseuse. History and English were her favorite subjects. For from history she could draw upon the stately images of queens and reconstruct scenes at Versailles and the pomp and vanity of the French and Viennese Courts. And from English she could absorb the living thoughts of dead poets, the immortal dreams of great men—and all of this would live again in her Art. She loved dramatics, too, of course, And gym because she knew that she must keep her body supple and fit.

She had a great many girls friends but no boy friends at all.

"I was," Myrna laughs now about it "a very plain little girl, to put it kindly. Carrotty hair. Freckles then, as now. Light eyelashes and eyebrows and unpleasantly skinny. I was a tomboy, too. Grubby hands and knees, torn dresses and socks, screechy voice. Not a trace of dimpled appeal. No one ever called me a 'little angel.' I was really quite hopelessly plain. It must have been hopeless if my mother gave up and did nothing about me. She evidently felt that you can't make a glittering brocade purse out of a little freckled sow's ear. She just saw to it that my hands and face were immaculately scrubbed at least once a day, my dresses tubbed and my reddish hair tightly braided into two pig-tails for neatness' sake. And let it go at that.

"And I suffered agonies in silence. I always have been inarticulate when it comes to personal pain. I wanted, passionately, to be beautiful. I read of Elaine and Guinevere and childish heroines like the 'Little Colonel' and I covered the pages with great globby tears of self-pity.

"I suffered all the more because, of all things, I had chosen for my best friend the little girl who lived next door. And she was a curly, golden-haired cherub who wore ruffles and ribbons. She had a peaches and cream skin and nary a freckle to her face, and a gurgly little giggle. She was feminine, soft and lovable—everything that I was not. She was a lace paper valentine, I was the comic variety! The boys made a great fuss over her—they carried her books to and from school for her. *I* trudged alone carrying my own. They shared their lunches with her, bought her ice cream and candies and sent her smudgy little notes covered with circular kisses. I ate my own lunch and never had a single note to my name. The contrast was really rather awful for me —it's a wonder it didn't give me an inferiority complex for the rest of my life. There was Amy, golden-curled and so pretty and there was I, pig-tailed and freckled!

THEN, to make the situation still more acute, I fell in love with a lordly lad of twelve, And *he* fell in love with Amy! I worshipped him. He worshipped Amy. And if adults bemoan the pain of unrequited love, they should remember the awful, inarticulate love of twelve!

"He would ride Amy home from school, this Romeo, on the back of his bicycle and I would tag along behind, taking little running steps in an effort to keep up with them, trying to pretend that I was having a glorious time, that it was fun and squeezing my eyes tight

shut all the while to keep the tears back! Amy would get me to telephone him, too, from my house, and invite him over to play with 'us.' And when he came he and Amy would go off and have secrets together and play games which never included me. I didn't try to compete. I think I knew I had no weapons with which to fight. It never occurred to me that I might try keeping my hands clean and curling my hair and softening my war-whoopish voice. I had none of the instinctive siren in me. I haven't now. Which is why the fact that I have played so many slinky exotic sirens on the screen strikes me as really funny . . .

"As a pay-off to that portion of my past . . . not very long ago I had a note from this very boy—*asking for my autograph!* He had been seeing me on the screen and realized, suddenly, that Myrna Loy and the small Myrna Williams were one and the same. He said very flattering and rather fulsome things, the kind of things that would have transported the child Myrna to Seventh Heaven. One might say that the Law of Compensation had worked in my behalf. It had—but too late.

"That was my first experience of being in love with someone who wasn't in love with me. I've had the same experience many times since. Unrequited love! I should be a poetess to sing that dirge. I've almost always fallen in love with the wrong man—or with a man who didn't know the state of my feelings.

"Gary Cooper lived a block in back of us in those days. I don't remember him. He says that he vaguely recalls seeing me about. And my mother knew his mother. Doubtless we went to the same grammar school together and must often have ridden the same ranges. It's just as well I didn't see him—I should probably have had another unrequited love to weep over !"

And so Myrna's childhood, up to the age of thirteen, was the childhood of any everyday little American girl in a happy home. Then, when Myrna was thirteen, came the flu epidemic. Myrna, her mother and brother were all stricken with the dread malady. Indeed, the whole town of Helena was laid low by the epidemic. Hospitals were filled beyond capacity in that first onslaught. Nurses were at a premium. In the Williams household a nurse was obtainable only for an hour or so each day. And for the rest of the time David Williams acted as nurse for his wife and two children. When Myrna became so ill that she was unconscious and had to be packed in ice, she would wake from a coma every now and again to be conscious that her father was sitting by her bedside, his strong hand holding firmly to hers.

He saved her life—and lost his own.

Gradually Myrna, her mother and brother recovered and then, with fatal swiftness, the malady struck David Williams. Myrna was sent to the house of a neighbor—to wait.

One day dragged by, two days. Myrna wandered restlessly about the house. On the third day, at high noon, she suddenly felt giddy, funny. She ran upstairs to an empty bedroom with her invariable instinct for hiding her heart from others. As she entered the room the thin blade of a knife seemed to enter her fast-beating heart. She said aloud "*Daddy is dead.*" She sat down to wait for the telephone to ring. Within five minutes it rang. Another few minutes and her hostess came slowly into the room. Myrna did not need to look at that compassionate face. She said, without raising her eyes, "You don't have to tell me, Mrs. Carter—*I know.*"

MYRNA said, "I can't explain, but with Daddy gone I never thought of anybody taking care of me. I knew that any care to be taken was up to me. Perhaps it was because I had always been identified so closely with my father that, when the reins fell from his hands, I picked them up. Perhaps, too, it was because mother had always been such a gay person, without ever having had to shoulder responsibility or know the meaning of making ends meet.

"In spite of which she was really magnificent in the months that followed. She rose to the sad occasion gallantly and competently. She decided that we would go to California, she, David and I. We had spent an occasional winter in La Jolla when we were younger and it had always agreed with her. Her health was precarious . . . Dad's death, her own illness and those of the friends who had fallen to right and to left of us had endangered it. There was a small amount of money left us from our lands in Montana and from insurance. We could manage until I should begin to work.

"We came to California and rented a small house in Culver City, not very far from here."

Myrna went to the Westlake School for Girls for a year. She wanted to study dancing and music. She wanted more history, French and English. She was too young, at that time, to do anything but prepare. Before the year was over, she had found a position, teaching dancing in a small private dancing school. She had thirty pupils, most of them older than herself, and she earned twenty-five dollars a month for her labors.

Myrna said, "Even in high school I never mingled much with the other girls. Alone the majority of the time, I always could be found, wearing a wisp of chiffon, in every May festival or amateur theatrical. But even in those moments you could hardly have called me companionable. For I was not being myself —I was somebody else!"

A little later Myrna decided to study sculpture. Both for its own sake and because she believed the plastic art would contribute to her dancing. She finally entered Venice High School in Southern California because she'd discovered that an artist of national renown, Mr. H. F. Winebrenner, was head of the art classes.

Not even then did boys, crushes or romance enter Myrna's life. She said, "I think my almost boy-less state at that time can be accounted for by the fact that I was consumed with a passion for *success*. My dreams were dreams of success. My daytimes were spent pursuing it. And then, there were things to do at home—helping mother, helping David do his homework. Occasionally I felt dreamily in love with some gilded youth but always one who did not know that I existed."

WHILE Myrna was sculpturing at Venice High, Mr. Winebrenner planned a sculptured group wherewith to grace the campus. He conceived the idea of an allegorical group of three figures, one to represent the Physical, another the Mental and a third the Spiritual. This classical group was completed and won the admiration of the art world. But a mystery hovered about it for five years —the mystery of the identity of the model who had posed for the Spiritual. Then, five years after the unveiling, the sculptor revealed the identity of his model—Myrna Loy!

Mr. Winebrenner is quoted as saying, "I had no difficulty in selecting the first two models. A football gladiator posed for the Physical and a pretty girl of high scholastic standing for the Mental. But the model for the Spiritual was not so easy. It required a girl with a beautiful body and if that were all it would have been easy. But animating the body the spirit had to be manifest, clear and idealistic. A prismatic refraction of intelligent understanding, beauty and grace combined into the term called spiritual. I was watching an interpretive dance at the school one day and happened to notice Myrna Williams, one of my own pupils. My eyes were opened. It took a good deal of persuading to induce her to pose for me but she finally consented to do so providing the work be done in the privacy of my own studio-home. Later, she asked me to keep her identity a secret. She said she would feel so silly, a little, unknown schoolgirl, being marbleized as Spirit!"

"My dancing school work," Myrna told me, "was getting me exactly nowhere. The twenty-five a month was getting us into debt. Funds were dwindling and drastic action was imperative. I had to take that action. I never wavered in my conviction that I was the man of the family. I wouldn't ask for help.

"I heard, then, that Fancho & Marco were putting on one of their revues at Grauman's Egyptian Theatre. I applied for the job and got it. I was one of thirty girls doing the dance numbers. I stayed there for one year and three months, made thirty dollars a week and was grateful."

And not then, not even then, did boys, good times, staying out late and partying figure in the life of Myrna Williams. Now and again she went dancing with some boy. Now and again she was in love with some youth who was unaware of her. The work was hard and constant and she had occasion many times, she told me, to be grateful to the Montana plains for the sound body they had given her. Now Myrna admitted, laughing, she never makes an athletic move. She is, she says, one of the laziest women living. A swim now and again is the sum total of her gladiatorial gaddings. And then, too, at that period of her life she had few clothes and when you have few clothes and must look smart all of the time, a considerable amount of home dry-cleaning, pressing and mending is necessary.

"Then—" said Myrna, "then something happened to me that was to be the turning point for me. Though, as is usually the case, I didn't know it for a turning point when I saw it. It was chance . . . and it is my belief that Chance is seventy-five per cent of success, the other twenty-five must be ability.

"Henry Waxman, the photographer, happened to have an idle evening on his hands. He dropped into the Egyptian. I chanced, that night, to be the central figure in the dance numbers. He happened to notice me, and thought I would make a good photographic subject. He came back stage and offered to photograph me. I was flattered and accepted the very kind offer, which was to be without cost to me. No one had ever wanted to photograph me before.

"The pictures were made. They turned out beautifully. A day or so later, Valentino happened to be in Waxman's studio. He saw my pictures and he asked about me. He went to see me at the Egyptian. The next day Henry Waxman called me. I was to go to the studio where Mr. Valentino would make a test of me—Natacha Rambova was preparing to screen "What Price Beauty?" and—and they wanted to test me!

"I couldn't sleep that night. I thought, *Ha, there, Amy!* The next day, carrying my heart in my hand, I walked into the presence of the most beloved man on the face of the earth. The most beloved and the kindest. Natacha was there, too, and they explained to me that they wanted me to test for the part of Intellect. Natacha was using all types of women in this picture which starred Nita Naldi.

RUDY himself made me up—and to this day and hour," Myrna said, a tremble in her low-pitched voice, "to this very hour I think there has never been an hour so terrific, so thrilling as that hour when Rudy's hands worked on me, when Rudy's eyes watched me, when Natacha brought me her own clothes to wear, when they both stood by and helped me make the test—both so friendly, so kind. Wherever Natacha is now, and if she reads my life story, I hope she will know that I am remembering her kindness . . . and Rudy's . . .

"Well, and so the test was made. A few days later I went to see it. I walked into that projection room alive and I walked out of it—*dead*.

"As I watched my screen self, stiff, absurd, ugly, I thought. 'They've done all these things for me and I'm *a complete flop!*'

"Imagine . . . imagine what it meant to me, not only to know that I had failed, lost my chance—but that I had failed *Valentino!* If there could be any young fate more heart-breaking, more nerve-shattering than that I should not like to know about it."

But there is something sturdy and substantial about this girl who has played so many "exotics." The freckles on that bizarre and beautiful countenance are the little brown badges of her independence. They give the lie to the lotus-lily soul. She is not languorous, of the night-blooming species. The pioneer spirit of Grandmother Annabelle beats valiantly in her blood. When she is down she is down only long enough to draw a full recuperative breath and then—she goes ahead and does things.

She went home from that projection room and stayed in bed for two weeks. That was the recuperative breath. When she rose, recharged, she decided that she must go to New York to dance and find new fields. But before she could go, there must be the wherewithal to go on. And wherewithals were earned, not given. Perhaps she could get some extra work at, say M-G-M. An extra didn't need to photograph beautifully.

Carfare was scarce in those lean days but fortunately Myrna was near enough to walk from her home to M-G-M. She found out where the casting office was, she entered it and, on those narrow wooden benches of hope so often deferred, Myrna sat patiently, long day after long day.

And there, again, the drama of this girl's story should smite the reader between the eyes. Her first entrance into M-G-M—as an applicant for extra work, a holder-downer of wooden benches. And now, a handful of years later, a star in that same studio, with the gates flung wide at her entrance!

Every now and again, in those days, a small wooden grille would open sharply and a man's cold eyes would slue about, eyeing the bench-sitters as though they were so many bolts of goods. Now and again his voice would bark, "Here, you Elsie de Smithers . . ." or, "You, there, in the black sateen, wanter work today?"

But no one called, "Here, you . . ." to the thin girl called Myrna Loy.

And then, one long day later, when funds were ebbing low and hope was having to fight for its life, the grille opened and the fateful voice boomed out, "Hey, you over there in the blue suit, wanter work?"

And Myrna said, "Oh, yes—yes, please—"

And she entered the portals of Metro-Goldwyn-Mayer.

What did she find awaiting her behind those magic doors? If you make seven guesses they will all be wrong.

(*This is the first of two articles on Myrna Loy's life story.*)

THE NEW MYSTERY OF
MR. AND MRS. CHAPLIN

[Continued from page 137]
dancing together were watched by hundreds of eager eyes in several night clubs. Their absorbed interest in one another's conversation was observed in this secluded corner and that. And the fact that Charlie, who is something of a hermit now, came out of his secluded estate and appeared at a few night clubs, without Paulette, was also noted.

There matters stood in late October when "The Great Dictator" was set to open both in New York and Hollywood and when Paulette did her disappearing act. She was neither in New York nor Hollywood. (Charlie was in New York, having left Hollywood.) Litvak was out of town, too.

This confirmed the whole situation for both sets of rumor reporters. Charlie had dropped Paulette and Paulette had dropped Charlie and the opening of "The Great Dictator" would be a frost because of it.

That was when the press agents of Warners and United Artists and Paramount all got busy. That was when the wires buzzed and the cables sang and the newspaper press stood waiting for headlines.

So what happened? On the opening night of "The Great Dictator," on Broadway, Mr. Charles Spencer Chaplin stepped out to acknowledge the crowd's applause. With him he brought

a beautiful girl, Miss Paulette Goddard, his co-star. He presented her to the audience.

"This is my wife," said Mr. Chaplin.

Paulette said nothing, as usual. She smiled that warm and sirenic smile of hers, as usual. But it was noted when she started back a day or two later to the Coast—without "the great dictator" that she wore a large and resplendent new diamond solitaire, a reward, it was whispered, for her New York trek. Charlie was to follow her shortly, but presently the plan changed and he was detained in the East.

When the news got back to Hollywood, several of the town's leading ladies chewed off their long fingernails in sheer aggravation. It was exactly like reading an installment of a serial in a magazine only to have it say "continued next week" just as one got into the most exciting chapter.

For, of course, this does mark the close of another chapter in the mystery mixup of Paulette and Charlie. And it does mean that the story will be continued. You know perfectly well that with such a dynamic beautiful heroine, a genius hero and a debonair, unattached "other man," it is bound to be.

I'M NOT MARRIED BECAUSE
[Continued from page 139]
I was only seventeen, and I thought marriage would be be a step into paradise. But even at seventeen, if I'd had to say to myself, 'This is forever. Are you sure?' I might have given myself time to realize that I wasn't sure and saved us all a lot of heartache."

She was speaking slowly, choosing her words, intent on presenting the facts in their true light, a light that reveals not heroes and villains, but the blundering humans most of us are.

YET I'm glad we married. Or perhaps I should put it this way. I'm sorry to have made my mother unhappy and Grant unhappy. But I'm glad for the lessons I learned—that marriage doesn't just work of its own accord, that it's got to be made to work. All humans are selfish, and we in this business are probably more selfish than most. We're pampered and fussed over. At first we're grateful, and then we begin to accept these things as our right. 'Why should I stand this, and why should I stand that?' we say and take that attitude with us into marriage. Of course it's ruinous. Of course you've got to give and take.

"Well, Grant and I may have hurt each other—not may have, we did—but only through youth and inexperience, not through ill will. There's no bitterness in my memories, and I hope and believe he would say the same. But if I hadn't learned about marriage through

that one, I might have stepped blindly into another that would have been bitter. Which is why I'm glad. It may be a selfish reason, but there it is. An actress friend of mine who waited till she was almost thirty to marry, once said to me, 'I waited because I wanted to be sure of what I was getting into. If I had to do it again, I'd do the same thing. And I'd train any children of mine to do the same thing. The only one important thing when you marry is to be sure he's the man you want to live with for the rest of your life.' That's what I didn't realize at seventeen. Now I do. And now I'll wait till I am sure."

A little relieved at having finished with that, she reached for a cigarette, then somewhat inexplicably murmured, "Salamander," and folded her hands demurely in her lap. I followed her warning eye to where a blue-uniformed guard had strolled on the scene. "No smoking," she explained. The guard smiled like a father and went his way. Miss Young stuck the cigarette back into its pack. "Be a good girl, Loretta," she admonished herself. "Don't betray that trusting grin. Anyway, wait until the effect's worn off."

I asked her if she carried in her mind any picture of the man she might one day marry. The answer came promptly, as if it were a matter she'd given thought to.

"Not a picture, no; but two things he's got to have. Moral courage and breeding. I can't stand a leaner. I don't want my husband to be my baby, too. Oh, in little ways, yes, but not in the essentials. If there's any leaning to be done, I'm old-fashioned enough to think the woman should do it. I'm no clinging vine. I'm used to being independent. I'm not one to hang fondly on a man and get a thrill out of being a slave to petty authority: 'Darling, you smoke too many cigarettes,' and so on. But I want to know that if I do feel like leaning all over him, I can, and he'll stand firm. Any woman wants that. She may love the other kind in a pitying way. But I want to love my husband plain, without pity, without feeling I have to apologize for him, even to myself—least of all to myself.

"And by breeding I don't mean a line of aristocrats behind him. There's a breeding of the heart, an instinctive good taste that aristocrats sometimes don't have and hod-carriers do. It includes a certain fastidiousness of mind and body. I don't like dirty finger-nails and uncouth language. He's got to be literate. I don't care whether he's a college graduate or not. He's got to love education for its own sake—not for the sake of some letters after his name, but because it opens new worlds and trains you to make the best of what you've been born with.

I HOPE I'm not sounding smug, making demands, as if I were a paragon of all the virtues myself. After all, they're not unreasonable demands, are they?" she pleaded with comic wistfulness. "Character and a certain degree of culture? And perhaps I can redeem myself by stopping there. The rest doesn't matter. I don't care what he looks like. Handsome or ugly, it's all the same to me. Of course, I'd be pleased if he weren't a Dracula. I'd be pleased if he were beautifully attentive and considerate and thoughtful of me. But if he weren't, I'd soothe my vanity by putting it down to absent-mindedness. Sometimes I think I'd like him to be in the motion picture business, and sometimes I hope to heaven he knows nothing about it.

"I'd be pleased, too, if his tastes were something like mine. For instance, I adore dancing. I studied it for eight years, and it's a passion with me. Well, when Albertina Rasch gives a recital at the Bowl, I'd like him to enjoy it with me. But if he'd rather go to the Stadium for the fights, that would be all right, too. When we got home, he could tell me who knocked out whom. And I could give him an imitatin of one of the Rasch girls dancing. That would probably amuse him.

"Money? Yes. Frankly, money is important. But only to this extent—that he should be able to make enough to keep his own self-respect. A million dollars has no attraction for me. The more money you have, the more you worry about it. I've got enough for myself. But for his own sake, I shouldn't want to marry a man who would have to take from me. If he were out of luck, I'd give with both hands. But however generously you give, taking humiliates a man—makes him feel inferior—which must never be. It's fatal to any marriage." Her kindling eyes softened as she said more quietly. "I couldn't bear to see my husband anything but proud."

Then again she sought relief in lightness. "I forgot," she smiled. "There's one more must. He must not be a practical joker. I can't stand a man who thinks it's funny to embarrass people—to electrify a chair, for instance, and then go haw-haw-hawing all over the place, as if he'd done something really noteworthy. I always feel like bashing him one," said the fragile-looking Loretta and eyed the slender hands in her lap as if to weigh their possible bashing power.

"And when I marry my non-practical joker," she went on, "I think I'd like to retire. I don't know, mind you, whether I will or not. I may feel quite differently about it tomorrow, and I've lived long enough to discover that keeping a flexible mind saves you a lot of self-torment. But if I feel as I feel now, I'd like to retire. Not because I believe marriage and a career won't mix. That's a subject I have no theories on. Whether they'll mix or not depends on the individual. But for myself, I'm inclined toward a normal home life, children and the rest of it. I'd like to run my house, work in my garden, be there when my husband comes home at night, look after my babies myself.

THERE'S always the danger, of course, that I'd miss the excitement and stimulation of this business. I've been in it for eleven years. I know how it's crept into my blood, become part of me. I know it would be hard to give up. If my husband were connected with pictures and came home and talked about them, I'd probably quiver like an old firehorse to get back. If he weren't connected with pictures, I'd feel cut off from all that's been most colorful in my life. Still," she said, thoughtful-eyed, "I do see the danger, so I might be able to avoid it.

"Because—and in relation to anything else I've said, you'd have to print this in letters a mile high—the only real happiness I've ever got out of life is contact with the people I love. Nothing else matters. Not money, not clothes, not looks, not being flattered and run after. All that's pleasant, but empty. If you had it all and lost your family and friends, it would just be a heap of nothing that would sicken you. Loving your own and being loved by them is the only happiness there is. If I know anything in this world, I know that. So it seems reasonable to suppose that a husband and children you loved more than anyone else would manage to compensate for the lost thrill of work that you love. After all, you can't love work as you love people.

"I've got a fair notion of how I'd feel about my own children, because I adore my niece and nephew so. D'you mind if I turn into a doting aunt? Try and stop me," she laughed. "James Carter Herrmann is only four months old and mostly sleeps. But Gretchen, my namesake, is all of ten months. I generally stop by from the studio to call on her. She's rather a high-strung baby, not especially calm except with her father and mother and nurse.

"Well, Sally and I look quite a bit alike, and the other day she mistook me for her mother. She cooed and gurgled, and she has a trick—when you stick your lips out at her, like this, she sticks her own right back—and she patted my face with those little hands of hers. If there's any lovelier feeling in the world, I haven't met it. I tell you I had the most wonderful time of my life. I try to get there every day now before Sally comes home, so the baby'll make the same mistake. Low trick to play on your own sister, isn't it? But she doesn't mind.

"She said to me the other day, 'Gretch, there's nothing like it. To feel the absolute dependence of that little creature on you. To know you're the one person in the world she trusts instinctively, turns to for everything. To feel her hands clinging to you. I can't describe what it does to you—makes you humble and strong and reverent all at once, so your heart almost bursts, and you want to get down and pray that you'll never fail her. I don't want to get maudlin over it,' Sally told me, 'and I've had thrills before. But this kind of quiet thrill it tops them all.'"

Her long, lovely hands, on which a blue sapphire gleamed, were lying in her lap again. Her gray eyes were serene, as when they'd been gazing out toward an imaginary sea. Serene, but illumined with such tenderness that she might have posed for a young madonna as she said, "That's a thrill I hope life isn't going to cheat me of."

Their friends say you can expect them to be married any day soon. But these two quarrel and make up, make up and quarrel, with Tony now being under the same handicap with Lana that he was with Alice Faye.

Tony's strongest medium is not dramatics. He is a personality, he is handsome, he has a swoon-making voice. In radio, in personal appearances, he's tops, but in pictures he's far from appearing at his best. Meanwhile Lana gets increasingly more important. It made a tough setup with Alice. It will probably mean a tougher setup with Lana, because Lana and Tony quarrel more. Even if they do marry, nobody in Hollywood would give you a plugged nickel on the success of the union.

You can tell, however, about Cary Grant and Barbara Hutton, or, in other words, unless all signs fail, there is nothing to tell. Despite their recent trip together into Mexico, this is one of those "as is" romances, similar to the Brent-Sheridan romance, the George Raft-Betty Grable romance. In the latter case, of course, nothing can be done. George is still undivorced. In the former two, Hollywood thinks nothing will be done.

You can discount that chatter about Laraine Day's marrying Ray Hendricks, the singer, any day now. The slim Miss Day knows how marriages slow down young actresses' careers and she wants nothing whatsoever to slow down hers. Don't put too much stock, either, in those Ginger Rogers-George Montgomery datings. They are intense and night-after-night currently, but it is often thus with Miss Rogers.

She seems to have as keen an ability to get in and out of romantic complications as does the aforementioned Mr. Brent Perhaps she even learned the trick from him, for once upon a time they too saw quite a bit of one another. Or maybe she learned some of it from Howard Hughes, to whom she was suppoesdly engaged a year ago, this same Mr. Hughes who lately has been ringing Miss Hedy Lamarr's doorbell, and prior to either Hedy or Ginger has dated every leading glamour girl in turn.

OF course, other gentlemen ring Miss Lamarr's doorbell, too. There is Mr. John Howard, who still calls frequently; Mr. Reginald Gardiner, who calls very occasionally, and amusingly enough, Mr. Gene Markey, who is an ex-husband, who has lately been re-calling. But Hedy's heart belongs to Johnnie. It honestly does. Johnnie is the only person that Hedy cares for passionately and completely. In case you have forgotten, Johnnie is the little boy she adopted nearly two years ago. Because of her divorce she still hasn't his legal custody. Until she has, you may be sure that there will be no romance in the Lamarr life. It is one of those unbelievable things that a girl like this should turn out to be all-mother, but it is absolutely true.

That's the current romance round-up, affairs of the Hollywood heart brought right up to the minute. Of course, I don't know how long this minute will last. They do say that Brent and Sheridan . . . they do say that that producer and his wife . . . no, no, I do not mean Arthur Hornblow and Myrna Loy . . . ah, well, I'll have to check up on those and tell you more in another couple of months, when I come back again armed with my beaux and arrows.

SO YOU'D LIKE
TO BE A STAR?

[Continued from page 143]
or a photographic sitting to be okayed.

AND these things must be done. We can't go temperamental, either, and scratch the paper off the walls or slam down our make-up boxes and take off. You, Sarah, can tell your boss off, slam down your desk or bolt of ribbon. You shouldn't, but you can. If you do, what happens? At the worst, you may get fired. That may be pretty bad but, at least, only your boss and the office force and a few of your friends need know about it. If I should get fired, the whole world and every producer in the industry would know about it.

"It would be blazoned in the headlines. The Finger would be on me. At the worst, your huff would be put down to a scrap with your boy friend, and a casual 'what's eating her?' would be the end of it. But I would be branded as

hard to handle. You may be able to pound the keys or sell merchandise with frazzled nerves, but you can't go before the camera that way. The camera catches everything.

"Perhaps a great many of you girls feel abused when your boss asks you to rewrite a letter. Perhaps you groan when you make a typographical error, have to take the sheet out of the machine and start all over again. I can feel for you, but I doubt that you have ever felt for me. For we, in pictures, 'take the sheet out of the machine and start all over again' ten, sometimes twenty times, before we complete a 'take.' Perhaps we fumble a line, perhaps someone sneezes or a bumble bee buzzes in, and then we have to do the whole scene over again. Perhaps it is the biggest love scene in the picture, a deathbed scene, something that makes far greater emotional demands than rewriting a letter. Whatever happens, I have to wear a bright, brave smile and pretend it doesn't matter.

"I just don't dare have a cold in the head. I have to be far more careful of myself than I would be, left to my own devices. After all, a gal from Montana isn't exactly a hot-house plant. I'm a pretty sturdy specimen. But I have to behave, most of the time, like a fragile orchid. For if I should catch cold, get a dose of sunburn or contract a nice dose of poison oak—well, if anything happens to me while I'm working, it isn't only *my* face that burns. It would cost the studio thousands of dollars while I held up production. It might keep hundreds of people, extras and so on, out of work. I'm not my own man, girls. I daren't take chances with Myrna Loy, for she isn't my property.

"Other girls," Myrna went on warmly, "write me like this: They say, 'What is there for me to do after hours? My boy friend and I may have dinner together or go dancing. Or my girl chums will come over and we'll talk about our boy friends or, if we are engaged, our coming marriages. But our parties, Myrna, would seem tame to a girl like you. You go to such glorious ones, don't you?'

"Hah!" said Myrna, "I'd give away two years of my life to be able to get together with girl friends and talk about my marriage and new house which are, naturally, the most thrilling topics in my life. If I could be the plain Myrna Williams I am at heart, instead of forever figuring out what Myrna Loy dare and dare not say, I'd talk about Arthur and our romance and marriage and new home. I want to, right now. I can't. It wouldn't be in good taste. It might sound like bragging, in public, about private matters. The studio mightn't like it. It would also be offensive to Arthur, who doesn't wish to be included in my

publicity. So, I can't have any of the he-sez-to-me and-I-sez-to-him chummy sort of talk that other girls can. You think that's fun? It isn't.

"I have to be self-conscious most of the time. The most normal, insignificant move I make may be magnified in the public prints tomorrow. As when, recently, I was knitting bootees for my maid's expected baby and read everywhere that I was not knitting bootees for my maid's baby—ah, no. Well, it happens that I *was* knitting them for my maid. You'd think I'd know better by this time than to be seen manufacturing 'little garments' in public. But I haven't learned yet.

WHEN I go home at night I can't have the fun of dining out or dancing or going to a show with my husband. We do all of our socializing over the weekend. Other nights, I'm too tired to know for sure whether I'm Myrna Loy, Mrs. Arthur Hornblow or Kitty O'Shea. I'm not much good as a wife, a hostess, a goer-outer. I just stumble into bed if, by some miracle, I don't have to memorize lines for the next day's takes. Fortunately for me," Myrna said, "Arthur takes the greatest possible interest in my work. He certainly doesn't want me to give up my career. And he understands perfectly the demands made upon me, which is the only way in which marriage to a screen player is even possible.

"I'm not interested in clothes as other girls are and should be. In fact, I hate clothes. I'm dressed up to the nines all day and every day on the set, every detail perfect, every hair in place, a mirror poked under my nose every time I turn around. I'm tired of looking my best. I loathe the very mention of shopping. I feel ill when anyone mentions fittings. There's nothing I'd like better than to slip into something loose, whether it fits or not, and relax. I can't. That's one reason why we built our home in the comparative wildness and isolation of Cold Water Canyon, so that I can wear slacks and shuffle about in slippers.

"I can't go anywhere when I'm working. Too tired even to go to a neighborhood movie or to the corner drugstore for a soda. I couldn't go even that far without looking 'right,' you see. Not because of any personal vanity, but because the studio has spent millions of dollars on the personality known as Myrna Loy. And I can't let the studio down by slipping off my expensive mask of glamor. I've got to be, on all public occasions, the personality they sell at the box office.

"It's a shaky business, too. A good break is likely to get you in, in the first place. And a bad break is just as likely to get you out. And if you're out, you're out. Then there is always someone coming along from the outside, someone newer, more colorful, more talented. Or you may have two bad pictures, fail to get the right material, and you're gone with the wind.

"'If I had the money you make!' girls write. Yes, for a limited time. On the premise, too, that the more you make the less you can keep. And also, what good is money unless you can spend it? And if I hate clothes, prefer to hike rather than roll about in cars, can't entertain much because of being too tired, can't get away from the studio to make trips, have to guard my home and possessions as though I were ashamed of them—well, so what?"

Myrna rose and walked to the windows, looking down on the Hollywood which she, a schoolgirl from Montana, has so triumphantly conquered. She turned to face me; her mouth was smiling. But there was something deeper than laughter in her eyes.

She said, "It's nine parts drudgery and fear and heartache to one part thrill and glamor. It's all the things I've said it is, and more. And I love it— I love it."

WHY THE PERFECT WIFE'S MARRIAGE FAILED

[Continued from page 145]
it. Certainly she would never have told what one of her friends did. Her friend explained, "If Arthur wants Myrna to eat and drink, she'll eat and drink. If those are some of the things that make him happy and they get in the way of her career, then it's too bad for the career. Myrna is a wife, first and foremost, and an actress long afterwards."

All Myrna's friends knew, too, how her interest in Arthur's productions quite outweighed her interest in her own. They knew, for example, how she carelessly let herself be manoeuvered, because of studio politics, out of the leading feminine role in "Boom Town" and into the very much less important "Third Finger, Left Hand."

If she'd been more aggressive about her own interests, she could undoubtedly have prevented that, but all that time she was fiercely studying every ad in every publication that came out, not looking for clothes or bargains that she could buy for herself, but looking instead at the pretty girl models who posed in them. This was because she was aware of Arthur's hunt for an unknown girl to go into one of his productions.

THOSE were some of the things Myrna Loy could have told.

But she had never told, and probably she never will tell, what it must have meant to her in terms of tears and sleeplessness, when she came to the realization that her romance was fading.

Perhaps Myrna will never tell any of those things because it looks as though even up until three months ago she would not admit the death of her marriage, even to herself. Three months ago, the whispers first started flying in Hollywood.

Three months ago, the whispers first began concerning Arthur's interest in still another actress. There were whispers and no more and there was no confirming the truth of them. It is highly possible that they were entirely compounded of imagination and fabrication; but there they were. A man as important, attractive and desirable as Arthur is always subject to such gossip.

Arthur was home ill when the whispers first began and all Hollywood knew how faithfully Myrna nursed him through that sickness. After he recovered, Myrna herself fell sick, badly enough for her doctor to insist upon hospitalization. It was "merely flu"— but any victim of that sly disease knows how weak and wretched it can leave you. It is at a time like that that a wife needs a husband around to protect and comfort her, but it was right after returning home from the hospital bout that Myrna finally confirmed those rumors.

Yes, she said, there would be a divorce. The grounds, she said, would be incompatibility of temperament.

That is all she said, this girl who had had a dream of being a perfect wife; this girl who had portrayed the perfect wife so charmingly, so truly, on the screen that a million wives and husbands had been inspired by that portrait to make their marriages more lasting and beautiful.

So salute her, this wife, who even at the end is still behaving perfectly. It will work out for her. It must work out for her if dignity and love and fineness mean anything in this life of ours.

MY HUSBAND IS MY BEST FRIEND

[Continued from page 147]
shipboard, at the festival in Panama, in Cuba.

"These pictures are frightful of Frank," she said indignantly, letting her luncheon grow cold. "Look at this! And do look at this! Why in this one he doesn't even look shaved! He mustn't pose for the news photographers again. They never make him look himself at all."

There also were clippings, clippings which heralded this trip as a second honeymoon.

"A second honeymoon," Irene laughed. "As if there ever could be such a thing with the same man!"

I asked exactly what she meant. And she told me, as simply and directly and honestly as it is her habit to say the things she thinks.

"A honeymoon is wonderful, of course," she went on, smoothing her sweater contemplatively. "It's the time two people go off alone and do their utmost to remain alone. Not only because they are so new and exciting to each other. But because it is their chance to draw closer and prepare for the intimacy of the every day married life which lies ahead of them.

"However, feverishly romantic though it may be, it's also apt to be something of a strain. Because the two people haven't yet learned to relax with each other. Because they haven't had time to become truly good friends. Because they don't know all the little things about each other which only the intimacy and affectionate understanding of years brings."

She began pulling a great flat package out from behind the sofa, untying the cord, crackling the big stiff sheets of paper which wrapped it.

"It's much more fun to have been married for a matter of years, I think," she went on. "Then you have a dozen little agreements about some things and a dozen differences of opinion about other things. Then you know more of what the other fellow is thinking and feeling, irrespective of what he may be doing or saying for courtesy's sake or some other good reason. Then you're both interested in meeting new people and speculating about them later when you're alone. Then everything that happens to you, even a triffling event, is enriched by some similar thing you've already shared."

She had the package undone. In it were architect's drawings of a house to be built in Holmby Hills, provided the studios remain in Hollywood. Holmby Hills lies beyond Beverly and Bel Air. It is where Freddie March has built his charming new house. And where, just across from the Griffin acres, Claudette Colbert is breaking ground for her new home.

THERE was one view of the house from the front. Another showed the side and the patio. There were views of the lawns and gardens. And detailed views of the different rooms as they would look when the house was completed and they were curtained and furnished, with fires burning on their hearths and flowers from the cutting garden standing about in bowls.

"Home of Doctor and Mrs. Francis D. Griffin," was lettered on each drawing. Not "Home of Irene Dunne," mark you. And not even "Home of Irene Dunne and Doctor Francis D. Griffin." But what it really is to be, what their architect knew it would be after talking to these clients of his only a few times. For away from the studios, in spite of all her increasingly bright fame, Irene Dunne isn't at all the movie star, the celebrity. She is Mrs. Francis D. Griffin. First, last and always. Which undoubtedly has a great deal to do with the greatest friendship in the business world which I'll come to in good time.

I kept remembering, a day or two previously, when Irene had entertained representatives of the Irene Dunne Fan Club at a tea party. There had been a pretty girl there who came with the Yonkers contingent, a pretty girl of about fifteen, with eyes as deeply blue as the dress she wore. A dozen times that afternoon, with an adoring nod in Irene's direction, this girl had gone out of her way to explain "She's my aunt, you know!" And later when I asked her, "How does it feel to have a movie star in the family," Dorothea Griffin admitted with lovely naïveté, "Well, sometimes I wish Aunt Irene wasn't a movie star. I get jealous when I have to share her with a lot of people. Like this afternoon, for instance."

And I had thought that movie stars, if not prophets, sometimes are appreciated in their own countries, even in their own families. And that's *something!*

"You'll notice," Irene indicated the patio on the drawing, "that we've planned this as an extra living-room. We like to have breakfast outdoors on Sundays. And to read outdoors in warm evenings. It's enclosed on two sides by the wings of the house and on the third side by the loggia. The front looks out over the lawn straight to the ocean. See, the hill drops off here, just beyond our property. There never can be anything to block our view, to shut off the sea."

Frank Griffin won't be in California to live in that house all the time. Many months of the year he is obliged to be in New York where his practise is located. But it pleases him, sentimental as the next Irishman, to think of Irene in their home. And to look forward to the years ahead when they'll both find lives less busy and be there together all the time.

IRENE and I talked of her marriage. Of how she had taken what so easily might have become a marriage of inconvenience and shaped it into something fine.

"I admit," she said, "the separations are pretty lonely at times. They'd be unbearable, really, if it weren't for Frank's frequent telephone calls, put through after midnight when we can afford to talk much longer. But now that we're together for the time being. and I'm able to view our months of separation with some perspective, I'm not sure but that they haven't served us well.

"Perhaps if we'd been together all the time during the last four years we wouldn't be such good friends. Perhaps together all the time we'd have come to take each other more for granted; and find less zest in each other's company. How can anyone tell? Frankly, I'd almost be afraid to have things any other way than they have been. For fear it wouldn't have worked out as much fun.

"A month from now, of course, when I'm back in California and Frank is here and I'm missing him more than ever because I've just left him, you'll find me singing another tune. I'll be complaining that it's absurd for married people to permit three thousand miles to separate them. For the hysterical moment I'm even likely to be considering giving up my work. Although I know in my heart that I couldn't, that it's become too much a part of me."

As she talked I remembered some of the things which have forged the bond stronger between her and Frank Griffin. There was the time, some years ago, for instance, when she spent an entire Sunday rehearsing for her screen tests of "Cimarron" which she was to take the next day, although RKO were giving her these tests simply to please her, having no idea that she, a musical comedy star in their minds, could properly play Sabra Cravat.

On that day Frank Griffin remained with her closed in her room. He knew how much this meant to her. He watched the different effects she tried out and, now and then, helped with a suggestion. His cronies kept the telephone ringing constantly. They wanted him to join them on the links. Suppose Irene did have to work, that was no reason why he had to stay home. They didn't understand.

I also remembered Irene's frantic trip across the continent after the telephone call which advisd her he had been rushed to the hospital for an appendicitis operation. At this time the newspapers insisted that, under cover of being in New York because he was ill, she had come on to ask for a divorce. Considering Frank Griffin's temporary weakened and depressed state those stories might have caused an upset. But because it was Irene who read him those stories, sitting close beside his bed, laughing, joking, meeting his eyes wth her own eyes level, they could do no harm.

So it goes. It isn't, after all, so much the number of hours two people spend together as what they do with those hours. For with the years, her marriage to Frank Griffin has grown into that which can only exist in marriage and is at the same time the ultimate of marriage, namely the greatest friendship in the world.

WHAT HOLLYWOOD IS THINKING
[Continued from page 155]

worry and possible squabbles over money."

Taking a rather different and not unsound point of view, one young actress suggested as adequate, "any steady income."

Besides the fifty-five and one-half per cent of the men who stipulated $100.00 as the lowest sum on which a married couple can live satisfactorily, there were the seventeen per cent who chose $75.00 a week; the ten per cent who said $50.00; the ten per cent who declined to set a figure on the grounds that circumstances alter cases, and the small group who mentioned $35.00 and $30.00.

"I need to make a hundred bucks to keep things going right!" wrote one married actor. "I've made less and we've lived on it, but I wouldn't call it adequate. Women are too expensive and a man likes his wife to have what she wants."

"At least $100.00 a week if there are children. This would provide funds for insurance, education, doctors' bills and emergencies," wrote another.

"As low as $30.00 a week, but it should be *sure!*" said another. He is a big star now, but a few years ago he was broke and hungry.

Of all who answered this question, only one, a woman, put the sum above an approximate $5,000.00 a year. She is the daughter of well-to-do parents and a ranking star. Her figure was— and understandably, after all—$10,000.00 a year.

Of the women who thought $100.00 a week necessary for marriage, two-thirds were married; of those who chose $50.00 a week or less, only one-fifth. Four-fifths of the men who specified $100.00 a week were married, as were two-thirds of those who selected $75.00. Only a fraction of the men who thought $50.00 a week adequate were married.

PHOTOPLAY'S sixth question was, logically: *Do you save a certain per cent of your income regularly?*

In response, eighty-four per cent of the feminine contingent said yes, and eighty-five per cent of the men.

"Of course," wrote one feminine star. "I'd be a fool not to. My big income can't last forever."

But, "Save? Tell me how!" wrote one perturbed contract player. "It costs *me* money to be in pictures!" This player, a beginner, has a private income. Apparently, she needs it.

Eighty-five per cent of the men also

save something regularly, PHOTOPLAY's questioning revealed.

"I have a business manager and he makes me save, whether I like it or not," declared one, recently risen to stardom.

"I should save, but I'm married and have two kids and I can't" wrote one of the small per cent who revealed himself *sans* a savings account.

Of the women who said they saved regularly, two-thirds were single. Of those who admitted they did not save, three-fifths were married. Among the men, approximately half boasting savings accounts were single. All of the men who said they could not save money were married.

EXTENDING its survey to embrace other phases of modern existence, PHOTOPLAY then asked: *"Were the time and money spent on your education worth while?"*

"Yes!" declared eighty-seven and one-half per cent of the women, but only sixty-two and one-half per cent of the men.

"I went to school only a few years. I wish it could have been three times that long!" wrote one feminine star.

"Not much money was spent for my education, but, as usual, the best things in life are free!" said a second. "Certainly," she added, "the *time* spent was worth it and then some!"

On the other hand, "I went to a so-called 'smart finishing school'," said one of the minority dissatisfied with the returns on their educational investment. "All I learned to do was to ride horseback, balance a teacup and look bored at any given social event! My real education has come since I began to make my own living. . . . And how!"

"Definitely!" wrote a large group of men who felt satisfied with their education. However, others in this class qualified their approval.

"Well—yes," wrote one, "but college less grammar and high school."

"No!" announced one of the masculine critics of modern education. "I was trained to be an electrical engineer, but I had a job in a filling station before the movies got me!"

FROM education, PHOTOPLAY turned to a question omnipresent in contemporary thought, to wit: *"What do you think constitutes the greatest danger of another world war?"*

Here, for the first time, the women proved hesitant about answering, with twenty-five per cent either leaving the space after this question blank or saying, frankly: "I don't know." The next largest group—twenty-two per cent—chose Fascism. After that came Communism, greed of dictators, bad economic conditions, aggression, overpop-ulation and discontent. In selecting Fascism and Communism, many expressed belief that attendant disregard of the church and principles of Christianity is far more dangerous than other phases of these "isms."

"The arrogance of rulers has been a vital factor in war-making of the past, and history repeats itself," wrote several others, in effect.

Without exception, the men had an answer to this question, with twenty-three per cent choosing dictators as the most formidable menace to peace; seventeen per cent selecting Fascism, its principles as well as dangerous greed of dictators; ten per cent, propaganda; eight per cent, Communism; and the rest being fairly well divided in the choice of dictators, capitalism, overpopulaton, upset economic conditions and "popular hysteria."

"All the 'isms' are dangerous," wrote another. "People should pay more attention to the blessings of democracy."

"Propaganda, carefully dished out by the Allies, led us into the last war. It will do it again if we are not careful," said a third, considering, particularly, Amerca's position in the case of war.

"ARE you interested, personally, in any of the outstanding social theories, such as Communism?"

To this inquiry, seventy-five per cent of the women and sixty-seven per cent of the men said no.

"No 'ism' but Americanism interests me!" said many of both sexes, emphatically.

"No! And it's too bad more people don't pay less attention to Communism and such and more to the principles of democracy!" said others.

Several were specific. "Neither Communism nor Fascism!" they said.

"No, I am an American!" announced one of the men, tersely.

Another thoughtful male star, taking a somewhat broader view of the question, said: "Democracy is, in reality, an 'ism.' I am vitally interested in Democracy. The others, only academically."

The majority of both sexes who said yes to this question qualified their answers by saying they were interested in, but not in sympathy with, the two outstanding 'isms'—Fascism and Communism.

"I am interested! I believe that the more thoroughly grounded I am in knowledge of these social evils, the more easily I can combat them!" was one answer.

Another: "Yes, in the sense that from studying all social theories we may achieve a truer and happier democracy. I do *not* believe that ignorance is bliss!"

PRESIDENT ROOSEVELT was the choice of forty-nine per cent of the women and fifty-five per cent of the men in answer to the query: *"Whom do you consider the outstanding figure in world affairs today?"*

Hitler was next, chosen by thirty-three per cent of the women and thirty-one per cent of the men. British Prime Minister Chamberlain was the selection of twelve and one-half per cent of both men and women. Mussolini was mentioned by many, but always jointly with Hitler. Henry Ford, Douglas Corrigan, Walter Winchell came in for a vote or two, each, from the women; Thomas Dewey and Charles Lindbergh were mentioned by the men.

"President Roosevelt because, while he has made mistakes, his combined idealism and ability are outstanding," said a feminine player.

"President Roosevelt because he is president of the United States—not because he is a great man," said several of the men.

Unanimously, Hitler was chosen, not because of personal greatness, but because of his unique position of power.

"I *hate* him, but I can't ignore him!" said one of the women who put him first in importance.

"Hitler and Mussolini because of their threats to democracy," said another.

The men seemed a little less resentful of the German *Fuehrer*, but equally inclined to rate him as a world menace.

"His attitude is similar to Napoleon's. He thinks he cannot be beaten," said one.

Choice of Chamberlain, without exception, was because of his contribution to world peace.

"He acted in the interests of his own country first, which was right. But he never forgot the welfare of the world," was one comment.

"I believe his ideal of peace at any price to be right. Nothing—no country's so-called 'territorial integrity' is worth the sacrifice of human life in war," was another.

The feminine star who voted for Winchell said, frankly: "I chose him because he is a great influence in my particular world—that of the stage and screen."

THE question put last by PHOTOPLAY was: *"Do you go to church regularly? . . . Occasionally?"*

To this fifty-nine per cent of the women said occasionally; twenty-two per cent regularly, and nineteen per cent not at all. The men's answers were: seventy-two per cent occasionally; fifteen per cent regularly and twelve per cent not at all.

"I only go occasionally, but my religion is always with me," remarked one woman star.

"Occasionally, yes," said a second.

"But I should go oftener. Mentally, I do!"

"I have never thought much about religion, but the infrequent times I attend church, I get something out of it," admitted one of the men.

"Church every Sunday brings me a certain peace of mind, inexplicable but definite," asserted one young actress declaring regular attendance.

Another said: "I think if more people went to church regularly, the world would be a better place—just as I am a better woman—for so doing."

On the other hand: "No, I do not go to church! I used to, but found nothing that I wanted in any of them," declared a certain famous woman star. "I believe in God, though," she added, "and try to practice a religion of my own."

"Neither my wife nor I go to church anymore," admitted another, "because we have not gotten much from it. But we send our children to Sunday School so that they may know what religion is all about and pass upon its value, themselves."

Yes—Hollywood does think about others things besides the movies!

HE WANTS TO BE ALONE
[Continued from page 158]
was trying hard to start a fight between the studio and me. It was too bad, really, that we had to spoil the fun. You see, the studio knew why I went to the desert, and it wasn't for the rumored reason.

"I went for a bit of convalescence. I had the flu, and it left me with a whisper instead of a voice. And I was giving this eye a rest." He exhibited an optic that, on close examination, was inflamed. "It's still giving me trouble. Last fall, the eyeball was sunburned. The immediate result was a flaking. And ever since, there has been a burning sensation, particularly after a siege in front of the lights. It's nothing serious, but it's annoying. After this picture, I'm planning to go East for some special treatment.

"From there, if the doctor says okay, I'm hoping to go on over to England for a picture. I can use a little travel, a change of scenery.

"My contract is up for renewal after this picture, and I'm hoping to settle for two pictures a year, one here and one, perhaps, in England. Anything I make over two pictures goes to the tax collector, anyway. Also, I've a hunch that with fewer pictures, the public won't weary of this physiognomy so soon. I still want to be around, years hence.

"How do I explain my 'recent success?' My friend, I've tried for years to figure out why I've been treated so

handsomely by the public, and it still has me puzzled.

"I'm doing the best I can, but I'm afraid I'm not quite as good as I'm supposed to be. God knows there are other actors who are better-looking, and better actors than I am. It all seems to simmer down to the idea that luck has a great deal to do with success. Luck—and a little privacy, a chance to keep your head, time to study your work.

"That's another reason why I want to be alone. To sort of preserve my luck."

DIETRICH IS STILL SELLING GLAMOUR
[Continued from page 159]
certain questions were asked, or evasive answers when the subject of her rumored romance with Douglas Fairbanks, Jr., was mentioned, or "We're just good friends," when the matter of Josef von Sternberg came up.

However, out of the various answers and tactful evasions one thing is certain and that is that Miss Dietrich is anxious to return to England as quickly as possible, even if the British newsmen, whom she likes better than their American cousins, did force her to grant a signed interview in the *London Leader* because of the numerous questions they pelted at her.

The reasons for this are several: (1) Von Sternberg is in London and she is anxious to return to make a picture under his direction. Incidentally, her loyalty to von Sternberg is carried almost to the point of fanaticism. In the *London Leader* story she said, "His enemies are mine also, and I would never number among my friends anyone who tried in any way to harm or discredit von Sternberg, though this has sometimes embarrassed Josef." (2) She prefers to have her daughter educated abroad, but what is more important in view of constant kidnapping threats that stars receive, probably feels that the child is safer in Europe than here.

THAT, then, is a fairly complete capsule portrait of the cinema's foremost exponent of glamour. But in order to understand the Dietrich of today—the Dietrich who enjoys the adoration of millions, likes to have them make a fuss over her in public, resents interviewers who pry into her private life and is human enough to make understandable mistakes as fibbing to reporters—it is necessary to know something of her background.

The story of Miss Dietrich's success is the story of one of the most amazing pieces of glamour-manufacturing ever perpetrated by Hollywood. Nine years ago Marlene Dietrich was a relatively obscure screen actress in Germany.

Daughter of a Prussian first lieutenant in the patrician Regiment of Grenadiers, she was born Mary Magdalene von Losch in the Duchy of Saxe-Weimar thirty-two years ago.

After the war, in which her father was killed early in the conflict on the Russian front. Marlene's mother took her to Berlin. But the revolution which followed the collapse of the German armies sent the bewildered family back to Weimar where Marlene was placed in a boarding-school.

In 1921 Marlene was back in Berlin a violin student at the *Hoschschule feur Musik* under the supervision of Professor Flesch. But an injury to her left wrist forced her to abandon a music career and as an outlet for her artistic energies she was given permission by her mother to embark upon a dramatic career in Max Reinhardt's school—but under a different name, the one by which the world now knows her today.

Her first appearance under Reinhardt's direction was as a bit player in *The Taming of the Shrew*. But progress on the stage was slow and she turned to the screen and obtained work at the UFA studios where, in 1923, she met and married an assistant director named Rudolph Sieber. Aften an interval she deserted the screen for the stage again, where she was discovered by Josef von Sternberg playing the role of an American society girl in a musical comedy called *Two Neckties* and signed for the leading role opposite Emil Jannings in *The Blue Angel*. And, incidentally, to Paramount.

FROM that moment on begins a success story that is among the most impressive in Hollywood. When she arrived in New York in 1929, she was introduced to the press at a champagne luncheon where the chief interest was in Marlene's already famed legs—the first stage in glamour building. In Hollywood, her movie career under the directorial guidance of von Sternberg, flourished rapidly until today she is one of the highest salaried stars on the screen.

But it is a career that has flourished on built-up glamour rather than talent.

Although Garbo submitted to the usual publicity stunts like posing with members of university track teams and such like matters and permitted herself to be built up as a glamorous mystery woman, she also indicated by her work that she was an actress of rare ability. Dietrich, on the other hand, except for one film, *The Blue Angel*, has never done anything from which one could judge whether she is a great actress or not.

How much of this is due to the fact that for the longest time she would work with no other director than von

Sternberg, is difficult to say. But this much it is reasonable to state without much fear of contradiction: By skilled lighting effects and magnificent photography, von Sternberg built Dietrich into a beautiful and glamorous figure on the screen.

However, by his stylized direction he also completely obliterated any latent acting ability his protege may have had. So much so that not even under the guidance of two other directors, Frank Borzage in *Desire,* and the late Richard Boleslawski in *The Garden of Allah,* has Miss Dietrich ever duplicated the promise she gave in *The Blue Angel.* The problem of her acting ability still remains in doubt.

BUT one thing Miss Dietrich does better than any other actress on the screen today: she has a genius for simulating glamour. Actually off the screen she is just a handsome woman with a lovely figure, neither more nor less beautiful than hundreds of other women on and off the screen. If you did not know she was the glamorous Dietrich the chances are you wouldn't be very much impressed with her beauty at a first meeting.

Just how true this is was brought home to the writer when he talked with Miss Dietrich when she arrived in New York recently and showed him some stills of herself in her new picture, *Knight Without Armour.* The difference between Miss Dietrich in real life and Miss Dietrich in the photograph was the difference between a handsome woman and one built up by studio artifice into a glamorous idol.

Now that Miss Dietrich has taken out her first American citizenship papers, the chances are that she will probably settle down in California with frequent trips to Paris, where she and her husband maintain an apartment, and to London where she is anxious to make films with von Sternberg.

AN OPEN LETTER FROM NORMA SHEARER
[*Continued from page 161*]

On the other hand, some people thought I was upset at the publicity given my friendship with Mr. Raft. No, indeed! On the contrary, I was very pleased that people were so interested. I've always maintained anything that is true about me can be printed in screaming headlines. And this is true, our friendship, I mean. It has now reached the point where most of the reports have it that we are either rifting or planning to be married. Neither is true, at least not at present. We are very devoted friends. My children adore him. Our friendship is growing, not diminishing. But marriage is, to me, a very important matter.

Not that I never intend to marry again, which answers another question you've all asked me. I'd certainly like to remarry. I think I should for the children's sake. For my own sake, too. But I'll wait awhile.

And now I'm going to attack the pile of "why don't you write to me?" questions. I could answer by saying, "My dears, it's time—merely time. But I won't let it go at that. I'm going into this matter thoroughly, once and for all. You're going behind the scenes, back home with me to see how things really are.

When I'm making a picture I am, literally, in over my head; I drown in it. Then time, my own time to do with as I please, simply isn't. I get up at six every morning, take no breakfast and, with no more than a too-hasty goodbye kiss to the children, I'm off to the studio. I arrive between seven and eight, have breakfast in my dressing-room and my hair dressed as I eat. I work all morning, then have my lunch and see the morning's rushes, all in an hour. I work all afternoon and when I get home I have my hair shampooed (it has to be done every night so it will always look the same), often eat my dinner under a dryer, have a massage at nine and go to bed.

YOU wouldn't expect me to write then, now would you? "But between pictures," some of you ask, "why can't you write then?" Well, I mean to, but here's what happens: There are people I want to see, friends I haven't had a chance to see while working. There are business matters, not pertaining to pictures, to be attended to. There are household details, such as repairs, redecorations, the kitchen linoleum to be shellacked, all sorts of things like that to be attended to. I'm really very domestic at heart; I like to do these things myself and I feel cheated if I can't.

There is, above all, the time I spend with the children, supervising their wardrobes, their lives. I plan treats for them. I take them to the movies, Zoo, concerts. I go walking and swimming with them. I read to them evenings. I sort of "catch up" with their interests. I ask them all the questions I want to ask and answer all they ask me.

Then there are the conferences for the next picture, tests with cameramen, portrait sittings, fittings, the new part to be studied. There is the dentist.

You do see, don't you? You realize that, by the time I begin another picture, not only have I NOT "taken up French," nor read many good books, but I haven't even caught up with your letters. Now, have I explained my failure as a correspondent? Tell me, please!

"What is your social life like?" I'm asked. Well, I'm afraid I'm going to be disappointing to those who like to think I live in the midst of glitter and night-life all the time. For my social life is the way I want it to be—cozy, warm and rather comfortable on the whole. I love to go to my friends' houses for an evening. I love to have them come to my house—Sylvia Fairbanks, Merle Oberon and Alex, the Mervyn LeRoys, the Charles Boyers, George, of course, and others. I don't care for huge parties. I seldom go to them and never, never give them. Sixteen is the largest number I ever entertain at home. This is because I'm allergic to crowds, a real victim of claustrophobia. I do love to go to Ciro's now and then, of course; love to dance, have fun. But—I also love to go to bed early, read a book and eat an apple, as I did when I was a child, and often do now. I don't play bridge or any parlor games. I like outdoor sports. I love seeing movies and, since I'm fortunate enough to have a projection machine at home, I always see four, sometimes five a week.

WHAT do you do with your old clothes?" is another question I'm asked. Well, for one thing, there are guilds here in Hollywood for girls who are trying to get jobs. I give some of my clothes to them. Some I give to friends and relatives. Sometimes we swap. No, the clothes we wear in pictures are not our own. We never take them off the lot. We can buy them when the picture is finished if we want to, but they are usually quite expensive and by that time we've grown pretty tired of them! They go back to the wardrobe department, are remodeled and used again in other pictures.

I'm often asked whether I am very clothes-conscious. No, I don't think I am. I never bother about complete wardrobes except when I travel. At home I always wear slacks and shirts and sweaters. To me, clothes are a convenience. I never like to be in that traditional feminine fix where I say, "I have nothing to wear!" I like to feel that I can be suitably and comfortably dressed for all occasions and that's about all. But I am very particular, even finicky, about my person. That is, I'm fussy about my nails, my hair, my skin.

I've been asked, "Do you smoke?" Yes, I like to smoke, but just occasionally.

"Do you diet?" is another common question. I don't go on fad diets, but I have lost considerable weight this past year by refusing second helpings and that sort of thing. I eat the simplest kind of foods and drink only fruit juices between meals. I eat a lot and eat frequently. I have to if I want to keep going, but I stick to the simple things.

A great deal of my fan mail has to do with the picture I am making, the picture I am going to make, the number I do a year and so on. Well, I've finished "Escape" with Bob Taylor. And—oh, I must tell you I dyed my hair for the part, something I've never done before. It's sort of a deep golden shade and I like it so much I think I'll keep it this way for a time. My next picture will be "The World We Make"—and I'll co-star with George Raft!

I am often asked whether we choose our own stories. No, we do not. And we should not even if we were given that privilege. We are not, for the most part, forced to play parts we don't believe in, or don't like—M-G-M is particularly lenient with us in this respect.

Many people ask how tall I am. For some reason, there seems to be the impression that I am a very tall person, I'm really only five feet three.

And now I come to a question asked me, often all too sadly. "When your husband died—how did you ever endure it?"

How did I "endure it?" I said at the time, and I say now, that there isn't any so-called consolation. I don't believe the "it's-all-for-the-best," "it-had-to-be" kind of comfort. I can only tell you that I worked things out because, first of all, I suddenly found myself feeling that life is very short and that we simply have to live it as best we may.

Gradually, then, everyday work, responsibilities begin to bring their satisfaction. It's not that you forget, it's that the business of life catches up with you.

Yes, I do believe that a woman, widowed, should marry again. Especially if she has had a very deep and great love. For once we have loved someone very deeply, we can't go on without loving another. We've learned to give our love to someone, and as long as we do, the unbearable becomes bearable.

And now I think I've told you most of the things you asked me about in your letters. I've asked some questions, too. Please—it's your turn to answer *me*.

TWO CLEVER FELLOWS WHO FOUND IT BETTER TO BEND THAN TO BREAK
[*Continued from page 163*]
his brother killed in the World War. He personally experienced all the horror, the heartbreak, the utter devastation brought on by man's inhumanity to man. It's ironical that Francis' own Czecho-Slovakia today should have been in the very heart of the agitation.

This personal earnestness almost cost Francis his career. When he established personal offices and paid the workers with his own check, he was accused of seeking publicity. His own studio refused to aid him in the work, because studios never like to take sides. But they

also made little effort to convince Hollywood that Francis was one of those rare individuals who was really on the level.

Francis worked before the camera in the day time. At night he'd drive to nearby towns, ofttimes making two hour speeches before having his dinner. Over weekends he often flew half way across the continent in order to make a speech. Doctors warned him about his health. His business manager pleaded with him to spend a little less, save a lot more. Then one day his interviews stopped. Hollywood columnists, who make the daily rounds of the sets, seemed to pass him by. His own studio branded him as a foolhardly dreamer of dreams.

Of course Francis despaired. Bad judgment in placing him in bad pictures, eventually found him without a contract. It was then they told Francis that movie stars must live in a little world apart. They must exist for the tired housewives, who get tired of looking at neglectful husbands. They must be dashing and handsome and make passionate love. They must not enter into world problems and become a party to the everyday struggle of life. Too late Francis came to the bitter realization that for Hollywood he had been all wrong.

Recently Francis Lederer finished an important role opposite Claudette Colbert in a picture called "Midnight." It is his first appearance on the screen in over a year. Mitch Leisen, the director, is lavish in his praise. Certain credit is coming to Mitch, because he is truly one of Hollywood's most intelligent souls. But in Francis, Mitch discovered an actor who was co-operative every second, who gives of himself till it hurts and turns in one of the finest performances ever seen.

Those who know him well, will tell you that Francis Lederer is a quieter person today. In place of that sparkle, that irresistible enthusiasm destroyed by Hollywood, there is a maturity and a stability that no one can doubt or criticize. There is also a note of sadness in his voice, when Francis sums it up in his usual honest way:

"I wish I could turn back the years, knowing what I now have learned. I have no misgivings. I alone am at fault. I was all wrong for Hollywood. I didn't make any adjustment, because at that time I didn't think it was necessary. I was much too easy-going and trusting in a city where the competition is so keen. Everyone always had a fine word to say for George. But somehow it was the other fellow who seemed to get the breaks. Then, overnight he changed.

Way back when he started in show business, it had always been George Murphy's policy to work like the devil,

never doublecross a pal and be a friend to everyone. All along the way George have changed—I hope for the better."

Unlike Francis Lederer, George Murphy's idealism presented no conflict with Hollywood beliefs. With George it was a strictly personal thing. Believe it or not, George was just too nice. That is, never failed himself. Many times they took unfair advantage of him. Once a manager skipped off with his salary. George was always Johnny on the spot when they asked him to do benefits. George was always trying to get someone a job. George was always fighting for the underdog. As a setup, George was one pretty swell human being. But he wasn't setting the world on fire with his unmistakable talent.

After listening to countless promises and believing in their fulfillment, George was finally signed by M-G-M. At last, this was it! His worries were over. No more blues and depressed moments. Six months went by and the studio didn't use him once. One day George got up and announced to his wife that he was driving back to New York with his good friend Roger Pryor. Knowing the depths of George's unhappiness, very wisely Julie Murphy encouraged him.

Seven days later George received a wire to fly right back to Hollywood. A picture was waiting for him. On wings of ecstasy George arrived, only to find they had cast him in a short. Still being a nice fellow, George spoke his piece. But he didn't carry on like most actors would have done. Over a period of years, George got a few fairly good parts. For eighteen months he didn't do a single picture for M-G-M. But on loanout he made five for other studios and was a big hit in each.

George was just on the point of asking for his release, when his son was born. After twelve years of married life, the Murphys' first son and heir was a pretty big thing. Their happiness knew no bounds. And the lovely Julie Murphy was especially thrilled with the way it affected George. Knowing just how talented and ambitious George had always been, it hurt Julie to see him wasted by the producers. But she knew everything was going to be all right when George suddenly announced one day:

"I'm going to stick it out and fight. Even if I have to go off the lot to do it, I'm going to prove to them how good I can be. I think a lot of it has been my fault. I've been too easy on myself. Now I'm going to show them what I can do.

This was just the start with George. Every day since, he has been changing before the very eyes of those who know and love him. George was never quite sure of his own judgment and used to ask others for their opinions. Now he makes up his own mind and he sticks to it. He used to be so low in spirits, it took days to snap him out of it. Now he knows everything will be all right. He used to sit around and "beat his brains" out when he had a picture to do. Now he does the best he can and refuses to worry about it. Arthur Lubin, who is directing George out at Universal, says he has never seen such confidence and enthusiasm. And Arthur is capable of rare judgment.

"I never could be anything but the way I am," says George. "But the baby has made a great difference. I haven't deliberately tried to change, but I guess I have because everyone seems to notice it. I seem to have a greater capacity for work. People say I am more dignified. If it's true, I'm glad. But it amuses me because I've never thought of myself as an overly-dignified person. My son makes everything seem less important.

"I used to worry when it was option time. When my last option came up for renewal, I hadn't even thought of it until the studio notified me that I was with them again for another year. Having worked in night clubs for so many years, if I didn't go two or three times a week, I always felt that I was missing something. Now my wife can't get me out of the house! She thinks it's good for me to get out and relax for an hour or two, after being on the closed sound stages.

In keeping with his new-found objectiveness, George has really set out to do things. Besides being a fine actor, a loving husband and father, George can add the following to his long list of accomplishments. He is master of ceremonies on the motion picture relief fund show. He's a member of the board of directors of the Screen Actor's Guild. He's chairman of the agency committee of the Guild. He's President of the West Side Tennis Club. He's a member of the board of directors of the Pacific Southwest Tennis Association. He's the associate editor of a new sports magazine. And he's writing a book on dancing!

And so, after long last, the Lederers and the Murphys of Hollywood bend to the exigencies of fame. There is no compensation and they suffer a personal loss. But on the other hand, in Hollywood nothing succeeds like success. There's only one way and that's the hard way—for those with ideals. But it's still better to bend before they break, than wait until it's too late.

WHY GIRLS SAY YES!

[Continued from page 165]
conrol your life? It's old-fashioned for girls to sacrifice domesticity for their careers. I've never had the actual situation to face, for I've never been in love. But—" and Sidney beamed angelically —"love will come first!"

"I sincerely think that if a girl is a good enough actress, has something to sell that the public wants, she'll climb the ladder on her own. Since the talkies the public doesn't care about the off-screen personality. They want their heroines vital and real in pictures. Helen Hayes, Ann Harding, Barbara Stanwyck—they are not glamorous or mysterious. And everyone admirers them tremendously!

"My convictions on the social angle? I'm absolutely against the 'being seen' idea. Oh, occasionally a director will see you at a party and announce, 'You're the girl I've been looking for!' But my opinion is that the less you are seen around Hollywood the better. A little partying goes a long way."

What's the unmarried but striving actress to do? As a last resort I went over to Marian Marsh's for tea.

"Who says that the married women are getting the best breaks?" she demanded. "Single girls are doing just as well—when they have equal ability. The public wants ability rather than beauty now." This from the beautiful Marian!

"The talkies follow the stage with respect to the idea that facial prettiness is less important than the quality of one's acting. Today most people go to see a star who can act. Not to see more beauty!

"If a girl has talent, she'll succeed. In the old days it was easier to make a star, because sheer personality was almost all that was necessary. Now the voice is of great importance.

"Hollywood girls marry for advancement in many instances, but not so often as formerly. Because no matter how much pull you may muster, you cannot last if you haven't the ability.

"I don't believe in social contacts either. Somebody may take a dislike to you and then they are always against you. But if you are not known personally you are judged by your screen work. It is your best reference."

Five who persist in remaining immune (so far!) to wedding bells have stated their opinions as to why girls in movieland marry.

What is *your* verdict?

HOLLYWOOD'S UNMARRIED HUSBANDS AND WIVES

[Continued from page 169]
He was Mister Broadway.

Virginia talked him into seeing Watson, one of Hollywood's most exclusive tailors. What's more, she talked him out of the theatrical clothes and into a more conservative taste.

All this is called "settling down." It usually happens to people after they've been married. He lives at the El Royale Apartments and Virginia lives in another building up the street. They just

go together. But she orders his meals. And he spoils her little girl to death.

No real father could be more infatuated than George with Virginia's five-year-old daughter, Joan. Nor would you call George the perfect picture of a family man, either. He has already paid up an insurance policy that will guarantee Joan a nice little stake when she is ready for college. He seems to lie awake nights planning something new and delightful to surprise her with whenever he sees Virginia, and that's usually all the time.

One of the stories the salesgirls still tell down at Bullock's-Wilshire, Los Angeles' swankiest store, is about the day Virginia Pine and little Joan came into the shop. Joan spied something she wanted right then. But Virginia, wishing to impress upon her daughter that a person isn't always able to have what he or she likes in this world, said, "But, Joan, you can't have that. You haven't the money to pay for it."

"Oh, that's all right," stated Joan in a loud, clear voice. "Just charge it to George Raft!"

When Bob Taylor docked in New York from England and 'A Yank At Oxford,' he waited around a couple of hours for a load of stuff he had bought over there to clear customs. Most of it was for—not Bob—but Barbara Stanwyck and her little son, Dion.

They've been practically a family since Bob bought his ranch estate in Northridge and built a house there.

Northridge, itself, is an interesting manifestation of how Hollywood's untied twosomes buy and build together. It lies in a far corner of the San Fernando Valley, fairly remote from Hollywood, all of fifteen miles from Bob's studio, Metro-Goldwyn-Mayer. No coincidence can possibly explain his choosing that side, pleasant and open though it is, right beside Barbara Stanwyck's place.

Barbara was there first. With the Zeppo Marxes, she established Marwyck Ranch to breed thoroughbred horses. She built a handsome ranch house and moved out. Bob Taylor had never been especially interested in either ranch life or horses until he started going with Barbara. But witness how quickly their interests—deep and expensive, *permanent* interests—merged after they slipped into the unique Hollywood habit. Marriage couldn't have worked more of a change.

Bob bought the acres next to Barbara's ranch. He started putting up a ranch house within a good stone's throw of hers. He bought horses. He spent every minute of his spare time working on the place. Overnight, he turned into a country squire. When, in the middle of it all, he was called to England, the work never stopped. Barbara supervised it. While Bob was away she ordered the things she knew he wanted. She oversaw the decoration and furnishing of the place. It was all ready when Bob came home.

Bob's house and Barbara's house stand now on adjoining knolls. The occupants ride together and work together and play there together in their time off. Bob trained and worked out for "The Crowd Roars" on Barbara's ranch. Almost every evening, after work at the studio or on the ranch, he runs over for a plunge in her pool.

If it isn't fight night—they've long had permanent seats together at the Hollywood Legion Stadium—or if they're not asked to a party—they're always invited together, just like man and wife—they spend a quiet evening together at either one or the other's place.

Or if Bob has a preview of his picture, Barbara goes with him to tell him what she thinks of it, and vice versa. Bob saw "Stella Dallas" four times. Once he caught it in London and bawled so copiously that when he came out and a kid asked him for his autograph he couldn't see to sign it! But he was a long way away from Barbara then.

When he's home, he's a little more critical. But never of Barbara's ice cream. Bob has never forgotten his Nebraska boyhood ecstasy licking the dasher of an ice cream freezer. That's why Barbara whips him up a bucketful every week, before they roll off to see the folks.

All in all, it's an almost perfect domestic picture. But no wedding rings in sight!

Even gifts and expressions of sentiment take on the practical, utilitarian aspect of old married folks' remembrances when these Hollywood single couples come across. Just as Dad gives Mother an electric icebox for Christmas and she retaliates with a radio, Bob Taylor presents Barbara Stanwyck with a tennis court on her birthday, with Barbara giving Bob a two-horse auto trailer for his!

THE gifts Carole Lombard and Clark Gable have exchanged are even more unorthodox. Whoever heard of a woman in love with a man giving him a gun for Christmas! Or a man, crazy about one of the most glamorous, sophisticated and clever women in the land, hanging a gasoline scooter on her Christmas tree!

For Clark, Carole stopped, almost overight, being a Hollywood playgirl. People are expected to change when they get married. The necessary adaptation to a new life and another personality shows up in every bride and groom. All Clark and Carole did was strike up a Hollywood twosome. Nobody said "I do!"

Clark Gable desn't like night spots, or parties, social chit-chat, or the frothy pretensions of society. He has endured plenty of it, but it makes him fidget.

Carole, quite frankly, used to eat it up. She hosted the most charming and clever parties in town. She knew everybody, went everywhere. When the ultra exclusive and late lamented Mayfair Club held its annual ball, Carole was picked to run things. It was Carole who decreed the now famous "White Mayfair" that Norma Shearer crossed up so wickedly by coming in flaming scarlet—an idea you later saw dramatized by Bette Davis in "Jezebel."

These things were the caviar and cocktails of Carole Lombard's life—before she started going with Gable. But look what happened—

Clark didn't like it, Carole found out —quickly. What did he like? Well, outside of hunting in wild country white men seldom entered, and white women never, he like to shoot skeet. Shooting skeet, of course, is an intricate scoring game worked out on the principle of trapshooting. It involves banging away at crazily projected clay pigeons with a shotgun.

Carole learned to shoot skeet—not only learned it but, with the intense proficiency with which she attacks anything, rapidly became one of the best women skeet shooters in the country!

Gable liked to ride, so Carole got herself a horse and unpacked her riding things.

He liked tennis, so she resurrected her always good court game, taking lessons from Alice Marble, her good friend and the present national women's champion. Playing with a man, Carole had to get good and she did—so good that now Clark can't win a set!

It goes on like that. Clark, tiring of hotel life, moved out to a ranch in the San Fernando Valley. What did Lombard do? She bought a Valley ranch!

Carole has practically abandoned all her Hollywood social contacts. She doesn't keep up with the girls in gossip as she used to. She doesn't throw parties that hit the headlines and the picture magazines. She and Clark are all wrapped up in each other's interests. While Gable did all the night work in "Too Hot To Handle," Carole, though working, too, was on his set every night. She caught the sneak preview with him and told him with all the candor of the little woman, "It's hokum, Pappy—but the *most excellent* hokum!"

Like any good spouse might do, Carole has ways and means of chastening Clark, too. When she's mad at him she wears a hat he particularly despises. Carole calls it her "hate hat."

Their fun now, around town, is almost entirely trips, football games, fights and shows. Their stepping-out

nights usually end up at the home of Director Walter Lang and his new wife, Madalynne Fields, "Fieldsie," Carole's bosom pal and long-time secretary. They sit and play games!

Yes, Carole Lombard is a changed woman since she tied up with Clark Gable.

But her name is still Carole Lombard. THE altar record, in fact, among Hollywood's popular twosomes is surprisingly slim.

Usually something formidable stands in the way of a marriage certificate when Hollywood stars pair up minus a preacher.

In Clark and Carole's case, of course, there is a very sound legal barrier. Clark is still officially a married man. Every now and then negotiations for a divorce are started, but, until something happens in court, Ria Gable is still the only wife the law of this land allows Clark Gable.

George Raft can't marry Virginia Pine for the very same good reason; he has a wife. Every effort he has made for his freedom has failed.

Some of them, like Constance Bennett and Gilbert Roland, go in a perfect design for living, apparently headed for perpetual fun with each other. Connie maintains one of the most luxurious setups of them all, with a titled husband in Europe and Gilbert Roland her devoted slave in Hollywood. Years have passed and the arrangement seems to please everybody as much now as it did at the start. Why should it ever break up?

On the other hand, the unmarried partners sometimes get a divorce—or at least a separation, a recess, a moratorium—whatever you care to call it. Calling the case of Charlie Chaplin and Paulette Goddard requires more than a bunch of handy nouns.

No one has ever been able yet to say definitely whether or not the gray-haired Charlie and his young, vivacious Paulette were ever married. Such things as public records exist for just such purposes, of course, but in spite of the fact that none can be unearthed, a strong belief hovers around Hollywood that Charlie and Paulette did actually take the vows, some say on his yacht out at sea.

But when, a few months back, Charlie was seen more and more in the company of other young ladies and Paulette began stepping out with other men, an unusually awkward contretemps was brewed. What was it? The breaking up of a love affair? Or the separation of a marriage? If a divorce was to be had, there had to have been a marriage. But was there? Charlie wouldn't talk; neither would Paulette. Hollywood relapsed into a quandary. It's still there as concerns the Chaplin-Goddard unmarried marriage. Meanwhile, both Charlie and Paulette seem to be having a good time with whomever they fancy. But the interesting thing is that Paulette still entertains her guests, when she wishes, on Charlie Chaplin's yacht. So maybe she has an interest in it that a mere separation couldn't efface.

THE most tragic, as well as perhaps the most tender match of them all gave way to an irresistible rival wooer, Death. At the time of Jean Harlow's untimely passing, she and William Powell had reached an understanding that excluded any one else from either's thoughts. Both had fought for happiness in Hollywood without finding it, until they found each other. Then Death stole Jean away and Bill has never recovered from the effect of that stunning blow.

There was only Jean Harlow's family, her doctor and William Powell in her hospital room the night she lost her fight for life. Jean died in Bill's arms.

In every way since he has acted as a son-in-law to Jean's mother. He bought the crypt where Jean lies today and arranged for perpetual flowers. This year, on the anniversary of her passing, Bill Powell and Mrs. Bello, Jean's mother, went alone to visit Jean's resting place. He sent Mrs. Bello on a trip to Bermuda last winter to recover from the severe grief she has suffered since Jean's death. She visited Bill regularly during his recent spell in the hospital. Both have one regret—that Bill and Jean never got to be man and wife.

And that, it seems, would point a lesson to the unique coterie of Hollywood's unwed couples—Bob Taylor and Barbara Stanwyck, who could get married if they really wanted to; George Raft and Virginia Pine, Carole Lombard and Clark Gable and the other steady company couples who might swing it if they tried a little harder. You can't take your happiness with you.

For nobody, not even Hollywood's miracle men, has ever improved on the good old-fashioned, satisfying institution of holy matrimony. And, until something better comes along, the best way to hunt happiness when you're in love in Hollywood or anywhere else— is with a preacher, a marriage license and a bagful of rice.

HOLLYWOOD JOINS THE NAVY

[Continued from page 171]
a studio in the business that wouldn't swap six glamour girls and an option on Hemingway's next three novels for Bob's services today.

But Lieutenant Montgomery likes his new casting director. Uncle Sam seldom makes mistakes in the roles he hands out and Montgomery's assignment to London was no accident. In the year he spent in England making films, the actor became one of the most popular Americans ever to carve his own niche in London life. The very men he is dealing with on an official basis today are the young Englishmen with whom, two years ago, he was batting cricket balls and shooting grouse.

If and when Goering's gangsters rain bombs on London again, it won't be the first time Bob Montgomery has been under German fire. Last year he drove an ambulance in France and twice, during the Nazi push around Amiens, Bob's mercy wagon was raked by machine guns. He came home when France fell, applied for a reserve commission in the Navy and, at the conclusion of his last film job, asked for active duty.

No hero's part he ever assumed in motion pictures rates more raves than Bob Montgomery's real-life role as ambulance driver, naval officer and diplomat.

SPEAKING of diplomats, Douglas Fairbanks Jr., who is a Lieutenant (junior grade) in the U. S. Naval Reserve, already has carried out with stunning success a major mission to the South American Republics.

Doug's tour of South America was no mere good-will gesture by movie makers seeking to promote box-office returns. Young Fairbanks, who has all of his father's flair for meeting and mixing with people, visited seven Latin American capitals as a personal emissary of President Roosevelt. In line with the Administration's desire to strengthen cultural relations as well as economic and military agreements between the Americas, Fairbanks spent two months talking with the top men of Argentina, Brazil, Chile, Peru, Uruguay, Paraguay and Panama and returned to give the White House and the State Department a confidential report on what the political and intellectual leaders of Latin America are thinking.

That Doug discharged his delicate mission with dignity and diplomacy is best attested by the fact that the foreign office of one of the countres he visited, Brazil, inquired unofficially of our State Department if the friendly film actor could not be sent back as a permanent member of the Ambassador's staff.

It is quite possible that Doug will return to South America on another official errand. Next time he soars South perhaps, like Montgomery, he will go as a naval attaché to one of our embassies. The reserve commission in the Navy for which Doug applied the day war broke out in Europe was recently signed by the President, and Lieutenant Fairbanks, when he completes his present studio chore, probably will ask for active duty.

The third actor to trade his dinner coat of dress sets for the khaki jacket of a naval aviator's duty uniform is Wayne Morris. Not many months ago Morris was filming the excellent air picture, "I Wanted Wings." He's got them now. Navy wings. And as a reserve Ensign he is serving as procurement officer at the Long Beach Naval Reserve Aviation Base.

The 26-year-old actor was a private pilot with about 80 flying hours to his credit before he put in his bid to the Navy for a commssion. In July he was called up for duty for the duration and assigned to the California base.

It is gratifying to note that Morris, who has symbolized the rugged young American in so many screen tales, should be one of the first actors to prove they can duplicate in reality the roles they romanticize in Hollywood's land of let's pretend.

IF there is anything of which big, blustering Wallace Beery is almost as proud as he is of his young daughter, Carol, it is the prized parchment which proclaims him a Lieutenant Commander in the United States Naval Reserve. Serveral years ago Wally, one of Hollywood's best private pilots, joined the Naval Reserve as a Lieutenant. Recently he was promoted to Lieutenant Commander.

Wally's initial interest in naval aviation came when he made "Hell Divers," a vivid picture of Navy aces which disclosed for the first time many of the activities aboard aircraft carriers and the dive bombing tactics invented by the Navy's air arm. In this connection, it is an interesting aside to note that when the picture was released in Europe, British military experts requested that certain scenes of highly complicated maneuvers be eliminated. The suggestions for the cuts came too late, however, and in Washington they'll tell you that the first military adaptation of the dive bombing methods shown in "Hell Divers" was made by the Russian air force, from whom the technique was borrowed and developed by the Nazis.

Regular officers of the Navy's air corps on the West Coast voice the hope that Beery will be assigned to a California base, if he is called up for active duty. He's a mess-mate they'd be proud to welcome, they say.

Another reserve Lieutenant Commander from Hollywood already has received his orders to report for duty. He is Gene Markey, writer-producer, and ex-husband of two of the most glamorous figures in the film capital's gallery, Joan Bennett and Hedy Lamarr.

One of the movie colony's more able yachtsmen, Markey has been a reserve officer for eight years. He joined the Atlantic Fleet in September and is now a deck officer on one of the big battle wagons based in the Panama Canal Zone.

Three other men whose fame in filmland has come from their activities behind rather than in front of the camera are reserve officers in the Navy, now awaiting possible calls. They are John Ford, who has directed several excellent sea pictures, including "Men Without Women" and "The Long Voyage Home"; Gregg Toland, crack cameraman; and Lloyd Bacon, another veteran director. Ford and Bacon, who served in the Navy in the last war, are Lieutenant Commanders; Toland, a Lieutenant in the photographic branch of the Naval Reserve.

Hollywood is represented in the Marine Corps by Captain James Roosevelt, the President's eldest son, who was fast making a reputation as a film producer before his return to active military service. During the time he was attached to the White House, as a secretary and aide to his father, Jimmy Roosevelt held a Lieutenant Colonel's commission. He resigned from this higher rank and took a captaincy when he went into active training at San Diego about a year ago and it was as a Captain that he made his extensive observation trip recently in the war zones of the Far East and Europe.

Captain Jimmy's superior officer at San Diego was Woody Van Dyke, known to film-goers as the director of the "Thin Man" series, who, after serving a tour of duty as a Major in the Marines, was retired for reasons of ill health and returned to his studio job.

Another marine of the First World War, who became somewhat better known for his fighting in the smaller arena of a prize ring, has shifted from the Marine Corps to the Navy. As Director of Athletics for all the Navy's training stations, Gene Tunney holds the rank of a Lieutenant Commader. His contact with Hollywood came in the days when he was still world's heavyweight champion and made a successful serial called "The Fighting Marine."

ANOTHER Lieutenant Commander in the Naval Reserve, who might lay claim to being a Hollywood "veteran" by reason of appearing in two pictures, "Wake Up and Live" and "Love and Kisses," would probably meet with violent protests from that landlubber Ben Bernie, did he also claim to be an actor.

Your correspondent, having enlisted as an apprentice seaman and served on the *U.S.S. Granite State* from April, 1917, to December, 1918, during World War 1, applied for a reserve commission in 1934, and was made a Lieutenant.

Advanced to the grade of Lieutenant Commander this summer, he spent a month on active duty and in four weeks learned more about just how great a service we have as our first line of defense than he could hope to tell you in four years.

But the story of the United States Navy isn't told in words. It's written in the skies by the slashing strokes of fire from the exhaust of fighting planes, by the rolling smoke screens that mask our mighty battleships on parade, by the faultless ranks of sailors and marines drawn up at attention when a President of the United States meets a Prime Minister of Great Britain in a history-makng conference at sea.

Most deeply, perhaps, is it written in the proud stirrings in the heart of every American who, on October 27, toasts the greatest fleet afloat and realizes that to the officers and men aboard its ships every day is Navy Day.

For the motion-picture industry's contribution to that Navy, both in manpower and morale, here's a salute and a toast from your New York correspondent, Walter Winchell: "Here's to the land you love—and the love you land!"